Land Rights

The Political Economy Forum

Sponsored by the Political Economy Research Center (PERC)
Series Editor: Terry L. Anderson

Land Rights: The 1990s' Property Rights Rebellion
Edited by Bruce Yandle

*The Political Economy of Customs and Culture: Informal
Solutions to the Commons Problem*
Edited by Terry L. Anderson and Randy T. Simmons

Property Rights and Indian Economies
Edited by Terry L. Anderson

*Public Lands and Private Rights: The Failure of Scientific
Management*
Edited by Robert H. Nelson

Taking the Environment Seriously
Edited by Roger E. Meiners and Bruce Yandle

Wildlife in the Marketplace
Edited by Terry L. Anderson and Peter J. Hill

Land Rights

The 1990s' Property Rights Rebellion

Edited by
Bruce Yandle

ROWMAN & LITTLEFIELD PUBLISHERS, INC.

ROWMAN & LITTLEFIELD PUBLISHERS, INC.

Published in the United States of America
by Rowman & Littlefield Publishers, Inc.
4720 Boston Way, Lanham, Maryland 20706

3 Henrietta Street
London WC2E 8LU, England

British Cataloging in Publication Information Available

Library of Congress Cataloging-in-Publication Data

Land rights: the 1990s' property rights rebellion / edited by Bruce
Yandle.
p. cm. — (The political economy forum)
Includes bibliographical references and index.
1. Environmental law—United States. 2. Eminent domain—United
States. 3. Right of property—United States. I. Yandle, Bruce.
II. Series.
KF3775.A75L36 1995 343.73'0252—dc20 95-3094 [347.303252] CIP

ISBN 0-8476-8028-2 (cloth: alk. paper)
ISBN 0-8476-8029-0 (pbk.: alk. paper)

Printed in the United States of America

♾™ The paper used in this publication meets the minimum requirements of
American National Standard for Information Sciences—Permanence of
Paper for Printed Library Materials, ANSI Z39.48-1984.

. . . nor shall private property be taken for public use, without just compensation.

Fifth Amendment,
U.S. Constitution

CONTENTS

Preface

Bruce Yandle

Today, all across America, there are people at the grassroots level, as well as some better-financed and better-organized groups, focusing on one major constitutional issue: the right of people to control the use of their own land and property. While a fundamental constitutional issue unites the property rights rebels, the trouble that has entered their lives varies from region to region.

Landowners in the East are concerned about restrictions on their land rights that follow historic park designations. Farmers nationwide are up in arms about the Corps of Engineers' wetlands program that forces them to abandon the use of farmland that is identified as sensitive habitat or becomes wet during part of the year. Ranchers in the West and timber operators in the East and West are threatened by enforcement of the Endangered Species Act, which gives superior occupancy rights to designated species but pays landowners nothing.

In some ways, the movement is a rebellion. Countless citizens are challenging the state's authority over their lives. Yet in the strict meaning of the word, the movement is more a revolution — a complete rotation that carries us back to a first constitutional principle.

Some of the groups that contest the state's authority describe their problems in simple terms. The land on which they live is theirs and often has been owned by family members for three generations or more. In their view, no one has the right to tell them what they can or cannot do on their land. Good stewards of the land in many cases, these ordinary Americans believe wholeheartedly that something is wrong. If they are to lose the right to use their land as they see fit, whether in the name of historic corridors, endangered species, or wetlands protection, then the owners should at least be paid for their loss. If the owners are truly harming others, then they should be sued under common law.

Others see the problem in more complex terms. They hold contracts, deeds, and easements that give them the legal right to graze cattle, cut trees, or build houses. They see a growing maze of federal, state, and local regulations that interfere with the terms of the contracts and deeds they hold. The rules are supposed to serve a public interest, but the burden for serving that interest falls directly on the shoulders of well-identified individuals who hold specified rights to land. In the view of those shouldering the load, their Fifth Amendment rights are denied. They believe what the U.S. Constitution says: *Nor shall private property be taken for public use, without just compensation.*

Corporate groups and some trade associations see yet another dimension of the property rights revolution. By now accustomed to the continuous expansion of government rules and regulations, in some cases, these groups are concerned about raising their voices. They fear the media backlash that will follow if they are tarred as being antienvironmental. At the same time, many in the business community recognize that private property rights form the keystone of a competitive capitalistic economy.

Critics of the property rights movement sometimes engage in ad hominem tactics, asserting that the whole property rights affair results from efforts by big business to push grassroots organizations to do battle in their antienvironmental efforts. The movement is depicted as a 'stop the environmentalists' effort. Other critics see the property rights movement as a last-gasp battle to support an obsolete constitutional structure that, in their view, was always more symbolic than real. The sooner the energies of property rights advocates dissipate, the quicker we can get on with centralized management of a complex world that has no room for such natural rights notions as private property rights.

The environmentalists who oppose and criticize the property rights advocates are also interested in property rights. But instead of seeking protection of existing rights, they seek to redefine rights. Sometimes the issue relates to how public lands will be used — for example, logging versus natural sanctuary. Sometimes the question has to do with private land rights — such as whether an individual can build a home on private beach property. No matter how land-use controversies are depicted, property rights, the legal ability to exclude others and control use, is the fundamental issue. The question that separates private property advocates from environmentalists who seek government control of land use is really about how rights are to be transferred. Will existing private rights be purchased or taken?

The origin of this book dates back to June 1992, when Clemson University's Center for Policy Studies joined efforts with PERC, a natural resources think tank in Bozeman, Montana, to bring together leaders of grassroots property rights organizations for a one-day meeting in Washington, D.C. The purpose of the meeting was simply to share ideas and to listen to individuals around the table tell how their group started, what they were doing, and what they expected would happen in the future. Around the room were groups with such names as Stop Taking Our Property, Fairness to Landowners Committee, Consumer Alert, and Alliance for America. Some were purely regional in their outreach. Others were national and international. About ten of the groups had started newsletters.

At the time of the June 1992 meeting, I had just completed a lengthy project that involved a study of how property rights had evolved for ordinary people over the centuries. My reading carried me back to tenth-century England and the rise of common law. I was struck by stories about common law rules of property and how they had evolved from communities of people in rural areas, not from constitutions and the seats of government.[1] Accounts of how country people, probably kinsmen, took annual oaths to be jointly and severally liable for maintaining community peace were joined by stories of country courts and judges who rendered decisions involving trespass, theft, and violent crimes.

My studies led me to the great English jurist Sir Edward Coke and then to a reading of his seventeenth-century Institutes, which was his attempt to compile all of the law of England.[2] Coke's explanation of the Magna Carta left little doubt in my mind that the Great Charter, as he termed it, was indeed a watershed document in the struggle of ordinary people to protect their natural rights, rights that evolved from common sense and community, from encroachments by government. One finds words in the Magna Carta that sound very much like the takings clause of the Fifth Amendment: *No freeman shall be deprived of his free tenement or liberties or fee custom but by lawful judgment of his peers and by the law of the land.*

At the time of the Magna Carta, "the law of the land" referred to common law, not to laws that might be written by some legislative body or king. Customary law, developed informally and rooted in community norms, was seen as the only logical way to protect property rights that had evolved over the centuries. Rights to land emerged from community and were transmitted to the nation/state. The lesson seems clear: People do not have rights because the state allows them; the nation/state exists because people have rights.

Constitutional Walls and Property Rights

From the Magna Carta to today, people have struggled with an endless paradox: A government strong enough to protect property rights is by definition powerful enough to take property. Constitutions that evolve from free people provide the means to wall off government, to define two economic domains —

one public, the other private. Of course, the lines often blur, but we can usefully consider the forces that dominate on either side of the wall.

One side of the wall is governed by the law of politics. There, the body politic engages in collective choice where voting rules and special interest struggles determine outcomes. The other side of the wall is governed by a rule of law where individual owners of property rights are forced to bear the cost of their actions while gaining the right to the fruits of their labor. Things are never perfect on either side. On one side of the wall, land use can be specified by statute. On the other side, the transfer of land rights requires purchase.

The rule of law gives individual owners the incentive to look ahead, to conserve, to avoid short-term actions that foreclose better longer-term outcomes, and causes each person to face the opportunity cost of his or her actions. On the other side of the wall, the rule of politics allows individuals to promote the public weal. Politics also enables the players to engage in opportunistic behavior, to call on government's redistributive powers to force the costs of their actions on others.

The Fifth Amendment is America's chief property rights wall. But like other walls, it must be maintained. At times cracks appear in the wall; new mortar must be applied and stones replaced. Otherwise the wall will fall to the ground. Were it not for the Fifth Amendment, those engaged in opportunistic actions would erase the wealth and property rights of those on the other side of the wall. No free people will allow that to happen. The wall conserves resources, making it possible for a society of human beings to prosper and flourish. The wall allows government and liberty to exist side by side.

Much of recent history can be described as a struggle around the constitutional wall. Those who successfully gain resources in political struggles understandably seek to expand the public domain where the law of politics prevails. Attractive arguments about the public interest and how it must be served accompany political struggles to expand government's ability to redefine property rights. Just as logically, those who have struggled to acquire and manage property logically oppose redefinitions of rights. They may understand the public interest arguments, but they are the ones who bear the cost of serving that interest.

Why Are Property Rights So Important?

Discussion of property rights in terms of law, politics, and benefits and costs may shed light on why they are so important to the functioning of a durable and strong market economy. Indeed, they are crucial. But the fact that property rights institutions are found across all societies, present and past, suggests they serve a far deeper purpose.[3] Indeed, the fact that many species seem to define and protect property rights implies that property rights are central to the biological survival and relative prosperity of many life-forms. In that sense, modern-day legal and political institutions that reinforce such natural tendencies are really biological artifacts, social inventions that have emerged over long periods of time. This deeper aspect of property may partly explain the outcry evoked when property rights are threatened.

How did these artifacts emerge? Stories of how early communities went about defining land rights generally start with land, or some element of it, as a common-access resource.[4] With increased competition for access and land use, often brought about by population growth or technological change, people collectively invented property rules that maintained order and conserved the scarce resource. Quite often, common or community property was the next evolutionary station.[5] At that point, property rules emerged that applied to and are enforced by well-defined members of a tribe or group. In some cases, as with feudalism, the landlord, the residual owner of all land rights, specified and controlled a bundle of rights that could be used by and transferred among members of the feudal estate.[6] In other instances, citizenship brought access to community or public property. As scarcity increases, and land access and use becomes more valuable, more resources are devoted to defining and managing property rights. Private property rights and transfers emerge, and the community provides for recordkeeping and enforcement.

The observed evolutionary process is also reversible. A resource with private rights that was once valuable can become obsolete and not valuable enough to justify property rights enforcement. For example, Anderson and Leal tell how the invention and application of barbed wire in the West led to a rapid decline of the value of horses (and cowboys).[7] Horses were released to the open range. The status of rights shifted. Horses became a common-access resource. The evolutionary path followed by property rights definition and enforcement parallels a biological path that seems to define the prospects for human survival and well-being.

Political forces can complement or compete with the natural forces that cause property rights to emerge. The resulting rights can be strengthened or weakened. Back at the constitutional wall, coalitions of interest groups can successfully persuade government to redefine rights. A resource-based activity can be passed from one side of the wall to the other. What was once public property, held in trust for the polity, can become private property. Homesteading is an example. Alternatively, rights once defined as private can be redefined as public property. Wetlands and endangered species habitat are examples. Paradoxically, recent transformations of rights have related to things that are claimed to be more valuable, not less. Instead of defining private rights that can be enforced by owners, interest groups have demanded that government claim the rights and then seek to enforce them. In recent years, the legal status of major categories of resources has moved from private to politically vulnerable public property, closer yet to becoming a commons where conservation incentives are weakest.

Seen in this light, today's property rights rebellion seeks to interrupt the trip to the commons. In many ways, property rights advocates are calling for a modern Magna Carta. Once again, ordinary people are seeking to restrain and contain government. But instead of having to settle differences with picks, swords, and arrows, the parties in the struggle now turn to courts and legislative bodies.

In the end, some form of private property rights will most likely survive in a stronger form. Natural law and biological theory suggest that. And if so, all parties to the struggle will win. With property rights enforcement, those who seek to protect sensitive wetlands and threatened species will bear more of the costs of their actions, but they will be more secure in their property. They will have less to fear about future political efforts to redefine land use. Those who seek to preserve their land rights also will gain new protection. Their rights will be enforced, and they will be required to respect the rights of wetland and habitat owners.

How the Book Is Organized

The chapters in this collection can be read selectively or in order. While there is some connective tissue, each piece can be viewed as a stand-alone essay. For that reason, there is obvious content overlap. The chapters are authored by individuals who have participated in the property rights struggle, have done research on specific dimensions of it, or have been longstanding students of land rights issues. Some are clearly property rights advocates. Others take a less passionate view. As noted in "About the Authors," most of the writers have been or are directly involved with PERC, which supported the development of the book.

Nancie Marzulla, president and founder of Defenders of Property Rights, begins the book with a chapter on the property rights movement itself, telling how the movement started, who is involved, and why the struggle is so important to the hosts of people included in it. She identifies themes seen later in the book, setting the stage for the chapters that follow and concluding her chapter with the thought that the property rights issue is the civil rights struggle of the 1990s.

As indicated in Marzulla's chapter, any bona fide constitutional question, such as matters involving the Fifth Amendment, eventually makes its way to the U.S. Supreme Court. Just in the past few years, the Court has rendered several significant decisions that give a richer definition of property rights. In Chapter 2 Erin O'Hara gives a detailed recounting and interpretation of Court decisions that involve regulatory takings — actions by government that diminish the value of private rights to property.

At the outset of her chapter, O'Hara asks if the words "regulatory takings" form an oxymoron. After all, the power to regulate is the power to take. Her careful examination of Supreme Court jurisprudence defines no enduring bright lines as to how the Court approaches the takings issue. But her discussions of takings theories and recent trends combine to show some emerging support for a stronger, perhaps more literal, reading of the Fifth Amendment.

No Supreme Court decision on takings has received more attention than the case involving David Lucas and his South Carolina beachfront property. For that reason, Chapter 3 by James Rinehart and Jeffrey Pompe logically follows O'Hara's discussion of the Court. Rinehart and Pompe, both economists, have done considerable research on beachfront land issues. By training and experience, they are able to relate the Lucas story in a different way. They focus on the law and economics of the issue and give numerous details about the land, the community, and the issues involved.

Few land rights issues have generated as much controversy as Section 404 of Clean Water Act, which is silent on the issue yet forms the basis for definition and protection of wetlands. In Chapter 4 on wetlands law and related property rights controversies, Karol Ceplo explains how pools and puddles that formed in fields following a season of rain became defined as navigable waters of the United States and how wetlands regulation followed. Ceplo describes major legal actions taken against individuals who failed to obtain Corps of Engineers licenses for placing soil on their own land and against others who encountered wetlands rules when seeking to build residential communities. She then discusses cases before the U.S. Claims Court, where in some instances, aggrieved citizens have won their suits against government.

The wetlands issues vies with the enforcement of the Endangered Species Act for first place on the list of land rights controversies. Chapter 5 focuses on the ESA in a specialized way. Lee Ann Welch, a biologist and now an aspiring lawyer, tells about the ESA and its somewhat convoluted history and then concentrates on a controversy involving the red-cockaded woodpecker and a large tract of timberland in eastern North Carolina. She explains how the federal government at first paid private landowners for sensitive habitat, but then, when budgets got tight, resorted to taking by regulation. Toward the end of her chapter, she offers several policy options that might be considered for resolving what is now a common property rights problem.

Some might argue with the earlier assertion that there is a property rights movement sweeping across the United States. But the fact that more than forty state legislatures are debating property rights legislation and thirteen have passed such statutes surely implies a movement is at work. In Chapter 6 Hertha Lund tells about the legislative efforts and the kinds of bills considered and passed, and discusses the coalitions that formed in the effort to obtain and to stop property rights legislation. She maintained close contact with participants in some of the legislative efforts and attended many hearings on the topic.

Chapter 6 lays a logical foundation for Chapter 7, which develops a special interest theory of the state legislation movement and then provides a statistical analysis of what has happened. In Chapter 7, Jody Lipford and Donald Boudreaux apply a public choice explanation of the property rights movement and, using data gathered from the fifty states, build a statistical model that predicts which states will entertain property rights legislation. Their analysis provides insights that reach beyond a legal or historical analysis of the issues and identifies economic and other characteristics related to the effort.

Most people applaud government efforts to protect property and to look out for the public welfare. Indeed, exercise of the police power of the state is often seen as absolutely necessary for protecting landowners and others from harmful pollution, unwanted noise, and a host of other obnoxious invasions. But few people seem to realize that long-held individual rights to environmental quality were protected decades before there was an Environmental Protection Agency. In Chapter 8, Roger Meiners discusses those rights, where they came from, and how they were enforced. He explains the origins of these rights and then presents summaries of a long series of common law cases that resolved land rights controversies. A careful reading of Chapter 8 leaves the impression that there is a workable alternative to centralized command-and-control regulation. Interestingly enough, recent Supreme Court decisions on takings have focused partly on common law rules and how they might be applied to protect environmental and private property rights.

Robert Nelson concludes the collection in Chapter 9. He reflects on the property movement and the issues raised in earlier chapters and then offers another perspective on the evolution of federal control of land. Widely recognized for his work on zoning, other forms of land control, and government land policy, Nelson sees the property rights struggle as more than a constitutional battle. It is a struggle of ordinary people in local settings to maintain their ability to manage their communities and settle land-use disputes. In that sense, the land rights movement again takes us back to the Magna Carta and efforts made by ordinary people to escape feudalism. Once again, as Nelson tells the story, the lord of the manor seeks to set the destiny of his tenants. As we approach the twenty-first century, we are reminded that property issues are never fully resolved. After all, the process underway is evolutionary.

Final Thoughts

A number of organizations and individuals almost too numerous to mention assisted in the development of this book. PERC, its staff, and those who support that organization are due a special note of appreciation. PERC provided funds and energy to support the writers and the researchers who assisted them. The Earhart Foundation assisted by providing summer support to me as the editor, making it possible for the book to proceed at a quicker pace. Over the years, E. I. DuPont has provided regular support of my research on environmental economics, and thus the work of my students. That much-appreciated stimulus assisted in nurturing an interest in property rights.

In addition to thanking these chief benefactors, I wish to thank Clemson University for providing an environment that promotes discussion, debate, and publication of ideas, even when controversial. Finally, I wish to thank my many students who have listened to (or endured) and sometimes challenged my ideas about the linkage between property rights and the survival and prosperity of a free society. In my view, that — the linkage between property rights and liberty — is the critical element in the story.

Notes

1. Reflections on these things are found in Bruce Yandle, "Organic Constitutions and Common Law," *Constitutional Political Economy* 2 (Spring/Summer 1991): 225-41.
2. See Bruce Yandle, "Sir Edward Coke and the Struggle for a New Constitutional Order," *Constitutional Political Economy* 4 (Spring/Summer 1993): 263-85.
3. On this point, see Edward O. Wilson, "Heredity," in *Law, Biology and Culture* (New York: McGraw-Hill, 1994): 76.
4. For a small sample, see Terry L. Anderson and P. J. Hill, "The Evolution of Property Rights: A Story of the American West," *Journal of Law & Economics* 18 (1975): 163-79; Terry L. Anderson and Donald R. Leal, "From Free Grass to Fences," *Free Market Environmentalism* (San Francisco: Pacific Research Institute for Public Policy, 1991): 24-36; and Armen Alchian and Harold Demsetz, "The Property Rights Paradigm," *Journal of Economic History* 13 (1973): 16-27.
5. The notion of a hierarchy of property rights stations, starting with a commons and ending with private property rights, is discussed in Hugh H. Macaulay and Bruce Yandle, *Environmental Use and the Market* (Lexington, Mass.: Lexington Books 1977): 67-80.
6. Bruce Yandle, "Escaping Environmental Feudalism," *Harvard Journal of Law & Public Policy* 15 (Spring 1992): 517-39.
7. Anderson and Leal, op. cit., 31-32.

References

Alchian, Armen, and Harold Demsetz. "The Property Rights Paradigm," *Journal of Economic History* 13 (1973): 16-27.
Anderson, Terry L., and P. J. Hill. "The Evolution of Property Rights: A Story of the American West," *Journal of Law & Economics* 18 (1975): 163-79.

Anderson, Terry L., and Donald R. Leal. "From Free Grass to Fences," *Free Market Environmentalism* (San Francisco: Pacific Research Institute for Public Policy, 1991): 24-36.

Macaulay, Hugh H., and Bruce Yandle. *Environmental Use and the Market* (Lexington, Mass: Lexington Books, 1977): 67-80.

Wilson, Edward O. "Heredity," in *Law, Biology and Culture* (New York: McGraw-Hill, 1994): 76.

Yandle, Bruce. "Organic Constitutions and Common Law," *Constitutional Political Economy* 2 (Spring/Summer 1991): 225-41.

———. "Sir Edward Coke and the Struggle for a New Constitutional Order," *Constitutional Political Economy* 4 (Spring/Summer 1993): 263-85.

———. "Escaping Environmental Feudalism," *Harvard Journal of Law & Public Policy* 15 (Spring 1992): 517-39.

Chapter 1

The Property Rights Movement:
How It Began and Where It Is Headed

Nancie G. Marzulla

In the waning days of the Carter administration, outgoing Secretary of the Interior Cecil Andrus bragged, "We have seen more wilderness and national parks, and more wildlife refuges than all other administrations combined."[1] Few members of the press who heard the remark realized that voters' reaction to the massive conversion of Bureau of Land Management holdings to the status of national parks and wildlife refuges during the Carter years was a major reason why his administration was not returning to office. Still more were puzzled as to why the 1980 election was such a landslide in the west.

Actions taken by the Carter administration more than doubled the size of the National Wildlife Refuge System. An additional five million miles of rivers went to the National Wild and Scenic River System, yielding a fourfold increase in size in just four years. The movement of open public lands to the more permanent status of parks and refuges reduced the likelihood of conversion to private ownership. The private tally yielded the massive increases shown in Figure 1.1 and elicited a sharp response. Perhaps, more than anything else, the Carter expansion of designated lands lit a tinderbox that became known as the property rights movement. But while land purchases and reshuffling may have been the initiating force, other events added fuel to the fire. Countless indivi-

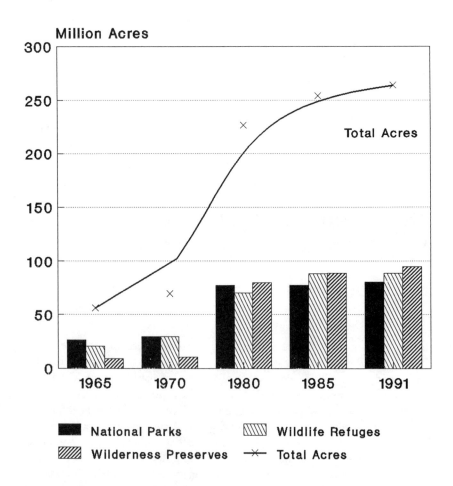

Figure 1.1 Federal public lands

duals seemed to be fed up with regulatory takings, this despite the Constitution's Fifth Amendment protection.

This chapter traces and describes the evolution of America's property rights movement, a rare event in the nation's history about land rights and countless ordinary people who have organized at the grassroots level to make their voices heard by legislative bodies nationwide.

How did it start? The chapter begins with a discussion of the roots of the property rights movement and describes the earlier Sagebrush Rebellion and the later Wise Use movement. Continuing the story, the chapter's next section focuses on the property rights backlash that gained national momentum as more people in more places became incensed about their loss of rights to their own land. A property rights response to the threats engendered by the environmental movement followed, and this is discussed in the section that follows.

While these various social forces were at play, small groups of people nationwide, sharing common concerns about the control of their land, began to organize. The rise of grassroots property rights groups is discussed in the next section. Finally, the chapter concludes with a discussion of property rights as civil rights. Here, a forecast is developed: The property rights movement is to the 1990s what the civil rights movement was to the 1960s. Indeed, there is more to the similarity than that. The property rights movement will not go away because property rights are linked to and are civil rights.

1. The Roots of the Property Rights Movement

In 1964 the Department of the Interior announced a moratorium on claiming desert land for farming purposes. That year was a turning point in the history of U.S. land policy. Since the founding of the republic, the federal government considered public lands as temporary holdings to be claimed, privatized, and homesteaded as the nation grew in population. The Great Society, which changed so many things about America, changed federal land policy as well.

The moratorium aroused little attention outside the American West, but provoked distinct outrage in the state of Nevada. The federal government administers approximately 46 million acres of the state, totaling roughly 87 percent of the land (much of which is classified as desert). If other states had been closed to land claims at a similar stage of their development, argued Nevadans, it certainly would have provoked a civil war. Robert List, Nevada's attorney general at the time, brought suit against the Interior Department in an attempt to force the agency to end its moratorium. Secretary Andrus finally capitulated and lifted the moratorium in 1978.

The suit had grown to become the focus of a populist movement in Nevada. Dubbed the "Sagebrush Rebellion" by the national media, it was founded on the principle that the federal government had a trust obligation to dispose of public lands. The momentum of the movement swept List into the Nevada governor's mansion.

Harry Swainston, who was Nevada's deputy attorney general under Governor List, decided to go one step further. Riding the support of the rebellion, he amended the original suit in an attempt to make the federal Bureau of Land Management completely relinquish public lands in Nevada.[2] A state so heavily dominated by federal control, he argued, could not be considered on an "equal footing" with other states (the federal government controls only about 3 percent of the land in other states).[3] He contended that such an overwhelming federal presence itself lessened the state's sovereignty, making it impossible for Nevada to be on a par with other states.

Swainston was not successful in his mission. In an unpublicized decision released in April 1981, U.S. District Judge Ed Reed ruled against the state of Nevada. He rejected the theory that the federal government is but a trustee of public lands, saying that Nevada lost its public domain to federal control when it achieved statehood. He wrote, "No state legislation may interfere with Congress' power over the public domain." Reed also ruled that Congress had the right to withdraw public lands from use for an indefinite period of time. When pressed, he denied a rehearing by the state.[4]

Judge Reed's decision, however, came too late to stem the tide of change. The Sagebrush Rebellion was spreading like wildfire across the West. From Nevada through Utah, Wyoming, and Montana, people were growing frustrated with the federal government's opposition to resource development in their region. Western states are a treasure trove of natural resources, containing an estimated 15 billion barrels of oil and 100 trillion cubic feet of natural gas, producing 40 percent of the nation's coal, holding enormous reserves of metals, and yielding vast productivity in the timber and cattle industries.[5] But with less than 5 percent of the nation's population, Westerners found themselves at the mercy of a Congress comprised of representatives from the more populous and urban states that saw the West as a wilderness playground that must be preserved and not developed—even at the cost of local poverty and unemployment. One national newspaper noted "a diffuse and ill-focused feeling of uneasiness, powerlessness, and anger that cuts through political and socioeconomic boundaries" among residents of the region.[6]

The first people to actively organize against the government were those dependent on federal lands for their livelihoods. Landowners being closed out of the productive use of their lands included farmers, ranchers, miners, loggers, and "inholders"—those with property bordering or surrounded by federal land. As the ability of these people to earn a living was infringed upon and their land increasingly threatened by federal control, they began to fight back. Trade associations representing each of these interest groups (such as the National Cattlemen's Association) fought specific regulations, but there was no real "network" connecting the organizations. The establishment of broader organizations like the Center for the Defense of Free Enterprise, National Inholders Association (now the American Land Rights Association), and People For the West! in the mid 1970s created a common network, and a name—the "Wise Use" movement. A coalition composed of real estate developers, hunters, fishermen, off-road bikers, 4-wheel-drive enthusiasts, and others formed the growing opposition to the environmentalist lobby.

Bill Burke of the left-wing Political Research Associates authored a highly critical report of the Wise Use movement, but, according to Scott Allen in the *Boston Globe,* even Burke had to admit the movement raises "valid issues about protecting property rights and about environmentalists' exaggerations."[7]

Property Rights Comes into Its Own

The focus on property rights rapidly began to emerge from the Wise Use movement to become a force in its own right. Infringement of the Fifth Amendment was not just a problem in the West anymore, but had grown to become a nationwide concern.

Just as infringement on the rights of the colonists led to the American Revolution in 1776, so it was that incursions on property rights in the name of the environment sparked the property rights revolt two hundred years later. Starting in the 1960s, federal, state, and local governments increasingly began to regulate property through environmental protection policies.[8] However, with the beginning of the decade of the 1970s, practically all environmental regulation was dictated from Washington.

The growth of environmental regulation can be reckoned in numerous ways, but dollar compliance costs tell an important part of the story. According to a definitive study by Thomas D. Hopkins of the Rochester Institute of Technology, environmental regulation costs rose from $41 billion annually in 1973 to $126 billion in 1993, stated in constant 1988 dollars.[9] But these estimates do not account for the productivity drag of regulation or the value of lost consumption that accompanies higher prices generated by regulation.

Of even greater importance to the average American, environmental rules brought intrusion into ordinary life. Whether it be repairing an auto air conditioner, replacing linoleum, or trying to dispose of tires and insecticides, countless people became aware of a new regulatory maze. Of course, loss of jobs because forest land and agricultural property were put off limits communicated the problem in even starker terms.

Counted in still other ways, the trend of regulation in the 1970s can be just short of startling. Figure 1.2 shows the annual number of pages, from before World War II to 1993, printed in the *Federal Register.* Of course, not all regulations are environmental, but much of the increase seen after 1970 reflects the environmental saga. Notice that the annual page count peaks in the last year

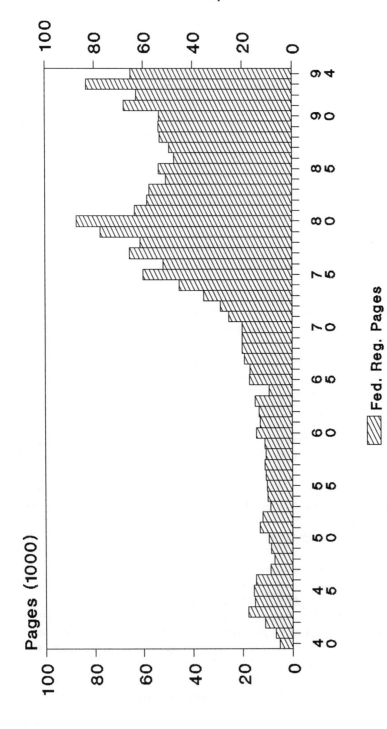

Figure 1.2 Federal register pages

of the Carter administration. In fact most of that occurred in the administration's last day, turned down during the Reagan years, and resumed its upward move during the Bush years. From the 1970s forward, the government printing presses were busy turning out new rules.

Roots of Today's Property Rights Movement

A more fundamental effect of regulation ignited the afterburner of the property rights movement. After rules appeared in the *Federal Register*, ordinary people confronted regulators, and in this case, the regulators wanted and were empowered to restrict the use of land, or take it, without compensation. Countless individuals across America felt they were singled out to bear the burden of implementing environmental policies, all in the name of serving the public interest.

Not concerned so much about the reasons for the rules, most individuals simply expected to be paid when their property was taken. But that was not the way the game was played. Government was simply not prepared to pay for valuable land, species habitat, historic corridors, and other land features that seemed so important to serving the public interest. Through its ability to regulate, the federal government increasingly chose to "take." When government takes by regulation, title to the property remains with the owner, so government argues it should not have to pay for it no matter the severity of the regulation.

It is this infringement of constitutional rights—not opposition to environmental protection—that provoked the property rights movement. The central idea is that no motive, no matter how laudable its purpose (including environmental protection), can justify violating the Constitution.[10] This includes the requirement to pay just compensation for takings. The strong antagonism between property rights activists and their environmentalist counterparts stems from the fact that environmentalism has supported the regulation that provides the majority of the rationale for the current attack on property rights. As Justice Oliver Wendell Holmes noted over seventy years ago, "a strong public desire to improve the public condition is not enough to warrant achieving the desire by a shorter cut than the constitutional way of paying for the change."[11]

2. Fueling the Property Rights Backlash

Federal environmental regulation, to some degree, can be traced back to early conservationists like John Muir, Gifford Pinchot, and Theodore Roosevelt. The birth of the modern environmental regime, however, can be traced back to April

22, 1970—the celebration of the first Earth Day. In rapid succession after that day, Congress, having created the Environmental Protection Agency in 1970, passed a string of environmental statutes that, when woven together, create a regulatory net covering virtually every aspect of property use and ownership. Not only do these regulations give the federal government the power to limit the exercise of private property rights, but they require, encourage, or serve as models for more stringent state and local regulation as well.

Even if we recognize that there is an important benefit side to the regulatory ledger, it is the maze of rules confronted by people far and wide that must be appreciated in order to understand the rising level of frustration that fueled the property rights movement. A survey of key environmental statutes and some of their provisions will help to communicate that dimension of the story.

The 1970 *National Environmental Policy Act* (NEPA),[12] one of the first comprehensive statutes, requires the preparation of an Environmental Impact Statement (EIS) for any "major federal action" significantly affecting the quality of the human environment. This encompasses permits and authorizations for things like road construction and mineral and timber sales as well as generic programs like oil leasing and gas exploration on federal lands. NEPA, in fact, also affects a broad array of private resource development. Opponents of such development rely on NEPA—often referred to as the "grandfather of all environmental statutes"—as a means of stopping projects on grounds that an environmental impact statement was not prepared or is inadequate.

Originally passed in 1970, significantly amended in 1977, and massively overhauled in 1990, the *Clean Air Act*[13] regulates the emission of pollutants into the atmosphere. It requires permits for "major sources" of air pollution. Regulations implementing the Clean Air Act of 1990 are still being written, so basic questions about operating permits and air quality requirements remain unclear. The Clean Air Act is primarily implemented through state legislation that must be submitted for federal review in the form of a State Implementation Plan (SIP). A state's failure to enact legislation to the satisfaction of the federal government may result in the imposition of a Federal Implementation Plan as well as sanctions like a cut-off of highway construction funds or punitive cutbacks in allowable emissions. The most expensive of the federal environmental regulatory programs to date, the Clean Air Act has spawned regulations that affect the siting of industrial plants and the expansion of communities, which is to say, the use of private property by its owners.

Discharge of pollutants into the waters of the United States is the target of regulations pertaining to the *Clean Water Act*.[14] Passed in 1972, the Clean Water Act has never been significantly amended, although amending legislation was proposed in the 103rd Congress. Like the Clean Air Act, Clean Water is implemented through state permitting programs called the National Pollution Discharge Elimination System (NPDES). Unlike Clean Air, however, Clean Water has no State Implementation Plan; instead, the federal government prescribes water quality standards that the state must achieve. Clean Water is also a principal vehicle for funding municipal wastewater treatment plants. Just as the Clean Air Act limits the uses to which private land can be put by requiring permits for new and expanding sources of emissions, the Clean Water Act limits land use where there is any meaningful form of wet discharge.

More to the point of the property rights movement, Section 404 of the Clean Water Act serves as authority for federal regulation of approximately 100 million acres of wetlands.[15] Congress has yet to establish a legal definition based on scientific or other criteria for "wetlands." Yet, under the Environmental Protection Agency's wetlands delineation, 75 percent of all wetlands in this country are considered privately owned. The unlucky private owner of a wetland, however, must leave his property untouched, and will rarely receive any payment from the government for so doing. Even in light of this imposition, he must still pay property taxes on the land, and on the passing of the land to heirs, they may pay inheritance taxes based on fair market value before the effects of the regulatory restriction.

The *Resource Conservation and Recovery Act* (RCRA)[16] prescribes a "cradle-to-grave" program for the management of hazardous waste. Drums of toxic waste must be labeled, manifested, and tracked to their ultimate place of disposal. Treatment, storage, and disposal (TSD) facilities must obtain RCRA permits and comply with stringent regulations concerning construction, allowable wastes, groundwater monitoring, closure plans, and financial responsibility. RCRA permitting programs are often delegated to states, which frequently impose additional requirements with regard to the handling of hazardous wastes.

The *Comprehensive Environmental Response, Compensation and Liability Act* (CERCLA, or "Superfund")[17] differs sharply from the Clean Air Act, Clean Water Act, and RCRA because it is a liability scheme rather than a permitting program. CERCLA imposes joint and several strict liability upon the owner, operator, transporter, or person arranging for the disposal of hazardous substances whenever those substances are released into the environment. Literally hundreds of firms and organizations, even EPA itself, can become counted among the potentially responsible parties in one Superfund site.[18] Each party has an incentive to sue the other in an effort to avoid paying the full site clean-up cost, which on average runs $25 million. More than a thousand Superfund sites have been identified nationwide, but fewer than one hundred have been cleaned since passage of the original 1980 statute. All the while, communities are disrupted, land values fall, and homeowners are left to wonder about health risks, which EPA itself says are generally minimal.

Massively overhauled in 1986 by the Superfund Amendment and Reauthorization Act (SARA), CERCLA also provides injunctive authority to the federal government to require private parties to "reclaim" sites that frequently were no part of the parties' operations or property. The federal government is involved in the design and implementation of cleanup programs that require runoff from a completed site to meet the drinking water standard, even if the site is located on industrial land. Most states also have their own clean-up program and mini-superfunds.

The *Surface Mining Control and Reclamation Act of 1977* (SMCRA),[19] administered by the Surface Mining Office of the Interior Department, requires reclamation of surface mine lands to conditions approximating their original natural contours. It also imposes penalties, to be deposited in the Abandoned Mineland Reclamation Fund, for reclamation of orphan sites. States also regulate surface mining under their own laws.

The *Endangered Species Act of 1973* (ESA)[20] forbids the "taking" of any species of animal or plant listed by the U.S. Fish and Wildlife Service as endangered, where "taking" is so broadly interpreted that making undue noise that might disturb a listed species can constitute a violation of the law. With some 1,200 species and subspecies listed, the ESA also covers the disturbance of species habitat. Initially funded with taxpayer dollars to acquire sensitive habitat from private owners, the Fish and Wildlife Service from 1966 through 1989 purchased 735,396 acres of private land for habitat and other protective purposes, but along the way the tables turned.[21] Under the ESA the Fish and Wild Service, now without funding, routinely engages in regulatory takings and in the process locks up hundreds of thousands of acres of privately owned land.[22] The protected species sometimes is found in competition with the provision of important public services, causing controversies that can agitate large groups of people who are understandably concerned primarily with their livelihoods and welfare.

For example, consider the case of a few innocent salamanders, feeding off the Edwards Aquifer in San Antonio, Texas. Their "protection" threatens the operation of a thriving city's water supply, with no compensation offered to those who bear the cost of maintaining biological diversity. A similar story is found in Cherokee County, Georgia, where a planned water reservoir "needed to alleviate water shortages" was blocked "when it was determined that two types of tiny fish living downstream from the dam would be endangered by the project."[23] As indicated in the news story, "[m]ost folks had never heard of the 2-inch Cherokee Darter and Etowah Darter and the stoppage of the project brought protests from residents and officials in Cherokee."[24] Such controversies, which are not uncommon, do little to engender support for protecting threatened species.

Property owners often find themselves targeted by ESA recovery plans that call for invocation of the Clean Water Act, the designation of a Scenic River, or encouraging local zoning as a means of seizing control of private property in order to protect the endangered species. Such plans are often blatant in their hostility toward property owners, containing mandates for "land acquisition" (not purchase); "zoning process" and "local ordinances" covering "non-federal lands"; and "control of land use."[25] To an ordinary citizen, or almost anyone else, the open-ended nature of ESA recovery can sound ominous. The plan for the painted snake coiled forest snail, for example, merely says, "If landowners are not in agreement, investigate other options for protecting habitat." For the swamp pink, the plan advises that "nontraditional avenues for endangered species protection . . . will be investigated."[26] In practice, these "nontraditional" options have included using everything from wetlands legislation to soil erosion control requirements to shut down private land use.

State and Local Regulation

Every state has adopted various sorts of environmental protection schemes that mirror, and in some cases exceed, the requirements of federal statutes. They logically adapt to the state's own ecological, economic, and social needs, but add another layer of rules and regulation. Some of these programs are federally mandated, while others are purely home grown. The variety and peculiarities of state environmental regulation cannot be catalogued in this brief survey, but it is important to note that it is often the state—rather than federal—regulatory scheme that most directly touches people on a daily basis.

A number of federal environmental statutes set minimums (or "floors") for state environmental protection on the rationale that states should not be allowed to create "pollution havens" where industry may flee to avoid environmental regulation. These federal statutes, however, provide substantial flexibility to states in determining how they will achieve compliance with the federal requirements, and allow states to adopt additional and more stringent regulations. State air pollution control laws often reach far beyond the basic requirements of the federal Act. California, New York, and Colorado have adopted highly specialized air pollution regulations to address their unique and very different climatic conditions, geographies, and population distributions. Indeed, the peculiar atmospheric conditions and population concentrations in a handful of cities, particularly Los Angeles, combine to generate tighter tailpipe emissions for all automobiles, no matter where they are sold. Instead of having to deal with the rising cost of environmental quality they generate in their own communities, people concentrated in a few places can export their costs to the rest of the nation.

Similarly, programs for controlling water pollution, wetlands, nonmunicipal drinking water supplies, underground injection, and other hazardous waste treatment or disposal programs must each be conducted in accordance with federal regulations, often denying flexibility and innovative home-grown solutions that might better suit a given group of people. Mineland bonding and reclamation, application of agricultural chemicals, and the protection of groundwater are effectively "state-led" programs where the federal government defers to local authorities as the more appropriate regulators of the activities in question. State "mini-superfunds," SEPA (the state equivalent of NEPA) requirements, recycling laws, labeling rules, and "community right-to-know" requirements are all examples of state analogies to federal statutes that either embroider federal regulatory programs or extend to activities not otherwise regulated.

The field of public health and safety has traditionally been the domain of the states, although recent years have seen significant federal encroachment on this formerly exclusive preserve. Similarly, zoning and land-use restrictions on private property are essentially a function of state and local governments, despite recent federal incursions of programs like wetland regulations. States have recently expanded their land-use regulations to include historic preservation, battlefield protection, scenic designations, setbacks along waterways and streams, farmland protection, establishment of "greenways," buffer zones, designation of parks and preserves, and restrictions on natural resource development. Finally, licensing and permitting schemes, economic incentives, and taxation are typical devices of state and local governments that serve as a means of encouraging or discouraging certain economic activities that ultimately affect the environment.

Taken together with a comprehensive battery of federal, state, and local regulations directly applicable to activities affecting the environment and land use, these economic incentive/disincentive policies can effectively prohibit or eliminate many otherwise feasible and productive human activities. But to focus again on the frustration problem, the rich and sometimes tortuous combination of rules makes it impossible for ordinary people to know the law, let alone abide by it.

Such was the case for Richard Delene and his 2,400-acre nature preserve in Upper Peninsula, Michigan.[27] Richard and his wife, Nancy, acquired their small wilderness for the purpose of reliving the life of Henry Thoreau whose words marked a sign on their property: "In the wilderness there is preservation of the world." Protected with lock and key were 26 acres of duck ponds and more than 100 acres of enhanced habitat the Delenes had built. More work was under way. But it was armed agents of the Michigan Department of Natural Resources who rudely disturbed their preserve. The Delenes had not obtained state permits for moving dirt. They now face potential fines in excess of $1.2 million and are under a permanent restraining order to cease all their construction activity.

The Burden of Environmental "Overkill"

Environmental regulation touches virtually every individual in this country on an almost daily basis. Environmental laws regulate the air we breathe, water we drink, food we eat, clothes we wear, and homes we live in. Likewise, nearly every sector of the economy is touched by environmental laws whose reach becomes increasingly global.

Environmental regulations currently in place reach from the depths of the sea to the heights of the stratosphere—from the rain forests of South America to the windswept heights of the mountains of Mongolia and back again, to include species from a whale to a blind salamander living in a single cave in Arkansas. No wonder individuals often feel incapable of protecting their rights against this massive regulatory steamroller. Yet while the goals of each environmental initiative may be praiseworthy and justified on some important public interest basis, the burden of providing the benefits often falls squarely and unjustly on the backs of individuals who are asked to yield their property without compensation to serve the greater good.

At some point, the burden becomes so heavy and the number affected so large that even the widely dispersed and politically weak find a way to respond. And when that happens, much of the good that might have been accomplished in the name of protecting the environment may be lost, all due to regulatory overkill.

2. The Property Rights Movement Responds

In simple terms, the current regulatory regime has pitted environmental protection against the individual's right to use and benefit from his own land. But there is more to the problem than the burden felt by individual landowners. When private land is taken for wetlands protection, a ten-year Superfund project is started, or land rental and resale values are reduced by endangered species restrictions, these regulations also challenge the ability of communities to maintain a tax base. These combined effects have left a bitter taste in the mouths of millions of people across the United States who, in the 1990s, are beginning to fight back yet again. These people are founding organizations and learning more about their rights, seeking relief from invasions of property that have become so rampant in this country.[28]

The embryonic ideas of the property rights movement were highlighted at the 1981 "Colonies in Revolt" conference sponsored by the Institute of the American West in Sun Valley, Idaho. "What we have been calling the revolt of the West," said Montana film writer and producer Annick Smith, "is an assertion of individual right[s]."[29] "[T]he more decentralized the decisionmaking, the faster and more valid decisions will be made," declared Montana rancher John Roush.[30] "Cowboys and Indians will be on the same side in the next fight because neither wants to be busboys in Ramada Inns,"[31] explained Vine Deloria, a member of the Standing Rock Sioux Tribe and author of the book *Custer Died for Your Sins*.

The Reagan Revolution

With the sentiments of the Sagebrush Rebellion raging through the West in 1980, many westerners felt drawn to the presidential campaign of former California governor Ronald Reagan, who ran on a campaign theme of "Get government off our backs! and out of our pockets." Using the support of these activists and others to propel himself into the White House, Reagan returned the favor by appointing a number of Westerners to key positions in his administration. These appointments included Bureau of Land Management (BLM) Director Bob Burford and Environmental Protection Agency Administrator Anne Gorsuch, both of Colorado. Reagan's most notable, and perhaps most controversial, Western appointment, however, was James Watt of Wyoming as secretary of the interior. Before coming to Washington, Watt was former director of the Mountain States Legal Foundation, a pioneer in property rights law.

When he started at Interior, Watt found it "to be in bad need of good management," noting in particular that national parks—land so zealously acquired by his predecessor—had deteriorated in "a shameful way" while wildlife refuges "had been ignored."[32] Word went out at Interior that these features of the nation's patrimony would not be compromised.

But it was Watt's property rights and Wise Use approach to environmental issues and numerous statements to that effect that made him the number one target of environmentalists. Watt's name and picture became the focus of environmental rallies and direct-mail campaigns nationwide, making him indirectly a major fundraiser for environmentalism.

"Some of the wild accusations really hurt," Watt admitted. One windfall of his notoriety, however, was that "exaggerated accusations forced Congress to see what Jim Watt is really doing"—resulting in what was considered to be a "phenomenally successful" tenure.[33] Constant pressure led to his resignation and that of Gorsuch during the early years of the Reagan administration. Although his time at Interior was short, Watt's legacy lived on. Many of his appointees at the department served through the Bush years and into the Clinton White House, continuing his agenda long after his departure.

Burford, on the other hand, held office for eight years. He resigned from the agency in 1989 after one of the longest reigns in BLM history. "We think he did a great job," noted Patty McDonald of the Public Lands Council.[34] Keith Knoblock of the American Mining Congress said Burford "ha[d] done a wonderful job of promoting and forging strong links between the BLM and the mining industry, something that has not happened in recent memory."[35] Even Johanna H. Wald, senior attorney and public lands expert for the Natural Resources Defense Council, grudgingly admitted, "I couldn't say Burford left the lands in absolutely worse shape than he found them."[36]

Property rights made substantial legal gains during the Reagan years, especially at the Supreme Court level. During his eight years in the White House, President Reagan had the opportunity to appoint a third of the Court—including elevating William Rehnquist to Chief Justice. He also appointed Antonin Scalia, who has proved to be a strong advocate of property rights.[37]

Prior to the Reagan years, the Court showed little interest in property rights law. In 1922, Justice Holmes announced the bedrock principle of takings law: "The general rule, at least, is that while property may be regulated to a certain extent, if regulation goes too far it will be recognized as a taking."[38] After this ruling, however, the Court showed no interest in cases that would actually enforce this doctrine. In 1978, the issue of regulatory takings had such little activity that Justice William Brennan declared he was simply "unable to develop any 'set formula' for determining when 'justice and fairness' require that economic injuries caused by public action be compensated by the government rather that remain disproportionately concentrated on a few persons."[39] The only guidance Brennan could offer was to order courts to review the circumstances of alleged takings—creating an ad hoc three-factor factual inquiry.

In 1987, following the appointments of Rehnquist, Scalia, and Sandra Day O'Connor, the Court seemed willing to again look at takings issues with favoritism toward the property owner. During the 1987 term, the justices agreed to hear the trilogy of *Hodel v. Irving*, *First English Evangelical Church v. County of Los Angeles*, and *Nollan v. California Coastal Council*.

During the 1980s, the courts fiercely struggled with these issues. They started by agreeing to hear more takings cases, but raised procedural hurdles in front of landowners, making it difficult to find a case to be ripe.[40] Cases the Supreme Court did hear brought increasingly positive news to property owners. The steps, while positive, were incremental. The Court deferred less to legislative determinations, taking on the role of balancing public and private interests.[41] It further held that a regulation must substantially advance a legitimate state interest. Even if a regulation does this, it cannot deny a landowner economically viable use of his land,[42] physically occupy any part of his land,[43] or provide free public access to his land.[44]

In the *First English* decision, the Court held that the county was required to compensate a church barred by a flood control ordinance from reconstructing summer camp buildings destroyed during a 1978 flood. In *Nollan*, the Court ruled that the California Coastal Commission could not require the owner of a home next to a beach to donate a third of his land to the state in order to obtain a permit rebuild the house. It required that just compensation be paid in order for the transaction to occur. *Hodel* secured property rights pertaining to future interest in a property.

In 1992, the Court again ruled for the plaintiff in *Lucas v. South Carolina Coastal Council*—giving the property rights movement a huge victory. *Lucas* represents the culmination of seventy years of regulatory takings jurisprudence.

After Lucas purchased two lots of beachfront property for the sole intent of development, he was told he could not do so because of recently enacted state environmental regulations.

The central holding of *Lucas* is that "[r]egulations that deny the property owner of all 'economically viable use of his land' constitute one of the discrete categories of regulatory deprivations that require compensation without the usual case-specific inquiry into the public interest advanced in support of the restraint." It is important to note that, because of this ruling, the court need not engage in ad hoc inquiry, thus keeping the government from introducing countervailing evidence to defeat the claim.

The Lucas decision also deals with the issue of ripeness. Instead of ducking the issue as it had previously, the *Lucas* court noted ripeness was a state concern that should not hold up Supreme Court review. It remarked: "In these circumstances, we think it would not accord with sound process to insist that Lucas pursue the late-created 'special permit' procedure before his takings claim can be considered ripe."

Reagan's legal legacy continued into the Clinton years. The appointment of judges like Jay Plager to the Court of Appeals for the Federal Circuit, and Alex Kosinski (1981-85) and Loren Smith (1985-present) as chief judges of the Court of Federal Claims as well as Moody Tidwell as a judge for the same court has brought property rights victories in 1994 in cases like *Loveladies Harbor v. United States* and *Florida Rock v. United States*. The Supreme Court also remains active on the issue of property rights, with the hearing of *Florence Dolan v. City of Tigard* in its 1993 term.

In *Dolan*, the Court reversed and remanded a decision by the Oregon State supreme court compelling a property owner to give almost 10 percent of her land to the city for the creation of a greenway and bike path. A permit for Mrs. Dolan to enlarge her plumbing supply business hinged on her agreement to donate the land. In his majority opinion, Chief Justice Rehnquist wrote: "We see no reason why the Takings Clause of the Fifth Amendment, as much a part of the Bill of Rights as the First Amendment and Fourth Amendment, should be relegated to the status of a poor relation in these comparable circumstances."[45]

The biggest boost Reagan gave to the property rights movement, however, was Executive Order 12630, entitled "Governmental Actions and Interference With Constitutionally-Protected Property Rights."[46] Executive Order 12630 recognizes that the government, short of the formal exercise of its eminent domain authority, can acquire private property through regulation or "inverse condemnation." Modeled after requirements for NEPA's "Environmental Impact Analysis," Executive Order 12630 requires "Takings Impact Analysis" of most government regulations to prevent unnecessary takings and allow the government to budget funds for compensating those actions involving necessary takings.[47] The executive order provides for an orderly accounting of the takings implications of government regulation, but does not necessarily hinder the enforcement of any environmental or other governmental program.

The purpose of the executive order is "to assist Federal departments and agencies in . . . proposing, planning, and implementing actions with due regard for the constitutional protection provided by the Fifth Amendment" and "to reduce the risk of undue or inadvertent burdens on the public fisc resulting from lawful government actions." The attorney general, in consultation with executive departments and agencies, is responsible for promulgating "Guidelines for the Evaluation of Risk and Avoidance of Unanticipated Takings." The head of each executive department or agency is required to designate an official responsible for ensuring compliance with the order, and requires agencies to report identified takings implications and actual takings claims to the Office of Management and Budget for planning and budgetary purposes. Supreme Court decisions serve as the touchstone for formulating these guidelines.

Executive Order 12630 does not enlarge or fix the scope or definition of regulatory takings. The Fifth Amendment itself still sets the floor upon which government may exercise its power in ways that adversely affect private property rights. The order simply requires decision makers to ascertain whether a proposed act will activate the Constitution's guarantee that private property not be taken for public use without just compensation before the act goes into effect.

The Bush U-Turn

By changing from an adversarial to a cooperative attitude with property owners, the Reagan administration took the wind out of the sails of the growing property rights movement—effectively disarming landowners and resource users. According to the *New York Times*: "Mr. Burford . . . said he helped end the 'sagebrush rebellion' . . . by seeing to it that the Federal Government . . . is sensitive to the needs of all users of the public range."" This left Westerners vulnerable to the an unexpectedly adversarial administration.

On the campaign trail, then-Vice President George Bush said he wanted to be known as the "environmental president." After his election, he appointed William Kane Reilly as administrator of the Environmental Protection Agency. Under his guidance, the EPA issued a new wetlands delineation manual in 1989. By broadening the definition of "navigable waters," it redefined land that held water for short periods of time each year as "wetlands"—almost doubling the amount of land over which the federal government exercises control (from 100 to 200 million acres), 75 percent of which is privately owned. This change vastly expanded federal control over private property under the Clean Water Act and habitat protection for migratory waterfowl. As Indiana Farm Bureau President Harry Reardon wrote at the time:

Few people realize that the laws governing wetlands and private property have not changed in 20 years. What has changed is the interpretation of those laws by several bureaucrats . . . The intent is to control all land, not just wetlands.[49]

The Bush administration was unable to cope with the property rights movement. Having distanced itself from the Reagan agenda through appeasement of environmentalists, it could not accommodate the revolt from the heartland. The *Washington Post* reported:

The Bush administration . . . finds itself straddling an awkward ideological fence. Many members of the core Republican constituency are active in the property rights movement. . . . However, President Bush has indicated support for the environment.[50]

What Has Regulation Wrought?

More than anything else, perhaps, federal wetlands regulations were the spark that ignited the renewed property rights revolt. The wetlands rules were the basis for many of the cases that have underscored the arbitrariness and injustices committed by the enforcement regime, under which people were sent to federal prisons for acts done on their privately owned land. For example:

• The EPA and FBI began to stake out the property of Marinus Van Leuzen after he challenged the government to "buy his land or put him in jail." Van Leuzen, who owns a house on stilts on the Bolivar Peninsula in Texas, put sand under his home to park his truck and set up lawn chairs. The U.S. Army Corps of Engineers and EPA ordered him to stop his development because it was deemed an illegal destruction of wetlands. After a six-hour meeting held in Washington with the assistant attorney general for the environment and natural resources and representatives of the Corps, EPA, and FBI, a decision was made to prosecute him.

• Ocie Mills and his son Carey served twenty-one months in jail and were fined $10,000 for the crime of dumping sand on Ocie's Florida property while building a home for Carey. The Mills' land contained a drainage ditch and pool. Federal District Judge Vinson later ruled that "at the time in question, Mills' land was probably not a wetland for the purposes of the Clean Water Act."[51]

• Marine engineer Bill Ellen was sentenced to six months' jail and six months' home supervision in 1990 for building a wildlife sanctuary on Maryland's Eastern Shore. The man who hired Ellen for the job, millionaire commodities trader Paul Tudor Jones II, escaped going to trial by paying a $1 million fine and making a $1 million donation to an environmental group. The "wetland" Ellen disturbed was so dry and dusty that construction workers were forced to wear surgical masks and keep the ground wetted down while they worked.

But not all stories of personal tragedies inflicted on individual property owners concern wetlands. Other well-known cases include:

• Wayne Hage, author of a history of the Sagebrush Rebellion entitled *Storm Over Rangelands*,[52] who after filing a takings suit against the federal government, was convicted of damaging or removing federal property. Hage had cut down trees blocking his right-of-way to maintain a ditch. Hage appealed, but his convictions were overturned by the 9th Circuit, U.S. Court of Appeals.[53] Additionally, the U.S. Forest Service's petition for a rehearing was denied in June 1994.

• Ann Corcoran, former National Audubon Society lobbyist, discovered that the National Park Service was engaged in secret maneuvers to incorporate her Civil War-era home and surrounding property into the Antietam National Battlefield. She and Ann Frobuch later founded the property rights *Land Rights Letter*.[54]

Stories like these have multiplied around the country in recent years. More often than not, each case gives birth to a local property rights organization established to fight the government. A good number of these organizations still exist today, even though their founding issue may be gone.

3. The Rise of the Grass Roots Property Rights Group

By 1992, property rights had become such an active issue at the grassroots level that even the *New York Times* took note of what was happening: "[T]he strength of the property rights movement, as it is often called, comes from joining the old wings of the 1970s Sagebrush Rebellion in the West—miners, loggers, ranchers and energy companies—with private landowners in the East and South."[55]

This was a trend picked up by a large portion of the establishment media, which had previously ignored the concerns of property owners and those who were dependent on land development and use for their livelihoods. The *Chicago Tribune* reported: "The issues that have increasingly brought aggrieved property owners together in the last one to two years read like an environmentalist's wish list: wetlands preservation, endangered species protection, public park and greenway expansions, scenic river corridors, land use planning, and zoning laws and growth management plans."[56]

One way landowners are fighting back is by taking their cases to court. In increasing numbers, they are emerging victorious. Property rights activists gained substantial legal muscle with the founding of the Pacific Legal Foundation (PLF) in 1973. PLF was the first nonprofit, public interest law firm litigating in defense of individual and economic freedoms on a national basis. This legal work includes protecting property rights and encouraging limited government. Over the next fifteen years, the Sacramento, California-based PLF participated in over a hundred cases—property rights and otherwise—before the U.S. Supreme Court, as well as countless other cases in lower courts.

In the wake of the victory in *Nollan v. California Coastal Council*, PLF set up the Nollan Follow-Up program to attempt to preserve the gains won in that decision. Besides work in the courtroom, PLF also participates in rulemaking proceedings to hasten regulatory reform.

At a time when many environmental groups are facing a decrease in contributions, PLF has been able to expand its legal staff by one-third as well as open up branch offices in Portland (Oregon), Seattle (Washington), and Anchorage (Alaska). PLF Founder and President Ronald Zumbrun proclaims: "We see the '90s as our decade. . . . We have the weapons — court precedent, experienced personnel, and credibility."[57]

Another result of the government's regulatory explosion has been a strong growth of property rights activism at the grassroots level. When property is affected, especially when a group is threatened, an organization is often formed to provide a unified front against the destruction of their lives and livelihoods. Oftentimes, this organization may go on to have a life of its own after the crisis that spawned it has been resolved. David Lucas, the plaintiff in *Lucas v. South Carolina Coastal Council*, received so many calls and letters from property owners with problems similar to his own that he formed his own groups called the Council on Property Rights. These groups range from small ones being run out of an activist's spare bedroom or den to larger organizations with dedicated staffs.

The Alliance for America serves as a loose confederation of over six hundred property rights organizations. Its first president, David Howard, lives within the boundaries of the Adirondack Park in New York. As a member of a tax grievance committee back in 1990, he stumbled on new state recommendations for land use in his region. While half the area that makes up the park is privately owned, the state sets restrictions on development. Disgusted with the plans, he formed the Adirondacks Blueline Confederation. Soon after that, he was helping to found the alliance at a meeting that included representatives of groups ranging from loggers to fishermen to developers. Howard describes those initial meetings as "so emotional, you could cut the air with a knife." The alliance communicates with its member organizations through a fax network, and hosts the Fly-In for Freedom, the group's annual lobbying excursion. Howard also edits the *Land Rights Letter*.

In Hollow Rock, Tennessee, Henry Lamb runs the Environmental Conservation Organization. He became involved when he read an article in *Outdoor* magazine about efforts to restrict farming because it conflicted with a species of bird's nesting and resting habits. He was appalled by the amount of people he found who considered private property to be a public resource. Professionally, Lamb was an officer in a contractors association. Realizing that any one organization's objectives could not easily be achieved, he set about linking groups together. From an initial seventeen organizations, the ECO coalition now boasts five hundred members. In addition to hosting conferences and publishing a magazine, ECO also maintains a computer network to aid its membership's information and networking needs.

Alice Menks lives near the Shenandoah Mountains in Virginia. She was concerned about what the state was doing in regards to land-use policy—especially the fact that the people who were most affected by it were not being consulted. It didn't take long before she discovered this sort of thing was happening all over the state, and she started running into other aggrieved property owners again and again. This group decided to band together to form Virginians for Property Rights. Menks was their first president. VPR acts as a clearinghouse for Virginians who need help on property rights issues. Although they lack the ability to fight for individuals, they can give information and hints at who fought for and passed SB 514 in 1992. This bill requires the state to involve landowners in land-use issues, and gives them the opportunity to vote on land-use designations affecting them.

Also working within their state is Oregonians in Action. Fred Nims, a career military man who took up farming in eastern Oregon, set up OIA in 1981. What was originally conceived to be a coalition grew into an education center focusing on property rights and land-use regulation reform that opened in 1989. In 1991, it expanded to include a legal center. OIA has been very influential in state politics, promoting ten bills in the 1993 state legislature to protect the rights of farmers and land users (with between eight and twelve planned for next session). Their legal center provided the lawyers for Florence Dolan when she recently took her case to the Supreme Court.

Through groups like these, the media has been forced to take notice of the burgeoning property rights movement. Grassroots activism has been highly effective as well. The property rights issue has unified many people and has been the catalyst for much coalition building. Large rallies and parades revolving around property rights have been held in state capitals from Boise, Idaho, to Tallahassee, Florida. On the federal level, the Alliance for America sponsors an annual "Fly-In for Freedom," bringing property owners from across the United States to meet and discuss their issues with representatives in Washington. The *Washington Post* noted "the growing number of small-scale property owners who, over the last two years, have coalesced into a political force aggrieved with government regulation of their land." It concluded that "the private property rights movement consists of 'moms and pops' who have joined together to fight to use their land as they see fit."[58]

In the midst of all the new lawsuits being filed and the burgeoning effort to translate Executive Order 12630 into legislation at the state level, it became clear that there was a need for a national foundation to formulate and execute a comprehensive litigative, legislative, and grassroots strategy. Hence Defenders of Property Rights was founded in 1991 with a set agenda to bring about a sea change in property rights law through strategically filed lawsuits and groundbreaking property rights legislation. This new initiative, designed to forge a unified national and state strategy in cooperation with existing grassroots forces, soon revealed that the wind had changed for the property rights movement.

What's on the Drawing Board

The 103rd Congress had pending before it proposals which would still further expand the reach of environmental statutes. Members of both houses introduced a broad array of bills to reauthorize and amend the Clean Water Act, ESA, RCRA, and Superfund. These bills would generally increase the penalties for violations, tighten regulatory requirements, and expand the reach of regulations over large groups of individuals and activities not currently subject to federal environmental jurisdiction. One bill, for example, would have defined an individual convicted of an environmental offense as a "bad actor," disqualifying him or his company from participation in government contracting, loans, or grant programs.[59] Another bill would authorize federal judges to compel corporations to adopt comprehensive environmental compliance programs designed by an outside consultant appointed by the court, and would punish infractions of the compliance plan as probation violations.[60]

The strength of property rights can definitely be felt in the 103rd Congress. Besides a number of property rights bills being introduced by Senators Bob Dole of Kansas, Phil Gramm of Texas, Richard Shelby and Howell Heflin of Alabama—joined by congressmen like Richard Pombo and Gary Condit of California (Pombo ran his campaign for Congress on a property rights platform), Billy Tauzin of Louisiana, John Mica of Florida, and many others— many of the bills the environmentalists were pushing were derailed.

Early in the session, Interior Secretary Bruce Babbitt sought approval for his National Biological Survey, an ambitious attempt to map out the United States in ecosystems (at the expense of the rights of property owners). The inclusion of property rights amendments calling for just compensation to be paid for takings and requiring permission for government workers to enter private property led Babbitt to abandon the bill (even though it passed the House) and to proceed with the project without approval. In an another early session vote, congressmen rebelled and voted down the rule on a bill to elevate the EPA to the cabinet because majority leaders in the House would not allow consideration of a risk-assessment amendment.

Environmentalists have felt the effects of these initiatives. A memo from a lobbyist to environmental leaders suggested that their movement "needs to focus more sharply on a limited number of pieces of legislation, and to put more substantial resources into winning [and strengthening] that legislation."[61] For almost all the pending bills to reauthorize environmental regulations, the memo recommended that the bills be held back for fear that property right amendments might be attached to them. To prove this concern, their best prospect—the Safe Drinking Water Act—was amended to include a risk-assessment requirement as well as mandates for "takings impact analysis" on future regulations.

The Clinton administration has given high priority to environmental issues. It is seeking to abolish the Council on Environmental Quality (an independent office established by Congress), replacing it with direct White House control over environmental issues. The administration, along with a majority in Congress at that time, also strongly supported elevation of the Environmental Protection Agency to cabinet status as the U. S. Department of Environmental Protection. Vice President Al Gore took direct charge of the newly created White House Office of the Environment and demonstrated a personal interest in virtually every environmental and natural resource policy issue. At the Timber Summit to discuss environmental issues in the northwest forests held in Portland, Oregon, on April 2, 1993, Clinton and Gore were joined by no fewer than seven members of the cabinet—each of whom offered his or her own suggestions for dealing with spotted owls, timber, and jobs.

Vice President Gore also personally proposed a new method of reviewing government regulations—and has shown a special interest in environmental regulations—to replace Office of Management and Budget review under Executive Order 12291. Although the outlines of the Gore proposal are not yet clear, the process he designs will undoubtedly be even more favorable to expansive government regulation. Indeed, the Clinton administration gives strong evidence of subscribing to Gore's exhortation that the world adopt a new "central organizing principle": to use every policy and program, every law and institution, every treaty and alliance, every tactic and strategy, every plan and course of action—to use, in short, every means to halt the destruction of the environment and to preserve and nurture our ecological system.[62]

The 1990s: The Tide Turns

Senator Ben Nighthorse Campbell of Colorado wrote to Interior Secretary Bruce Babbitt: "People working under your command at the Interior Department seem bent on offending and double-dealing everyone west of Oklahoma City."

These bureaucrats, wrote Campbell, are on a "crusade to push through public lands reforms that fit their own elitist vision of the world. "[63]

By then, even Cecil Andrus, whose 1981 quote as Interior secretary extolling the growth of federal lands started this chapter, had enough. Clinton BLM Director Jim Baca, wrote Andrus (who was now governor of Idaho), "didn't know what he was talking about." An angry Andrus wrote a letter to Babbitt warning him, "Frankly, my friend, you don't have enough political allies in the western United States to treat us this shabbily."[64] (Babbitt was governor of Arizona before he ran for president in 1988. Prior to his move to Interior, he served as president of the environmentalist League of Conservation Voters.)

Baca resigned shortly after the date of Andrus's angry letter. The "Greenwire" environmental press service asked Babbitt what happened. Replied Babbitt: "The Western governors were unhappy with Jim Baca."[65]

Those who once felt powerless to protect their rights are now aggressively seeking relief. They are filing lawsuits seeking the enforcement of their rights, and passing laws requiring prior assessment of the potential "takings" implications of new regulations before they go into effect.

State Legislation: A New Hope

Property rights activists of the 1990s have chosen to fight back in the forums they know best—state and local government. There, they have introduced property rights bills in forty-four states across the United States. As of August 1994, eleven states passed such laws. These bills are leading the federal government in turning the tide to favor private property rights.

It is at the state level that property owners have become most active in efforts to gain new protection for land rights. There are two types of property rights bills at the state level: (1) "planning" bills, and (2) bills that actually identify a numerical percentage of diminution in value that will trigger the constitutional requirement of just compensation.

4. Property Rights: The Civil Rights Issue of the 1990s

Although rooted in the agrarian land-based Sagebrush Rebellion of the 1970s, the property rights battle has now become a fight for freedom and individual rights, with property recognized as more than just land. Just as segregation led to the civil rights movement of the 1960s, government intrusion on property rights—largely in the name of protecting the environment—has sparked a new crusade to protect an individual's right to use and own all forms of and interests in private property. As noted by Noah Webster, the great eighteenth-century American educator and linguist, the link between liberty and private property rights is intrinsic: "Let the people have property and they will have power—a power that will forever be exerted to prevent the restriction of the press, the abolition of trial by jury, or the abridgment of any other privilege."

Steadily increasing regulation at the federal, state, and local levels now touches every conceivable aspect of property use. Through its ability to regulate, the government now more than ever takes the uses and benefits of property rather than condemn it and pay its owner fair market value—violating the Fifth Amendment's guarantee that "nor shall private property be taken for public use, without just compensation." Like civil rights movements of the past, people have also organized to pressure the government through their elected representatives and the courts to change current policies and promote property rights protection.

Today, property rights has become the line drawn in the sand between tyranny and liberty. As a result, the American public is also coming to realize that the environmental ethic is based less on environmental protection and more on the false pretense that people should have only limited rights to own and use their property, when it is deemed acceptable to government regulators. Indeed, the environmental movement is predicated on the notion that the world would be better off without people and their activities:

> Legal experts like Joe Sax and John Echeverria envision a future in which land is treated not as individual castles behind a moat, but as cooperating units of larger natural and economic systems. In fact, says Echeverria, it is inevitable that a crowded Earth will demand more of each of its citizens. "I think this (environmental backlash) is sort of a burp," he says, "an anachronistic movement appealing to the myth of the Boone frontier, which is not what we have anymore."[66]

A close look at the statutes that have been passed to protect the environment reveal how they reflect this antihuman animus. For example, the Clean Water Act is designed to restore the chemical and biological integrity of our nation's waterways. In actuality, it sets a goal of *zero* discharge into our nation's waterways. Needless to say, virtually all human endeavors—including taking a shower—involves the discharge of water into the nation's waterways. The Superfund statute addresses cleaning up soils and groundwater, but it has no limit on the extent of this cleanup. Basically, it requires that land be restored to the way it was when there were no people.

Their policy of making criminals out of ordinary people, who in the course of using their land for such ordinary activities as attempting to build a house on a subdivided lot, illustrates how a wetlands criminal enforcement program has gone far astray of protecting the environment. It again reflects a regulatory scheme that is fundamentally opposed to humans and their activities. A wetlands enforcement program created by bureaucrats and never authorized by

Congress—which sentences people to jail for violation of vague and arbitrary rules and even though there may be no actual harm to the environment by the act, sends people to jail even if they never had any intent to harm the environment, and requires property owners to spend hundreds of dollars to create new wetlands as so-called mitigation—calls to mind a passage from Ayn Rand's classic novel, *Atlas Shrugged*, when government bureaucrat Dr. Ferris tells industrialist Hank Rearden:

> There's no way to rule innocent men. The only power government has is the power to crack down on criminals. When there aren't enough criminals, one makes them. One declares so many things to be a crime that it becomes impossible for men to live without breaking laws. Who wants a nation of law-abiding citizens? What's there in that for anyone—but just pass the kind of laws that can neither be observed nor enforced nor objectively interpreted—and you created a nation of law-breakers—and then you cash in on the guilt . . .

The environmental ethic denies the natural human impulse to own things and protect one's right to ownership as well as shuts out and makes enemies of the majority of Americans. Under it, almost everybody who owns something is doomed to failure. The notion that government can do things better than people can, that federal bureaucrats and local comprehensive planning that deprives property owners of their rights is a better way of doing things, is a failed premise that is increasingly being discredited.

The property rights movement of the 1990s is rooted in the recognition that the "better" way to do things is to recognize property rights and acknowledge the importance of working together with the property owner to achieve environmental protection.

The "commons" will always be at the mercy of politically powerful special interests who hold no stake in the land. Exclusive ownership of property creates the only effective, long-term incentive to conserve resources and minimize pollution. A property owner who blights his land destroys his own estate and that of his heirs; when a bureaucrat blights "public" land, he bears no cost whatsoever. When land belongs to everyone, it really belongs to no one, which is the source of the "tragedy of the commons."

On the other hand, experience teaches that uncompensated takings in the name of environmentalism often creates perverse disincentives that are themselves antienvironmental in effect. If the price of creating habitat is losing property without compensation, where is the motivation to create or maintain habitat? The property rights movement is not seeking less environmental protection; it asks only that the few unlucky landowners who do lose their property to regulation will no longer be forced to bear an unfair share of the burden.

Ultimately, uncompensated takings are not just a problem of economic efficiency, but of justice. The danger was outlined by Chief Justice Holmes in 1922:

> The protection of private property in the Fifth Amendment presupposes that it is wanted for public use, but provides that it shall not be taken for such use without compensation. . . . When this seemingly absolute protection is found to be qualified by the police power, the natural tendency of human nature is to extend that qualification more and more until at last private property disappears.[67]

As the Supreme Court further noted in 1972:

> The dichotomy between personal liberties and property rights is a false one. Property does not have rights. People have rights. The right to enjoy property without unlawful deprivation, no less than the right to speak or the right to travel, is in truth a "personal" right. . . . In fact, a fundamental interdependence exists between the personal right to liberty and the personal right to property. Neither would have meaning without the other.[68]

To defend human rights and to ensure that we live in a world where the environment is protected pursuant to the rule of law as embodied in the Constitution, we must ensure that forced transfers of property—not just through the power of eminent domain, but also through regulatory takings—be allowed only when just compensation is paid. We are already at a major constitutional and governmental crossroads. Property rights advocates are committed to see to it that property rights are vigorously protected.

Notes

1. Cy Ryan, United Press International, January 6, 1981.
2. The Federal government owns 82.265 percent of Nevada's total state acreage. U.S. Department of the Interior, Bureau of Land Management, *Public Land Statistics*, Tables 4 and 5.
3. These include Ala., Conn., Ill., Ind., Iowa, Kans., Maine, N.J., N.Y., Ohio, Okla., Pa., R.I., S.C., Tex., Mich., Minn., Mo., N.C., N.D., Tenn., Wis. Ibid at Table 4.
4. Cy Ryan, United Press International, July 28, 1981.
5. David F. Salisbury, "Energy: The Varmit that May Spoil America's West," *The Christian Science Monitor*, September 3, 1981, p. B26.
6. Ibid.
7. "'Wise Use': Groups on Move Against Enviros in New England," *Greenwire*, October 22, 1992.
8. Although all government regulation can potentially violate the Fifth Amendment, this chapter is limited to a discussion of environmental regulation. (See *Hodel v. Riving*, 481 U.S. 704 (1987) (federal law that provided for escheat of tribal property interests);

Richardson v. City and County of Honolulu, 759 F. Supp. (D. Ha. 1991) (city ordinance that set a dollar ceiling on renegotiated historic rental property); *Seawell Assoc. v. City of New York*, 542 N.E. 2d 1050 (N.Y. 1989) (city ordinance prohibiting the demolition, alteration, or conversion of single-room occupancy rental properties): and *United Artists Theater Circuit v. City of Philadelphia*, 595 A.2d 6 (Pa. 1991) (city ordinance designating property as historic).

9. Thomas D. Hopkins, *Cost of Regulation* (Rochester, N.Y.: Rochester Institute of Technology, 1991) Table 5A.

10. U.S. Constitution, amendments V and XIV; *Pennsylvania Coal Co. v. Mahon*, 260 U.S. 393, 416 (1922).

11. *Pennsylvania Coal*, 260 U.S. at 416.

12. A useful compendium of the various federal statutes discussed in this text is *Federal Environmental Laws* (St. Paul, Mn.: West, 1993).

13. 42 U.S.C. §§ 7401-7671q (1988 & Supp. 1991).

14. 33 U.S.C. §§ 401-26p, 441-54 (1988).

15. For an in-depth discussion of wetlands, see Chapter 2 by Karol Ceplo.

16. 42 U.S.C. §§ 6901-91i. (1988).

17. 42 U.S.C. §§ 9601-75 (1988).

18. See Brett Dalton, "Superfund: The South Carolina Experience," in Roger E. Meiners and Bruce Yandle, eds., *Taking the Environment Seriously* (Lanham, Md: Rowman & Littlefield, 1993), Chapter 5.

19. 30 U.S.C. §§ 1201, 1202, 1211, 1221-30a, 1231-43, 1251 to 1279, 1281, 1291-1309, 1311-16, 1321-28 (1988).

20. 16 U.S.C. §§ 1533-44 (1988).

21. See Thomas R. Dunlap, *Saving America's Wildlife* (Princeton: Princeton University Press, 1988). Also, National Research Council, *Setting Priorities for Land Conservation* (Washington, D.C.: National Academy Press, 1993).

22. On this and more, see Chapter 5 by Lee Ann Welch.

23. Paul Kaplan, "Those Little Fish Still Delaying Cherokee County Reservoir," *The Atlanta Journal/The Atlanta Constitution*, July 3, 1994.

24. Ibid.

25. National Wilderness Institute, "Going Broke? Costs of the Endangered Species Act as Revealed in Endangered Species Recovery Plans," p. 27.

26. Ibid.

27. See Margaret Ann Reigle, "FLOC Members Under Armed Siege Over Duck Ponds," *News from the FLOC*, Cambridge, Md: Fairness to Landowners Committee, February 1994.

28. See Dixy Lee Ray and Lou Guzzo, *Environmental Overkill: Whatever Happened to Common Sense?* (Washington, D.C.: Regnery Gateway, 1993). Also, see Joseph L. Bast, Peter J. Hill, and Richard C. Rue, *Eco-Sanity* (Lanham, Md.: Madison Books, 1994).

29. David F. Salisbury, "Energy: The Varmit that May Spoil America's West," *Christian Science Monitor*, September 3, 1981, p. B26.

30. Ibid.

31. Ibid.

32. Robyn C. Walker, United Press International, January 23, 1982.

33. Ibid.

34. Philip Shabecoff, "Washington Talk: Farewells, Fond and Otherwise, for Land Director," *New York Times*, July 5, 1989.

35. Ibid.

36. Ibid.

37. The Supreme Court Justices during the 1993 - 94 term were Chief Justice William Rehnquist (sworn in January 7, 1972), Henry Blackmun (June 9, 1970 — he retired at the end of the term), John Paul Stevens (December 19, 1975), Sandra Day O'Connor (December 25, 1981), Antonin Scalia (October 6, 1986), Anthony Kennedy (February 18, 1988), David Souter (October 9, 1990), Clarence Thomas (October 23, 1991), and Ruth Bader Ginsburg (August 10, 1993). President Clinton nominated Steven Breyer to fill Blackmun's seat on the Court.

38. *Pennsylvania Coal v. Mahon*, 260 U.S. 393, 415 (1922).

39. *Penn Central Transp. Co. v. City of New York*, 438 U.S. 104, 124 (1978).

40. *San Diego Gas & Electric Co. v. City of San Diego*, 450 U.S. 621 (1981) and *McDonald, Sommer & Frates v. Yolo County*, 477 U.S. 370 (1986).

41. *Agins v. Tiburon*, 447 U.S. 255 (1980).

42. *Keystone Bituminous Coal Ass'n v. DeBenedictis*, 458 U.S. 419 (1982).

43. *Loretto v. Teleprompter Manhattan CATV Corp.*, 458 U.S. 419 (1982).

44. *Kaiser Aetna v. United States*, 444 U.S. 164 (1979).

45. *Dolan v. City of Tigard*, No. 93-518, Slip Op., at 17 (U.S. June 24, 1994).

46. Upon assuming office, President Clinton and Vice President Gore immediately expressed their intent to rescind Executive Order 12630. 53 *Fed. Reg.* 8859 (1988).

47. See Roger J. Marzulla, *The New "Takings" Executive Order and Environmental Regulation — Collision or Cooperation?* 18 *Envntl. L. Rep.* (Envtl. L. Inst.) 10254 (July 1988). Mr. Marzulla, also a westerner and former president of the Mountain States Legal Foundation, was the chief architect of the executive order and appointed by President Reagan to serve as assistant attorney general for the then Land and Natural Resources Division of the United States Department of Justice.

48. Philip Shabecoff, "Farewells, Fond and Otherwise, for Land Director," Phillip Shabecoff, *New York Times*, July 5, 1989, p. A18.

49. Harry Pearson, *Hoosier Farmer*, September - October 1991, p. 3.

50. "A Conservative Supreme Court Addresses Property Rights," Kirstin Downey, *Washington Post*, February 16, 1992, p. H1.

51. *United States v. Mills*, 817 F. Supp. 1546, 1548 (1993).

52. Wayne Age, *Storm Mover Rangelands* (Bellevue, Wash.: Free Enterprise Press, 1989).

53. "Three for Stewards, Zero for Feds," *Cornerstone*, April 1994, p. 2.

54. Wallace Kaufman, "The Cost of 'Saving': You Take It, You Pay for It," *American Forests*, November/December 1993.

55. Keith Schneider, "When the Bad Guy Is Seen as the One in the Green Hat," *New York Times*, February 16, 1992.

56. Rob Rossi, "Conservative Groups See '90s as Decade of Opportunity," *The Reporter*, May 1, 1992.

57. H. Jane Lehman, "Owners Aren't Giving Ground in Property Battles," *Chicago Tribune*, February 9, 1992, p. E1.

58. H. Jane Lehman, "A Changing Tide in Wetlands Decisions: Violators Caught in a Tug of War Over Property Rights, Environmental Protection," *Washington Post*, January 18, 1992, p. E1.

59. H.R. 908, 103d Cong., 1st Sess., The "Bad Actors" bill.

60. H.R. 3461, 103d Cong., 1st Sess.

61. Draft Legislative Strategy Paper developed by Environmental Group Lobbyists dated March 5, 1994, Bureau of National Affairs, March 16, 1994.

62. Al Gore, *Earth in the Balance: Ecology and the Human Spirit* (New York, N.Y.: Plume, 1992), p. 273.

63. Letter from Senator Ben Nighthorse Campbell to Interior Secretary Bruce Babbitt, March 5, 1994. For contrast, see "'Wise Use': Groups on Move Against Enviros in New England," *Greenwire*, October 22, 1992, in which the idea of "land-grabbing elitists" is depicted as a "right-wing" fantasy.

64. Letter from Idaho Governor Cecil D. Andrus to Interior Secretary Bruce Babbitt, August 25, 1993.

65. "Babbitt Outlines Priorities for Coming Year," *Greenwire*, March 28, 1994.

66. "Landowners turn the Fifth into Sharp-Pointed Sword," *High County News*, February 8, 1993, vol. 24, no. 2, p. 12.

67. *Pennsylvania Coal Co. v. Mahon*, 260 U.S. 393, 415 (1922).

68. *Lynch v. Household Finance Corporation*, 405 U.S. 538, 552 (1972).

Chapter 2

Property Rights and the Police Powers of the State: Regulatory Takings: An Oxymoron?

Erin O'Hara

Private property is often viewed as a hallmark of our American legal, political and economic systems. To a greater extent than most other countries, the various governments of the United States are both structured and required to protect that bundle of rights—to possess, use, exclude, and dispose of both tangible and intangible "things"—that we call property.[1] Yet at the same time we seem to accept, at times even welcome, limited governmental interference with this bundle of rights to protect others' property rights or to achieve important policy objectives. The police powers of the state seem inevitably to clash with the notion of private property.

The Bill of Rights to the U. S. Constitution itself reflects a property rights conflict faced by the Founders. In drafting the Bill of Rights, which was a compromise to satisfy the Antifederalists, James Madison saw the need to protect individual rights to property from the excessive use of the powers otherwise granted to the new federal government.[2]

To strike an appropriate balance, the takings clause was included in the Fifth Amendment. The clause provides, in pertinent part, "nor shall private property be taken for public use, without just compensation. "[3] Similar provisions are also found in all the state constitutions.[4]

Over the years, the courts have interpreted takings clause provisions to include two broad requirements: (1) the government can take private property only for public use; and (2) the government must provide the owner with "just compensation" for any property it does take. While these requirements as stated seem to settle a host of issues faced by ordinary citizens, that is indeed not the case. There is obviously much more to the story.

This chapter focuses on the takings issue as seen through the eyes of the courts. By examining decisions of various lower courts, and more importantly, the Supreme Court, one is able to identify patterns and puzzles that may be reflected in today's property rights movement, a movement that seeks strong legislation as a guide for court rulings.

Part One of the chapter takes up the "public use" and "just compensation" principles just mentioned and illustrates how creative interpretations of these common words lead to unexpected outcomes that can erode a common-sense interpretation of the Fifth Amendment. This part of the chapter forms a brief foundation for a more systematic review of takings case law.

The courts have developed two ways to view the claims of property owners seeking compensation for regulatory takings. These form a basis for the chapter's sections two and three. In some instances, the courts rely on a nuisance theory, which suggests that the state has the power to regulate without compensation those private actions that impose costs on the general public. In another category of cases, the courts rely on a notion of reciprocity when upholding uncompensated takings. Under this theory, an aggrieved property owner is seen as bearing the same common burden as everyone else, a burden that presumably generates collective net benefits.

Part two of the chapter uses the nuisance theory as a template for organizing an analysis of Fifth Amendment case law, paying particular attention to Supreme Court decisions. Part three focuses on the reciprocity theory. The cases discussed begin with the late nineteenth century and end with 1994 decisions. Over the years, and with some important exceptions among a few states, the courts have expanded the government's regulatory powers almost infinitely under the guise of preventing harm to others.[5] At the same time, the Supreme Court and a few state courts have come to recognize the importance of reciprocal benefits and burdens to the fundamental fairness of imposing uncompensated regulations on a given property owner.

While some recent court decisions are understandably celebrated by landowners who seek a stricter property rights interpretation, even the more celebrated cases leave serious property rights uncertainties. Part four of the chapter discusses some of these uncertainties and offers concluding thoughts.

1. Some Initial Thoughts on the Takings Clause

As mentioned earlier, the takings clause includes two hurdles a state must clear before interfering with private property rights. The first safeguard allows private property to be taken only for public use. Richard Epstein offers a rationale for this public use requirement based on the fact that a property owner is ordinarily entitled to retain any surplus value his property can command from a willing purchaser. "In sharp contrast, the state's exercise of its eminent domain power forces the private party to accept damages by way of just compensation, equal to the owner's best use of the property before condemnation. The state is thereby allowed to capture without negotiation all the transactional surplus, but only for the benefit of the public at large."[6] The public use requirement should help to ensure against these "naked wealth transfers" from the politically weak to the politically powerful.[7]

However, the public use requirement is presently toothless as interpreted by the federal courts.[8] Even when property is taken by the federal government and given to other private individuals, the Supreme Court finds a public use so long as a legislature stated the public would benefit from the taking. For example, in *Ruckelshaus v. Monsanto Co.* (1984),[9] the government required companies dealing with hazardous chemicals to report specific data to the Environmental Protection Agency, and the data was then given to other companies for their own reporting uses. Monsanto asserted, among other things, that the regulation effected an unconstitutional taking of its trade secrets because they were appropriated for private rather than public uses. The Supreme Court disagreed, and rejected "the notion that a use is a public use only if the property taken is put to use for the general public. . . . So long as the taking has a conceivable public character, the means by which it will be attained is for Congress to determine."[10]

The same year, in *Hawaii Housing Authority v. Midkiff* (1984),[11] the Court was confronted with a challenge to Hawaii's Land Reform Act of 1967, which consisted of a land condemnation scheme under which certain lessors were forced to sell their land to their lessees to reduce the high concentration of land-ownership. The Court concluded that the legislation satisfied the public use requirement, stating that it "will not substitute its judgment for a legislature's judgment as to what constitutes a public use unless the use be palpably without reasonable foundation."[12] After *Midkiff*, it is hard to think of any government action that would violate the public use requirement. Indeed, the Supreme Court asserted as much three decades before *Monsanto* and *Midkiff*: "when the legislature has spoken, the public interest has been declared in terms well-nigh conclusive. . . . The role of the judiciary in determining whether that power is being exercised for a public purpose is an extremely narrow one."[13]

Consequently, any federal constitutional constraint on governmental interference with private property must be found in the second requirement of the takings clause, that the government provide just compensation for its takings. The extent to which the courts actually mandate compensation for interferences with private property depends on the context of the government's action. For example, if the government takes title to property, thereby taking the entire bundle of rights associated with that property, then the government must pay the owner the fair market value of the property taken.[14]

The courts also require the government to provide compensation for interferences short of outright condemnation when the government physically invades private property or requires the owner to allow his property to be physically invaded by others. For example, in *United States v. Causby* (1946),[15] the U.S. military had been frequently and regularly flying army and navy fighter planes close to the ground over the Causby family's property. The planes' startling noises and glaring lights at night left the family frequently deprived of sleep. Moreover, the flights interfered with the family's chicken farm; 150 chickens died after flying into the walls with fright. The Supreme Court held that because the government's flights were so low and frequent that they directly and immediately interfered with the Causby family's use and enjoyment of their land, the government effected an unconstitutional taking of property requiring compensation.

Loretto v. Teleprompter Manhattan CATV Corp. (1982),[16] provides another example. A New York City statute required landlords to permit the cable television company to install cable facilities in their buildings, and an accompanying regulation allowed the landlords to charge the cable company no more than one dollar for installation rights. The Supreme Court held that even though the physical invasion of space was quite small, any permanent physical occupation of property authorized by the government is a taking without regard to the public interest served. According to the Court, even if the government invades only an easement in property, it must nevertheless provide compensation.[17]

Compensation issues become thorny, however, when the government attempts to regulate the uses a private property owner can make of his property. On the one hand:

> government regulation . . . involves the adjustment of rights for the public good. Often this adjustment curtails some potential for the use or economic exploitation of private property. To require compensation in all such circumstances would effectively compel the government to regulate by purchase. Government could hardly go on if to some extent values incident to property could not be diminished without paying for every such change in the general law.[18]

At the same time, the Supreme Court has recognized that the takings clause must provide some protection from governmental efforts to force a few individuals to bear all the costs of governmental programs:

The Fifth Amendment's guarantee that private property shall not be taken for a public use without just compensation was designed to bar government from forcing some people alone to bear public burdens which, in all fairness and justice, should be borne by the public as a whole.[19]

Two centuries of litigation and scholarship have failed to resolve this tension. Indeed, the issue has been described as "the most haunting jurisprudential problem in the field of contemporary land-use law . . . one that may be the lawyer's equivalent of the physicist's hunt for the quark."[20] Most commentators agree that some amount of uncompensated regulation is consistent with the takings clause, but they disagree on where to draw the line.

Probably the most well-known theory of regulatory takings was developed by Frank Michelman, who proposed a utilitarian approach to the constitutional interpretation in his celebrated *Harvard Law Review* article.[21] According to Michelman, property takings and compensation issues involve three fundamental concerns, which he labeled efficiency gains, demoralization costs, and settlement costs. Efficiency gains were defined as "the excess of benefits produced by a measure over the losses inflicted by it."[22] Demoralization costs were defined as "the total of (1) the dollar value necessary to offset disutilities which accrue to the losers and their sympathizers specifically from the realization that no compensation is offered, and (2) the present capitalized dollar value of lost future production (reflecting either impaired incentives or social unrest) caused by demoralization of uncompensated losers, their sympathizers, and other observers disturbed by the thought that they themselves may be [later] subjected to similar treatment."[23] Finally, settlement costs were "measured by the dollar value of the time, effort, and resources which would be required in order to reach compensation settlements adequate to avoid demoralization costs."[24]

Under Michelman's approach, the efficiency gains from interfering with established property rights are compared with the demoralization and settlement costs. If both the two cost types exceed the efficiency gains of the interference, then the property transfer should be forbidden as unconstitutional. The transfer should be permitted if the efficiency gains exceed either of the two cost types. However, compensation should be required only if the settlement costs are lower than both the efficiency gains and demoralization costs. If the settlement costs are higher than the demoralization costs, then it is socially cheaper, or more efficient, to forgo compensation and accept that some property owners will feel exploited by their government. Michelman's balancing approach has gathered widespread support since its publication,[25] although a few commentators have suggested minor revisions or clarifications.[26]

Probably the most recent use of an efficiency criterion as a tool for constitutional interpretation has been developed by Thomas Miceli and Kathleen Segerson.[27] They propose that the balance regarding regulatory takings be drawn to eliminate both (1) the moral hazard problem of overinvestment by landowners who are guaranteed full compensation for regulatory takings and (2) the risk of excessive regulation without compensation.[28] Two different compensation rules will produce efficient outcomes. Under the first rule, a landowner receives compensation if the regulated land use was efficient at the time it was first engaged in. If not, compensation should be denied to deter the moral hazard problem. Under the second rule, the state must compensate the owner if it imposes a regulation inefficiently, and the risk of overregulation from "fiscal illusion" is thereby eliminated.[29] The authors note that since both of the proposed rules produce efficient land-use incentives, some other criterion, such as "fairness," must provide the rationale for choosing whether to require compensation in many individual cases.

A very different approach was proposed and later rejected by Joseph Sax. In 1964, Sax suggested that the compensation issue turn on the purpose of the government's regulation.[30] When the government acts in an enterprise capacity and attempts to enhance its resource position, then compensation to losing parties should be required. But compensation should not be required whenever the government acts as a mediator between two private parties with conflicting property claims, because the government does not directly benefit from the regulation.[31]

Aside from its questionable meaning, the Sax test would apparently allow the government to take all the property of a politically powerless minority so long as it gave the property to other, more powerful, private individuals. At a minimum, virtually everyone would interpret the Fifth Amendment to prevent this extreme democratic tyranny.

Sax himself largely abandoned his approach in 1971,[32] but for different reasons. In the later article, Sax embraced environmental regulation and the concept of "public rights." Sax advocated a redefinition of property to focus on competition among resource users rather than on the physical boundaries of property. Sax claimed to put competing resource users in a position of equality with his proposed rule that any demand of a right to use property that has spillover effects may be constitutionally restrained without competition. Sax's "spillover effects" include using property that in any way affects the health or well-being of any other individuals, even those who lack rights under conventional property law.[33] Assuming, arguendo, that the public is better off with regulatory interference in these cases, Sax seems to have forgotten that the Constitution requires public use *and* just compensation for property taken. His efforts to circumvent this second requirement by redefining "property" are contrary to the entire history of American constitutional law.

Alternative normative approaches have been offered more recently by commentators supporting the Land Rights movement.[34] The most well known is found in Richard Epstein's *Takings*,[35] where he constructs his conclusions on a natural right to retain the fruits of our labor. The state may act only to increase the size of the pie representing total social wealth, and should preserve the relative wealth entitlements among the members of society.[36] From there he presents his argument that the public use requirement is satisfied only when the government's regulation of property is necessary to create a public good or public rule the benefits of which all have a right to enjoy on the same terms.[37] Even when the public use requirement is satisfied, however, the state usually must compensate the property owner. An uncompensated taking is justified as an exercise of the state's "police power" only in response to a property owner's "common law wrongs involving force or misrepresentation, deliberate or accidental, against other persons, including private nuisances."[38] Otherwise, explicit monetary compensation should be required whenever an owner does not receive adequate, implicit, in-kind compensation as a result of the regulation. A property owner receives adequate in-kind compensation only if the regulatory plan leaves him at least as well-off constrained along with the others regulated than he was before the regulation. For example, if the value of an owner's land rises after zoning restrictions are imposed in his neighborhood, then no compensation is required for his restricted land use. However, if he is left worse off under the regulation, he must be compensated.[39]

While these are probably the best-known approaches to takings law, they are by no means exclusive, and the alternatives vary widely.[40] The Supreme Court has fared no better in its attempts to strike a consistent balance. Indeed, the Court has repeatedly refused to provide any reliable guidelines for regulatory takings, preferring instead ad hoc determinations of whether compensation is required.[41] Nevertheless, some patterns or trends can be ascertained by tracing the development of takings clause jurisprudence.

2. Regulatory Takings to Prevent Nuisances

Nuisance has been defined as "that activity which arises from unreasonable, un-warranted, or unlawful use by a person of his own property, working obstruction or injury to the right of another, or to the public, and producing such material annoyance, inconvenience and discomfort that the law will presume resulting damage."[42] The government has always had a common law right to take actions to prevent such "noxious" uses of property in the United States.[43] And early in the Supreme Court's development of takings jurisprudence, it held that the government need not compensate a property owner when actions are taken to prevent nuisances.[44]

While the doctrine by itself makes much sense, it has been applied to actual cases over time in a fashion that has allowed the government to adopt virtually any regulation without compensating injured property owners. This part traces the historical development of the nuisance doctrine and then illustrates how its expansion has influenced more recent cases.

Early Treatment of Nuisance Regulations: The Die Is Cast

The Supreme Court first reconciled nuisance regulations with the takings clause in *Mugler v. Kansas* (1887).[45] The state of Kansas had adopted a constitutional provision providing that the manufacture and sale of intoxicating liquors would be forever prohibited in the state. To effectuate this provision, the state legislature passed a statute making it a crime for anyone to manufacture, sell, or barter intoxicating liquors within the state.[46] Mugler had built a $10,000 brewery in Kansas and operated it profitably before the constitutional provision was adopted. Because his land and brewery under the prohibition were worth only $2,500, Mugler claimed that the statute effected an unconstitutional taking of his property. The Supreme Court disagreed, labeling his brewery a classic public nuisance, and noting that an individual's property rights have never included a right to use property in ways injurious to the community.

> The power which the States have of prohibiting such use by individuals of their property as will be prejudicial to the health, the morals, or the safety of the public, is not—and consistently with the existence and safety of organized society, cannot be—burdened with the condition that the State must compensate such individual owners for pecuniary losses they may sustain, by reason of their not being permitted, by a noxious use of their property, to inflict injury upon the community.[47]

The *Mugler* Court's result was not surprising, and indeed contains considerable logical appeal. However, its opinion included dicta that foreshadowed the present breadth of the nuisance doctrine even in 1887. For example, the Court made it clear that the state can act pursuant to its "police powers" to protect the safety, health, and morals of the community even though the chief value of property—here 75 percent—is frustrated. More important, the Court leaves to the legislature a determination of when such protection is needed: "A prohibition simply upon the use of property for purposes that are declared, by valid legislation, to be injurious to the health, morals, or safety of the community, cannot, in any just sense, be deemed a taking or an appropriation of property for the public benefit."[48] From its very first case, then, the Court has placed the legislatures in the position of foxes guarding henhouses. By making most regulation considerably less expensive to the government, the Court began to pave the way for an extensive regulatory state.

The trend continued the following year, with the Court's decision in *Powell v. Pennsylvania* (1888).[49] Pennsylvania had passed a statute forbidding the manufacture or sale of imitation butter in the state. Powell, a grocer, was indicted under the statute for selling two five-pound cases of oleomargarine butter to a customer. Powell challenged the statute, arguing, inter alia, that because he purchased the oleomargarine prior to passage of the restrictive statute, his property was effectively taken from him when he was prohibited from selling the two cases. Powell further argued that the uncompensated taking was unjustified because the statute represented nothing more than naked special interest legislation favoring butter producers over their valuable competitors.

The Supreme Court ultimately validated the statute on nuisance grounds by quoting legislative statements that the statute was intended to protect the public health and prevent the fraudulent adulteration of dairy products. Despite Powell's attempts to prove that the product he sold was as wholesome, safe, and nutritious as butter, the identification of a nuisance, as well as its appropriate treatment, was given entirely and explicitly to the legislature. The Court stated:

> Whether the manufacture of oleomargarine . . . involves such danger to the public health as to require, for the protection of the people, the entire suppression of the business, rather than its regulation, in such manner as to permit the sale of articles of that class that do not contain noxious ingredients, are questions of fact and of public policy which belong to the legislative department to determine.[50]

Without further explanation, the Court concluded that the state had not effected an unconstitutional taking, and cited *Mugler*.

It is possible the Court thought that Pennsylvania, like Kansas, was attempting to protect its citizens from unscrupulous or immoral businesses and their noxious practices. However, it became clear that no such moral judgments are necessary when the Court decided the famous case, *Miller v. Shoene* (1928).[51] Virginia law required that red cedar trees located within two miles of any apple orchard be cut down when found to carry cedar rust, a communicable plant disease. Although the disease left the cedar trees unaffected, it destroyed the leaves and fruit of apple trees, which had much greater commercial value in Virginia than did the cedar trees. Schoene, the state entomologist, ordered Miller to cut down a large number of cedar trees growing on his property. Because the statute contained no provision for compensating owners for the value of their standing cedar trees or for the reduced market value of their land with fewer trees, Miller brought an action claiming that the state, through Schoene, took his property in violation of the Constitution. The Supreme Court held that no compensation was necessary, reasoning that "the state does not exceed its constitutional powers by deciding upon the destruction of one class of property in order to save another which, in the judgment of the legislature, is of greater value to the public."[52] The fact that the owners of red cedar trees were not at all to blame for the predicament faced by the apple orchard owners did not alter the Court's conclusion.[53]

The same result had been reached in 1915 when the value of property taken was much greater than that of a few trees. In *Hadacheck v. Los Angeles*,[54] a city statute made it illegal to operate a brick yard or brick kiln within specific areas of the city. Hadacheck continued to operate his brick kiln in the forbidden area because his land contained ideal clay for making bricks, and the clay could not feasibly be removed from the land to a kiln located outside the prohibited area. When he was arrested and imprisoned for his actions, Hadacheck challenged the statute, claiming it effected an unconstitutional taking of his property. He claimed that his operations were harmless because they omitted no noises or noxious fumes. In contrast, the city alleged that his kiln's fumes, gas, smoke, soot, steam, and dust sometimes caused sickness and discomfort to area residents. Although the brick yard served a valuable market function, its operation in this particular location had become incompatible with the developing residential character of the immediate community. The Court stated "there must be progress, and if in its march private interests are in the way they must yield to the good of the community."[55] Thus, the city was not required to compensate Hadacheck, despite the fact that his property with brick manufacturing was worth $800,000, while without it the property was worth only $60,000, a reduction in value by more than 90 percent.[56]

These opinions, taken together, gave both the state and federal governments nearly complete latitude to launch a regulatory state beginning with the New Deal. And the regulatory powers were probably enhanced by a Supreme Court case reviewing extreme regulation during World War II. In *United States v. Central Eureka Mining Co.* (1958),[57] the mining company brought a takings challenge to a 1942 order by the federal War Production Board that it cease operating its gold mines. The U.S. military needed skilled labor to work in the copper mines, and it hoped that by closing the gold mines, it could attract the workers it needed. The copper mines also needed scarce equipment used by the gold mines, and hoped the closings would help bring down the price of the equipment and increase its availability. Despite Justice Harlan's dissenting argument that the mine closings constituted temporary takings requiring compensation, the Court ruled otherwise. To the Court, the board merely made a reasoned decision that the unrestricted use of mining equipment and manpower in the gold mines was so wasteful of wartime resources that they must temporarily be suspended. The Court did recognize that regulatory action could diminish the value of property to the point where it constituted a taking, but the mere fact that a property owner is deprived of the property's most valuable use was insufficient to require compensation.

Note that the board's order was an attempt to indirectly confiscate the equipment and labor it needed for wartime efforts.[58] Perhaps the case is confined to its peculiar wartime facts, for the Court did express a reluctance to conclude that wartime losses of income require compensation. Indeed, it suggested that if the United States had lost the war, the property owners would have forfeited much greater freedoms than those interfered with by the government. Nevertheless, *Central Eureka* has been cited by the Court to support more general propositions about the government's ability to take property without compensation.[59]

More Recent Cases

During the 1970s and early 1980s, the Supreme Court continued its reluctance to require the government to compensate property owners for regulatory takings. In the last five to ten years, the Court has placed limits on the most extreme, or complete, regulatory interferences with property rights. However, at present a few state courts offer the only real protection from governmental regulatory takings.

Two inconsistent mining cases help illustrate the first proposition. In the 1987 case, *Keystone Bituminous Coal Association v. DeBenedictis*,[60] an association of coal mine operators in western Pennsylvania challenged a state law which prohibited coal mining that caused subsidence[61] damage to pre-existing buildings, dwellings, and cemeteries. The plaintiff coal miners had already obtained explicit releases of liability from the surface owners affected by their mining. In other words, when purchasing the mining rights from property owners, the miners also purchased the right to alter the surface of the property. By contract law, the surface owners no longer had rights against subsidence damage that the state needed to protect. Nevertheless, the Court found that the state was acting to prevent a public nuisance caused by the shifting land surface.

The Court's *Keystone* decision conflicts with its decision in *Pennsylvania Coal Co. v. Mahon* (1922).[62] In that case, the Court found that an essentially identical law constituted an unconstitutional taking. As in *Keystone*, the owners of mining rights had previously obtained releases from the owners of surface rights. While the *Pennsylvania Coal* Court recognized a public interest in the legislation, compensation was required because the law had abolished the entire interest in land owned by the miners. According to the *Pennsylvania Coal* Court, "a strong public desire to improve the public condition is not enough to warrant achieving the desire by a shorter cut than the constitutional way of paying for the change," at least where the extent of property interference is great.[63]

The *Keystone* Court tried to distinguish the two cases with a trick it used in *Hodel v. Virginia Surface Mining & Reclamation Association* (1981),[64] by stating that since the new law had not yet been enforced, and no evidence was presented showing how extensively the law would interfere with the association members' mining rights, the Court had no basis on which to find a taking. The distinction rests on mere formality, however, because the new law was just as likely to prevent coal mining as the *Pennsylvania Coal* law was. As noted by the four dissenting justices, the *Keystone* Court used the nuisance exception to allow the complete extinction of the value of a parcel of property, something it had never done before. The dissenters also pointed out that *Pennsylvania Coal* had earlier concluded that this type of statute did not fall under the nuisance exception to takings in the first place.

Property owners may find some solace in the fact that at least one state has rejected the government's right to circumvent explicit contractual provisions in a different context. In *Bino v. City of Hurley* (1956),[65] the owner of all the land surrounding a lake granted the city a 15-foot wide easement in order to bury pipes to extract the city's water supply from the lake. The easement expressly stated that Bino was to retain all riparian rights in the lake. Later, the city tried to circumvent this provision by adopting an ordinance forbidding swimming, bathing, and boating in the lake. The supreme court of Wisconsin, interpreting a state constitutional provision, concluded that the ordinance effected a taking of Bino's riparian rights requiring compensation. Although the court recognized that the city was acting in the interests of public health and welfare to prevent contamination of the water supply, condemnation was the only constitutionally acceptable means of extinguishing this property owner's rights.[66]

Police Powers and Aesthetics: A Nuisance?

The U.S. Supreme Court's reluctance to consider regulatory takings challenges until recently is further illustrated with *Penn Central Transportation Co. v. New York City* (1978).[67] That case involved New York City's Landmarks Preservation Law, which restricted the development and destruction of historic landmarks and neighborhoods. One provision required the owner of a designated landmark to keep the exterior of his building in good repair, and prohibited him from altering its exterior without the prior approval of the city's Landmark Preservation Commission. Penn Central owned the famed Grand Central Terminal, a designated landmark site, and brought this takings action after the commission denied two sets of plans it had submitted to add a fifty-plus story building at the top of the terminal.

At this point in the Court's takings jurisprudence, it will come as no surprise that it concluded the city had not unconstitutionally taken Penn Central's property. After all, Penn Central was not denied any of the present uses of the terminal, and was permitted to transfer its development rights to eight of its nearby lots. The Court also relied on the unsupported possibility that the commission would allow a more modest addition to the terminal in the future.

The Court's doctrinal reasoning, however, was somewhat surprising. The Court equated this regulation to zoning law, and noted that zoning laws have been found permissible even when they prohibit the most beneficial uses of property and the owners are disproportionately burdened by the regulation. The Court then cited several nuisance cases to support its conclusion, including *Mugler, Hadacheck,* and *Miller.* The Court had finally done explicitly what its cases had been foreshadowing for a century: it extended the nuisance rationale to any land-use regulation with a potentially public character, a determination long ago left to the legislature itself. And the Court picked the most extreme situation in which to extend the nuisance rationale, because nothing about the landmarks law protected the health, safety, or morals of the people of New York City. Indeed, the regulation served purely aesthetic concerns.

Luckily for landowners, not all state courts would reach the same result. At least one state, Pennsylvania, has used its own constitutional takings provision to reject purely aesthetic land use limitations. For example, in *Redevelopment Authority of Oil City v. Woodring* (1982),[68] the city redevelopment authority had required all electrical wires on a particular street to be relocated underground. The city installed underground service conduits ending at each owner's property line, and the owners were required to provide encasement conduits for electrical service from their buildings to the property lines. Mrs. Woodring, who owned some buildings on this street, spent more than $5,000 complying with this requirement, and sued the city, claiming that the expense constituted an uncompensated taking of her property. According to the supreme court of Pennsylvania, the city could exercise its police powers to promote the health, safety, or general welfare without compensation, even if an owner's property is taken or destroyed. However, when, as here, the city acts on the basis of aesthetic considerations only, it must act under its eminent domain power. To do that, the Pennsylvania constitution guarantees property owners compensation for property taken, injured, or destroyed.[69]

Nuisance and Complete Deprivations: Is "Regulatory Takings" An Oxymoron?

Returning to the U.S. Supreme Court, once the Court began upholding virtually any land-use regulation with the nuisance rationale, it had to shift its focus to the extent of the deprivation suffered. Otherwise, the government could circumvent the takings clause entirely by requiring a landowner to put his land to a particular use, or nonuse, so long as the regulation did not constitute a physical invasion of the property. Indeed, the federal government did just that in *Central Eureka*. Recall that instead of taking over the gold mines and their equipment, which would be an actual taking of property requiring compensation, the government simply ordered the gold mines to shut down, hoping it could effect the same result without compensation. Now that the government's regulatory powers during peacetime had likewise expanded, the Court needed to concern itself with regulations so pervasive or restrictive that they resembled thinly veiled actual takings.

The Court seized its opportunity in *First Lutheran Church v. Los Angeles County* (1987).[70] The plaintiff church owned a 21-acre parcel of land on which it operated a retreat center. In 1978, after a forest fire denuded the surrounding hills, the church's buildings were completely destroyed by a flood. Thereafter, the county issued an interim order prohibiting all reconstruction in a flood protection area, which included the church's land. Despite the dissent of three justices who characterized the prohibition as just another health and safety regulation designed to prevent injurious land uses, the Court reasoned that the fact that the order could be a nuisance regulation did not end the constitutional inquiry. According to the Court, even a justified temporary taking of property requires compensation when the government denies a landowner all use of his property:

> It would be a very curious and unsatisfactory result, if . . . it shall be held that if the government refrains from absolute conversion of real property to public uses it can destroy its value entirely, can inflict irreparable and permanent injury to any extent, can, in effect, subject it to total destruction without making any compensation, because, in the narrowest sense of the word, it is not *taken* for the public use.[71]

Given the procedural history of the case, the Court was required to assume the truth of the church's allegation that it was denied all effective use of its property for a considerable period of years under the county's order. The church was therefore constitutionally entitled to compensation.

The Court strengthened its conclusion in the context of permanent regulation in *Lucas v. South Carolina Coastal Commission* (1992).[72] Lucas had purchased two residential lots on the Isle of Palms outside Charleston, South Carolina, in 1986 for $975,000, and he intended to build a single-family home on each of the lots. At that time, development was regulated in "critical areas," where beach erosion was likely, but since Lucas's land was 300 feet from the beach, no special building permits were required. However, when the South Carolina Beachfront Management Act was enacted in 1988, the critical area was moved to landward of Lucas's property, and all construction of occupiable improvements in this area was flatly prohibited. Lucas challenged the regulation as effecting an unconstitutional taking of his property, and the trial court found that because the 1988 Act barred him from erecting any permanent habitable structures on his parcels, his property was rendered "valueless." The state claimed that even if this were true, no compensation was constitutionally owed Lucas because the legislation was reasonably necessary to prevent "harmful or noxious" uses of property near the coast.

The Court disagreed with the state's legal conclusion, adopting reasoning similar to that used in *First Lutheran Church*. Moreover, this time the Court specifically expressed concern with upholding regulations tantamount to outright condemnation on the basis that it prevents harmful uses of property when every regulation can be so characterized. The Court therefore held that where a state adopts regulation that deprives land of all economically beneficial use, it may resist compensation only if the proscribed use interests were not part of the owner's title to begin with.

Was Lucas *a Victory for the Land Rights Movement?*

Lucas signals a continued, perhaps strengthened commitment to the notion that even important regulatory measures will not be sustained without compensation in the extreme case where the owner is deprived of all beneficial use of his property. If the owner is placed in a position no better than if his property were condemned, then the government must pay for the deprivation.

While property rights advocates thus won a battle in the *Lucas* case, they may have lost the war in the Court's opinion. Justice Scalia, who authored the majority opinion, left three glaring loopholes that could weaken *Lucas*'s purported protection of property rights, even in the context of extreme deprivation.

First, as Justice Blackmun points out in his dissent and the majority opinion candidly concedes, the Court fails to describe criteria for characterizing the property interest that will be evaluated for loss of value. To illustrate the problem, the Court asks the following: if an owner must leave 90 percent of a rural tract in its natural state, has the owner been deprived of all economically beneficial use of the burdened portion of his tract, entitling him to compensation? Or has the owner suffered a mere diminution in the value of the tract as a whole? Justice Scalia admitted that this confusion has produced inconsistent pronouncements by the Court itself, but claimed that the *Lucas* case presented no uncertainty.[73]

The *Lucas* opinion leaves a great deal of uncertainty in this regard, however, and the ambiguity leaves courts with tremendous latitude to sustain regulations that effect a gross interference with an owner's use of his land. A few state court cases illustrate the difficulty. For example, compare *Burrows v. City of Keene*, (1981)[74] with *Gardner v. New Jersey Pinelands Commission* (1991),[75] and *Brecciaroli v. Connecticut Commissioner of Environmental Protection* (1975).[76] In *Burrows*, the plaintiff had purchased 124 acres of land, and had planned to convert the land into a subdivision. The city wanted the land left as open space and offered to purchase the tract for less than half its market value. After Mr. Burrows refused its offer, the city denied approval of his subdivision application and placed 109 of his acres in a conservation zone, where all building was prohibited. According to the supreme court of New Hampshire, arbitrary or unreasonable restrictions that substantially deprive an owner of economically viable use of his land in order to benefit the public in some way constitute a taking requiring compensation within the meaning of the New Hampshire constitution. Because the permitted conservation zone uses were economically impractical as applied to Burrows's land, its value was substantially reduced, and Burrows was prevented from enjoying any worthwhile rights or benefits in the land. Thus, the city's actions effected an unconstitutional taking.

The *Burrows* court may have been influenced by the city's apparently questionable tactics surrounding its rezoning of the property. In any event, the court found an effective taking with respect to part of the parcel sufficient to require compensation. However, in *Gardner*, a more recent decision by the supreme court of New Jersey, a similarly onerous zoning regulation was found not to contravene the New Jersey constitution's takings provision.

Mr. Gardner owned a 217-acre farm in the New Jersey Pinelands. He wanted to turn the land into 10-acre "farmettes," but found he was prohibited from doing so under regulations promulgated by the Pinelands Commission. According to the regulations, residential units could be constructed on Gardner's tract, but at a density no greater than one unit per 40 acres. Moreover, those homes built were required to be clustered in one-acre lots with the remaining 39 acres allocated to each residence permanently dedicated to agricultural use by recorded deed restriction. Although Gardner was required to leave at least as great a fraction of his land undeveloped as Burrows was, the *Gardner* court found no unconstitutional taking. Because a portion of his land could still be used for residential building and Gardner was permitted to continue his existing use of his land, the court concluded that the beneficial use of his property as a whole had not been substantially destroyed by the regulations.

The supreme court of Connecticut, in *Brecciaroli*, took a similar approach. Mr. Brecciaroli owned a 20.6-acre parcel of land abutting a river. In 1971, the state designated 17.5 acres of his tract as tidal wetland, meaning that he could not dig, build, or fill on this land without the permission of the state commissioner of environmental protection. Brecciaroli thereafter asked for permission to fill in 5.3 acres of his property to establish a six-lot industrial subdivision, but his application was denied. The court found the denial was not an unconstitutional taking of his property, reasoning, in part, that Brecciaroli could still use his property for unregulated activities. It is difficult to conceive of any practicable unregulated use of his property, however, because the applicable regulated uses included:

> draining, dredging, excavation or removal of soil, mud, sand, gravel, aggregate of any kind or rubbish from any wetland, or the dumping, filling or depositing thereon of any soil, stones, sand, gravel, mud, aggregate of any kind, rubbish, or similar material, either directly or otherwise, and the erection of structures, driving of pilings, or placing of obstructions, whether or not changing the tidal ebb and flow."

Thus, the court's conclusion must turn on its remaining argument, that Brecciaroli might still be permitted to either fill a smaller portion of his land or fill some portion for a different purpose. This second rationale implies that this court, like the *Gardner* court, considered the tract as a whole to be the relevant property interest to evaluate retained beneficial uses.

This malleability of the definition of a property interest has plagued courts for well over a century. Although the problem does not lend itself to any easy solution, the Supreme Court's simultaneous adoption of a complete interference litmus test with its casual dismissal of the issue has exacerbated the difficulties. More importantly, it leaves lower courts an almost unbridled ability to circumvent the *Lucas* holding, as illustrated above.

The second problem with the *Lucas* opinion is closely related to the first: even when the relevant property interest is well defined, it is often difficult to determine whether the challenged regulation precludes all economically beneficial or productive uses of that property. Several conflicting state court cases help illustrate this problem.

For example, compare *Sibson v. State* (1975)[78] with *Bartlett v. Zoning Commission* (1971).[79] In *Sibson* the owner of a four-acre tract of land found his development plans frustrated two years after he purchased the property, when his land was included in the definition of marshland under state law. Mr. Sibson was later denied a required permit to fill his property, after the zoning commission determined that the filling would be "bad for the wetlands" and "for mankind." While the court acknowledged that some courts have denied or restricted governmental attempts to prevent marshland filling without compensation, it nonetheless found that Sibson's permit denial was not an unconstitutional taking. According to the court, "an owner of land has no absolute and unlimited right to change the essential natural character of his land so as to use it for a purpose for which it was unsuited in its natural state and which injures the rights of others."[80] The court therefore found it constitutionally sufficient that Sibson retained all normal traditional uses of his marshland, including wildlife observation, hunting, having of marshgrass, clam and shellfish harvesting, and aesthetic purposes.

In contrast, an equally restrictive wetlands regulation was held unconstitutional in *Bartlett*. Like Sibson, Mr. Bartlett also owned a 4-acre tract of land that he purchased in 1961 for a nominal amount of money. In 1964, Bartlett applied to the local zoning commission for a permit to fill his land, but permission was denied. In 1968, the town adopted new zoning regulation that restricted the uses of Bartlett's land, designated as tidal marshland, to wooden walkways, duck blinds, public boat landings, and public ditches. Exceptions were permitted only to (1) dig a channel or build a boathouse large enough for the owner's boat only, or (2) build piers, docks, piles for lifelines, rafts, or jetties.

The Connecticut court concluded that the 1968 regulations effected an unconstitutional taking of Bartlett's property, even though the previous denial of his filling permit in 1961 could have indicated his feasible land uses had already been drastically restricted. The court focused instead on the fact that Bartlett's land, if usable for commercial purposes, was worth $32,000, but under the regulations, was worth only $1,000. The court noted that the town's objective to preserve the marshlands from encroachment or destruction was laudable. Indeed, the court found the preservation of our natural environment to be an issue of "critical concern."[81] However, the regulations went so far that they became confiscatory, and consequently, the town would have to achieve its goals with compensation.

The difficulty is further illustrated by comparing *Turnpike Realty Co. v. Town of Dedham* (1972)[82] with *Dooley v. Town Planning & Zoning Commission* (1964).[83] In *Turnpike*, the plaintiff had purchased 61.9 acres of land in 1947 when it was zoned for general residential uses. In 1963, the town amended its zoning bylaws, designating almost all of plaintiff's property in a flood plain, and forbidding all building on the land. Nevertheless, because the plaintiff was still permitted any woodland, grassland, wetland, agricultural, horticultural, or recreational use of the land or water not requiring filling, the supreme court of Massachusetts concluded that the amendment did not effect an unconstitutional taking of his property. Instead the court found persuasive the trial court's conclusion that because the property was located in a flood plain, building was not economically feasible to begin with. Consequently, the plaintiff retained all the economically feasible uses it had before the amendment.

In contrast, the supreme court of Connecticut rejected similar ex post reasoning in *Dooley*. Mr. Dooley's land classification was also changed from residential to flood plain district, but Dooley retained more land uses than did Turnpike Realty, including parks, playgrounds, marinas, boathouses, landings and docks, clubhouses, wildlife sanctuaries, farming, and motor vehicle parking. Nevertheless, the court found that each of the permitted uses was either impracticable or greatly reduced the value of Dooley's land.[84] As a result, the new zoning, while attempting to achieve "laudable" goals,[85] was unconstitutional without compensation.

Finally, compare *Annicelli v. Town of South Kingstown* (1983)[86] with *Hall v. Board of Environmental Protection* (1987).[87] The *Annicelli* case is very similar to the *Dooley* case. Mrs. Annicelli brought her suit after a new zoning ordinance designated various segments of the town's shoreline, including her property, as "high flood danger" districts and limited their development to protect the beach. Annicelli was unable to obtain a permit to build a single dwelling house on her property, because the ordinance restricted her property to such uses as a horticultural nursery or greenhouse, a park or playground, a wildlife area or nature preserve, a golf course or marina, raising crops or animals, storing commercial vehicles and repairing boats. The supreme court of Rhode Island held that the regulation was unconstitutionally confiscatory after it concluded that each of the permitted uses were impracticable as applied to Annicelli's property.

In contrast, the *Hall* court considered one more fact that altered the outcome. The Hall family bought a lot and summer cottage on the beach in 1970 for $30,000. In 1976, they lost their cottage to beach erosion, and placed a motorized vehicle in the lot to stay in while visiting. In 1979, a new law was enacted that required sand dune permits prior to building on certain lands, including the Halls' property. In 1982, the Halls unsuccessfully applied for a sand dune permit to build a house. When the Halls challenged the permit denial, the trial court concluded that while the property was worth $50,000, with an option to build a year-round structure, it was worth no more than $500 without the option. Thus, the denial reduced the Halls' land value by approximately 100 percent.

The supreme court of Maine nevertheless concluded that the permit denial did not effect a taking, and characterized the trial court's findings as clearly erroneous. The court's conclusion turned on the fact that the Halls had been using a motorized camper on the property and could continue to do so under the new regulations. Indeed, the court found that the family could profitably rent their camper on the property if they so chose. The Halls were thus still permitted economically beneficial use of their property, so that no compensation was required.

Interestingly, Annicelli most likely would have been permitted a motorized camper on her property as well, and had the court considered this possibility, the result in her case might have been reversed. The result in any given case, therefore, may well turn on the imagination of the reviewing court in considering alternative property uses. As the cases above illustrate, the *Lucas* Court's failure to elaborate a point at which courts must find a complete deprivation of property leaves future courts with yet another means of circumventing the compensation requirement.

The third limitation of the *Lucas* opinion is that even if a regulation deprives land of all its economically beneficial uses, its owner need not be compensated if a court finds the proscribed use was not part of his title to begin with. The majority opinion indicated that the Court will uphold a law or decree giving effect to nuisance principles if it does "no more than duplicate the result that could have been achieved in the courts under state private nuisance law, or by the state under its complementary power to abate nuisances that affect the public generally, or otherwise."[88] The Court also provided two examples of this exception. First, the owner of a lakebed is not entitled to compensation when he is denied the requisite permit to engage in landfilling operations that would flood his neighbor's land. Second, the owner of a nuclear generating plant is not entitled to compensation when it is directed to remove all improvements from its land upon discovery that the plant sits astride an earthquake fault.

These examples make sense, given the present common law of nuisance and necessity. However, Justice Scalia went further to add that new common law prohibitions on property use may arise through changed circumstances or new knowledge that may make what was previously permissible no longer so. This vaguely described possibility could further erode whatever property rights the *Lucas* opinion purportedly protects. After all, new information about environmental and ecosystem hazards has led to vastly increasing regulatory restrictions on property use. It seems the common law can also be used to effect similar results in the future, in which case the *Lucas* exception could swallow its own rule.

Consider, for example, the supreme court of Wisconsin's decision in *Just v. Marinette County* (1972).[89] The county adopted a shoreland zoning ordinance required by the state that prevented, with the exception of narrow special permit situations, the changing of the natural character of any land within 1,000 feet of a navigable lake or within 300 feet of a navigable river. The Just family owned lakefront property in the county and claimed the ordinance effected an unconstitutional taking of their property. While other states have struck down similar ordinances, the *Just* court found those cases uncontrolling. The difference, according to the court, was that the state of Wisconsin has an active public trust duty in respect to navigable waters that requires it to protect and preserve the waters for fishing, recreation, and scenic beauty. According to the court, owners of land adjacent to or near these navigable waters must hold their property subject to the state's public trust powers. The challenged ordinance "preserves nature, the environment, and natural resources as they were created and to which the people have a present right."[90] Moreover, the court had never previously held that "destroying the natural character of a swamp or a wetland so as to make that location available for human habitation is a reasonable use of that land when the new use, although of a more economical value to the owner, causes a harm to the general public."[91]

Thus, the court found a common law right of the people that must be carried out by the state to maintain certain lands in their natural state, and further concluded that a landowner's common law right to property cannot extend to the point where it thwarts the public right. While it is not entirely clear that the *Lucas* Court would find the *Just* court's reasoning constitutionally sufficient, the case illustrates the ease with which courts can create even severe common law limitations on property rights to support restrictive statutory and administrative regulations.

Takings and Nuisance: A Summary

To summarize the Supreme Court's use of the nuisance doctrine, once the Court permitted uncompensated regulations that purport to prevent any harmful use of property as determined by the legislature, the term "regulatory taking" became somewhat of an oxymoron. At this point the Court will require compensation only when governmental regulation effects a complete interference with an owner's right to the beneficial uses of his property. However, the Court's most recent declaration of this principle enables state and lower federal courts to easily circumvent even this limited exception. One might therefore conclude that any real takings clause limitation on governmental regulations must be found in state court interpretations of the various state constitutions. Part four of this chapter considers whether there may still be some federal constitutional protection from regulatory takings found in the Court's consideration of reciprocity. That is, the nuisance doctrine, as well as other takings principles, are often justified by their delivery of reciprocal advantages to those regulated. Perhaps a burdensome regulation becomes confiscatory if it provides no reciprocal benefits to those singled out to carry the burden.

3. Regulatory Takings and Reciprocal Benefits

Courts sometimes justify the burden imposed on a property owner's rights by reference to the benefit that person enjoys from similar burdens placed on the rights of other property owners. In these cases, a court usually concludes that the owner's property has not been taken, but Richard Epstein uses reciprocity to point out that while the restrictions do constitute "takings," the reciprocal nature of the burdens provides "just compensation."[92]

Traditional nuisance-preventing regulations provide a classic example of reciprocity. After all, if everyone in a given neighborhood must respect the land-use and enjoyment rights of his neighbors, then everyone is better off, and everyone's land values are higher.[93] Many of the Court's early cases were consistent with this principle, including, for example, *Plymouth Coal Co. v. Pennsylvania* (1914).[94] In *Plymouth*, the Court upheld a state statute requiring the owners of adjoining coal properties to leave boundary pillars sufficiently wide to safeguard employees of either mine in case the other should be abandoned or fill with water. While the case was not given as a rationale for upholding the regulation at the time, later courts have justified the law at issue in *Plymouth* as one securing a reciprocity of advantage to the adjacent mine owners.[95]

The reciprocity issue has been a factor, although sometimes only implicitly, in several more recent cases. For example, comprehensive zoning plans are upheld as constitutional unless they are clearly arbitrary and unreasonable.[96] Where the plans are applied generally across a given geographic area, they are uniformly upheld. In *Agins v. Tiburon* (1980),[97] for example, Mr. Agins purchased land for residential development shortly before the city of Tiburon adopted general zoning ordinances limiting the number of houses that could be built on a given acreage. The Court held that the regulation did not effect an unconstitutional taking because the city has police powers to protect its residents from the ill effects of urbanization. In its reasoning, the Court identified an element of reciprocity in the zoning regulation, stating that Agins "will share with other owners the benefits and the burdens of the city's exercise of its police power. In assessing the fairness of the zoning ordinances, these benefits must be considered along with any diminution in market value that [Agins] might suffer."[98]

Misuse of Property: Where Property Value Declines

The Court upholds general zoning provisions even when the plans greatly reduce the market value of some properties,[99] and several state courts have upheld onerous zoning restriction on the basis of reciprocity as well. For example, recall *Gardner v. New Jersey Pinelands Commission* (1991),[100] the case in which Mr. Gardner was prevented from breaking his property into farmettes after a regulation was adopted prohibiting the building of more than one home every 40 acres. The supreme court of New Jersey held that the commission's attempt to maintain the sparse agricultural nature of the pinelands was constitutional. Because other landowners in the area would be burdened by the same restrictions and comparable regulations, Gardner and his neighbors would share in the benefits from preservation of the natural environment and protection of the water supply.

Note that the court's theoretical justification does not apply to Gardner. He does not appreciate any benefit to preserving the environment in its present state, given his other opportunities, and his plans to sell farmettes would not have conflicted with the regulations' stated goal to preserve agriculture. Indeed, those New Jersey residents who drive through and vacation in the pinelands were much more likely beneficiaries of the regulation than were any of the residents in the pinelands. The *Gardner* case helps illustrate the degree to which the reciprocity rationale can be improperly expanded to justify regulatory restrictions on property.[101]

There is a limit to this rationale, however. At least one state has used due process principles[102] to strike down arbitrary or unreasonable zoning restrictions. According to the supreme court of Pennsylvania, even if zoning restrictions can be characterized as reciprocally beneficial to the residents in a community, they are unconstitutional if they have an exclusionary purpose or effect on outsiders. This idea was expressed by the court in *Appeal of Kit-Mar Builders* (1970).[103] The plaintiffs planned to purchase a 140-acre tract on which they would construct homes on one-acre lots. However, their plans were frustrated when they learned of a preexisting lot requirement of 2 to 3 acres for residential development in the town of Concord, where the property was located. The plaintiffs apparently realized they were not well situated to challenge the regulation under the takings clause, so they instead claimed that the zoning scheme violated the due process clause of the Fourteenth Amendment and won. This court rejected the very arguments used by the *Gardner* court, that an increased population would strain resources or change the character of the community. For this court, where there are alternative methods for dealing with the problems that attend population growth, zoning that has an exclusive purpose or effect on those who desire to move into the area is not acceptable. The fact that the current residents of Concord might reciprocally benefit from exclusionary restrictions was not relevant in the due process context.

A Reciprocity Requirement Ensures Pareto Optimality

Moreover, a lack of reciprocity has been used to strike down extremely burdensome zoning restrictions under the takings clause, as seen in *Lucas*. While not technically labeled a zoning case, recall that the council's prohibition of building on Lucas's lots was very similar to a zoning regulation. One of the reasons the Court gave for striking down the prohibition was the fact that the purported nuisance regulation secured no reciprocal benefits to Lucas. Justice Scalia noted the Court's suspicion that when no beneficial use of land is permitted, the legislature is probably not simply adjusting the benefits and burdens of life to secure an "average reciprocity of advantage" to everyone concerned. Rather, in this context there is a "heightened risk that private property is being pressed into some form of public service under the guise of mitigating serious public harm."[104]

Indeed, in the last few years the Court has gone further and found that a small reciprocity aspect is insufficient to justify a serious interference with property rights. *Hodel v. Irving* (1987),[105] involved the Indian Land Consolidation Act, a federal statute aimed at the extreme fractionation of Indian lands. The Act prohibited those Indians who owned only very small interests in reservation land tracts from passing their interests to their heirs. Instead, the land was to escheat to their tribe, which could lease the land more profitably in bigger pieces. Even though the Court identified an "average reciprocity of advantage" in the law because the landowners maintained a nexus with the tribe benefited, it held that monetary compensation to the owners was constitutionally necessary. Its decision turned on what the Court characterized as the extraordinary character of the legislation; indeed, the ability to pass on property to one's heirs has been part of our Anglo-American legal system since feudal times.

In the foregoing cases, the Court used reciprocity to ensure that the government was benefiting everyone on net by helping to reduce the transactions costs of multiparty bargaining. The Court occasionally uses a reciprocity requirement in a slightly different sense as well: to protect individuals from being singled out to donate their property to the general public. In these cases, the Court more carefully scrutinizes the state's interference with property rights.

A Reciprocity Requirement Protects Those Singled Out

Indeed, even lesser interferences with property rights occasionally require compensation if the Court finds that state action lacks both reciprocity and substantial justification. The principle was recently enunciated in *Nollan v. California Coastal Commission* (1987).[106] The Nollan family owned oceanfront property and sought to replace their small bungalow with a single-family permanent dwelling. The coastal commission agreed to grant the Nollans the required permit to build, but only on the condition that the Nollans grant a permanent right of easement to the public to pass along their beach. The Court held that the condition amounted to a taking requiring compensation, because the commission effectively eliminated their right to exclude others, one of the most essential sticks in the bundle of property rights. The Court stated that similar land-use regulation would not amount to a taking if it substantially advances legitimate state interests and does not deprive the owner economically viable use of his land. However, the Court found none of the state's claimed interests substantially advanced with the condition.

While the *Nollan* majority never discussed reciprocity, the lack of reciprocity in the state's condition may well be driving the Court's opinion. First, as the dissenting justices point out, the Court could easily have found a legitimate interest in enhancing public beach access.[107] The Court recognizes this interest, but concludes that the state must pay for this increased access. According to the Court, the state would be required to pay for any easements it imposed outright, so it should also pay for any easements granted as a condition to building. It's reasoning is nonpersuasive, however, because easements required by towns for sidewalks are routinely upheld without compensation, as noted in Justice Brennan's dissent.[108]

There is a distinction between this case and the sidewalk example, however: the commission's condition in this case lacks reciprocity. That is, the Nollans get little or nothing in return for their easement because even if their neighbors are also required to eventually grant easements, the Nollans already enjoy beach access and so benefit little from the restrictions of others. Furthermore, California law already allows the public, including the Nollans, access to all beach areas on the oceanside of the historic mean high tide line. In the sidewalk example, however, all neighboring landowners benefit from a common path on which to walk. Indeed, the benefits of sidewalk easements remain largely in the immediate neighborhood.

Government-imposed conditions on an owner's attempt to build on or otherwise improve his property generally lack reciprocal benefits because the property owner is by definition singled out to make a public donation. The Supreme Court seems to recognize the problem and, consequently, continues to carefully scrutinize conditions attached to building permits. In its most recent takings case, *Dolan v. City of Tigard* (1994),[109] the city agreed to issue a permit to Mrs. Dolan to expand her plumbing and electric supply store and pave her parking lot, but only on condition that she (1) transfer title to the portion of her property immediately adjacent to a creek to improve flood drainage and (2) dedicate an additional 15-foot strip of her land for a pedestrian/bicycle pathway to help reduce traffic congestion that would be intensified by her proposed expansion.

The Supreme Court, reinforcing *Nollan*, held that an essential nexus must exist between a legitimate state interest and the permit condition. The Court went further, however, and held that the exactions demanded in a permit condition must be roughly proportional to the projected impact of the proposed development. Turning to the *Dolan* facts, the Court concluded that while the city may restrict development in the flood plain along the creek, the city was not justified in confiscating title to the property. With respect to the second condition, the state had not found that the pathway dedication would reduce traffic congestion, but only that the congestion *could* be reduced. Without more certain benefits from the dedication, the second condition failed the Court's requirement. *Dolan* may well signal that there is some hope for Supreme Court support of the land rights movement in the context of state-imposed conditions on land-use improvements.

Another example of a takings clause violation based on a lack of both reciprocity and substantial justification is found in *Granat v. Keasler* (1983).[110] The case involved a Seattle ordinance subjecting owners of moorages within the city to rent controls and regulating the eviction of floating home tenants from their moorages. The ordinance allowed the moorage owner to evict a floating home tenant only to use the moorage for the owner's personal residence, and severely regulated the evictions. Most importantly, the moorage owner was required to give his tenant four months' notice of the eviction and to locate a replacement moorage within the city for his tenant. This second requirement was quite burdensome because residential moorages were exceedingly scarce.

In any event, Mr. Granat, the owner of some city moorages, sought to evict two of his tenants by moving them to alternative moorages he owned elsewhere in Seattle. The tenants claimed the attempted eviction was invalid because Granat intended to use their moorages to rent two of his own houseboats, at unregulated rents, rather than to use them for his personal residence. Granat claimed the restriction was so onerous that it effected an unconstitutional taking of his property, and the supreme court of Washington agreed. The court's reasoning is quite scant; it stated simply that under the ordinance the landlord is prohibited from the intended use of the property, but not the tenant.

Although the matter was not discussed, the court was presumably concerned about the lack of reciprocity in the Seattle ordinance. The landlords are required to incur severe burdens, yet the benefits are enjoyed solely by the tenants. Of course, many, perhaps most, regulations lack reciprocity in the sense that some portion of the population is burdened to benefit others.

However, here, as in *Nollan*, the challenged ordinance lacked substantial justification for the burden. The tenants were permitted to keep their houseboats at rent-controlled moorages and rent out their houseboats for a profit, while the landlords were prohibited from using their own moorages to rent houseboats. Although guaranteeing affordable moorages to those who live on houseboats might be an acceptable objective to many courts, the actual regulations discriminate against property owners without any sensible basis.

Occasionally a state court goes further and strikes down a lesser restrictive regulation that lacks reciprocity even though substantially justified. Consider *State v. Herwig* (1962),[111] for example. The Wisconsin Conservation Commission promulgated a rule prohibiting hunting on 2,800 acres of land the commission found attractive to waterfowl. Thereafter, Mr. Herwig was convicted of shooting a duck on his land, which was located within the prohibited area. Herwig appealed his conviction, claiming that the prohibition was invalid because it effected an unconstitutional taking of his property. The hunting prohibition in the area of his land had increased the presence of waterfowl that foraged Herwig's corn, alfalfa, and rye fields. This foraging cost Herwig $500 each year. The prohibition was intended to improve hunting conditions in the general area by attracting the birds initially to the prohibited area. Moreover, the increased presence of birds in the area would expand opportunities for people who wanted only to watch or photograph the birds.

The supreme court of Wisconsin found the commission's purposes laudable, but held that the regulation was nevertheless unconstitutional without compensation. In effect the state was establishing a game refuge without making any efforts to maintain or provide the waterfowl with food. If a landowner was prohibited from protecting his fields by shooting the waterfowl, the state must compensate the owner for the crop damage the waterfowl caused. Notice the critical fact that this regulation lacked reciprocity. Herwig was expected to endure a burden of fattening up the birds to provide a benefit to other landowners who were permitted to hunt on their property, but Herwig was prohibited from enjoying the benefit himself.

Reciprocity: A Summary

The point of this part has been to show the reader that the reciprocity rationale that is often used to justify uncompensated regulation can and sometimes is used as a sword to strike down regulations lacking reciprocal benefits to the burdened property owners. It is important not to make too much of the courts' progress in this regard, however, for the lack of reciprocity in a regulation is often ignored, especially when the burdens imposed are not particularly onerous. *Penn Central Transportation Co. v. New York City* (1978)[112] provides an excellent example. Recall that the Supreme Court treated

New York City's Landmarks Preservation Law as a zoning law and noted that even very extensive zoning is generally justified on nuisance grounds. In his dissent, however, Justice Rehnquist pointed out the essential distinction between this preservations law and the general zoning ordinances usually upheld: unlike the other laws, this law as applied burdened only a few physically separated landowners rather than an entire neighborhood or community. Thus, this regulation lacked the reciprocity of advantage found to accompany general zoning laws. And while the Court had, in the past, upheld government action singling out one owner to prohibit a noxious use of his property, no comparable nuisance was present in this case.[113]

However, the reciprocity argument has been used successfully to challenge regulations that otherwise could have been upheld under the nuisance doctrine. This point is more tentative than the conclusion regarding the nuisance cases, because reciprocity grounds are often implicit rather than explicit in the courts' opinions, and some opinions that explicitly consider the lack of reciprocity also consider other factors, such as physical invasion, that can contribute quite substantially to the court's holding. While doing so is not foolproof, landowners might do well to note a lack of reciprocity in challenged regulations whenever possible.

4. Final Thoughts

The Supreme Court has not yet rendered the term "regulatory takings" an oxymoron, but the Court has not extended property rights protections very far, even considering recent decisions in favor of landowners. The nuisance rationale, originally intended to justify uncompensated restriction of only the most noxious or illegal uses, has, by virtue of dicta from even the earliest cases, been extended to include any harmful use of property, as determined by the state itself. Although "nuisance regulation" that effects a complete deprivation of an owner's use and enjoyment of his property must be accompanied by compensation, vague definitions of "property" and "complete deprivation," as well as an expanding common law, enable most courts to circumvent even this token protection of property.

Justices Rehnquist and Scalia have been marginally successful in infusing reciprocity concerns into recent takings jurisprudence, however. The idea is that when a few isolated individuals are forced to endure heavy burdens for the benefit of others without receiving any or scant benefit from the regulations themselves, then those burdens, as expressed in *Armstrong*, should "in all fairness and justice" be "borne by the public as a whole." Even lesser burdens should not be borne by individuals who receive no benefit from the regulation if they do not bear a substantial relation to some important public purpose. In these cases the regulation begins to resemble naked transfers from the politically weak to the politically powerful, and this exploitation can be discouraged only by requiring the powerful to pay for their takings.

The reciprocity argument is by no means pervasive or consistently applied in the Supreme Court's decisions. However, aside from a few more protective state court interpretations of state constitutional takings provisions, it offers the only real weapon against increasingly burdensome land-use restrictions promulgated by an ever-growing regulatory state.

Notes

1. William Blackstone, *Commentaries on the Laws of England* 134 (Chicago: University of Chicago Press, 1979); Richard Epstein, *Takings: Private Property and the Power of Eminent Domain* 22 (Cambridge: Harvard University Press, 1985) (citing Blackstone).

2. The takings clause was adopted in the very form Madison submitted it, and was accepted by Congress without debate. See Veit, Bowling, and Bickford, *Creating the Bill of Rights: The Documentary Record from the First Federal Congress* 3-4, 180 (1991). The inclusion of a takings clause was originally and vigorously advocated by Thomas Paine. See Brant, *The Bill of Rights: Its Origin and Meaning* 240 (1965).

3. U.S. Constitution, Amendment V. The Fifth Amendment originally constrained only the actions of the federal government. However, the U.S. Supreme Court has more recently determined that the Fourteenth Amendment due process clause, which states, "nor shall any state deprive any person of life, liberty or property without due process of law," requires that state and local governments also abide by the constraints of the takings clause. *Chicago Burlington & Quincy R.R. v. Chicago*, 166 U.S. 226, 241 (1897).

4. Dennis J. Coyle, *Property Rights and the Constitution: Shaping Society Through Land Use Regulation* 280 n.50 (1993) (hereinafter Coyle). See, for example, Conn. Const. art. I, sec. 11 ("The property of no person shall be taken for public use, without just compensation thereof."); Calif. Const. art. I, sec. 7(a) ("Private property may be taken or damaged for public use only when just compensation, ascertained by a jury unless waived, has first been paid to, or into court for, the owner."); Pa. Const. art. I, sec. 10 ("Nor shall private property be taken or applied to public use without authority of law and without just compensation."); Maine Const. art. I, sec. 21 ("Private property shall not be taken for public uses without compensation; nor unless the public exigencies require it."); Wisc. Const. art. I, sec. 13 ("The property of no person shall be taken for public use without just compensation therefore.")

5. The federal Constitution, as interpreted by the Supreme Court, delineates the minimum property rights that the government must respect. However, states can interpret their own constitutional takings clauses to require more protection of property than that provided by the federal constitution. See Brennan, "State Constitutions and the Protection of Individual Rights," 90 *Harv. L. Rev.* 489, 498-502 (1975).

6. Epstein at 164.

7. G. Stone, L. Seidman, C. Sunstein, and M. Tushnet, *Constitutional Law* 1447-48 (1986). See also Levmore, "Just Compensation and Just Politics," 22 *Conn. L. Rev.* 285, 306-7 (1990) (as ad hoc group, victims of takings unlikely to be well represented in political process because they lack logrolling abilities of repeat players).

8. State courts, interpreting state constitutions, sometimes impose more stringent public use requirements on government takings. See Munzer, *A Theory of Property* 463 n.46 (1990) (citing Merrill, "The Economics of Public Use," 72 *Cornell L. Rev.* 61, 65, 93-109 (1986)).

9. 467 U.S. 986 (1984).

10. 467 U.S. at 1014.

11. 467 U.S. 229 (1984).

12. 467 U.S. at 241.

13. *Berman v. Parker*, 348 U.S. 26, 32 (1954). The Supreme Court's interpretation has been supported by some constitutional scholars. See, for example, Ackerman, *Private Property and the Constitution* 190 n.5 (1977) ("any state purpose otherwise constitutional should qualify as sufficiently 'public' to justify a taking.").

14. See, for example *Bothwell v. United States*, 254 U.S. 231 (1920).

15. 328 U.S. 256 (1946).

16. 458 U.S. 419 (1982).

17. For more invasion cases, see *Kaiser Aetna v. United States*, 444 U.S. 164 (1979) (government could not force private marina owner to provide public access without compensation); *Griggs v. Allegheny Co.*, 369 U.S. 84 (1962) (regular low-altitude flights over property, frequently disrupting owners' conversation and sleep, constituted taking); *Portsmouth Co. v. United States*, 260 U.S. 327 (1922) (frequent firing of guns over land could amount to taking); *United States v. Cress*, 243 U.S. 316 (1917) (government's damming of river, which subjected property permanently to periodic flooding, effected partial taking of property requiring compensation). The right to exclude others can be limited without compensation, however, if the property owner already provides access to the general public. See *Pruneyard Shopping Center v. Robins*, 447 U.S. 74 (1980) (state could require shopping center owner to allow mall access to individuals to solicit signatures for petitions in opposition to a United Nations resolution).

18. *Andrus v. Allard*, 444 U.S. 51, 65 (1979).

19. *Armstrong v. United States*, 364 U.S. 40, 49 (1960).

20. Peterson, "The Takings Clause: In Search of Underlying Principles," 78 *Calif. L. Rev.* 53, 56 (1990) [quoting C. Haar, *Land-Use Planning* 766 (3d ed. 1976) and *San Diego Gas & Electric Co. v. San Diego*, 450 U.S. 621, 649 n14 (1981) (Brennan, J., dissenting)].

21. Michelman, "Property, Utility, and Fairness: Comments on the Ethical Foundations of 'Just Compensation' Law," 80 *Harv. L. Rev.* 1165 (1967) (hereinafter Michelman).

22. Michelman at 1214.

23. Ibid.

24. Ibid.

25. As of 1985, Michelman's was the eighth most cited law journal article on any subject. Fischel, "Exploring the Kozinski Paradox: Why Is More Efficient Regulation

a Taking of Property?," 67 *Chicago-Kent L. Rev.* 865, 881 n.52 (1991) (citing Shapiro, "The Most Cited Law Review Articles," 73 *Calif. L. Rev.* 1540, 1550 (1985).

26. See, for example Fischel & Shapiro, "Takings, Insurance & Michelman: Comments On Economic Interpretations Of 'Just Compensation Law," 17 *J. Legal Stud.* 269 (1988).

27. Miceli & Segerson, "Regulatory Takings: When Should Compensation be Paid?," 23 *J. Legal Stud.* 749 (1994).

28. Several scholars have raised these concerns. See, for example, Blume, Rubinfeld & Shapiro, "The Taking of Land: When Should Compensation Be Paid?," 99 *Q.J. Econ.* 71 (1984); Fischel & Shapiro, "Takings, Insurance & Michelman: Comments on Economic Interpretations of 'Just Compensation' Law," 17 *J. Legal Stud.* 269 (1988); Kaplow, "An Economic Analysis of Legal Transitions," 99 *Harv. L. Rev.* 509 (1986); Knetch & Borcherding, "Expropriation of Private Property and the Basis for Compensation," 29 *Univ. of Toronto L.J.* 237 (1979); Baxter & Altree, "Legal Aspects of Airport Noise," 15 *J. Law & Econ.* 1 (1972).

29. William Fischel adopted a conflicting position. To him, efficient regulation of immovable assets by local government should receive more extensive takings scrutiny because the taking is less likely to be corrected through legislative means. Fischel, "Exploring the Kozinski Paradox," supra note 25.

30. Sax, "Takings and the Police Power," 74 *Yale L.J.* 36 (1964).

31. Ibid. at 62-63.

32. Sax, "Takings, Private Property and Public Rights," 81 *Yale L.J.* 149 (1971).

33. Ibid. at 162.

34. See, for example, Epstein, supra note 1; Coyle, supra note 4; Paul, *Property Rights and Eminent Domain* (New Brunswick, NJ: Transaction Press, 1987).

35. Epstein, supra note 1.

36. Ibid. at 3-18.

37. Ibid. at 161-81.

38. Ibid. at 111.

39. Ibid. at 263-73.

40. Alternative approaches can be found in Ackerman, *Private Property and the Constitution* (New Haven: Yale University Press, 1977); Blume, Rubinfeld & Shapiro, "The Taking of Land: When Should Compensation Be Paid?" 99 *Q.J. Econ.* 71 (1984); Farber, "Economic Analysis and Just Compensation," 12 *Int. Rev. of Law & Econ.* 125 (1992); Radin, "The Liberal Conception of Property: Cross Currents in the Jurisprudence of Takings," 88 *Colum. L. Rev.* 1667 (1988); Tideman, "Takings, Moral Evolution and Justice," 88 *Colum. L. Rev.* 1714 (1988); Rose-Ackerman, "Against Ad Hocery: A Comment on Michelman," 88 *Colum. L. Rev.* 1697 (1988); Levmore, "Takings, Torts and Special Interests," 77 *Va. L. Rev.* 1333 (1991).

41. See, for example *Andrus v. Allard*, 444 U.S. at 65 ("There is no abstract or fixed point at which judicial intervention under the Takings Clause becomes appropriate. Formulas and factors have been developed in a variety of settings. . . . Resolution of each case, however, ultimately calls as much for the exercise of judgment as for the application of logic.").

42. *Black's Law Dictionary* 961 (5th ed. 1979) (citing *State v. Cardon*, 23 Ariz. App. 78, 530 P.2d 1115, 1118).

43. See, for example, Michelman, supra note 20 at 1191; Epstein, supra note 1 at 112 ("Supreme Court cases have repeatedly referred to control of nuisances as a proper end of the state, and there is no doubt today, as in times past, that this proposition is sound in principle."). See also IV William Blackstone, *Commentaries on the Laws of England* 167-69 (Chicago: University of Chicago Press, 1979) (discussing various common law nuisances punishable by the king).

44. *Mugler v. Kansas*, 123 U.S. 623 (1887).

45. 123 U.S. 623 (1887).

46. 123 U.S. at 655. The statute did permit the manufacture or sale of alcohol for medical, scientific or mechanical purposes. Ibid. Despite this exception, however, Mugler was effectively prohibited from operating his business.

47. Ibid. at 669.

48. Ibid. at 668-69.

49. 127 U.S. 678 (1888).

50. Ibid. at 685.

51. 276 U.S. 272 (1928).

52. Ibid. at 279.

53. For an interesting public choice discussion of the *Miller* facts, see Buchanan, "Politics, Property and the Law: An Alternative Interpretation of *Miller et al. v. Schoene*," 15 J. Law & Econ. 439 (1972); see also Samuels, "Interrelations Between Legal and Economic Processes," 14 J. Law & Econ. 435 (1971).

54. 239 U.S. 394 (1915).

55. Ibid. at 410.

56. As will be shown, infra, property value reductions this severe have been upheld in more recent cases even when the public harm identified is much less direct than that identified in *Hadacheck*.

57. 357 U.S. 155 (1958).

58. The Supreme Court has found direct wartime confiscation to constitute a taking requiring compensation. See *United States v. Pewee Coal Co.*, 341 U.S. 114 (1951) (federal government's temporary seizure and operation of coal mine to avert nationwide miners' strike in 1943 was compensable taking).

59. See, for example, *Penn Central Transp. Co. v. New York City*, 438 U.S. 104, 126 (1978); *Goldblatt v. Hempstead*, 369 U.S. 590, 593 (1962); *Heart of Atlanta Motel v. United States*, 379 U.S. 241, 261 (1964).

60. 480 U.S. 470 (1987).

61. Coal mine subsidence is the lowering of strata overlying a coal mine, including the land surface, as a result of extracting the underground coal. Ibid. at 474.

62. 260 U.S. 393 (1922).

63. Ibid. at 416.

64. 452 U.S. 264 (1981) (rejecting takings challenge to more comprehensive federal mining regulations).

65. 273 Wis. 10, 76 N.W.2d 571 (Wis. 1956).

66. See also *People v. Hulbert*, 91 N.W. 211 (Mich. 1902). The supreme court of Michigan held unconstitutional a similar ordinance without any evidence that the city was attempting to circumvent contractual promises. The city owned a parcel of land

bordering the lake, but each of the other lakeshore owners had an equal right to use the water for ordinary household uses even if the water's purity was to some degree affected.

67. 438 U.S. 104 (1978).

68. 498 Pa. 180, 445 A.2d 724 (Pa. 1982).

69. See also *National Land & Investment Co. v. Kohn*, 419 Pa. 504, 215 A.2d 597 (Pa. 1965) (aesthetic considerations alone not enough to sustain zoning regulations under due process clause).

70. 482 U.S. 304 (1987).

71. 482 U.S. at 316-17 (quoting *Pumpelly v. Green Bay Co.*, 13 Wall. 166, 177-78 (1872)) (emphasis in original).

72. 112 S. Ct. 2886 (1992).

73. Justice Blackmun does not criticize the majority for failing to provide better guidelines. Instead, he laments that the majority's rule is incapable of objective application. According to Justice Blackmun, "any land use regulation can be characterized as the 'total' deprivation of an aptly defined entitlement. Alternatively, the same regulation can always be characterized as a mere 'partial' withdrawal from full, unencumbered ownership of the landholding affected by the regulation." 112 S. Ct. at 2913 (quoting Michelman, "Takings, 1987," 88 *Colum. L. Rev.* 1600 (1988)).

74. 121 N.H. 590, 432 A.2d 15 (N.H. 1981).

75. 125 N.J. 193, 593 A.2d 251 (N.J. 1991).

76. 168 Conn. 349, 362 A.2d 948 (Conn. 1975).

77. 362 A.2d at 949 n.2.

78. 115 N.H. 124, 336 A.2d 239 (N.H. 1975).

79. 161 Conn. 24, 282 A.2d 907 (Conn. 1971).

80. 336 A.2d at 243.

81. 282 A.2d at 910.

82. 362 Mass. 221, 284 N.E.2d 891 (Mass. 1972).

83. 151 Conn. 304, 197 A.2d 770 (Conn. 1964).

84. The court estimated that the value of Dooley's parcel had declined by a total of at least 75 percent.

85. 197 A.2d at 773.

86. 463 A.2d 133 (R.I. 1983).

87. 528 A.2d 453 (Me. 1987).

88. 112 S. Ct. at 2900.

89. 56 Wis. 2d 7, 201 N.W.2d 761 (Wis. 1972).

90. 201 N.W.2d at 771.

91. Ibid. at 768.

92. See Epstein, supra note 1 at 195-216.

93. Epstein provides other examples: The general creditor who cannot collect from his debtor receives compensation because the parallel restrictions imposed upon other creditors assure that there is a pool of assets available to satisfy claims on a pro rata basis. The landowner who cannot erect a large sign is assured that his neighbor cannot put up a sign that will block his own. So long as the property received by the owner equals or exceeds the value of the property he surrendered, explicit compensation is unnecessary; indeed it is wholly improper overcompensation, which is itself a taking of property from someone else. Ibid. at 196.

94. 232 U.S. 531 (1914).

95. See, for example, *Pennsylvania Coal Co. v. Mahon*, 260 U.S. 393, 415 (1922) (*Plymouth* regulation "secured an average reciprocity of advantage that has been recognized as a justification of various laws.").

96. See *Euclid v. Ambler*, 272 U.S. 365, 395 (1926).

97. 447 U.S. 255 (1980).

98. 447 U.S. at 262. Epstein has argued, however, that Agins did not receive a sufficiently large benefit from the zoning restrictions to excuse the city's compensation requirement. Epstein, supra note 1 at 272-73.

99. See, for example *Euclid v. Ambler Realty Co.*, 272 U.S. 365 (1926) (residential zoning restrictions reduced market value of property 75 percent).

100. 593 A.2d 251 (N.J. 1991).

101. See also Coletta, "Reciprocity of Advantage and Regulatory Takings: Toward a New Theory of Takings Jurisprudence," 40 *Amer. Univ. L. Rev.* 297 (1990). Coletta actually advocates using the reciprocity rationale to "provide broad justification for land use regulation and thereby substantially limit the accessibility of inverse condemnation actions." Ibid. at 303. He argues:

> Reciprocity demands should be deemed to be met, and the regulation therefore deemed to be a legitimate exercise of the police power, in any case where the land use restrictions affirmatively enhance the community's welfare. Therefore, rather than requiring that direct individualized benefits accrue to the burdened individual, reciprocity defenses would focus on the benefits gained by the community at large. Individuals' use of property could legally be restricted even where their properties received no reciprocal, or offsetting, enhanced value; insofar as the individual landowners, in their roles as members of society, could be characterized as sharing in the restriction's benefits, they would be denied legal redress. Ibid.

102. Both the Fifth and Fourteenth Amendments provide that the government cannot deprive individuals of their property without due process of law.

103. 439 Pa. 466, 268 A.2d 765 (Pa. 1970). Dennis Coyle provides an extended and useful discussion of the Pennsylvania court's treatment of this and other cases in *Property Rights and the Constitution: Shaping Society Through Land Use Regulation* 53-61 (1993).

104. 112 S. Ct. at 2894-95.

105. 481 U.S. 704 (1987).

106. 483 U.S. 825 (1987).

107. See 483 U.S. at 865 (Blackmun, J., dissenting).

108. See 483 U.S. at 854 (Brennan, J., dissenting), and cases cited therein.

109. 1994 WL 276693 (June 24, 1994).

110. 99 Wash. 2d 564, 663 P.2d 830 (Wash. 1983).

111. 17 Wis. 2d 442, 117 N.W.2d 335 (Wis. 1962).

112. 438 U.S. 104 (1978).

113. 438 U.S. at 138-45 (Rehnquist, J., dissenting).

References

Ackerman, Bruce. *Private Property and the Constitution*. New Haven: Yale University Press, 1977.

Baxter, William and Lillian Altree. "Legal Aspects of Airport Noise." 15 *Journal of Law and Economics* 1 (1972).

Blackstone, William. *Commentaries on the Laws of England*. Chicago and London: University of Chicago Press, 1979.

Blume, Lawrence, Daniel Rubinfeld, and Perry Shapiro. "The Taking of Land: When Should Compensation Be Paid?" 99 *Quarterly Journal of Economics* 71 (1984).

Brant, Irving. *The Bill of Rights: Its Origin and Meaning*. New York: New American Library, 1965.

Brennan, William. "State Constitutions and the Protection of Individual Rights." 90 *Harvard Law Review* 489 (1975).

Buchanan, James. "Politics, Property and the Law: An Alternative Interpretation of *Miller et al. v. Schoene*." 15 *Journal of Law and Economics* 439 (1972).

Coletta, Raymond. "Reciprocity of Advantage and Regulatory Takings: Toward a New Theory of Takings Jurisprudence." 40 *American University Law Review* 297 (1990).

Coyle, Dennis. *Property Rights and the Constitution: Shaping Society Through Land Use Regulation*. Albany: SUNY Press, 1993.

Epstein, Richard. *Takings: Private Property and the Power of Eminent Domain*. Cambridge and London: Harvard University Press, 1985.

Epstein, Richard. "Property, Speech and the Politics of Distrust." 59 *University of Chicago Law Review* 41 (1992).

Farber, Daniel. "Economic Analysis and Just Compensation." 12 *International Review of Law and Economics* 125 (1992).

Fischel, William. "Exploring the Kozinski Paradox: Why Is More Efficient Regulation a Taking of Property?" 67 *Chicago-Kent Law Review* 865 (1991).

Fischel, William, and Perry Shapiro. "Takings, Insurance, and Michelman: Comments on Economic Interpretations of 'Just Compensation' Law." 17 *Journal of Legal Studies* 269 (1988).

Fischel, William, and Perry Shapiro. "A Constitutional Choice Model of Compensation for Takings." 9 *International Review of Law and Economics* 115 (1989).

Fisher, William. "The Significance of Public Perceptions of the Takings Doctrine." 88 *Columbia Law Review* 1774 (1988).

Kaplow, Louis. "An Economic Analysis of Legal Transitions." 99 *Harvard Law Review* 509 (1986).

Knetch, Jack, and Thomas Borcherding. "Expropriation of Private Property and the Basis for Compensation." 29 *University of Toronto Law Journal* 237 (1979).

Levmore, Saul. "Just Compensation and Just Politics." 22 *Connecticut Law Review* 285 (1990).

Levmore, Saul. "Takings, Torts, and Special Interests." 77 *Virginia Law Review* 1333 (1991).

Merrill, Thomas. "The Economics of Public Use." 72 *Cornell Law Review* 61 (1986).

Miceli, Thomas, and Kathleen Segerson. "Regulatory Takings: When Should Compensation Be Paid?" 23 *Journal of Legal Studies* 749 (1994).

Michelman, Frank. "Property, Utility, and Fairness: Comments on the Ethical Foundations of 'Just Compensation' Law." 80 *Harvard Law Review* 1165 (1967).

Michelman, Frank. "Takings, 1987." 88 *Columbia Law Review* 1600 (1988).

Munzer, Stephen. *A Theory of Property.* Cambridge: Cambridge University Press, 1990.

Paul, Ellen. *Property Rights and Eminent Domain.* New Brunswick, N.J.: Transaction Press, 1987.

Peterson, Andrea. "The Takings Clause: In Search of Underlying Principles." 78 *California Law Review* 53 (1990).

Radin, Margaret. "The Liberal Conception of Property: Cross Currents in the Jurisprudence of Takings." 88 *Columbia Law Review* 1667 (1988).

Rose-Ackerman, Susan. "Against Ad Hocery: A Comment on Michelman." 88 *Columbia Law Review* 1697 (1988).

Samuels, Warren. "Interrelations Between Legal and Economic Processes." 14 *Journal of Law and Economics* 435 (1971).

Sax, Joseph. "Takings and the Police Power." 74 *Yale Law Journal* 36 (1964).

Sax, Joseph. "Takings, Private Property and Public Rights." 81 *Yale Law Journal* 149 (1971).

Stone, Geoffrey, Louis Seidman, Cass Sunstein and Mark Tushnet. *Constitutional Law.* Boston and Toronto: Little, Brown, 1986).

Tideman, Nicholas. "Takings, Moral Evolution and Justice: 88 *Columbia Law Review* 1714 (1988).

Veit, Helen, Kenneth Bowling, and Charlene Bickford. *Creating the Bill of Rights: The Documentary Record from the First Federal Congress.* Baltimore: Johns Hopkins University Press, 1991.

Chapter 3

The Lucas Case and the Conflict over Property Rights

James R. Rinehart and Jeffrey J. Pompe

As Nancie Marzulla explained in an earlier chapter, conflicts between property owners and regulatory agencies over environmental controls have reached a high-pitched level in recent years. The land rights movement has come of age. Federal, state, and local government agencies find themselves caught in a crossfire between environmentalists, who want tougher environmental standards, and property owners, who want greater protection of their property rights.

The stakes are high on both sides. Environmenalists seek control of huge amounts of natural resources, control that they believe to be a legitimate function of government. Property owners are equally dedicated to protecting what they believe is theirs. For them, protection of property rights is a fundamental function of government. At present, winners and losers are determined largely by who can muster the most political support in implementing or blocking passage of new environmental laws. Property owners, or environmentalists, who lose out in the legislative battles often look to the judicial system for redress. Such was the case with David Lucas, a developer in Charleston, South Carolina, who ran afoul of property regulations imposed by the South Carolina Coastal Council.

In 1986 David Lucas paid $975,000 for two oceanfront lots in a development referred to as "Wild Dunes" located on the Isle of Palms near Charleston. (See Figure 3.1.) The two lots were near an inlet erosion zone with a shoreline that changed dramatically, sometimes accreting, sometimes eroding. At the time of purchase, the lots were several hundred feet from the mean high tide mark and were zoned for single-family homes, with houses already constructed on adjoining lots as well as most other oceanfront sites in the development. (See Figure 3.2.) No federal, state, or local regulations in effect at the time would have denied Lucas the right to build on his lots the houses he had planned.

In 1988 South Carolina enacted the Beachfront Management Act, which established a new exacting building setback line. All portions of Lucas's two lots were found to be situated seaward of the setback line; consequently, no legal way existed for him to use his lots for single-family houses. The value of his properties vanished along with his right to build. The Act contained no variance procedure that might have allowed Lucas to request and possibly receive a special building permit. Lucas's response to the regulation was to file a $1.2 million lawsuit against the South Carolina Coastal Council, the agency that established the building setback line. Lucas argued that the legislation had rendered his property worthless, and he was therefore entitled to compensation under the takings clause of the Fifth Amendment of the U.S. Constitution.

Although governments routinely use the power of eminent domain to force landowners to relinquish land for the public good, a fair market value is paid to property owners. The Lucas case constitutes a "regulatory taking" since the government did not occupy the land. As the controversy developed, the coastal council took the typical position: Compensation was not due; as a duly constituted arm of government, the council was acting to prevent public harm.

When *Lucas v. South Carolina Coastal Council* (91-453) went before the U.S. Supreme Court in February 1992, the outcome of the litigation was anticipated with considerable interest on the part of Lucas partisans and detractors. Many property rights advocates saw *Lucas* as a critical test case that would better define the rights of property owners. Indeed, in light of what appears to be a recent move by the Court toward greater protection of property owners, some saw *Lucas* as having the potential of being one of the most important cases of the century. In the summer of 1992 the U.S. Supreme Court rendered an opinion that favored Lucas and cheered property rights advocates.

This chapter reviews and analyzes the Lucas story. In what follows, considerable attention is devoted to institutions and how they affected the controversy. There is less attention given to Fifth Amendment jurisprudence, which is covered extensively by Erin O'Hara in Chapter 2. The Lucas story we present begins with a discussion of land-use controls, property rights, and coastal zone management. There, attention is given to economic concepts that

Figure 3.1 Location of Lucas's properties

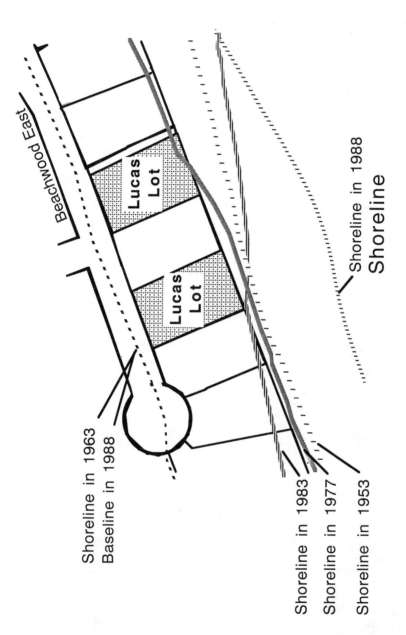

Figure 3.2 Lucas's properties in the Wild Dunes development

relate to markets and regulation. The chapter's next section brings David Lucas face-to-face with South Carolina's Beachfront Management Act and the coastal commission and recounts key elements of the Lucas story. Here, we develop the short- and long-run implications of the *Lucas* decision for shaping future land-use controls. Given the intense interest in *Lucas* and the likely effects the ruling will have on land-use planners, we offer some alternatives to regulatory takings in the next-to-last section. Finally, we conclude the chapter with a discussion of political economy, the relationship between social welfare, majority rule, and restrictions on property rights.

1. Land Use, Property Rights, and Coastal Zone Management

Land-use controls are as old as the United States.[1] But because of the great abundance of land, the actual taking of land for public purposes was until recently a rare occurrence. Even if regulatory controls deprived the owner of all use of his land, while leaving the owner with title and possession, as in the 1826 case of *Brick Presbyterian Church v. the City of New York*, the courts held that no taking had taken place (Cullingworth, 1993, 21-22). It was not until the 1922 *Pennsylvania Coal v. Mahon* decision, in which Justice Holmes held that a state must compensate owners when regulation "goes too far," that American courts accepted the idea that remuneration may be required in a regulatory taking.

Conflicts over land-use regulation are principally a twentieth-century urban phenomenon. As populations became more concentrated and space more limited in urban centers, cases involving costs imposed on one neighbor by another increased in frequency. In 1916, New York City implemented the first comprehensive zoning law that restricted the use of private property without providing compensation. The U.S. Supreme Court supported such zoning limits on property use in two landmark decisions, first in 1926 (*Euclid v. Ambler Realty Co.* 272 U.S. 365) and again in 1928 (*Nectow v. City of Cambridge*, 277 U.S. 183).

Although state courts ruled on numerous land-use conflicts over the next fifty years, until 1974 the Supreme Court had relatively little to say on the matter. Beginning with *Village of Belle Terre v. Boraas* in 1974, the Supreme Court renewed its attention to zoning, although the high court did little to interfere with local government decisions on zoning (Fischel, 1985, 40). The Lucas case is one of a growing number of recent instances where the Supreme Court has shown increased interest with regard to property rights protection.

Real Estate and Scarce Resources

Real estate, whether it is located near the ocean, in the mountains, or on scenic rivers and swamps, is a scarce resource with alternative uses. Consequently, as is the case with all resources, choices must be made as to which use or uses any particular property will satisfy. Advocates of the American enterprise system recognize private property rights as a fundamental tenet of a free market economy. Property use in market-driven economies is dictated by the choices made by owners as they attempt to use their property to satisfy consumer demand and earn the highest return on their investment.

During the past half century the police power of the state has expanded from simple zoning restrictions to voluminous regulations limiting how property owners may use their land. And for most of these limitations on property use, as long as the state did not physically take possession of the property, the constraints were enforced without providing compensation. Presently, it is a common practice to prohibit property uses that destroy or impair certain kinds of scenery, animals, plants, trees, air, water, wetlands, and beaches. Even the right to set property prices such as rent on apartments falls under the purview of local governments in many places.

All scarce resources, including land, by their very nature involve forgoing a particular set of benefits when some other set of benefits is selected. It is in society's best interest to find ways to allocate resources and define uses so that all resources taken together produce the greatest net benefits, that is, to obtain Pareto optimality. Under the Pareto criterion, efficiency occurs when it is impossible to make someone better off by reallocating resources without simultaneously making someone else worse off. Evidence demonstrates that private ownership and control of property under of a rule of law coupled with competitive markets lead to the highest and most efficient use of resources. Since users deriving the highest benefits from a particular piece of land can repeatedly outbid other potential users, the property in question automatically goes to its highest and best use. In addition, actions taken by a private landowner that impose costs on a neighbor can be subject to legal action at common law. However, some exceptions to the rule arise, thus leading to possible justification for some type of governmental involvement in the regulation of private land.

An inefficient outcome may result when property owners have little incentive to take into account all of the economic consequences resulting from the use of their property. A negative externality may be created when a market participant does not bear all the consequences of his or her action. For example, an owner of a beachfront lot may have little reason to factor in any potential damage to property on the same beach when clearing sand dunes to be closer to the water or building a seawall for greater protection of the owner's beach. The existence of such externally imposed costs causes the injured parties to seek redress in the legislature and courts.

Another possible market-generated inefficiency, one that has been used in defense of government regulation of coastal development, is the problem of a public good. A pure public good provides nonrival and nonexcludable benefits to all individuals. Enjoyment and consumption of a public good by an individual is available to everyone without cost and such availability does not prevent others from having access without paying. For example, efforts by one landowner to reduce beach erosion will benefit the owner *and* all other users of the beach, but the owner has no way of securing payment from the "free riders." As a result, an efficient amount may not be provided by the market-place without government intervention. Although beaches may not be a "pure" public good, they do meet the criteria to a certain degree and therefore might justify some government involvement.

There is yet another problem confronted by market participants. If access to common property resources such as coastal areas is not controlled, pollution and depletion of resources may result. When a resource is open to all, the "tragedy of the commons" is a likely result (Hardin, 1968). When a single individual or group is not able to capture all of the gains from conserving a resource, which is to say property rights are not defined and enforced, the resource tends to be abused and overused.

Finally, if land costs and the cost of development are distorted by government subsidies, such as with flood insurance, then market participants receive faulty market signals when making land-use plans. In short, government-provided incentives or a failure to define and enforce property rights can combine to yield a call for more detailed government controls.

Management of the Coastal Zone

For a multitude of reasons, concerns about coastal development and public access to beach areas have produced a clamor for governmental involvement in the decisions property owners make concerning the use of their property. The rising demand for access to coastal areas has exacerbated these concerns. Part of the rising clamor can be explained by population patterns and growth. The number of people living within 50 miles of the coastline rose from 61 to 130 million from 1940 to 1988 (Long, 1990, 6), representing an increase from 46 percent of the total U.S. population in 1940 to 53 percent in 1988. Concomitantly, the number of nonresident tourists traveling to coastal areas has grown substantially with rising demands for leisure-related activities. This trend is expected to continue, and the resulting conflicts over land use will not abate.

Growing populations in coastal areas coupled with development that fails to take all costs into account can lead to significant environmental and economic

damage. Overdevelopment and building too close to the water lead to the loss
of vegetation and sand dunes, which in turn reduces the beach's capacity to
resist erosion, causing further destruction of land, buildings, and infrastructure
(Neal et al., 1984, 54). Oceanfront structures suffer the most severe damage
but land and buildings farther inland also experience losses that are to a
considerable extent caused by the initial loss of oceanfront property. Additionally, shoreline erosion threatens recreational benefits that accrue to tourists and
other coastal residents and ruins the natural habitat for plants and animals.

Coastal erosion does not occur solely from manmade activities. Natural
forces such as wind and water cause coastal shorelines to be in perpetual motion
between erosion and accretion. This process can be drastically altered due to
catastrophic storms and global sea level rise. Some evidence indicates that the
rise in sea level has accelerated since the 1930s, perhaps by a vertical rise rate
of more than one foot per century (Neal et al., 1984, 23). This could be the
result of the greenhouse effect, which suggests that a gradual warming of the
earth's atmosphere is occurring. Should global temperatures rise, the resultant
melting of polar ice caps would raise ocean levels and thus inundate coastlines
worldwide. Whether right or wrong, the widespread view that ocean levels are
rising increases the public's concerns about the future of coastal resources.

Barrier islands, such as the Isle of Palms, on which the Lucas lots were
located, are especially dynamic landforms. They protect estuaries and the
mainland from the direct force of ocean waves and their shorelines are
constantly eroding or accreting because of changing energy conditions (Leatherman, 1988). The Isle of Palms shoreline has changed dramatically over the
years. Indeed, the Lucas lots were under water between 1957 and 1973. (See
Figure 3.2.)

Various erosion control techniques have been practiced in an effort to protect
property, some by private landowners and others by government on behalf of
private citizens.[2] Although the use of "hard" shoreline protection devices such
as jetties and seawalls to impede the loss of sand is widespread, serious
questions have arisen recently regarding the indirect consequences of such
structures. While jetties and seawalls may shield property from erosion in the
immediate vicinity of the barriers, such devices tend to cause greater damage to
neighboring properties. As a result, most localities now either ban them
completely or significantly restrict their use.[3]

A second approach to control the damage from shoreline erosion is to simply
renourish the beach by trucking sand from inland sand pits or pumping sand
from the rivers or ocean floor. Although beach nourishment is a viable and
popular option, the practice is expensive and the benefits are ephemeral. For
instance, Ocean City, Maryland, replaced nine miles of oceanfront at an
aggregate cost of $51.2 million, only to see the bulk of it wash away during the
heavy storms in the fall of 1992 (Pope, 1992, 8d). Kana concludes that

nourishment of South Carolina's eroding beaches will require $65 million in the decade of the 1990s alone (1990, 21).

Some, such as geologist Orrin Pilkey (1987), are of the opinion that replacing sand on beaches that are meant to move is a losing battle. Despite the critics of the nourishment practice, the economic benefits for areas relying on the revenues created by wide beaches may be very large. Indeed, a cost-benefit examination demonstrates that beach nourishment projects can be economically viable (Pompe and Rinehart, 1994). However, raising the millions of dollars for such projects is not an easy task, and the equity issue concerning who pays and who benefits plagues advocates.

In recent years, federal, state, and local government agencies have been turning to a third option that involves placing restrictions on coastal development such as disallowing construction in certain areas and upgrading building standards in others. Land-use regulation is aimed principally at preventing the encroachment of developmental activities on the natural defenses of the shoreline.

The recognition of the fact that a decision to use property in a particular way may impact negatively on some other property owner or individual has fed the movement to limit land use. Federal, state and local government agencies have responded to the concerns of injured parties by enacting laws and establishing policies aimed at controlling how coastal land is used, especially with respect to erosion effects.

Government Regulaton of Coastal Zone Development

Coastal zone management, which is a relatively recent attempt by the federal government to deal with problems of coastal development, began with the federal Coastal Zone Management Act (CZMA). The purpose of the Act, signed into law on October 27, 1972, was to "preserve, protect and where possible, to restore or enhance the resources of the nation's coastal zone for this and succeeding generations" (P.L. 92-583). These lofty objectives were to be achieved by encouraging the affected states and local governments to become involved. Although the Act allowed the federal government to protect and manage development in the coastal area, specific management policies were placed in the hands of state and local governments. The Act specifically sought state involvement by providing federal funding for states to establish a federally approved program for coastal management.[4] Concerned that erosion problems were not being contained, the federal government amended and strengthened the original legislation on July 26, 1976. The states were directed to "prevent or significantly reduce threats to life and the destruction of property by eliminating development and redevelopment in high hazard areas" (CZMA, 160 S.C. Soc. 1451 et seq.).

In 1982, the federal government followed up with the enactment of the Coastal Barrier Resource Act (CBRA), which removed federal subsidies to construction on barrier islands and other areas specifically susceptible to erosion. For areas designated as undeveloped by the Department of Interior, the Act provided for the elimination of federal funding for flood insurance, infrastructure, such as bridges and roads, and federal disaster relief. The area covered by CBRA was expanded in 1990 to include land along the Great Lakes, the Florida Keys, Puerto Rico, and the Virgin Islands.

South Carolina and Coastal Zone Controls

South Carolina became involved in coastal regulation when the General Assembly enacted the Coastal Management Act in 1977. This Act was in direct response to the federal initiative discussed above, and the state has participated in the federal program since that date. The Act established the South Carolina Coastal Council to oversee the implementation of the law's provisions. Along with the Council, the Act set in place a permitting and management process for activities occurring in the "critical coastal zones" of eight coastal counties, which allowed the state to exert management authority over all development in areas such as tidelands, coastal waters, beaches, and oceanfront sand dunes.

Despite this initial effort on the part of South Carolina to control erosion, it was clear by the mid-1980s that the policy was falling short of its adherents' expectations. Erosion was continuing and the "hard" erosion control devices allowed by the coastal council actually had exacerbated the problem. In response the state established a Blue Ribbon Committee on Beachfront Management to study the situation. Subsequently, the committee concluded that there was inadequate protection of the state's fragile beach/dune system, and operating on the principle that the public has rights to beaches that supersede those of property owners, the state legislature passed the 1988 Beachfront Management Act (S.C. Code, Sec. 48-39-250, et seq.).

The Act broadened and better defined the powers and jurisdiction of the coastal council in controlling the development of coastal lands and focused on preserving the beach/dune system primarily by establishing building setback lines, barring future construction of "hard" devices such as seawalls, limiting the size of structures in the predicted erosion zone, and initiating a retreat from the beach over a forty-year period. The beach/dune system was considered to be in "both the public and private interests" since it provides storm protection, tourism benefits, habitat protection, and a natural healthy environment for South Carolina residents. The Act further emphasized the elimination of unwise development, offered greater public access to beaches, and provided additional funding for the law's implementation and development of a long-range comprehensive management plan for the entire coastal area. The retreat from the beach was to be accomplished by prohibiting the building of new structures and the rebuilding of old or damaged structures in high hazard areas.

To define a high hazard area, a baseline, approximately at the point of the highest ridge line of the primary dune, was established. A setback line then was drawn 20 feet landward of the baseline.[5] Seaward of this setback line no new structures could be built nor severely damaged structures repaired. This area of the beach became known as the "dead zone," and in time became the most controversial portion of the legislation. (See Figure 3.3.) The only exceptions to the new regulations were for those property owners who had building permits issued by local government licensing agencies not later than March 1, 1988, or those with master development plans approved or with site development under construction before March 1, 1988, in pursuant to approval of a plan. David Lucas fell prey to the South Carolina Beachfront Management Act by not being able to meet these provisions.

2. *Lucas v. The South Carolina Coastal Council*

Recall that Lucas purchased two beachfront lots in 1986, prior to the passage of the 1988 Beachfront Management Act and formation of the coastal council. (See Table 3.1 for chronology.) After being denied a permit to build the two residences he had planned, and with no avenue for obtaining a variance, Lucas brought suit. However, he did not challenge the constitutionality of the South Carolina Beachfront Management Act (BMA), thereby in essence admitting that the legislation was adopted to prevent serious injury to the community. He simply thought that he should be compensated for his loss since the building restrictions on his property resulting from the BMA amounted to a "regulatory taking." In his view, the failure to compensate violated his constitutional rights.[6]

The South Carolina Coastal Council, in accordance with the Beachfront Management Act, argued that construction on the lots would cause serious public harm. In addition to possible erosion caused by building in a sensitive area, it was argued that during a major storm, when houses closest to the shore were damaged, debris from these houses would cause further damage to property inland. In August 1989 the South Carolina Circuit Court heard the summons and complaint, and ruled that a regulatory taking had occurred and required the state to pay Lucas more than $1.2 million in compensation.

South Carolina Supreme Court Decision

The coastal council's appeal to the South Carolina supreme court resulted in a three-to-two decision, in February 1991, to reverse the lower court ruling.

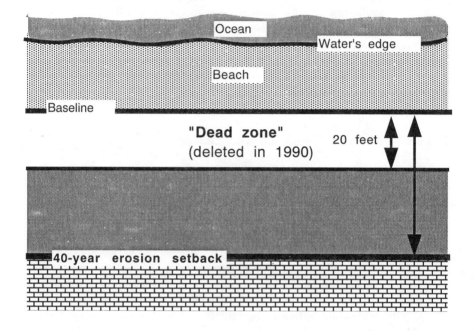

Figure 3.3 Setback zones established by the South Carolina Beach Management
Act of 1988

Table 3.1
SYNOPSIS OF THE LUCAS CASE

1986   Lucas purchased two vacant lots on the Isle of Palms for
       $975,000.
1988   The South Carolina Beachfront Management Act (BMA) is passed,
       restricting any development of Lucas's property.
1991   Lucas is awarded $1.2 million by the District Court; the
       Coastal Council appeals.
1991   State supreme court reverses the lower court ruling; Lucas
       appeals to the U.S. Supreme Court.
1992   U.S. Supreme Court reverses the decision, the case is remanded to
       the state supreme court
1992   State supreme court ruled a temporary taking has occurred and
       ordered the lower court to determine damages.
1993   The coastal council purchased Lucas lots, paying $1.5 million.
1993   The coastal council auctioned off lots for $785,000
       to Congaree Construction Company.
1994   Purchaser plans to build on one lot and sell the other.

The state supreme court concluded that a regulatory taking had not occurred
even though the court did not challenge Lucas's contention that his property was
worthless. Relying on the U.S. Supreme Court's 1987 decision in *Keystone
Bituminous Coal Association v. DeBenedictis* (480 U.S. 470, 107 S. Ct. 1232,
94 L. Ed. 2d 472 (1987), the court concluded that since the Beachfront
Management Act was designed to prevent serious public harm, no compensation
was necessary. In deciding the case, the state justices also relied on the decision
they had rendered previously in *Carter v. South Carolina Coastal Council* (281
S.C. 201, 314 S.E. 2d 327 (1984). This decision denied compensation to an
owner of coastal wetlands who was deprived of all economically viable use of
his property when the coastal council would not allow Carter to build on a
wetland site. In this case, the court held that "the state may properly regulate
the use of property where uncontrolled use would be harmful to the public
interest; and this regulation, even though it prohibits all beneficial use, will not
necessarily be deemed a taking in the constitutional sense."

   The South Carolina supreme court decision in the Lucas case was not
unanimous. Justice A. J. Harwell in his dissent wrote that he did not think the
Beachfront Management Act had "as its primary purpose the prevention of a
nuisance." He went on to state that the purpose of the Act was to "prevent and
foster the regeneration of the beach/dune system, the benefits of which enure to
the State of South Carolina by among other things, promoting tourism, creating
a habitat for indigenous flora and fauna, creating a place which harbors natural

beauty, and providing a barrier and buffer from high tides, storm surge, hurricanes and normal erosion. . . . I conclude that none of these intended purposes can fairly be said to resemble a nuisance." In Judge Harwell's view the lack of a nuisance basis for the court's ruling did not mean that the Act was invalid since a legitimate state interest was involved; however, it did mean that David Lucas should be compensated for his loss (Opinions of the Supreme Court and Court of Appeals of South Carolina, February 16, 1991, Columbia).

In 1990 while the case was being heard by the state supreme court, but before the justices rendered a verdict, the Beachfront Management Act was amended. Following Hurricane Hugo, which struck the South Carolina coast in September 1989, causing extensive damage to properties in the Charleston area, many property owners discovered the Beachfront Management Act for the first time when they were prevented from rebuilding their damaged houses. Because of numerous relief petitions from property owners, the coastal council felt compelled to put in an appeal and variance system allowing some building, under special conditions, in the previously off-limit areas. Although the commitment to retreat from the beach in the long run remained, a "special permit" could be issued to build seaward of the baseline if (1) the structure was not on an "active beach" or primary oceanfront dune, (2) the landowner agreed to remove the structure should erosion cause it to rest on an active beach, and (3) the use would not be detrimental to public health, safety, and welfare (Watters, 1993, 878). Although several of Lucas's neighbors did apply for and were granted variances, Lucas chose not to apply.[7]

U.S. Supreme Court Decision

Lucas appealed the state supreme court decision to the U.S. Supreme Court, which decided the case on June 29, 1992. The U.S. Supreme Court ruled six to three to reverse the state decision and remanded the case to the South Carolina supreme court, arguing that the state court had erred in basing its decision on the "harmful or noxious uses" principle. The Court asserted: "To win its case, respondent cannot simply proffer the legislature's declaration that the uses Lucas desires are inconsistent with the public interest, but must identify background principles of nuisance and property law that prohibit the uses Lucas now intends in the property's present circumstances" *Lucas v. South Carolina Coastal Council* (60 U.S.L.W. 4842, Supreme Court of the U.S., June 29, 1992). The Court specifically advised that the coastal council must demonstrate that the regulations placed on Lucas's lots were part of the property title or show further evidence that there is serious harm to the public if building takes place in the restricted areas as defined by the Beachfront Management Act. Otherwise, Lucas is due full compensation for any losses sustained.

The U.S. Supreme Court in reversing the lower court's ruling in the Lucas case was unable to consider the question as to whether Lucas's property had been rendered completely worthless; indeed, the state supreme court never contested the lower court's ruling that Lucas's property had become worthless. Instead, the Supreme Court dealt only with the constitutionality of the state supreme court conclusion that the use Lucas intended for his property constituted a public nuisance.

The South Carolina Supreme Court on Remand

On November 20, 1992, the South Carolina supreme court issued its response to the U.S. Supreme Court decision. The state court chose to allow the coastal council the opportunity to review the case in an effort to "identify background principles of nuisance and property law by which Lucas could be restrained from constructing a habitable structure on his land" (*Lucas v. South Carolina Coastal Council,* Order on Remand, Supreme Court of South Carolina, Columbia, November 20, 1992 p. 3). However, the coastal council was unable to persuade the state supreme court that a common law basis exists by which Lucas could be restrained from building on his property, nor could the court find through its own investigation any such basis. Therefore, the state justices concluded that the only thing left for them was to determine the actual damages suffered by Lucas and order the state to pay him. The Court concluded that only a *temporary* taking had occurred since the coastal council now had a permitting process in place that presumably would allow a variance for Lucas to build. On the other hand, should the coastal council refuse to grant the permit or impose undue restrictions on the use Lucas intends for his land, the Court made it clear that "Lucas might contend a subsequent unconstitutional taking has occurred" and initiate new litigation. The state supreme court directed the trial judge to make the specific findings of damages due Lucas and furthermore refused to dictate to the circuit court judge the specific method for calculating the damages except to order that the compensation commence with the enactment of the 1988 Beachfront Management Act and continue through the date of their order.

Final Disposition of Lucas

Lucas's legal saga did not end with the state supreme court decision. Lucas made a request for a special building permit and got it from the coastal council; however, it was laden with building restrictions. The coastal council imposed conditions that limited structure size, location, and additional structures. The permit also contained a clause that orders the removal of the structure under certain circumstances, for example beach erosion. Lucas found the terms to be unacceptable, arguing that he was entitled to the unrestrictive type of building permit that was permissible at the time he bought his lots. Lucas maintained that the state should compensate him for the temporary taking of his property and issue him an *unrestricted* building permit or purchase his property.

In January of 1993 Lucas brought another lawsuit against the South Carolina Coastal Council, seeking punitive damages in addition to $2 million in actual damages for the value of the property. Finally, in August 1993 on the eve of a trial to determine damages owed to Lucas, the two parties agreed to an out-of-court settlement. The Coastal Council consented to pay Lucas a total of $1.5 million for the two lots, legal fees, back interest, and other related costs. Despite the size of the settlement, Lucas says that he netted less than $100,000. The bank holding the mortgages on the property received $900,000 and the attorneys got $514,000. Lucas summed up his thoughts this way: "Litigation is not a way to get whole again. It is a salvage operation" (Lehman, 1993, El).

After four years of litigation, the battle between Lucas and the coastal council ended, but not without a bit of irony. Once title to the land passed, the coastal council put the lots on the market, eventually selling them for development to the Congaree Construction Company for $785,000 (*The State,* November 12, 1993). In trying to justify the decision a spokesperson for the State's Budget and Control Board was quoted as saying, "We felt that we had an obligation to offer the property to the public and get the highest price" (*The State,* September 1, 1993).

The final disposition of the land may be the most significant aspect of the Lucas case. It points up the ease with which government is willing to impose restrictions on property owners when the cost is borne by the owner, but the reluctance to subject the state to the same restrictions when the cost burden falls on a government agency budget.

Commenting on the sale, John Echeverria, chief counsel for the National Audubon Society, summed up things this way: [The decision to sell the lots] "opens the state to charges of hypocrisy when it is willing to have an economic burden fall on an individual but not when the funds have to come out of an agency's budget" (*Washington Post,* August 17, 1993). The Lucas decision certainly took on a new kind of gravity for the council when the agency had to bear the cost. In the final analysis it is a healthy development when decision makers are forced to weigh the benefits and costs of their actions.

The Significance of the Lucas Ruling

At issue in this case is whether anyone suffering an economic loss as a result of a "regulatory taking" is compensable under the Fifth Amendment's taking clause. Lucas argued that any regulation that totally diminishes value is a taking, a justification that courts have recognized in requiring states to pay compensation. Land-use restrictions such as zoning regulations that adversely affect the value of property do not automatically require compensation. Such restrictions currently are considered a legitimate exercise of the police power of the government not requiring compensation if the use of that power promotes the public health, safety, and welfare. However, a precise equation has not been identified as a basis for the calculation.' The U.S. Supreme Court has considered each case coming before it separately, weighing the public and private interests. Often the primary consideration is whether the property owner can receive a "reasonable return" despite the use limit imposed. Still, there exists no clear definition of what constitutes a Fifth Amendment taking.

For most of this century, states and localities have imposed property restrictions based on a very broad interpretation of the "nuisance" basis for 1denying the property owner certain uses for his property. According to Williams and Lyman (1992) the U.S. Supreme Court, once ruling favorably in the 1920s on behalf of the government's right to restrict land use without compensation, abdicated any responsibility in the area and left the matter up to the state courts. And over the decades the states have established a large body of law "toward a broader interpretation of the public power to regulate" (1116).

Although the Lucas decision was not the definitive ruling that many had anticipated, the Court advanced the rights of property owners to some degree, perhaps continuing a trend that has been in evidence for some time. Justice Blackmun certainly was of that opinion. In a strongly worded dissent, he maintained that the Supreme Court "takes the opportunity to create a new scheme for regulations that eliminate all economic value. From now on, there is a categorical rule finding these regulations to be a taking unless the use they prohibit is a background common-law nuisance or property principle" (Bagley and Haubegger, 1993, 150).

In fact, in delivering the majority opinion, Justice Scalia makes it clear that this is how the majority of the justices see their decision. He writes: "Where the state seeks to sustain regulation that deprives land of all economically beneficial use, we think it may resist compensation only if the logically antecedent inquiry into the nature of the owner's estate shows that the proscribed use interests were not part of his titles to begin with" (Bagley and Haubegger, 1993, 151).

In order for a state to avoid compensating a property owner who has been injured by land-use restrictions, the Supreme Court is insisting that three elements must be examined. First, the state must show that the use the property owner intended was not part of the original bundle of rights that go with ownership. Justice Scalia writes: "South Carolina must identify background principles of nuisance and property law that prohibit the uses he [Lucas] now intends in the circumstances in which the property is presently found. Only on this showing can the state fairly claim that, in proscribing all such beneficial uses, the Beachfront Management Act is taking nothing" (Bagley and Haubeg-ger, 1993, 152).

Second, the Supreme Court asserts that in the absence of sufficient background principles of nuisance the state must prove the property's use constitutes a public nuisance in order for the state to avoid compensation. In other words, the state cannot simply assert that a particular use of one's property is inconsistent with the public interest. Presumably, the ruling will require states imposing new property regulations (not part of the rights inherent in the original title) to present evidence of the degree of public harm alleged to result from the claimant's anticipated use. No longer can the state simply infer that the intended use of the property constitutes a nuisance. Hard evidence must be presented to that effect.

Third, these higher, more lucid standards articulated by the Court apply only to a "total taking," not a "partial taking." In the Lucas case this issue was never seriously evaluated because the state supreme court in rendering its opinion never contested the lower court's finding that Lucas had, indeed, suffered a "total taking."

Trying to predict how a somewhat less than definitive ruling on a case such as *Lucas* is apt to play out in subsequent years is a hazardous business. However, since the U.S. Supreme Court rendered its opinion on *Lucas* more than two years ago and the state of South Carolina finally settled with Lucas in 1993, one might ask, what has been the effect of the case on government regulation of property use? In one commentator's view, "Lucas is a shift in the legal landscape, a realignment of tectonic plates substantial enough to alter at least some of the foundations of takings law and litigation," although he admits "its potential for causing further upheaval is not yet known" (Hollister, 1993).

The Short-Run Effect of the Lucas Decision: What Has It Been?

In an effort to ascertain what immediate effects Lucas may be having on environmental policy at the state level, the authors surveyed all fifty states. In January 1993, a short questionnaire, asking if any new regulations or directives had been enacted or were planned as a result of *Lucas*, was mailed to each state's environmental agency and governor's office (Rinehart and Pompe, 1994). Almost half the states (twenty-three) confirmed that either new rulings or legislation had been enacted or that bills were recently introduced to address the property rights issue.[9]

Although many states expect the Lucas case to have a narrow effect on land-use regulation, since most restrictions on property do not result in a total taking, most expressed the view that a variance procedure is considered to be a necessity to avoid Lucas-type cases.

Moreover, the survey shows clearly that *Lucas* has led to greater caution where new environmental policy initiatives are involved and (especially in the west) to greater emphasis on measuring the economic impact of new regulations. Further, a movement towards a priori cost-benefit assessment of new regulatory policies is under way. More than thirty states have introduced legislation that would require compensation for a regulatory taking.

The Long-Run Effect of the Lucas Decision: What Will It Be?

Questions about long-run effects cannot be answered definitively. Experts do not agree on just how far the Supreme Court decision has deviated from past rulings, but clearly the Court itself believes it has made some shift in its position. (See Blackman's comment above.) A majority of the legal experts who have published opinions on the subject feel that the Lucas decision was a significant one, especially when viewed within the context of other recent decisions of the court. Specifically we refer to the Court's rulings in *First English Evangelical Lutheran Church of Glendale v. County of Los Angeles, California* (107 S. Ct. 2378 (1987) *Nollan v. California Coastal Commission* (483 U.S. 825, 97 L. Ed. 2d 677, 107 S. Ct. 3141 (1987).[10]

The *Nollan* and *First English* cases, both decided in the 1986-87 term of the Supreme Court, elicited significant speculation as to the effects these decisions would have on land-use regulatory policy. Eaton (1990) notes a trend of increased scrutiny on the part of the Court since these 1987 decisions, and expects more litigation, greater justification of benefits by regulatory agencies, and greater caution on the part of planners. Bailey (1992) and Michelman (1988), however, argue that the heightened scrutiny of the Court in regulatory takings cases following *Nollan* is less significant than it might appear.

Similarly, a variety of views regarding the impact of *Lucas* exist. According to one observer, "*Lucas* will likely join a short list of modern Supreme Court decisions that will influence, for better or worse, the relationship of public and private interests in land use well into the next century and its political impact, particularly at the state and local level may well outweigh its legal impact" (Platt, 1992). Burke (1992, 24) contends that the ruling shows a Supreme Court trend toward greater protection of property owners against governmental regulation. He finds it significant that Scalia defines two types of categories of regulatory action that require compensation without case-specific inquiry (27). In addition to a physical taking of property, the Court now recognizes a taking when regulation denies "all economically beneficial or productive use" of one's property.

Pollot (1993) agrees that the U.S. Supreme Court in recent years has moved toward limiting government regulation of land use, and believes that the Lucas decision is an extremely important ruling representing a continuation of this trend. He also finds it significant that the majority in *Lucas* states that *Lucas* is only one example of a deprivation case (191). Further, Pollot feels that the decision in *Lucas* on what constitutes a nuisance places the burden on government to clearly show that the nuisance exists (191). Berger (1993, 30) concurs that the nuisance exception has been narrowed and that the playing field has been leveled now that the government must offer real evidence of the harm that justifies the land-use restriction.

One thing that most observers agree on is that *Lucas* has and will encourage landowners to challenge public land-use regulations with more frequency. Hollister (1993) expects increasing numbers of property owners to make claims. He states: "*Lucas* enhances the rights of property owners and creates a new area of takings litigation, the 'total takings inquiry'" (14). He also believes "there is a distinct possibility that *Lucas* will engender a whole new jurisprudence of nuisance and property law" (15). Hollister cautions planners to be more exacting and exhaustive in collecting evidence that indicates the need for protection of critical areas (14). Blumm (1993) agrees, making the point that lawyers are already willing to take on such cases on the basis of contingency fees.

Lucas also will be applied to a wide range of cases and not just to ones that affect the coastal environment. Sax (1993) thinks the target of *Lucas* is much broader than concern over coastal erosion. Sax believes the Court is looking ahead to the possibility of multitudes of cases brought to the courts with regard to wetland problems, endangered species problems, etc. He sees the Scalia opinion as a farsighted one. Sax believes that "the majority opinion correctly recognizes that a fundamental redefinition of property was possible in *Lucas*. In this light *Lucas* represents the Court's rejection of pleas to engraft the values of the economy of nature onto traditional notions of the rights of land ownership. Justice Scalia assumes that redefinition of property rights to accommodate ecosystem demands is not possible. The Court treats claims that land be left in its natural condition as unacceptable impositions on landowners" (1446). Sax believes the Court is saying that "a state should compensate landowners who, through no fault of their own, lose property rights because of scientific or social transformations" (1449). While Sax believes the Court majority in *Lucas* relied on an "outdated view of property" and therefore "is not satisfactory in an age of ecological awareness," he praises the Supreme Court for recognizing for the first time "the profound implications of the ecological perspective on traditional property rights" (1455). Funk (1993, 891) thinks Lucas "is the foot in the door for a property rights revolution" (p. 891). He believes environmental statutes such as the Endangered Species Act, section 404 of the Clean Waster Act (pertaining to wetlands), and various historic preservation laws may serve as the basis for future litigation.

By requiring the coastal council to show the damages that result from the Lucas construction, the Court limits the ability of state governments to regulate land use. The Supreme Court's insistence that the coastal council come up with evidence of nuisance is already making legislators nervous about having to document the existence of harm associated with the use or uses intended by the property owner. As indicated above lawmakers in some states are already enacting laws requiring some attention to weighing costs and benefits. We expect this trend to continue.

Sullivan (1993, 923) contends that the Court has instituted an "incipient property rights revolution" with the Lucas decision. He believes "the opinion of the Court, though fairly narrow in its scope, contains, especially in the footnotes, the seeds of a far more expansive change from current takings jurisprudence" (919). He specifically thinks the nuisance exception has been significantly narrowed (920). Also, even if a physical invasion does not occur and despite the degree of public interest, if all economic use allowed under common law is taken, then compensation is required. Furthermore, he asserts that in certain circumstances a partial loss may constitute a taking (921).

Large (1993, 885) believes a key element of the U.S. Supreme Court decision "redefined the concept of a harmful or noxious use." In essence, the Court wants to make it less easy for the state to take private property on the basis of the nuisance rule. Payne (1993, 318) concurs, saying that Scalia believes that courts not legislatures should be making decisions on when compensation should be paid.

Writing in the *State Legislative Report* in September 1993, White and Alberts (1993, 3) provide an assessment along these same lines.

> The significance of the *Lucas* decision to state legislatures is that the courts will have a greater role in determining what constitutes public harm (nuisance property use) and that, for the first time, the courts have determined that the economic impacts of a regulation can, in come cases, pre-empt the public benefit advanced by government regulation. Legal scholars believe the court's new philosophy has affected the balance between the public good and economic value factors used to decide when compensation is due. The weighing of private and public interest is increasingly more likely to favor the property owner, [and] therefore, state legislators must analyze all proposed environmental legislation for the potential far-reaching fiscal impacts of compensating land owners.

We believe it is such an interpretation of *Lucas*, along with the general drift of the Supreme Court in the past few years toward greater protection for property owners, that accounts for the fact that more than thirty states now have bills pending that would make environmental regulations that severely restrict a property's use tantamount to a taking. A movement is clearly afoot to protect the rights of property owners and is being pushed along by property rights defenders such as the American Legislative Exchange Council and Defenders of Property Rights (Lavelle, 1993). David Lucas himself is presently contributing time and his name to further the property rights agenda. Lucas thinks that he is "just the tip of the iceberg" and there is a growing backlash against the state's intrusion on the rights of property owners (Schulte, 1993, p.1-A). According to Lucas his aim is to become the property rights movement's Ralph Nader.

Even those who see a more modest effect for *Lucas* are not totally sure of their position. Halper (1994) is of the opinion that the Lucas decision may have limited effect because the ruling pertained only to land and it involved only a 100 percent taking. However, she does believe that Justice Scalia may have left the door open for future courts to award compensation for a partial taking. Halper writes: "If the difference between a regulation that prevents harm and one that confers a benefit is indeterminate and unprincipled, it is so whether the loss caused by the regulation is 100 percent, 50 percent, or even 10 percent. If only courts can tell whether a legislative act is legitimate, there is no inherent reason to limit their oversight to the case where the loss inflicted is total" (39). Epstein (1993), with a similar assessment of the Scalia opinion, points out that Justice Scalia himself noted that the question of a partial taking was unresolved and out there on the horizon. Epstein is puzzled as to why the line is drawn "to distinguish total from partial takings, as well as the physical from the regulatory" (1374).

There is also the problem yet to be resolved as to whether we are talking about a partial restriction on a parcel of land or a total restriction on a specific piece of the property. Huffman (1993) puts this point in perspective with a good example. He says that if a regulation declares 12 acres of a larger parcel of land to be wetlands, then he thinks one could assert that those 12 acres are a total loss "regardless of the size of the original parcel" (903). If in the future the court views a takings in this way, a significant shift toward property rights protection will have occurred.

Some critics believe *Lucas* alone will do little to shackle state legislators. One may discern from the opinion of the majority of the Supreme Court justices in the Lucas decision a certain distrust of state legislators and a willingness to provide some degree of protection for property owners. However, the Lucas decision alone is not definitive enough to *guarantee* such protection. State decision makers will likely attempt to document more completely what they perceive as benefits from any new proposed property regulations (as the Supreme Court suggested) in order to avoid a compensatory taking. Additionally, the policy makers probably will go to extra lengths to point out that all uses of the affected property have not been taken away. As Fisher (1993) points out: "When imposing severe restrictions on land use, they [legislators] will simply enumerate the activities in which the affected owners are still permitted to engage. In *Lucas* itself, for example, the South Carolina legislature could have included in its 1988 statute a provision assuring the owners of the affected beachfront lots that they could still 'picnic, swim, camp in a tent, or live on (their) property in a movable trailer.'" Such property uses would surely be of some economic value and, therefore, perhaps provide a basis for not having to compensate the owner since a 100 percent taking did not occur.

Lazarus (1993) thinks the Lucas decision will in fact make it easier for policy makers to enact environmental protection laws without falling prey to the takings clause because the Supreme Court made it clear that its ruling pertained only to a 100 percent taking, and it will be relatively easy for environmentalists to demonstrate some remaining viable economic use.

One of the most interesting observations on *Lucas* was made by Joseph Sax (1993). Sax's view is "that the current Court takes property rights seriously, believes government abuse of regulatory power is a problem, and feels the takings issue has been ignored too long by the Supreme Court. The Court, however, shows no taste for overturning the vast structure of regulatory government . . . On another level, I suspect the Court is frustrated with the takings issue. It wants to affirm the importance of property, but it cannot find a standard that will control regulatory excess without threatening to bring down the whole regulatory apparatus of the modern state."

While the exact impact of *Lucas* cannot be predicted at this time, it is clear to the authors that *Lucas* represents another step toward greater protection of property rights. The widespread debate that has ensued and the growing caution on the part of state legislatures and bureaucrats attest to this fact.

The June 1994 U.S. Supreme Court five-to-four ruling in *Dolan v. Tigard* continues the trend toward protection of property rights. The city of Tigard, Oregon, demanded that Florence Dolan turn over, without compensation, 10 percent of her property to the city for a bicycle path in exchange for permission to expand her hardware store. The Court ruled five to four in favor of Dolan, contending that a "rough proportionality" between the harm caused by the development and the expected benefit of the government action is necessary (*Wall Street Journal*, June 27, 1994) The decision could well lift the takings clause of the Fifth Amendment to a level of importance attached to the First or Fourth Amendment.

3. Alternative Approaches to Regulatory Takings

Conflicts over the use of scarce natural resources are perennial. Numerous special interest groups (old and new) continue to work toward limitations on private property use in ways compatible with their interest. And government policy makers enact and implement rules and regulations that they deem to be in the interest of their constituents. Given the recent Supreme Court decisions and the combative nature of the growing property rights movement, planners and policy makers are likely to proceed circumspectfully and prudently as they seek out alternatives that may avoid or mitigate regulatory takings and the concomitant litigation. In those cases where societal welfare may be enhanced by resolving the spillover problems that impose costs on neighbors and other users of natural resources, alternatives to regulatory takings may be more popular and desirable than they were in the past.

Remove Subsidies to Development

Less government involvement rather than more may sometimes be the answer to a spillover or externality problem, as in the case of federal subsidies that encourage construction in sensitive areas such as flood plains or coastal zones. Numerous programs provide taxpayer dollars to defray the costs of building in hazardous areas. For example, the 1968 National Flood Insurance Program provides subsidized flood insurance to flood-prone communities.[11] The program's goal was to reduce the expensive government payments that result when disasters such as hurricanes occur, and was to be achieved through stringent building codes that would make homes more storm resistant.

Unfortunately, the subsidized insurance program led to increased construction in sensitive and dangerous coastal and flood plain areas, as well as increased federal liability. The program created an incentive to build more numerous and expensive homes in hazard-prone areas since residents are not required to bear the full costs of their lifestyles. Further, since no regulations prevent homeowners from rebuilding and getting the same inexpensive insurance, houses that are destroyed by storms are simply rebuilt at taxpayer expense. Following major disasters, federal and local governments also replace infrastructure, offer FEMA disaster relief, and pay cleanup costs, further reducing the costs to those who wish to live in dangerous coastal areas. Removing such government-provided subsidies would go far toward reducing property damage and concomitantly lessen the need for property regulation.

Beach nourishment, which provides a combination of recreational and property protection benefits, also encourages coastal development. When undertaken by the Army Corps of Engineers, such projects are funded by the government and often protect private developments that have been built in precarious areas. In general, the federal government will pay up to 65 percent of nourishment costs over the life of a project, requiring taxpayers across the nation to contribute substantially to these projects. State and local governments cover the remaining 35 percent. Clearly, the principal beneficiaries of these nourishment projects are property owners near the ocean and perhaps local governments enjoying increased revenues from tourists and higher property taxes. Beach access fees and a special tax assessment on properties near the ocean would be a more appropriate way to fund such projects and would have the direct effect of eliminating this subsidy to coastal developers, thereby diminishing the need for property regulation.

The 1982 Coastal Barriers Resource Act (CBRA) redlines undeveloped coastal areas, thereby denying developers access to government subsidization. Attempts have also been made to remove the below-market-value flood insurance, thus requiring those who choose to live in these hazardous areas to pay for the true costs of their decisions. A bill currently in the U.S. Senate would help in the relocation of houses in flood-prone areas and limit government liability in the event of future flood damage. The legislation would reduce construction in erosive areas, while gradually removing the current insurance subsidy. At this writing strong lobbying interests have successfully managed to defeat this bill. Finally, grandfathering, that is, offering permits to landowners based on the rules in effect at the time of land purchase, is a form of variance that avoids the taking problem.

Taxes and Subsidies

A carefully implemented system of taxes could allow the government to achieve desired environmental goals. For example, instead of using command-and-control regulation, the government could announce a per unit charge for pollution or other activities that impose costs on the ecosystem. Then, polluters or users with high costs of controlling pollution will pay the tax, while polluters with low abatement costs will prefer instead to control pollution or relocate. But while offering the prospect of improving the management of sensitive environmental assets, the development of a system of taxes is a political event that can suffer from special interest abuse.

Government-Purchased Land

The government can directly purchase areas that are necessary to public welfare, as is the case in eminent domain or acquisition programs. Public land ownership is necessary for the provision of sites for schools, hospitals, and airports. When the needs are for the public use, just compensation, as required by the Fifth Amendment, is paid. As discussed in Chapter 5 by Lee Ann Welch, the Endangered Species Act, when first introduced in 1963, included a funding that enabled the U.S. Fish and Wildlife Service to purchase tracts of habitat for the protection of species. With land purchases, the takings issue is avoided.

Privately Purchased Land

Private organizations can, and do, purchase valuable and sensitive natural areas. One of the best known is the Nature Conservancy (TNC), which owns the largest system of nature preserves in the world—more than 1,300 as of 1992 (Endicott, 17). TNC began in 1950 as an international nonprofit organization dedicated to establishing reserves to preserve plants, animals, and natural areas that have special scientific, educational, or aesthetic merit. The organization purchases or receives as donations these sensitive areas, often preserving the land for government. Private purchase of land has certain advantages over government purchase since dealings can be speedier and more flexible. Many of the transactions of TNC are joint projects with local, state, or federal government agencies. Deblinger and Jenkins (1991) provide examples of how interagency cooperation protected an endangered Atlantic coast seabird and a coastal dune plant community.

The Coase Theorem, Private Interests, and Market Solutions

In many cases involving spillover costs or externalities, a more secure and specific system of property rights may be an alternative to government regulation. The Coase Theorem tells us that if transaction costs are not too great and property rights are well defined, affected parties have an incentive on their own to negotiate an efficient solution. Although this approach is not applicable to all land use problems, the process is an effective solution in many circumstances.[12] Ellickson (1986) found an illustration of this principle in Shasta County, California, where rural landowners resolved disputes to mutual advantage, without government involvement. Agreements between farmers and ranchers limited the damage to crops, a negative externality caused by open-range cattle grazing.

Market-oriented solutions that are based on property rights offer valuable alternatives to government regulation. Marketable permits for nonpoint source pollution can reduce the costs of improving water quality (Yandle, 1993). Planned coastal communities such as Seabrook and Dewees Islands in South Carolina protect beaches and wildlife without government regulation. Near Yellowstone National Park, sheep owners are paid for any sheep killed by wolves, so that wolves are protected while farmers are compensated. In other cases, landowners lease their land for hunting and fishing, as well as cultivate seafood and wild game for markets.

As suggested here, the definition and enforcement of property rights can solve the "Tragedy of the Commons." Anderson and Leal (1993) illustrate how the assignment of property rights to fish, a traditional common property, can improve the efficiency of fishing effort, while preventing the decimation of the fish population. They present examples of property rights approaches, such as individual transferable quotas, that offer alternatives to the current regulatory regimes that have proved inadequate for fisheries.

Some institutions provide compensation to landowners who suffer from harsh regulatory policies. Transferable development rights can be used as an alternative to zoning in order to mitigate costs imposed on landowners by regulation. With this method the government offers credits that allow a landowner to be compensated for development restrictions. Beginning in 1980, Pineland, New Jersey, issued Pineland Development Credits to landowners in areas where development was prohibited or restricted, which could be sold to landowners in designated growth areas (Tripp, 1987).

Alternative strategies internalizing the costs and benefits of market transactions serve as a powerful substitute for government regulation. Market incentives can be used to achieve results clearly superior to command and control techniques (Cropper and Oates, 1992).

4. Some Final Thoughts on *Lucas*

In an ideal world, democratic governments strive to maximize the welfare of its citizens. But as James Madison reminds us, the process is not necessarily neat and pretty. Nonetheless, in discussions involving property rights restrictions the focus should always be on the question, does the regulation make things better for all people taken together? From a theoretical and a practical point of view this is the bottom line. Although it is relatively easy to contemplate what maximizing social welfare might mean in the theoretical sense, admittedly, it is quite another thing to actually engineer such an outcome in the real world. But despite the difficulty in translating theory into practice, this fact should not prevent us from striving toward the goal. To do otherwise is to make policy without the benefit of a rudder.

Most governmental policy actions that limit property use create both benefits and costs. The trick is to limit property use only when benefits are clearly high enough to warrant the costs and an equitable distribution of costs and benefits can be determined. To illustrate, suppose there are fifteen property owners each with a house on a lake. Also assume that one of the property owners begins to operate a powerboat on the lake to the great consternation of the others. Since powerboats are noisy and dangerous and represent a source of pollution, it may occur to some residents that an ordinance banning the use of powerboats on the lake might be a good idea. In order to simplify the problem, suppose that all property owners, including the one operating the boat, voluntarily accept such a regulation, the reason being that they all love the peace and quiet of the lake and recognize that if everyone operates a boat that tranquillity will be threatened. Such a restriction on the use of private property clearly leads to a higher welfare level for the community since benefits of the policy for each owner exceed costs, otherwise unanimity on the ban would not result.

The problem with this scenario is that in reality things are not so simple. Suppose there are 2,000 property owners located around the lake and some of the owners have been there for many years and historically have owned and operated powerboats for a long time. Because of the higher number of residents, any attempt on the part of the community to impose regulations on the use of powerboats is apt to be met with resistance from some property owners. Property owners seeking tranquillity may favor a ban on powerboats while fishermen and water skiers may oppose such a policy. It would be safe to say that as the number of property owners rises from fifteen toward 2,000 it would become increasingly more difficult to get unanimity on any practice. So, should powerboats be prohibited on the lake or not? Majority voting rules can decide the issue, but cannot determine whether the community is better or worse off with the policy decision.

Since some members of the community would be injured by the regulation (i.e., costs exceed benefits) and others would gain (i.e., benefits exceed costs), it is not readily apparent that a majority rule would produce a net welfare gain to the community. However, if winners were required to compensate losers, the situation would change dramatically. If gainers are "willing" to compensate the losers for all of their losses, then it is obvious that a net gain to the community occurs from the powerboat ban. If the reverse is true, then the ban would not lead to higher social welfare.

Herein lies the crux of the property regulation problem. When property regulations inflict pain on some while generating benefits for others, which is the situation most of the time, what is the appropriate rule in deciding on the overall merits of the regulation? To say that we want the regulation if it maximizes social welfare is certainly the correct answer, but it does not give us an operational basis for deciding the issue. From an efficiency and equity point of view some means must be devised to measure the benefits and costs, and if the former exceed the latter a scheme must then be implemented for compensating losers and taxing winners. This is something that markets do automatically when property rights are clearly defined. Constitutional rights for property owners guaranteeing compensation for public use of their property would force policy makers to look at costs as well as benefits.

From the origin of zoning regulations in the early 1900s, the government's approach has been primarily one of using the democratic rule of the majority to impose property restrictions. Laws restricting land use are passed at the city, county, state, and federal levels whenever a majority of the elected representatives can be convinced to vote in favor. And only when the property is physically occupied by the government is compensation paid to the property owner. Special interest groups have used their money and lobbying skills, assisted by rational voter ignorance and the short-term orientation of politicians, to push through a myriad of property use regulations. Taking advantage of the Court's unwillingness to protect property owners under the Fifth Amendment, the state has been able to accomplish this at little expense to the government and the special interests. Recent decisions of the Supreme Court, *Lucas* and *Dolan* being the latest, are beginning to change that.

The main problem with majority rule in formulating and enacting land-use regulations is that the state can literally take private property (through reductions in the property's market value), by denying use. Whether it is a partial or complete taking the result is the same. Little, if any, incentive exists on the part of the state to take into account costs incurred by the property owner. In other words, the majority sees a way of reaping benefits at the expense of a few property owners, whose costs are not factored into the decision-making process. To return to our lake example, if rule is by majority, when a majority perceives a net gain for themselves from a ban on the use of powerboats, they will seek to vote in such a requirement irrespective of the degree of harm that might be done to the minority of property owners.

The ability of government policy makers to shift much, if not all, of the costs of their actions to a minority of property owners encourages aggressive pursuit of land-use restrictions as remedies to a host of environmental problems. Environmental groups who expect to receive benefits (they may be entirely nonmonetary) from tougher standards, let's say on water quality, will lobby legislators very hard for new laws restricting property rights without regard to the costs imposed on property owners or consumers. They do take into account, however, their own costs, such as campaign contributions and time spent lobbying, but personal benefits generally are large relative to personal costs. An individual who bought a tract of land in the middle of a wilderness for logging purposes many years ago with no objections from anyone regarding what and how many trees might be cut may suddenly find restrictions imposed on his logging operation.

In fact, that was exactly Lucas's problem. He bought two lots for the purpose of building houses, which at the time was perfectly legal, only to discover a few years later that the government had changed the rules of the game, making his property essentially worthless. The South Carolina Coastal Council felt no obligation to compensate him, and since the council expected to pay nothing for the devaluation in Lucas's property, it had no reason to factor in the cost to Lucas in meeting the objectives established by the state legislature. The state legislature certainly did not weigh the costs to Lucas in its efforts to implement more stringent restrictions on the use of oceanfront property. Therefore, with policy makers looking only at the benefit side of the equation and not at the cost side, things easily get tilted toward excessive property regulation. Any positive benefit for any newly proposed regulation serves as sufficient grounds for putting the measure through, despite the level of costs incurred by property owners and society at large. However, just because the state is able to use its police power to avoid compensating a property owner, it does not mean that the cost is not real and incurred by someone. Also, because there is a real cost borne by the property owner, there is no assurance before the fact that the property regulation, even though there are benefits associated with it, leads to a net gain in human welfare. In other words, the aggregate gain to society in better erosion control produced by denying Lucas the right to build on his lots may be less than the cost to Lucas. If this is the case, then societal welfare suffers a net decline as a consequence of the new setback requirements assigned to his property. When decision makers are not required to take into account all of the costs stemming from their policies, the result is often multitudinous and intricate laws restricting property use.

Viewed in this particular way, perhaps one can begin to see why property rights enthusiasts were so anxious about the Lucas case. The welfare of society hinges so much on how the courts view the constitutionality of property regulation, especially in light of the rather recent increases in environmental limits that are being placed on property. From a purely equity point of view, Lucas should not have been required to bear the full cost of a rule on property use that generates benefits for society at large, even if aggregate benefits exceed Lucas's costs. Huffman (1993, 906) put it this way: "Government regulators and advocates of regulation view the takings clause as an unfortunate obstacle to the pursuit of the government's important business, but it does not in any way prevent us from protecting endangered species or saving wetlands or preventing pollution. We can do anything we want; we just have to pay. Somebody's going to pay. These are real costs. If we impose the cost of regulation on Lucas, it will be a real cost to him and a real impact on the economy. So it is only a question of who pays. Why should Lucas pay? Is there any principle of justice that says Lucas ought to pay to protect a beach in which all of us are interested?" Moreover, whatever scheme is used to fashion environmental laws where the effect is to benefit some and harm others, both costs and benefits must be measured and weighed before an overall assessment of the policy can be determined. Otherwise, there is no assurance that the measure will produce a net benefit to society. Furthermore, without a careful look at benefits and costs of alternative proposals there is no assurance that even if a net benefit does arise from the proposed policy, this particular policy is better than some alternative approach.

If the effect of the Lucas decision (and other future rulings of the Supreme Court) is to require government bodies to compensate injured property owners when the rules of the game are changed in pursuit of higher environmental standards, lawmakers would find it necessary to look at costs along with the benefits of any proposed legislation affecting property rights. This would be a first step toward achieving a greater level of accountability on the part of legislators enacting laws governing property use, and a first step toward ensuring that such laws do indeed enhance social welfare. Funk (1993, 892) said it succinctly: "If the government has to pay for things which it has previously gotten for free, it may start to think about whether these things are worth the cost. Is it really worth it to preserve wetlands? Is it really worth it to preserve beaches or species or historical things if we have to pay for them?" The Lucas decision surely did not clear up the "takings" problem, and it is not certain which government actions constitute a taking and which ones do not. But *Lucas* seems to be consistent with a grassroots movement demanding greater respect for property rights and with recent decisions of the Court itself that offer more protection for property owners. *Lucas* will likely provide an impetus toward greater market incentives as an alternative strategy to government regulations.

Notes

1. Land-use controls began with the Virginia House of Burgesses in 1631.

2. The first concerted effort of erosion control was an 1829 Army Corps of Engineers project to protect Ft. Moultrie, which incidently is located about 10 miles from the property purchased by Lucas.

3. At Edisto Beach, South Carolina, some want to repair the groins while others, fearing increased erosion of their property, have taken legal action to stop the repairs. (*The State,* March 20, 1994).

4. Most states and territories bordering oceans or the Great Lakes are participating in this program. Since 1972, twenty-nine of thirty-five possible participants were receiving CZMA funds.

5. Setback lines are in place for more than one-third of the coastal states (Griffin, 1992).

6. A few days after the Lucas decision, the U.S. Supreme Court refused to hear the case of twenty-four Hilton Head property owners who challenged the constitutionality of the Act.

7. The South Carolina Coastal Council argued that because of the new variance procedure, Lucas was no longer a total takings case. The Court, however, found that since the issue had not been relied on at the state level, and that there could still be a total interim taking, the case should be determined on its merits (Epstein, 1993, 1373).

8. Historically the U.S. Supreme Court has relied on four principles in deciding cases involving harm to property owners from state regulation. In cases having to do with eminent domain where the government physically occupies the property, the Supreme Court consistently has held that the property owner must be compensated. A second standard requires compensation if most of the economic value of a property is eliminated. A third type of case involves compensation if the economic loss incurred by the landowner exceeds the aggregate benefits accruing to the public. The fourth situation requires no compensation, regardless of the damage sustained by the property owner, if the regulations prevent the public from being harmed. (Fischel, 1985, 154)

9. See Chapter 7 in this book for an analysis of the recent property rights legislation at the state level.

10. In *First English* the property owners were awarded damages for income lost as a result of land-use regulation and in *Nollan* the Supreme Court ruled that the state could not require public access over the Nollan's beachfront property without compensation. For an excellent review of these two cases see Eaton (1990) and Michelman (1988). Also, other chapters in this book look at these cases in greater detail.

11. For a beachfront house valued at $200,000 a homeowner pays as little as $950 for flood insurance. Without the government-subsidized insurance the policy could cost $18,000 (Culliton).

12. See Siegan (1972) for a discussion of the success of how covenants have been used in Houston, rather than the traditional zoning approach.

Acknowledgments: Lucas's lawyers, Lewis, Babcock, and Hawkins and Finkel, Goldberg, Sheftman, and Altman.

References

Anderson, Terry L., and Donald R. Leal. 1993. "Fishing for Property Rights for Fish." In Roger E. Meiners and Bruce Yandle, eds. *Taking the Environment Seriously* Lanham, Md.: Rowman & Littlefield, 161-83.

Bagley, C. E., and C. A. Haubegger. 1993. *Cutting Edge Cases* in the *Legal Environment of Business.* Minneapolis: West.

Bailey, Sandra. 1992. "Land Use Regulations and the Takings Clause: Are Courts Applying a Tougher Standard to Regulators After Nollan?" *Natural Resources Journal* (Fall): 24-30.

Blumm, Michael. 1993. "Property Myths, Judicial Activism, and the Lucas Case." *Environmental Law*, 23: 907-17.

Burke, Barlow. 1992. "A First Look at Lucas v. South Carolina Coastal Council." *Real Estate Appraiser* (December): 24-30.

Callies, David, ed. 1993. *After Lucas: Land Use Regulation* and *The Taking of Property Without Compensation.* Chicago: American Bar Association.

Coase, Ronald. 1960. "The Problem of Social Cost." *Journal of Law and Economics,* 3 (October): 1-44.

Cropper, M. L., and W. E. Oates. 1992. "Environmental Economics: A Survey." *Journal of Economic Literature* 30: 675-740.

Cullingworth, J. B. 1993. *The Political Culture of Planning: American Land Use Planning in Comparative Perspective.* New York: Routledge.

Deblinger, R. D., and R. E. Jenkins 1991. Preserving Coastal Biodiversity: The Private, Nonprofit Approach. *Coastal Management* 19: 103-12.

Dimento, J., ed. *Wipeouts and Their Mitigation: The Changing Context for Land Use and Environmental Law.* Cambridge, Mass.: Lincoln Institute of Land Policy, 1990.

Eaton, J. D. 1990. "A Decade of U.S. Supreme Court Decisions—An Appraiser's View," *Appraisal Journal* (July): 334-46.

Ellickson, R. 1986. "Of Coase and Cattle: Dispute Resolution Among Neighbors in Shasta County." *Stanford Law Review* 38: 623-87.

Endicott, Eve. *Land Conservation through Public/Private Partnerships.* Washington, D.C.: Island Press, 1993.

Epstein, Richard A. 1993. "Lucas: Tangled Expectations," *Stanford Law Review* 45 (May): 1369-92.

Fischel, W. *Do Growth Controls Matter?* Cambridge, Mass: Lincoln Institute of Land Policy, 1990.

Fisher, William W. III. 1993. "The Trouble with LUCAS" *Stanford Law Review* (May), 45: 1393-410.

Funk, William. 1993. "Revolution or Restatement? Awaiting Answers to Lucas' Unanswered Questions." *Environmental Law* 23: 891-900.

Glickfeld, M. J. 1990. "Wipeout Mitigation: a Judicial Primer," In J. Dimento, ed., *Wipeouts and Their Mitigation: The Changing Context for Land Use and Environmental Law.* Cambridge, Mass.: Lincoln Institute of Land Policy: 61-85.

Griffin, R. 1992. "Threatened Coastlines." *CQ Researcher* 2: 97-120. Halper, Louise A. 1994. "A New View of Regulatory Takings?" *Environment* (JanuaryFebruary): 2-5, 39-40.

Hollister, T. S. 1993. "The Shifting Landscapes: Planning for and Litigating Takings Claims after Lucas." *Municipal Attorney* 34: 12-18.

Huffman, James L. 1993. "Lucas: A Small Step in the Right Direction" *Environmental Law* 23: 901-6.

Large, Donald. 1993. "Lucas: A Flawed Attempt to Redefine the Matton Analysis" *Environmental Law* 23: 883-9.

Lavelle, Marianne. 1993. "'The Property Rights' Revolt" *National Law Journal* (May 10), 15(36): 1.

Lazarus, Richard J. 1993. "'Spinning' Lucas" *Stanford Law Review* (May), 45: 1411-32.

Leatherman, S. *Barrier Island Handbook.* College Park: University of Maryland Press, 1988.

Lehman, H. Jane. 1993. "Accord Ends Fight Over Use of Land" *Washington Post* (July 17): El.

Long, L. 1990. "Population by the Sea." *Population Today* 10: 6-8.

Malloy, R. P. 1992 "A Classical Liberal Critique of Takings Law: A Struggle between Individualist and Communitarian Norms," In N. Mercuro, ed., *Taking Property and Just Compensation: Law and Economics Perspectives of the Takings Issue,* Norwell, Mass.: Kluwer.

Michelman, Frank. 1988. "Takings." *Columbia Law Review* 88: 1600-29.

Neal, W., W. Blackeney, O. Pilkey Jr., and O. Pilkey Sr. 1984. *Living with the South Carolina Shore.* Durham, N.C.: Duke University Press.

Payne, John M. 1993. "From the Courts." *Real Estate Law Journal,* 21: 312-21.

Pilkey, Orrin Jr. 1987. "A Time for Retreat." In R. Platt, S. Pelczarski, and B. Burbank, eds., *Cities on the Beach: Management Issues of Developed Coastal Barriers.* Chicago: University of Chicago Press: 275-80.

Platt, R. H., T. Beatly, and H. C. Miller. 1991. "The Folly at Folly Beach and Other Failings of U.S. Coastal Erosion Policy." *Environment* 19: 6-9, 25-32.

Platt, Rutherford H. 1992. "An Eroding Base" *Environmental Forum* (September/October): 10-15.

Pollot, M. L. *Grand Theft and Petit Larceny: Property Rights in America.* San Francisco: Pacific Research Institute for Public Policy, 1993.

Pompe, J., and Rinehart, J. 1994. "The Value of Beach Nourishment to Property Owners: Storm Damage Reduction Benefits." Florence, S.C.: Department of Economics, Francis Marion University.

Pope, C. 1992. Coastal Clashes. *The State* (Columbia, S.C.): November 22, 1D.

Rinehart, J., and J. Pompe. 1994. "Property Rights and Coastal Protection: Lucas and the U.S. Supreme Court" *Society & Natural Resources,* Forthcoming, Vol. 8, 1995.

Rinehart, J., and J. Pompe. 1994. "State Reaction to Lucas: Planning and Policy Implications." Under review.

Sax, Joseph L. 1993. "Understanding Lucas," *Stanford Law Review* (May) 45: 1433-55.

Schulte, Brigid. 1993. "Property Rights Fight Finds Symbol in S.C." *The State,* (Columbia, S.C.), December 25, 1-A.

South Carolina Beachfront Management Act. 1988. SC 49-39-250.

South Carolina Blue Ribbon Committee on Beachfront Management. 1987. Report. Charleston, SC.

The State (Columbia, S.C.), November 12, 1993. "State Sells Beach Property That Was Part of Lawsuit": 3B.

The State (Columbia, S.C.), September 1, 1993. "State's Plan to Sell Lots Criticized": 4B.

The State (Columbia, S.C.), March 20, 1994. "Edisto Beach Homeowners against Renourishment Plan": B10.

Sullivan, Edward J. 1993. "Lucas and Creative Constitutional Interpretation" *Environmental Law* 23: 919.

Tripp, James. 1987. "Transferable Land Rights on Developed Coastal Barriers." In R. Platt, S. Pelczarski, and B. Burbank, eds., *Cities on the Beach: Management Issues of Developed Coastal Barriers*, Chicago: University of Chicago Press: 295-98.

Waters, L. 1993. "Introduction and Decision." *Environmental Law* 23: 869-82.

White,, Carolynne C., and Alberts, Gerard G. 1993. "The Lucas Case and Modern Takings Theory," *State Legislative Report* (September) 18 (9): 1-3.

Williams, Norman, and Lyman, R. Jeffrey. 1992. "Where Are South Carolina and the Supreme Court Taking Us?" *Vermont Law Review* 16: 1111-25.

Yandle, Bruce. 1993. "Community Markets to Control Agricultural Nonpoint Source Pollution." In Roger E. Meiners and Bruce Yandle, eds., *Taking the Environment Seriously*. Lanham, Md: Rowman & Littlefield: 185-207.

List of Cases

Carter v. South Carolina Coastal Council, 281 S.C. 201, 314 S.E. 2d 327 (1984).

Dolan v. City of Tigard, June 24, 1994.

Euclid v. Ambler Realty Co., 272 U.S. 365 (1924).

First English Evangelical Lutheran Church of Glendale v. County of Los Angeles, California, 107 S. Ct. 2378 (1987).

Keystone Bituminous Coal Association v. DeBenedictus (480 U.S. 470, 107 S. Ct. 1232, 94 L.Ed. 2d 472 (1987).

Lucas v. South Carolina Council, 60 U.S.L.W. 4842 (June 29, 1992).
Nectow v. City of Cambridge, 277 U.S. 183.
Nollan v. California Coastal Commission, 483 U.S. 825, 97 L. Ed. 2d 677, 107 S. Ct. 3141 (1987).
Pennsylvania Coal Company v. Mahon, 260 U.S. 393, 43 S. Ct. 158 (1922).
Village of Belle Terre v. Boraas.

Chapter 4

Land-Rights Conflicts in the Regulation of Wetlands

Karol J. Ceplo

A property rights battle is raging in every state over the control of wetlands on private land. On one side of the struggle, we find the environmental lobby along with the Environmental Protection Agency, the Fish and Wildlife Service, and many legal academics. On the other side stand private property owners—farmers, timber companies, and ordinary individuals encountering federal land-use controls for the first time. Allied with these interests are land-use and property rights advocates and, in a rather ambivalent position, the U.S. Army Corps of Engineers.

Why the struggle? And why now? During the past thirty years, the property rights protections afforded private land, traditionally based on the common law and the takings clause of the Fifth Amendment, have changed, and the rate of change has accelerated. New methods of land-use planning, environmental regulations, and restrictions that come with the historic preservation movement have seriously eroded the certainty of land rights. Recently, however, the property rights backlash has scored some notable successes that may form a basis for a return to a rule of law and renewed respect for private property rights. Meanwhile, environmentalists search for strategies to maintain the momentum that has, since the 1960s, effectively redefined rights to land.

Federal control of private wetlands provides a vivid picture of how land rights have eroded.[1] Until the mid-1980s, the federal government relied on the market and taxpayer money to purchase and protect sensitive wetlands. Environmental goals were achieved quietly through the market. In the 1990s, a new stance was adopted. Command-and-control regulation replaced fair market value purchases as a means of protecting wetlands. A rule of interest group politics replaced the rule of law and markets.

This chapter traces the the evolution of federal control of privately owned wetlands. The chapter focuses ultimately on regulatory actions taken by the Army Corps of Engineers, which at first acted reluctantly and then enthusiastically. Under the permit requirements of Section 404 of the Clean Water Act, the Corps is the chief enforcer of wetlands law. Attention is also paid to the role played by the Environmental Protection Agency, because that agency has chief responsibility for enforcing the Clean Water Act.

To begin the story, section one describes the political economy of wetlands protection in the context of an unfolding property rights controversy. The current enforcement of wetlands rules is explained using several theories of regulation. Section two gives a brief history of the Army Corps of Engineers' mission to control the discharge of materials into U.S. waters. The roots of wetlands regulation, and the evolving definition of wetlands, which becomes ever more narrow and specialized, are identified in this section. The section ends with a detailed discussion of the agency's permitting process.

Regulatory takings of property rights becomes an inevitable issue in the story of wetlands, and in many cases, citizens seek redress through the U.S. Claims Court.

Section three focuses on the Claims Court and how it has dealt with regulatory takings. Recently, public attention was drawn to a series of criminal actions brought against citizens who violated wetlands law. Some of the more gripping stories involve ordinary people who may have unwittingly triggered a serious legal action that placed them in prison. Section four focuses on criminal enforcement of wetlands law and discusses a series of these cases. Finally, the chapter ends with a discussion of property rights policy, offering final thoughts on the controversial enforcement of wetlands regulation.

1. The Political Economy of Wetlands Protection

From the mid-nineteenth century to the 1960s, federal policy strongly supported the draining, filling, and clearing of swamps and wetlands so that the "improved" land could be used by landowners, or the government itself, for economic development purposes. The forces of economic development also dominated actions by state governments, which encouraged wetlands development. The federal government not only encouraged the private development of wetlands (see, e.g., the Swamp Land Acts of 1849, 1850, and 1860), it also undertook massive development projects of its own. These actions, such as building the levee system along the banks of the Mississippi River, led to the draining and filling of vast numbers of acres of wetlands. Additionally, the federal government has, for decades, subsidized agriculture. These subsidies contributed significantly to the conversion of wetlands to agricultural production.

The political economy changed in the 1960s. Rising personal incomes, population growth, and newly recognized environmental scarcity combined to counterbalance demands for further economic development. Along the way, scientific data on the benefits of wetlands led environmentalists to question the wisdom of continued wetlands destruction.

In 1972, in a move that was to have a major effect on wetlands protection, the federal government passed the federal Water Pollution Control Act, now known as the Clean Water Act.[2] The official purpose of the Act was to protect the integrity of the waters of the United States, and concomitantly, to eliminate pollution in navigable waters by 1985. A rather obscure section in the Clean Water Act, Section 404, provided the basis for controversial government actions that had little to do with pollution or navigable waters, as ordinary people might define them. Wetlands entered the environmental saga.

The Evolution of Section 404 Actions

Section 404 of the Clean Water Act states that any person wishing to discharge fill or dredging materials into the waters of the United States must first obtain a permit issued by the Army Corps of Engineers.[3] Most likely, the original intent of Section 404 was merely to maintain navigation in the nations rivers, canals, and harbors.[4] However, "waters" of the United States is now broadly defined to include wetlands, which may be as small as a puddled area on a farmer's field, and so the use of wetlands resources is governed by the Clean Water Act.[5] Over the past twenty-five years Section 404 has become such a powerful regulatory tool that it may now be seen as federal zoning law, limiting the use of privately owned wetlands.

Over the years, the nature of civil and criminal enforcement efforts under Section 404 has also changed dramatically. Throughout much of the past twenty-five years, the Army Corps was a rather lax enforcer of Section 404, despite pressures from the EPA, the Department of Justice, and the environmental lobby, to engage in more stringent enforcement efforts. This changed in the mid-1980s. The Corps now readily accepts calls to enforce Section 404, readily denies development permits when appropriate conditions are not met, and occasionally, together with the EPA and Department of Justice pursues criminal prosecutions.

Theories of Regulation Applied to the Problem

Because the Corps is an agent of Congress, its stronger regulatory stance reflects a shift in demand for political actions that focus on wetlands resources. Public Choice theories of government help to explain this change. The *public interest theory* suggests that government has responded to information delivered by well-organized environmental groups, and weaker efforts by others, to determine that scarce wetlands are more valuable to society at large if kept in their undeveloped state.[6] This public interest reaction, by itself, is a legitimate response to citizens' improved knowledge of ecosystems, increased population pressures, and rising income. Changing policy in the face of new evidence is a rational public interest response.

The *special interest* (or Public Choice) *theory* of government offers a different explanation. The environmental lobby, populated by individuals with higher than average incomes and stronger preferences for wetlands protection, discovered its political strength in the late 1970s and used that strength to impose the costs of environmental protection on politically weak property owners, who are widely dispersed across the country. In effect, the benefits of additional wetlands protection could be purchased at a zero price. At a zero price, the quantity demanded expands until those who supply the benefits—the widely dispersed landowners in this case—rise up and organize a counterforce.

When the public interest and special interest theories are combined, we have a richer explanation of modern wetlands regulation. New scientific knowledge demonstrated that private landowners were not fully aware of the ecological value of their wetlands. Thus, these owners inadequately estimated this value when making private development decisions. A public interest theory suggests that those who understand the true social value of wetlands resources can either purchase the land or organize and lobby government to offer private landowners incentives to change their use of land. Sensitive lands, or easements, can be purchased with private or public funds, thereby protecting the lands valued by the lobby.

But the special interest theory tells us that outright purchases can be avoided. Taking the moral high ground, the environmental lobby can demand that "greedy" (or ignorant) landowners be instructed (via regulation) to change their land-use plans.[7] Land rights formerly held by landowners, such as rights to farm or build homes, are taken by the government at zero price by regulating the use of property. For those seeking control of a resource, gaining such control without paying for it is a preferred arrangement. Should regulatory takings fail, wetlands might be purchased with tax revenues, paid for by citizens, not just members of the special interest group.

Herein lies the crux of the wetlands problem. The federal government, strongly supported by the environmental lobby, prefers to protect wetlands resources in the cheapest possible manner, in terms of fiscal impact. Given limited government revenues, this desire to protect wetlands without dipping into the treasurer's purse, makes perfect sense. The cheapest way for the government to accomplish its goal of "no net loss" of wetlands is not to buy wetlands on the open market, nor is it to buy wetlands through an eminent domain action, where it would have to pay the private owner fair market value of the property.[8] Rather, the cheapest way for government to get these resources is to take the property via regulation and without just compensation.[9] For well-organized environmental groups, and the politicians they support, this is the best of all worlds.[10]

There are obvious problems with this outcome, aside from the property rights dilemma it creates. First, when a valuable good such as undeveloped wetlands is provided to consumers at little to no cost it is overconsumed. Because protection is "costless," little effort is made to determine which wetlands are most sensitive, and which might be protected at least cost to all parties. Excessive wetlands protection is the result. If government officials were required to face the full costs of wetlands protection, a more efficient level of wetlands protection would occur. In the long run, both environmental and other land-use interests would be better served.[11] We have but one system of property rights to land. Taking property rights protections away from landowners without paying just compensation empowers the state to take these same rights from groups wishing to protect sensitive wetlands.

Competition for Regulatory Benefits

There is yet another theoretical wrinkle to consider in the regulatory story. The rent-seeking theory of regulation tells us that even the most dedicated political agent is likely to be influenced disproportionately by well-organized special interest groups when that agent has the ability to bestow benefits on such groups via regulatory action.

The Army Corps, under Section 404, has valuable benefits to bestow on interest groups: the ability to engage in property development on the one hand, and the ability to have and enjoy pristine wetland resources on the other. Private property owners want to develop their land. Environmentalists want as much undeveloped land as possible. Government responds most effectively to the desires of the most powerful interest groups. Interest groups lobby effectively when the cost of lobbying is shared by group members who directly enjoy the benefits of these actions. Group members are, in such cases, willing to support the lobbying efforts.

In contrast, private property owners as a group traditionally lack political organization, are disbursed, and are therefore politically ineffective. Wetlands owners seeking to organize for political action encounter substantial problems— identifying other wetlands owners, gaining consensus on what should be done, and avoiding free-rider problems—that arise when the benefits of successful lobbying accrue to one and all, even those who did not join the rally. The rent-seeking story tells us that politicians respond to what (and who) they hear and see, which means they assign less importance to the desires of private property owners. Faced with competition from well-organized interest groups, private property owners lose out in the race for political rents.

The Property Rights Issue

The question of whether, or to what extent, government should limit the ability of a landowner to use her land in whatever manner she so desires is purely a property rights question. Typically, landownership includes the right to buy and sell property and to freely use and enjoy that property. These rights are considered basic elements, or "sticks," in the bundle of property rights. Under common law, property rights were theoretically "absolute," though in fact were subject to three specific exceptions: (1) a property owner may not harm the property of another, (2) the sovereign may engage in eminent domain actions, and (3) private property rights could be infringed if done in a lawful fashion.[12] The question of what is lawful is crucial to the last exception.

Our founding fathers considered property rights to be a basic civil liberty, without which prosperity and personal freedom would be impossible. To protect these rights, they clearly defined the boundaries within which government may operate. The Constitution was written, in large part, to *restrict* government's ability to infringe upon the rights of property ownership. The bedrock of this protection is found in the Fifth Amendment's takings clause. The amendment does not forbid the government from taking private property; rather, it requires government to pay for what it takes. This requirement that government pay for what it takes creates important incentives for government to carefully weigh the need for a particular acquisition against the purchase price. Requiring government officials to face the costs of property purchases forces them to accept market discipline. In a democratic society, this discipline results in a more equitable use of limited resources: if taxpayers are willing to fund projects through general revenue, these projects are more likely to represent society-wide preferences than are projects funded out of agency budgets (which are more subject to special interest group lobbying pressures).

Despite the Fifth Amendment, the government has, over the course of this century, increasingly taken private property without paying compensation. The politically preferred method for such a taking is regulation, which restricts the uses to which a property owner may put her property, but typically does not require compensation. When the government regulates land use, title to the land is not transferred from the owner to the government (as is the case in an eminent domain action). The owner retains title, but some of the sticks in her bundle of property rights are taken.

Environmental Feudalism

The ever-increasing use of regulation to restrict private property rights represents a profound change in the politics of land use. This movement has been described as a "new feudalism of regulation."[13] The management of environmental resources has shifted from the private owner to a centralized bureaucracy, much as land use in medieval times was controlled by centralized royal or ecceleciastical powers, rathern than by the people who lived on and worked the land.

Property rights protections, which took centuries to obtain, afford an antidote to such developments. With the Magna Carta, property rights became fundamental rights. They should remain so. Their strong protection is necessary for a number of reasons. As Coyle notes: "Property rights are at the core of liberalism, the political vision of individual freedom and limited government that animated the American Revolution."[14] Property rights protect individuals from excessive government intereference. Strong property rights protection means that government is less likely to become tyrannical. In addition, a government that faces strong property rights provisions is less likely to be discriminatory because it will be more difficult to transfer (or restrict the use of) the property of one, disfavored group, to another, favored group.

In addition, a strong property rights regime provides significant economic advantages. If an individual (or corporation) owns property, and is confident that the judicial system will protect the rights that adhere to the property, the owner—who enjoys the gain and bears all losses—is more likely to protect the property than is a nonowner. In other words, property owners have incentives to use their resources wisely and to act creatively to improve the value of such resources. It is the ability of property owners to use, invest in, and improve their property that makes property ownership so valuable. And from this ability to profit from property ownership, we derive our economic well-being. When property rights break down, all citizens ultimately suffer. We need only point to the lessons of the Soviet Union and Eastern Europe.

In the case of wetlands protection, we should ask, "Does central planning, in the form of government regulation of land use, protect wetlands resources more efficiently than would a strong property rights regime?" This question introduces the role of the Army Corps of Engineers.

2. The Corps of Engineers and Wetlands Jurisdiction

The Army Corps of Engineers was created in 1802 by Congress.[15] Established originally to build and maintain coastal fortifications for the new nation, the Army Corps was also given powers to maintain the navigable waters of the United States.[16] Federal jurisdiction over such waters comes from Congress's constitutional powers to regulate interstate commerce.[17] Because of the correlation between freedom of navigation and commercial activities, Congress laid claim to control over navigable waterways at an early date.[18] This control was delegated to, and continues to be handled by, the Army Corps. Throughout the nineteenth century, the Army Corps concentrated on its mission of building and maintaining coastal fortifications and of improving the nation's harbor and river facilities.

The Corps received further authority to maintain the navigable waters of the United States following the landmark Supreme Court decision *Williamette Iron Bridge Co. v. Hatch* (1888).[19] The *Williamette* Court held that common law did not prevent states from constructing obstacles in the navigable waters of the United States. In response to this decision, in 1890 Congress passed federal legislation designed to prevent the erection of obstacles in navigable waters of the United States, unless such projects received explicit government approval.[20] In addition to requiring explicit federal government approval for all construction activities taking place in the navigable waters of the United States, the 1890 Act also prohibited the dumping of waste matter into such waters unless the secretary of war granted approval. In 1899, Congress passed the Rivers and Harbors Appropriations Act, which amended the 1890 Act.[21] The 1899 Act gathered together under one title both the 1890 Act and all other navigation-related laws of the federal government.[22] The goal of the 1899 Act corresponded to that of its predecessor: protect and promote freedom of navigation within the United States.[23] The 1899 Act also shifted the center of approval for construction projects from the secretary of war to Congress.

Perhaps the most important contribution of the 1899 Act to the Army Corps' administrative authority was its creation of a permitting system, requiring persons to obtain both an Army Corps permit *and* congressional approval if they wished to build a bridge, dam, causeway, or dike.[24] Actions typically covered by this section of the Act include the building of jetties, docks, piers, and wharves, and the dredging and filling of harbor areas and adjacent wetland areas.

The Army Corps' permitting system also applies under Section 13 of the Act, known as the Refuse Act. The Refuse Act is an early example of environmental legislation, which requires that a permit be issued for the dumping of any waste matter (with the exception of liquid sewage) into the navigable waters of the United States. The Army Corps' permitting system created under the 1899 Act served as the blueprint for the later Section 404 permitting system.

While jurisdiction under the 1899 Act was clearly focused on navigable waters, the Corps, through interpretive regulations, expanded its review powers to cover nonnavigable waters such as tributaries. Nonnavigable waters were covered if construction, dredging, or filling activities on such waters would adversely affect the free flow of navigation or the condition of connected navigable waters.[25]

It was not until the early 1960s that the Corps experienced a significant expansion of its jurisdiction, resulting in what one pair of commentators has termed "A Corps of Engineers Renaissance."[26] This expansion of jurisdiction shifted focus in the Army Corps from its traditional concern with determining the effects of proposed actions on navigation, to a concern with the effects of proposed actions on the environment at large, and on wetlands particularly.

Expansion of Army Corps Jurisdiction and Wetlands Protection

Several factors led to the expansion of Army Corps jurisdiction in the 1960s. First, in 1960, the Supreme Court interpreted Section 10 of the 1899 Act as applying to industrial pollutants, without regard to the pollutants' effects on navigation.[27] This ruling expanded the definition of discharge affecting navigable waters and thereby broadened the scope of Corps jurisdiction under the Rivers and Harbors Act, giving the Corps an environmental-protection function similar to the one it held under the Refuse Act.[28]

Second, in December 1968, the Corps significantly shifted its focus for permit review by promulgating its "Public Interest Review" regulations.[29] These regulations were issued in response to an agreement reached by the secretaries of the army and the interior,[30] requiring the Army Corps to give effect to the Fish and Wildlife Coordination Act of 1958.[31] Under the terms of the agreement, the Army Corps agreed to consult with the Department of the Interior's Fish and Wildlife Service when making permit determinations. The Public Interest Review regulations amended and further expanded the Corps' jurisdiction under Section 10 of the 1899 Rivers and Harbors Act.

The Public Interest Review regulation requires the Army Corps to grant or to deny permit applications based on "all factors which may be relevant . . . including the cumulative effects thereof . . . on conservation, economics, aesthetics, general environmental concerns, wetlands, historic properties, fish and wildlife values . . . and, in general, the needs and welfare of the people."[32] Thus, permits for the dredging and filling of property may be rejected by the Army Corps not only because of whatever adverse effects such activity might have on navigation or water quality, but also because of factors such as "aesthetics" and "the needs and welfare of the people." This expansion of jurisdiction has received the blessing of all branches of the federal government.[33]

Importantly, however, the general Public Interest Review no longer applies to wetlands, which are considered special areas, and now are subject to stricter review criteria. Under the stricter standard of review applied to wetlands, the Army Corps has created a presumption *against* any permit that involves a nonwater- dependent fill of land.

Finally, in 1969, the National Environmental Policy Act (NEPA)[34] was enacted, further expanding Army Corps jurisdiction. NEPA requires federal agencies to prepare environmental impact statements whenever they take actions that significantly affect environmental quality. NEPA requires agencies to consider the possible economic and social costs of proposed actions, in addition to the possible environmental costs, thus complementing the requirements of the Army Corps' Public Interest Review regulation. Because its permitting procedure constitutes an action by a federal agency, the outcome of which may significantly impact the environment, the Army Corps' Section 404 program is subject to the legal requirements of NEPA.

By the time the federal Water Pollution Control Act (hereinafter the Clean Water Act, or CWA) was passed in 1972,[35] the Army Corps had far more extensive jurisdiction over waters of the United States than the 1899 Rivers and Harbor Act suggests. This jurisdiction was further increased by the 1972 legislation.

Split Jurisdiction under the Clean Water Act

The stated goal of the CWA is "to restore and maintain the chemical, physical and biological integrity of the Nation's Waters."[36] Section 404 of the Act provides that the Army Corps shall be responsible for issuing permits for actions that involve the dredging or filling of the nation's waters.[37] Dredging sediment and filling waters or wetlands disturbs the integrity of those resources and, therefore, constitutes activity within the purview of the CWA. "Dredged spoil" (dredged sediment) is defined by the Act as a pollutant. Thus dredging and filling that produce such spoil (actions commonly involved in agricultural activities or commercial or residential property development) are covered by the Act.[38]

Section 404 of the CWA is the only section of the act that is administered by the Department of the Army, acting through the Army Corps. Primary responsibility for monitoring water pollution rests with the Environmental Protection Agency (EPA). The EPA may, pursuant to the National Pollutant Discharge Elimination System, issue permits for the discharge of materials into the nation's waters so long as statutory requirements are met.[39] Section 404 represents an important exception to the general rule of EPA control of the federal water pollution program (though the agency does have veto power over Army Corps permit determinations).[40]

Despite the fact that Army Corps jurisdiction had expanded during the twentieth century to include control over nonnavigable tributaries, the Corps restricted its jurisdictional reach and resisted the urge to become an environmental regulator. Until 1975, the Army Corps' position was that its jurisdiction extended only as far as the high water mark of bodies of fresh water and to the mean high water mark for tidal waters. Some commentators suggest that the Army Corps took a "laissez-faire" approach to its jurisdiction because its own dredging and filling activities might come under unwanted scrutiny.[41] But as discussed below, there may be more to the story.

Unlike the Corps, the EPA responded to the Clean Water Act's mandate by making sweeping jurisdictional claims.[42] An interesting question is posed by the conflicting jurisdictional claims of the Army Corps and the EPA: why would the Army Corps eschew a congressional grant of greater jurisdictional power? The EPA happily accepted this widened jurisdiction. And it is the EPA's response that, on the surface, makes more sense.

In thinking about the question, consider the age of the two agencies and the interest groups supporting them. The old Corps had served agricultural and development interests for almost a century. Farmers were not generally interested in seeing wetlands protection surface as a national issue. Further, under the pre-1986 federal tax code, farmers could deduct as a current-year expense the costs of land clearing associated with converting wetlands into farmable drylands. They were allowed a 25 percent soil and water conservation deduction for activities associated with draining or filling wetlands, and they (or other investors) could claim a 60 percent capital gains deduction for the conversion of wetlands to cropland if such land was then sold as a capital asset (See, 26 U.S.C. §§182, 175, 1257 (1986).) In contrast, the newer EPA was supported primarily and significantly by national environmental groups who adamantly opposed old-line Corps activities. Environmentalists wanted a more aggressive agency. Farmers and the Corps' traditional constituencies wanted a different approach. The support of the two agencies was polarized from the start.

Extending the Reach of the Corps

The conflict between the reserved jurisdictional approach of the Army Corps and the expansive approach of the EPA was settled in 1975 in the case of *Natural Resources Defense Council v. Callaway.*[43] The plaintiff sought a judgment declaring that the Army Corps *had* to expand its jurisdiction to match that of the EPA. The U.S. District Court for the District of Columbia determined that EPA and Army Corps jurisdiction under the Clean Water Act covered the "navigable waters" of the United States, and that by "navigable waters" Congress meant "the waters of the United States."

Congress's definition of navigable waters as all "waters" indicated to the court that the government wanted the agencies to accept and use broad jurisdictional powers to combat water pollution at its sources, wherever they might be.⁴⁴ The court agreed with the plaintiffs that the Army Corps was exercising excessively limited jurisdiction under Section 404. The Corps was ordered to issue new regulations reflecting a broader jurisdictional reach. In response, in 1975 the Corps issued interim regulations that revised its previous definition of "waters of the United States" to include all waters and wetlands (both freshwater and saltwater) that are either interstate or that could affect interstate commerce.⁴⁵ The Calloway decision forced a reluctant Army Corps to expand its jurisdiction.

Throughout the 1970s the Army Corps continued to amend its permit process to better reflect calls for its increased jurisdiction and protection of wetlands resources. These calls included the 1977 Clean Water Act Amendments,⁴⁶ which embraced the Calloway decision. The Corps' expanded jurisdiction resulted in increased work burdens on the agency, as well as greater use of general, as opposed to individual, permits for development.⁴⁷ However, increased use of general permits proved to be an unsatisfactory solution to the problem of expanded jurisdiction.⁴⁸

In December 1980, the Army Corps promulgated its final guidelines for issuing permits under Section 404. These guidelines reflected a significant change in Army Corps focus. They called for much greater protection of wetlands and created a new presumption in favor of wetlands protection over wetlands development.

The added protection for the nation's wetlands did not satisfy the environmental lobby, which brought suit against the Corps in 1982 seeking to terminate the Corps' use of nationwide general permits for isolated wetlands. As a result of *National Wildlife Federation v. Marsh*,⁴⁹ the Corps issued new regulations specifying that nationwide general permits would only apply to isolated wetlands of one acre or less. In the case of isolated wetlands between one and ten acres, the Corps created a new review process that further expanded its jurisdictional authority. The Corps was on its way to becoming a wetlands-use regulator.

The Glancing Goose Test

In 1985, despite its ever-growing jurisdictional claims, the Corps came under fire from Congress, the EPA, and environmental groups. All wanted the agency to monitor wetlands more closely, especially isolated and nonadjacent wetlands. In a memorandum of agreement signed by the Corps and the EPA in September 1985, the Corps agreed to extend its jurisdiction to include wetlands that could *possibly* be used by migratory birds or other endangered species.⁵⁰ The so-called "glancing goose" test says that the Army Corps has jurisdiction over any wetland, no matter how attenuated its claim to be a "water" of the United States, *if* a goose might look down in flight and consider landing there. The hypothetical bird could, the government argued, be considered in the stream of commerce because it could conceivably be caught, eaten, or hunted.

This tie to interstate commerce, slim though it might be, was enough for the government to bring the regulation of isolated wetlands under the auspices of federal agencies. The expansion of Army Corps jurisdiction to adjacent and isolated wetlands was upheld by the Supreme Court in *United States v. Riverside Bayview Homes, Inc.* (1985).[51] By expanding the definition of "wetlands," the Corps has extended its jurisdictional reach over more and more private property merely by relabeling the property "wetlands."[52] Property owners are now hard-pressed to determine what might be tomorrow's definition.

The Army Corps' claim to jurisdiction over isolated wetlands has not gone unchallenged.[53] In the 1992 case *Hoffman Homes, Inc. v. EPA*,[54] the court determined that (1) the Clean Water Act provides no statutory basis for Army Corps jurisdiction over non-adjacent and isolated wetlands, despite the Riverside Bayview decision, and (2) the exercise of such jurisdiction is both unreasonable and invalid under the Act. The *Hoffman* court questioned the validity of the "glancing goose" test, noting that mere overflight (with nothing more tangible) does not place a bird in the stream of commerce. Furthermore, the court stated, exerting jurisdiction based on the possibility that a migratory bird might use an isolated wetland "is even more far-fetched."[55] This decision provides some hope for owners of isolated wetlands, insofar as it expresses a sense of frustration with endless expansions of jurisdiction based on the most tenuous of claims for connection with interstate commerce, and it may signal a small step toward common law protection of property rights.

How Section 404 Process Works

The Army Corps issues individual permits and general permits. In those cases where only a very small number of acres are involved, where projected environmental impacts will be minimal, or where "isolated" waters are involved,[56] an applicant may ask for either a state, regional, or nationwide general permit.[57]

Certain types of activities are exempted from the provisions of Section 404. These activities include normal farming, harvesting, or ranching; maintaining or conducting emergency repairs to dams; building or maintaining farm and stock ponds, irrigation ditches, drainage ditches (maintenance only); building and maintaining farm or forest roads; and building temporary sediment basins on construction sites.[58]

However, Congress does not provide a blanket exemption for these activities. Section 404 restricts the ability of farmers to engage in "normal" farming activities if these activities have the effect of "bringing an area of the navigable waters into a use to which it was not previously subject, where the flow or circulation of navigable waters may be impaired or the reach of such waters be reduced . . ."[59] This "recapture" provision is designed to reduce the drainage of wetlands for farming or ranching purposes, and means that farmers and ranchers may, after all, be required to comply with the Section 404 permitting process.

An applicant must seek an individual permit for dredging or filling 10 or more acres of property. Army Corps standards of review for granting individual permits are much stricter than those for granting general permits. Not surprisingly, the cases reviewed later in this chapter involve the denial of individual permits.

To obtain a Section 404 permit, an applicant must first make an application to the appropriate district engineer of the Army Corps.[60] This formal request must include a detailed description (though oftentimes "rough drafts" are accepted) of the applicant's proposed development project, as well as the kinds, composition, source, and amounts of material to be dredged or used as fill. Information must be included concerning the "physical, biological, and chemical nature of the materials" to be discharged, their disposal site, and a description of the ecosystem receiving the materials.[61] Additionally, the application should include appropriate architectural or other drawings, sketches, or plans of the applicant's land. The applicant must explain and justify the proposed activity. A development schedule is required, as are the names and addresses of adjacent landowners.

Often, property owners wishing to develop land will need to obtain permits from local or state agencies, in addition to federal permits. If local or state authorizations are necessary, applicants must present the district engineer with evidence that the property owner has obtained the necessary state or local approval before a Section 404 permit will be granted.

After the application is filed with the district engineer, the Army Corps, acting through the district engineer, will issue a public notice calling for comments on the proposed activity. Following receipt of public comments, the district engineer will comprehensively review the application, based on Army Corps regulations, paying particular attention to the Public Interest Review requirements of these regulations, and balancing the potential benefits of development against possible harms. The district engineer must consider whether practical alternatives to the proposed activity exist.

After this review, the district engineer will then issue a memorandum discussing whether the permit should be granted.[62] (Permits may be granted retroactively for work already completed). Based on these findings, a higher-level officer at the Army Corps will make the final determination concerning approval, denial, or approval with modifications.

Any action taken in the Section 404 permit process must comply with EPA regulations and take into account the views not only of the EPA, but also of the

Department of the Interior. Finally, it is possible that the EPA will veto an Army Corps permit determination.[63] Vetos may be based on a finding by the EPA that permit approval will result in "an unacceptable adverse effect" on water quality.[64] Persons who dredge or fill any water without a permit are subject to EPA jurisdiction, while persons who violate the terms of an existing permit are subject to Army Corps jurisdiction.[65]

The EPA handles wetland issues through its Office of Wetlands Protection. The functions of this office include expediting Section 404 policy development; improving state and local wetland protection; improving coordination between state and federal protection efforts; promoting public awareness about wetlands; increasing scientific knowledge about wetlands resources; and developing "anticipatory approaches" to protection efforts.[66] EPA staff assigned to the protection of wetlands resources are located in each of its ten divisional offices, as well as at its Washington, D.C., headquarters.

3. The U.S. Court of Claims and the Takings Issue

Property owners denied a Section 404 permit to develop their land may sue the government, claiming that government regulatory activity has taken their property. Because the government typically does not pay for regulatory takings, the property owner claims a Fifth Amendment violation and these are heard by the U.S. Claims Court. The jurisdication of the Claims Court arises by virtue of the Tucker Act.[67] This Act specifies that all legal actions involving sums greater than $10,000, in which the federal government is the defendant, and which involve nontortious constitutional issues, must be heard by the Claims Court. Fifth Amendment takings cases fall squarely within this category. Appeals from Claims Court decisions are heard by the Court of Appeals of the Federal Circuit, with a grant of writ of certiorari possible, though unlikely, by the U.S. Supreme Court.[68]

The Tucker Act bars suits in which the government's activity was illegitimate. In other words, plaintiffs must admit that the Corps acted within its powers when it denied a Section 404 permit. However, because federal takings jurisprudence has defined the police power of the state rather broadly, it is almost foolhardy for a plaintiff to argue against the validity of a taking.[69] Given the current state of takings doctrine, as discussed in Chapter 2 by Erin O'Hara, it is fair to say that the government may take what it wishes. The real issue in takings cases is this: how much, if anything, does the government owe to the property owner whose land has been devalued through regulation?

The Claims Court has heard twenty-eight cases involving wetlands and takings claims.[70] The majority of these cases involve a claim that Army Corps denial of a Section 404 permit to fill a wetland constitutes a compensable taking.[71] Of these 28 cases, twelve are currently pending and sixteen have been

decided: twelve in favor of the government, three in favor of the plaintiff, one
was settled before a final determination was reached.

Cases in Which There Was No Compensable Taking

In twelve cases the Claims Court dismissed the plaintiff's suit, finding that
government action did not constitute a taking, and therefore the government had
no obligation to pay the plaintiff just compensation. A dismissal may occur after
one of the parties, typically the government, files a motion to dismiss while the
suit is in progress. Alternatively, at the close of the case the court may issue
a determination in favor of the government, which acts to dismiss the plaintiff's
suit. A discussion of a few typical cases will serve to identify a few common
elements.

The first Section 404 takings case brought before the court was *Deltona
Corp. v. United States* (1981).[72] This case involved a developer who purchased
10,000 acres of land in Florida for $7,500,000.[73] The developer planned to
create a "water-oriented residential community" on Marco Island, Florida. The
company divided its development plan into five stages and completed stages one
and two before the enactment of Section 404 in 1972.

The land on which Deltona was building contained mangrove swamps and
wetlands, which the company planned to fill, permanently destroying much of
the natural mangrove vegetation.[74] The initial stage of the project received Army
Corps approval under its 1899 Rivers and Harbors Act powers. At the time, the
Corps was concerned only with the effects of dredging and filling on navigation.
Deltona's application was approved because its planned development posed no
threat to navigation. After promulgation of its Public Interest Review standard
in 1968, the Corps issued another permit to complete the second stage of the
Deltona development, subject however to certain conditions.[75]

In April 1973, following the passage of the Clean Water Act and its Section
404, the Corps granted a permit for one of the three remaining parcels Deltona
hoped to develop, but denied permission to dredge and fill Deltona's two
remaining parcels of land. Deltona brought suit against the government, alleging
that its property had effectively been taken without compensation, by virtue of
the Corps' denial of the dredge and fill permit.

The *Deltona* court first determined that Section 404 advanced legitimate
government purposes.[76] The requirement that a regulation advance a legitimate
state interest was specified by the Supreme Court in its 1980 case *Agins v.
Tiburon.*[77] The *Agins* decision involves a multistep process for determing when
a government action requires compensation. The second step in the *Agins* test
requires a court to determine whether a government act, albeit legitimate, denies
a property owner *all* economically viable use of her land.[78] The determination
of economic viability may only be resolved by first establishing which piece or

part of a plaintiff's land has been affected by government regulation. As another Supreme Court takings decision, *Penn Central Transportation Co. v. City of New York* (1978),[79] specified, when considering a takings claim, a court must consider the whole parcel of land owned by the plaintiff, not just a discrete section of that land. Economic viability will be based, therefore, on the entire holding of the plaintiff, not simply on a plaintiff's wetlands holdings.

In the Deltona case, the plaintiff had completed sales contracts for 90 percent of the lots it intended to develop in the two undeveloped parcels of land.[80] Denial of Section 404 permits meant, of course, that the company could not develop any of the wetlands in these parcels and thus had to forgo the income that could be derived from fulfilling many of its extant sales contracts. However, the court noted that the two tracts of land for which permits were denied amounted to only 20 percent of Deltona's total acreage.[81] Furthermore, this 20 percent of Deltona's land contained 111 acres of uplands which could be developed.

The developable parcel of the land at issue was valued by the court at $2.5 million.[82] The court noted that while some of Deltona's investment-backed expectations had been frustrated by the changing law regarding wetlands, the company nonetheless retained "enormous" residual value for its land.[83] The court cited *Agins* for the proposition that "the question (whether a compensable taking has occurred) requires a weighing of private and public interests."[84] The *Deltona* court held that the scales tipped in favor of the government; no compensation was due because the government had not denied *all* economically viable use of the plaintiff's land.

The court also rejected the plaintiff's argument that it deserved compensation because it was denied the "highest and best economic use" of its land. Based on the Supreme Court's decision in *Penn Central*, the *Deltona* court determined that it is "simply untenable" to permit property owners who have been denied the ability to pursue or exploit a particular property interest to argue that a compensable taking has occurred.[85] This argument, the court stated, is nothing more than the diminution in value argument dressed differently.[86]

The *Deltona* court's standard for determining when a compensable takings occurs is an extremely difficult one for plaintiffs to meet. Indeed, under such a standard it is surprising that courts ever find that a government regulation has taken all economically viable use of land.[87] Presumably one could always permit passive activities, such as birdwatching, on one's land and charge a small price for such activity, thereby engaging in an "economically viable" use of land. The *Deltona* plaintiff was denied just compensation because, in the court's opinion, economic viability remained: that is, Deltona had made what the court determined to be a sufficient profit on its investment.

The *Deltona* court further justified its ruling by referring to the nationwide application of Section 404, and by stating that Deltona's loss of property value was not inequitable because across the country property owners were bearing similar burdens. These property owners, the court said, were benefiting from the Section 404 program, and these benefits were sufficient compensation for the burden of property devaluation.[88]

What the court fails to note, however, is that the perceived benefits of the Section 404 program, for example undeveloped wetlands, accrue to *all* of society. Wetlands owners cannot keep for themselves the value of their resource; the benefits provided by wetlands necessarily flow to innumerable people in the form of better water quality, flood protection, wildlife-habitat protection, and various aesthetic gains. However, the Supreme Court has clearly stated that when the government takes property to provide a public benefit, compensation is due to the property owner. This rule was clearly enunciated in the 1960 case *United States v. Armstrong.*[89] Although the *Deltona* court recognized that wetlands provide public benefits, it nonetheless ignored the reasoning of *United States v. Armstrong.*

In 1981 the Claims Court also heard the case of *James J. Jentgen, Trustee v. United States.*[90] In *Jentgen* the plaintiff purchased 101.8 acres of land near Everglades City, Florida, in 1971 for $150,000. Mr. Jentgen intended to develop this property as a residential community. Much of the property consisted of mangrove swamps and other wetlands. Completing the project would require extensive dredging and filling of land.

At the date of purchase, the Clean Water Act was not in effect, although the 1899 Rivers and Harbors Act was. Section 10 of the 1899 Act applied to some of the plaintiff's proposed activities. Accordingly, in 1973, the plaintiff applied for a Section 10 permit. In 1975, he applied for a Section 404 permit covering approximately 80 percent of his land. Under the Corps' Public Interest Review standard, Jentgen's applications were denied, although the Corps offered a permit for development of 20 acres. The plaintiff rejected the Corps' offer and filed suit for a compensable taking.

In its holding, the court again employed the *Penn Central* test,[91] assessing the economic impact of the permit denial on Jentgen's investment-backed expectations. The court focused its inquiry on the whole of Mr. Jengten's property, not on a discrete part, and found that Jentgen retained economically viable use of his land. The court noted that while the permit denial reduced the value of the plaintiff's property, a compensable taking had not occurred because the government did not take *all* of the property's value. In this case, "justice and fairness" did not require the court to find a taking.[92]

In the 1989 case of *Ciampetti v. United States,*[93] the plaintiff sued the government, alleging a compensable taking of property following a Section 404 permit denial. This case centered around a piece of property located in Cape May County, New Jersey, which the plaintiff wished to develop into a residential community. The Army Corps determined that most of the northern section of this property was wetlands and so development would require a Section 404 permit.

Mr. Ciampitti applied for Section 404 permits to dredge and fill the northern half of his land. The Army Corps informed him that he needed to obtain a determination from the state of New Jersey that his proposed development would be consistent with that state's coastal management policies.[94] Additionally, he needed a New Jersey water-quality certificate before a Section 404 permit could be issued. Ciampitti obtained neither the water-quality certificate nor the letter of compliance from New Jersey. The Corps denied his Section 404 permit.

On the basis of (1) a cease and desist order issued by the Army Corps against the plaintiff after the Corps learned that Ciampitti was illegally dredging and filling wetlands on his property and (2) the Section 404 permit denial, Ciampitti filed suit in the Claims Court alleging that the government took his property without paying for it.

The Claims Court noted that the Corps' decision to deny Ciampitti's permit was based on the "unnecessary permanent disruption to the environment" that would result from the proposed development, and not on the missing paperwork from the state of New Jersey.[95] Indeed, the court determined that even had Ciampitti received the necessary state documentation, the Corps may well have denied the permit based on its "public interest" in the protection of wetlands.

The government argued, however, that it did not have to compensate Ciampitti because New Jersey had not issued the necessary permits for development. Because New Jersey created an impediment to development, the federal government could not be responsible for a compensable taking. The court rejected this argument and held that the plaintiff's taking claims was based on an independent federal regulatory action. The federal government was not able to shift its constitutional responsibilities for compensable takings by relying on a botched paperwork argument.

Alternatively, the government argued that Ciampitti's proposed development would create a nuisance. Thus, denial of the permit should fall under the nuisance exception to the Fifth Amendment and should be dismissed.[96] While noting that the "public interest in preventing activities similar to public nuisances is a substantial one,"[97] the court determined that the nuisance exception cannot be "viewed in isolation."[98] The court held that even if Ciampitti's actions did constitute a nuisance, because of the severe economic impact of the permit denial and the permit denial's impact on his investment-backed expectations, it would be improper to summarily dismiss Ciampitti's suit based on this defense.

Finally, the Claims Court noted that when a federal taking claim is made, a court must look to the rights of the landowner in the parcel as a whole, not just to component parts of that land. Single parcels may not be divided into discrete units to determine whether a taking has been effected.[99] In this case, a critical question remained: which parcel of land should be considered for purposes of determining a taking—the entire tract, or simply the northern Phase II tract? For these reasons, the Claims Court denied the government's motion for summary judgment and a full trial was held.

In the follow-up case *Robert Ciampitti v. United States* (1991),[100] the Claims Court dismissed Ciampitti's case on conclusion of the trial. The court held that the government's denial of a Section 404 permit had not taken all economically viable uses of Ciampitti's property. Therefore, no compensation was due. Once again, a property owner suffering a partial taking of property was denied compensation.

Recent takings cases in the Claims Court follow the pattern established in *Deltona* and *Ciampitti*. In the 1993 case of *Tabb Lakes, Ltd. v. United States*,[101] the plaintiff sought compensation for a temporary taking. Tabb Lakes based its claim on an Army Corps cease and desist order that effectively delayed the plaintiff's development plans for three years. The order was issued because the plaintiff was filling wetlands located on its property without a Section 404 permit.

This case, involving development of land in York County, Virginia, was heard on appeal by the federal Circuit Court, which affirmed the decision of the Claims Court.[102] The Claims Court dismissed the case because it found no compensable taking of property.

Much like the Deltona case, *Tabb Lakes* involved a real estate developer with a multistage development plan. The initial stages of the development received the necessary state and federal approval. However, after lengthy negotiations, Tabb Lakes and the Army Corps were unable to reach an agreement for further development. The developer then withdrew its application for a Section 404 permit and sought judgment declaring that its property was not subject to Army Corps jurisdiction. In October 1986, the Army Corps issued a cease and desist order requiring Tabb Lakes to stop filling wetlands on its property.

Tabb Lakes argued at trial that the Army Corps improperly determined that its land consisted of isolated wetlands because the Corps failed to comply with the notice and public comment requirements of the Administrative Procedure Act. Thus, the plaintiff argued, the Army Corps did not have jurisdiction over the case.[103] This argument was accepted and affirmed by the 4th Circuit.

Tabb Lakes then began filling and developing its property as planned.[104] The Corps took no further action against the property owner, and all lots in the development were sold. In November 1990 Tabb Lakes filed suit in the Claims Court, alleging a temporary taking of property by the Corps based on the delay imposed by the cease and desist order.[105]

The Claims Court found in favor of the government, stating that because the plaintiff had engaged in economic activity connected with its land during the pendency of the cease and desist order, no compensable taking occurred. Additionally, the court found that the government had not acted in bad faith in issuing the order, and that the delay imposed by the order was not "extraordinary." For these reasons, compensation was denied.

On appeal, the federal Circuit Court determined that the only issue to be tried was whether the cease and desist order constituted a compensable taking.

The court noted that temporary takings, if they meet the required criteria, are compensable.[106] In this case however, the court rejected the plaintiff's argument that it was denied "all economically viable" uses of its property after issuance of the cease and desist order.[107] The court also held that although a regulation may work a taking of property, this will be the case only if the regulation, in the words of Justice Holmes, "goes too far." Here, the cease and desist order did not go too far, thus there was no regulatory taking.

Also decided in 1993 was *Plantation Landing Resort, Inc. v. United States.*[108] The plaintiff was a joint venture, created to develop a resort on Grand Isle, Louisiana. In November 1985, the developers filed a permit application with the Army Corps to dredge and fill the 220 acres of land they owned on Grand Isle. After the application was filed, the Corps held a public hearing on the proposed development. Public response to development was favorable.

The plaintiff contended that in April 1987 the Corps suggested the group modify its development plans, reducing the number of acres involved from 220 to 59, so that the time and expense of an environmental impact statement could be avoided. Accordingly, in October 1987, the plaintiff revised its Section 404 permit and requested permission to dredge and fill 59, rather than 220, acres. Of the 59 acres included in the permit application, 37 were shallow bay bottom and 22 were salt marshes.

The Corps held another public hearing on the revised proposal. Again the response was positive. In December 1988, the district engineer responsible for the project issued a draft statement approving the project. The draft statement contained specific recommendations for mitigation measures the plaintiff should take to limit the destruction of wetlands. This draft statement was forwarded to the EPA. Following EPA review of the statement, a determination was made to review the plaintiff's application at the Washington office of the Army Corps. In April 1989, Washington advised the New Orleans district engineer to reevaluate the application. In January 1990, more than four years after its initial filing, the Corps informed the plaintiff that a much more extensive mitigation effort would be necessary in order to win permit approval. (Rather than create five new acres of marsh, the group was now asked to create 22 acres *prior* to any dredging or filling activity.)[109] The plaintiff made a counteroffer to buy and restore 22 acres of freshwater wetlands in another section of Louisiana, but this offer was rejected by the Corps. Negotiations over appropriate mitigation efforts were unsuccessful, and in December 1990 the district engineer denied the plaintiff a permit.

The plaintiff sued in the Claims Court, alleging that a denial of the permit took its property. The court dismissed the case, finding that no compensable taking took place because the plaintiff had an inadequate property interest in the land it sought to develop. The court determined that 51.5 of the 59 acres of plaintiff's land were located under the mean high water mark, and were, therefore, subject to the jurisdiction of the state of Louisiana, which requires a special permit for development on tidal land. At the time of the alleged taking, the plaintiff possessed no such permit, so it could not legally develop the land it owned. In addition, the ownership of several more acres was in question. Given these factors, the court held that it did not need to discuss the takings claim in detail. The plaintiffs were denied compensation.

Cases Settled Before a Final Determination Was Rendered

The 1992 case of *Beure-Co. v. United States*[110] was settled after the government and the plaintiff reached a settlement agreement following denial of a government motion to dismiss the suit. Under the terms of the settlement, the government agreed to pay the plaintiff a total of $761,818: $425,000 in just compensation, $236,818 in interest, and $100,000 for the plaintiff's lawyers' fees.

Beure-Co. arose after the plaintiff was denied two Section 404 permits to fill a tract of land containing a calcareous fen. Such fens are classified by the Corps as "important wetlands," and applications for permits involving these types of wetlands are subject to a high level of scrutiny.

During the permit process, the Army Corps indicated to the plaintiff that chances of winning approval would increase if the plaintiff reduced the scope of its development plans from all 13 acres that it owned to 9.75 acres. Beure-Co. accepted this advice, submitting a permit application for the lesser number of acres.

The Army Corps denied the plaintiff's application to fill the 9.75 acres, based on its determination that the project's benefits were outweighed by its likely detriments. The plaintiff then applied to develop the 3.25 acres not included in its initial application. This application was likewise denied, based on the fact that the plaintiff did not have the necessary state authorization for the project.

Following the second rejection of its permit application, the plaintiff sued in the Claims Court, alleging that the two permit denials, taken together, constituted a regulatory taking of all 13 acres of its property, resulting in the deprivation of all economically viable use of its land. This was the case, the plaintiff argued, because *any* development of the land necessitated filling the property, and the Army Corps would not permit such activity.

It was, however, unclear to the court whether the Corps' denial left the plaintiff with any profitable use for its land. The court found it was reasonable for the plaintiff to interpret the Corps' permit denials as indicative of the fact that no future approval would be forthcoming. However, even if the Corps' actions did not indicate that all future permit applications would be denied, the court said that the actual permit denials could "still have such far-reaching effect" that they could be considered a reviewable action by a court (thereby rejecting the government's claim of unripeness).[111]

Beure-Co. was a victory for the plaintiff and should be classified with those cases in which a final determination in favor of the plaintiff was reached. Denying Beure-Co. the right to develop its land forced the company alone to provide society at large with a precious resource, a rare fen. In cases where a private individual, or legal entity, is forced to provide such a benefit, costs should, in all fairness, be borne by society as large, not by a single landowner. The *Beure-Co.* settlement represents a more equitable and efficient allocation of resources.

Cases Where a Compensable Taking Was Found

In the 1990 case of *Florida Rock Industries, Inc. v. United States*,[112] the plaintiff sought compensation from the federal government following denial of its Section 404 permit. The plaintiff was a commercial producer of limestone that owned 1,560 acres of wetlands in Dade County, Florida. Florida Rock purchased this tract of land expecting to mine a large limestone deposit found on the property. Denial of the permit rendered Florida Rock unable to develop this resource, thereby greatly reducing the value of the property.

In 1972, when the plaintiff purchased its property, it secured all permits necessary to mine the underground mineral deposits. As a result of a weak construction market, the plaintiff did not develop the limestone mine immediately, but waited until 1978 (after the passage of the Clean Water Act and its 1977 amendments) to mine the property. In 1978, the plaintiff sought approval from the Army Corps to mine its land. The Corps determined that the plaintiff's proposed mining activities would harm the wetlands by creating a public nuisance.

In its holding, the Claims Court rejected the government's public nuisance argument. The court noted that ongoing mining operations existed in the same area, and were not subject to public nuisance charges. Indeed, the court pointed out that if the plaintiff had applied for its dredge and fill permit before enactment of the 1977 amendments to the Clean Water Act, the likely result would have been approval for the permit and a grandfathering of the mining activities.[113]

Importantly, the government provided little in the way of concrete evidence to prove its claim that mining the Florida Rock property would ravage wetlands or contaminate a local aquifer. After visually inspecting the Florida Rock property, the court held that the government failed to prove that the proposed mining operation would damage either the wetlands or the underlying aquifer. Based on this finding, the court held that the government's denial of a Section

404 permit "took" the value of the limestone from the plaintiff. The court awarded Florida Rock a total of $3,616,339 in compensation and costs.[114]

In a companion case to *Florida Rock*, *Loveladies Harbor, Inc. v. United States*, the Claims Court once again found for the plaintiff and held the federal government liable for a compensable taking of private property.[115] The plaintiff in *Loveladies Harbor* was a residential property developer. In 1956, Loveladies purchased 250 acres of undeveloped land in coastal New Jersey. Some of this property was wetlands. Between the date of its purchase and the date on which its complaint was filed, April 14, 1983, Loveladies filled in and developed 199 of its 250 acres. Although Loveladies received state permission to fill and develop 11 of its remaining 51 undeveloped acres, federal permits to develop this land were steadfastly denied.[116] The plaintiff sued the government, contending that denial of a Section 404 permit for these 11 acres was a compensable taking of private property.

The Claims Court focused on the plaintiff's intended use of its property. Loveladies purchased its land so that it could build a housing development. Therefore, the plaintiff had investment-backed expectations for the property. By denying a Section 404 permit the Army Corps forced Loveladies to turn its remaining 51 acres into a natural preserve. This government action took from the plaintiff the value it could have received for the property in a developed state, approximately $200,000 per acre.

In *Loveladies*, the Claims Court was less concerned with the issue of a causal connection between the government's denial of a Section 404 permit and the proposed use of the plaintiff's property. In *Florida Rock*, the Corps rejected a permit based on proposed mining activities, presumably because the mining itself would harm the integrity of the physical environment. In *Loveladies*, on the other hand, it was not the development per se that caused the Corps to reject the permit. Rather, the Corps' primary concern was with the protection of wetlands qua wetlands. To the court, it seemed that the Corps' primary concern was not with possible pollution, but was instead with preserving an ecosystem that the Corps considered valuable. The court did not question the government's power to regulate land use for such purposes; it did, however, deny the government's power to force private landowners to bear the full costs of such regulation.

Again, the government argued that compensation was not due because Loveladies was not robbed of all economically viable uses for its undeveloped 51 acres. The government suggested that the remaining acreage could be used for birdwatching or hunting.[117] The court was unimpressed by this argument, focusing instead on the fact that the government dramatically reduced the value of the plaintiff's property by restricting its ability to develop its land as it had planned. In the court's view, the government seized Loveladies' property for a public use and was under a constitutional obligation to pay just compensation for this taking. The court awarded the plaintiff $2,658,000.

The final case in which the Claims Court found a taking is *Formanek v. United States* (1989).[118] The plaintiffs here were denied a Section 404 permit to fill 112 acres of land they owned in Savage, Minnesota (approximately 90 percent of which was classified as wetlands),[119] after the District Engineer determined the development would be contrary to the public interest. The government argued that the claim was not ripe for judicial review.

The plaintiffs purchased their land in 1959, well before state and federal permit requirements existed. The property was part of larger tract of land known as the Savage Fen, "a rare, ecologically significant calcareous fen plant community."[120] This land had, nonetheless, been zoned for industrial use since 1962. Between 1983 and 1985, the Army Corps changed the requirement for obtaining dredge and fill permits in this area, creating a significantly more restrictive atmosphere for development. In October 1985, plaintiffs filed for a Section 404 individual permit to place fill material on their property so that an access road could be built.

Under its Public Interest Review standard, the Army Corps denied the Formaneks' a Section 404 permit. Their property contained 11 acres of "important wetlands," so a higher level of scrutiny applied to their permit application. This higher level of scrutiny required the Corps to deny the permit if the detriments that might result from filling or dredging the land would equal or exceed the benefits of such action.[121] The Corps also determined that a practicable alternative existed to this proposed development scheme.

The government's claim of unripeness rested on its allegation that (1) all possible uses of the plaintiff's property had not been enjoined and (2) only 11 of the 112 acres of plaintiff's property were subject to the permit denial.[122] Additionally, the government argued that it had not rendered a final determination on all of the plaintiff's property, adding weight to the argument that the claim was not ripe for judicial review. The ripeness defense was rejected by the Claims Court.

The court also rejected the government's argument that denial of the Formaneks' application did not necessarily imply that all future permit applications, and hence development, would be denied. The Formaneks responded that the Corps clearly indicated to them that their land could only be used as a nature preserve; that it must be maintained in its "undeveloped, natural condition."[123] Such a factual allegation, which if true would provide a clear basis for a Fifth Amendment takings claim, also argued strongly in favor of finding the case ripe for review.

In addition to its request to dismiss the case based on unripeness, the government argued that the case should be dismissed because the permit denial affected only a small percentage of the plaintiff's property. The government insisted that is was "speculative" for the plaintiffs to assert that they would be denied all viable economic use of the remainder of their land.[124]

The court rejected this argument also, noting that the plaintiff's permit application included a "rough plan" calling for a comprehensive development of its 112 acres, not merely for the laying of an access road. In denying the permit, the Corps gave the Formaneks "no encouragement regarding any commercial use of their property."[125] The Formaneks could reasonably assume that all development of their property would be disallowed. Thus, the government's attempt to limit the takings claim to 11 acres was rejected.

Unlike *Deltona*, the 12 upland acres of the Formaneks' land were completely surrounded by wetlands. The court, however, had previously determined that permission to engage in any development (i.e., installing access roads to the uplands) was unlikely.[126] Thus, in the court's determination this case was analogous to *Loveladies*, where a similarly isolated upland was considered "taken" by the court. Quoting the *Loveladies* opinion, the *Formanek* court said: "A taking of such property [an isolated wetland] is found where the government's regulations imposed on the surrounding wetlands have cut off all the routes of access to the property or have cut off all the property's routes of access which remain."[127]

Finally, the government argued that because the Formaneks had purchase offers, the case had to be dismissed because an economically viable use of the land remained, (i.e., it could be sold). This meant, the government contended, that the plaintiffs failed to prove that their property had been stripped of all economically viable use.[128] However, the two possible purchasers of the land were the Nature Conservancy and the Minnesota Department of Natural Resources, both of whom would maintain the land as a natural preserve. This land use was significantly different from the industrial use for which the land was zoned. The Corps' action significantly diminished the value of the Formaneks' land and left them with only a few possible purchasers. In such a situation, the existence of possible buyers does not refute the claim of a regulatory taking.[129]

Comparing the value of the plaintiff's property before the Section 404 permit was denied and after denial, it was clear to the court that the Formaneks were denied all economically viable use of their property. The court agreed with the Formaneks' claim that they were forced to provide a public benefit, a calcareous fen. In such cases, government regulations were a taking of property for which compensation is due.

The cases discussed above, *Florida Rock*, *Loveladies*, and *Formanek*, represent an important stage in the evolution of the takings doctrine in the Claims Court. Although the language of *Florida Rock* speaks of a complete taking of property, the case suggests a willingness of the Claims Court to compensate property owners for partial regulatory takings. In *Loveladies*, the court shows greater flexibility in the way it defines the "whole" of a parcel of land. Finally, in *Formanek* the court recognizes that when property owners are forced by government to provide a public benefit, the government must pay compensation for its taking. (Signally a return to the kind of reasoning expressed in *United States v. Armstrong, supra* page 120.) Taken together, these cases point to an important shift in takings jurisprudence toward a greater concern with the rights of property owners and with limiting the excesses of government regulation.

What Can We Learn from the Claims Court Cases?

A general review of Claims Court takings decisions reveals a common logical thread. This court has been, throughout its dealings with Section 404 takings claims, mindful of the takings doctrines of the Supreme Court. As the takings doctrine has evolved at the Supreme Court, so too has it evolved at the Claims Court. Note that all of the cases in which a final determination of compensable takings was found were decided *after* the landmark 1987 Supreme Court term during which *First English Evangelical Lutheran* and *Nollan*[30] were decided.

The court's jurisprudence may properly be interpreted as a direct response to the somewhat greater deference being paid by the Supreme Court to property rights. While it is arguable that the Claims Court has, since 1987, been more sympathetic than the Supreme Court to property rights cases, it is a mischaracterization to argue that the court has taken a jurisprudential wrong turn; it has merely followed the lead of its superior.

The common thread running through recent Claims Court takings jurisprudence is this: in cases where *all*, or practically speaking all, viable economic use of property is removed as a result of a Section 404 permit denial, the court is most likely to find a compensable taking. In contrast, in cases where some nonminimal economic use of land remains after a permit denial, the court will most likely dismiss the case, finding no compensable taking. *Florida Rock, Loveladies*, and *Formanek* fit into this broad classification. Essentially, a partial taking worked a near total diminishment of property value in all three cases.

The approach of the Claims Court tracks very nicely with the Supreme Court approach to takings as expressed in the 1992 *Lucas* decision. (For more detail, see Chapter 3 by Rinehart and Pompe.) Rather than acting like a rebel and instigating a property rights revolution in takings jurisprudence, the Claims Court is more accurately seen as a faithful, if somewhat more flexible, interpreter of the Supreme Court's guidelines.

Additionally, it is also possible to discern, between the lines, a concern at the Claims Court with equitable issues. Thus, plaintiffs who come to the court with "unclean hands," who knew when they bought property that Section 404 permits would be needed, or who engaged in willful violations of Army Corps cease and desist orders (see, for example, *Ciampitti, supra* pages 121-22), are less likely to succeed before the court. Concomitantly, plaintiffs who come with "clean hands," who purchased property before the 1972 Clean Water Act and its

Section 404 provisions took effect, who did not know they needed a federal permit to develop their land, and who attempted to work with the Corps to reach a mutually satisfactory solution to the problems presented by federal wetlands regulation, are more likely to receive compensation from the court for a permit denial (*Florida Rock* is a good example).

It seems that the Claims Court is primarily concerned with cases where a severe economic hardship is worked by a permit denial. If such a hardship case is brought by a well-intentioned plaintiff, the court will most likely weigh the equities of the case in favor of that plaintiff and not lay the burdens of the government's regulatory policy squarely on the back of the plaintiff. Importantly, the Claims Court can be sympathetic to the argument that the provision of a public benefit in the form of undeveloped, natural wetlands, by a private landowner acts as a regulatory taking deserving of compensation (*Formanek*). Given the state of takings jurisprudence during the past sixty years, the recent Claims Court approach to takings claims represents a limited victory for property owners and property rights.

The question of whether the Supreme Court, and therefore the Claims Court, is correct in its takings analysis is an altogether different one, and one that may only fleetingly be addressed here. If wetlands owners correctly assert that their land is a valuable resource, one that if left undeveloped provides significant benefits to society at large, then it seems highly problematic that owners denied a Section 404 permit are not compensated under the Fifth Amendment. The Supreme Court has stated, quite clearly, that private property owners who are forced by the government to provide society with a benefit must be compensated (*Armstrong v. United States*). Such an outcome is not only fair, it is efficient. Yet this line of reasoning is, with the exception of the Formanek case, absent in Section 404 cases. Perhaps wetlands owners are not making the case of public benefit as strongly as they should. A large body of scientific evidence exists to support the proposition that wetlands are extremely valuable resources. Property owners need to stress this element in takings cases they bring against the federal government.

A Reply to Some Critics

Critics argue that the Claims Court has seriously erred in finding that compensable takings occurred in *Loveladies*, *Florida Rock*, and *Formanek*.[131] These decisions are wrong, according to such critics, because the Claims Court misapplied Supreme Court takings jurisprudence. One critic accuses the court of having "an undue bias towards landowners in its consideration of a section 404 permits denial's economic impact upon the plaintiff's property."[132] This allegation would certainly be news to the twelve landowners who were denied compensation by the court after the Corps rejected their Section 404 permit application. (In only three cases has the court found a compensable takings.)

This same author suggests that in Section 404 cases there should be a presumption *against* development in order to "significantly counterbalance the private claimant's interest in profiting from its regulated property."[133] But since when has an interest in making a profit from one's own land been so ignoble that a court must adopt a presumption against the activity? The very justification of private property (an institution much favored by America's founders) is that private ownership gives owners proper incentives to use their resources wisely. (Bureaucrats *do not* have these same incentives.) The argument of Claims Court critics assumes that wetlands owners do not properly internalize the value of their resource and, therefore, the government should step in and stop the misuse of wetlands. However, even assuming that this is so, it is not an argument against compensating wetlands owners who are denied development permits.

Adoption of a presumption against development will lead to inefficient resource use. Wetlands will become less valuable and their price will fall. Thus, some wetlands that should be developed will remain undeveloped because of the consequent legal risks. Further, these critics betray an unfortunate naivete. The reason the United States can afford the luxury of environmental protection is precisely because individuals have long enjoyed private property rights protection, thereby enabling each to make land-use and investment decisions disciplined by the market. Creating a presumption of the kind advocated above sneaks central planning and command-and-control oversight by government in through the back door.

Other critics are equally disdainful of the Claims Court's jurisprudence. For example, the Florida Rock decision, in which the court undertook a vigorous defense of property rights, is characterized in the following way:

> the court lapsed into the wooden dichotomy of distinguishing between regulation that secures a public benefit from that which prevents a public harm. Worse, the court classified preserving the wetlands at issue as falling into the former category.[134]

Labeling the court's attempt to distinguish between police-power actions requiring government compensation and those that do not as "wooden" is no genuine criticism of the court. Rather, drawing such distinctions is the court's constitutional duty. In order for the Fifth Amendment to have any meaning, courts *must* distinguish between compensable and noncompensable regulations. If such distinctions were not drawn, one of two outcomes would obtain: (1) all regulation would result in compensation (as Justice Holmes noted, an untenable proposition), or (2) all regulation would be declared "police-power actions" and would result in no compensation ever for government takings (equally untenable). To give the Fifth Amendment meaning, courts must decide when the government has to pay for property it takes. Using the public benefit/public harm dichotomy is a perfectly valid means of reaching this determination.

Beyond this, the "wooden" argument has other serious flaws. First, the proponents of this argument recognize that undeveloped wetlands *do* confer public benefits.[135] It is logically inconsistent to argue that an undeveloped resource confers public benefits, but that forcing owners of the resource to cede all future development rights does not create a public benefit. Either a thing is a benefit or it is not. If undeveloped wetlands are valuable, then forced provision of the resource by its owners gives society something of value for which owners should be compensated.[136] More disturbing, however, is the complete disregard for property rights exhibited by such critics. As an example, Blumm and Zaleha state that:

> denials of 404 permits do not represent seizures of property interests or attempts to secure public benefits without payment. Instead, they are the product of a broad-based set of comprehensive environmental guidelines designed to prevent public harms associated with wetlands losses.

This statement is false on its face. Prohibiting property owners from building on or otherwise developing their property does indeed represent a seizure of a traditional property right. The fact that the property rights at issue are seized by means of "comprehensive environmental guidelines" doesn't make such seizures any less of a taking. Merely relabeling seizure as avoidance of "public harms" does not change the fact that one of the sticks in the bundle of traditional property rights *has* been taken. Such recharacterization of property rights represents an attempt to undermine the very meaning of the Fifth Amendment.

As a final point, we should ask, why is it "too late in the day"[137] to recognize those rights that property owners have traditionally held under the common law of property? Does the average citizen really believe that if government makes a determination about how that citizen may and may not use her land, this decision outweighs her constitutional and common-law rights? If not, don't the arguments of those who wish to deny takings claims smack of elitism and paternalism? Critics of the Claims Courts' takings jurisprudence are all too ready to trade away Fifth Amendment protections for cheap wetlands. But they should beware. Trading away constitutional liberties is a dangerous path to tread.

4. Criminal Actions Involving Wetlands Protection

Most wetlands enforcement efforts by the Army Corps and the EPA involve civil prosecutions. However, over the past fifteen years the Corps, the EPA, and the Department of Justice have prosecuted a handful of criminal cases.

Some of these have been highly publicized. The criminal enforcement of environmental laws emerged after statutory deadlines for achieving compliance with the Clean Water Act and the Clean Air Act took effect in 1977.[138] One should not conclude, however, that criminal prosecutions for violations of environmental rules were previously unknown. For example, long before there were environmental statutes, criminal charges could be brought at common law in cases involving public nuisances.[139] Additionally, under the Rivers and Harbors Act of 1899, violations of Section 13, the Refuse Act, could result in criminal charges.

Criminal sanctioning mechanisms exist under the Clean Water Act and may be applied to persons who violate the permit process under Section 404. Sanctions were strengthened in the 1977 amendments to the Act, which authorized additional penalties for persons who illegally tamper with materials, falsify documents, or make false statements concerning their activities.[140] Persons who knowingly endanger others are subject to strict penalties. Criminal violations under Section 404 are based on a finding of knowing or negligent discharge of a pollutant into the waters of the United States without, or in violation of the terms of, a permit. Under the knowledge standard, persons may only be convicted of criminal charges if they *knowingly* engaged in proscribed behavior.[141]

A conviction for discharging into a wetlands may result in a felony conviction of no more than three years in prison and/or a fine of not less than $5,000 and not more than $50,000 per day of violation.[142] A conviction for negligently discharging will result in a misdemeanor charge, subject to up to one year in prison and/or fines of not less than $2,500 and not more than $25,000 per day of violation. In both cases (knowing or negligent discharge) repeat offenses garner more severe punishments.

As noted above, only a small number of criminal prosecutions involving Section 404 have occurred. Unlike civil proceedings, there is no special court to which prosecutors must bring these cases. Rather, they are initially filed at a federal district court and may be appealed through the federal court system. A brief review of several of these cases follows.

Cases Involving Individuals

In the first Section 404 criminal case, *United States v. Holland* (1984),[143] the owner of a Florida construction company pled guilty to eight counts of illegally filling and dredging wetlands in violation of the Clean Water Act, as well as to three counts under the 1899 Rivers and Harbors Act for illegally building piers and bulkheads. As part of his plea agreement, the defendant agreed to undertake large-scale restoration work in exchange for a suspended sentence and probation. In 1988, the defendant's suspended sentence and probation were revoked when it was discovered that he had illegally destroyed a mangrove swamp and illegally constructed docks and bulkheads. Mr. Holland was sentenced in 1988 to six months in prison, fined $10,000, and forbidden to engage in the construction business until 1990.

In *United States v. Bieri* (1987),[144] an independent contractor was given a ninety-day prison sentence (all but one week of which was suspended), two years' probation, and a $500 fine for filling wetlands without a Section 404 permit. Mr. Bieri received warnings from the Army Corps that he needed a Section 404 permit to fill his wetlands. Despite these warnings, Bieri failed to obtain the necessary permits and, additionally, placed other fill materials on wetlands he had previously been ordered to restore.

In *United States v. Mills* (1988),[145] the government charged a father and son who owned property in Florida with knowingly filling wetlands without a Section 404 permit. The defendants were charged with unlawfully excavating a canal in the East Bay, a navigable water of the United States, a violation of Sections 10 and 12 of the 1899 Rivers and Harbors Act. They were charged with five counts of knowingly discharging pollutants into the waters of the United States by filling their wetlands property adjacent to the East Bay. This despite the fact that the men had received state permission to place fill on their land. The filling activity consisted of dumping sand on a quarter-acre lot on which the defendants' intended to build a home.

The EPA claims that the case against the Mills was pursued because "Mills was adamant he wanted to take on [federal wetlands officials] about the violation."[146] In other words, Mills knew, when he purchased his land, that it was a wetlands subject to a cease and desist order, and he wanted to challenge this previous order. Other versions of this story suggest that the Mills were subjected to federal prosecution because they were "uppity," something federal regulatory officials may not like.[147]

Each defendant was sentenced to twenty-one months in prison with one year's probation, a $5,000 fine, and special assessments. Additionally, the defendants were required to restore those wetlands they filled.

In the 1990 case of *United States v. Jones*,[148] the defendant, Paul Tudor Jones —an investment banker who purchased real estate in Maryland in the hopes of creating a private wildlife preserve—was charged with negligently filling wetlands in violation of the Clean Water Act. The defendant pled guilty to the misdemeanor charge under a plea arrangement (thus avoiding trial) and was sentenced to eighteen months' probation, $1 million in fines, and $1 million in restitution. This $2 million fine represents the largest fine ever paid by a single individual for an environmental crime.[149] The sum paid in fines represented a "donation" to a wildlife refuge. The other $1 million was earmarked for a wetlands restoration project involving 2,500 of the defendant's 3,200 acres. In addition, the defendant agreed to grant the federal government a conservation easement over his property, limiting all future use and development of the restored 2,500 acres.

In the much publicized companion case to *United States v. Jones, United States v. Ellen*,[150] William Ellen, Jones's project manager, was charged with five felony counts of knowingly filling wetlands. Mr. Jones hired Ellen in 1986 to help him create a natural preserve on his Dorchester Country, Maryland, property. Before working for Jones, Ellen had been employed for approximately twenty years as an environmental consultant in Virginia and Maryland, and therefore had extensive experience with the array of local, state, and federal permits required to develop property.

Despite his expertise, Ellen ran into significant legal trouble with the Jones property, apparently because part of the land was "heavily forested areas that had been subject to the most prolonged drought in Maryland's history."[151] Thus Ellen, who was unfamiliar with identifying nontidal wetlands, had difficulty recognizing what the Army Corps determined were in fact wetlands. It was not only Ellen who had trouble identifying the "wetlands." State officials responsible for mapping Jones's land also failed to identify much of the property as wetlands. Additionally, the Soil Conservation Service identified the land Ellen was working on as uplands not subject to federal wetlands regulations.[152] When the Army Corps arrived on the Jones farm to investigate the construction activity, it determined that much of the land (even bone-dry land) should be classified as wetlands. Ellen made the mistake of challenging this determination, questioning the wisdom of the Army Corps/EPA classification, and then allowing his crews to dump two truckloads of dirt on the site before a final determination was reached concerning the status of the land.[153]

It is ironic that Ellen's goal for Tudor Farm was "to create a duck haven on the 3,000-acre tract by building large ponds and improving wildlife habitat."[154] Over the course of the ill-fated project's life, Ellen *created* approximately 45 acres of wetlands. The government never determined the exact number of wetlands Ellen filled, but one former Army Corps official concluded that nine acres of nontidal wetlands were filled.[155] Despite Ellen's intentions to create a wetlands haven for wildlife, his conflict with the Army Corps and EPA over what constitutes a wetland resulted in a jail sentence. Interestingly, in an interview on a national news program, an Army Corps official familiar with Ellen's case said: "It's a matter of a person flaunting the federal government. Forget the wetlands issue."[156]

Ellen pled "not guilty" to all counts. He stood trial before a jury and was sentenced to six months in prison, one year of supervised release, which included four months of home detention, $250 in special assessment, and sixty hours of community service.

A much discussed case from 1991, *United States v. Pozsgai*,[157] involved a defendant who filled a 14-acre tract of land he owned in Pennsylvania. When Mr. Pozsgai purchased his land in 1987, he was told by engineering consultants that the property qualified as wetlands under federal regulations and so would be subject to the provisions of Section 404.

Pozsgai was charged with forty-one counts, under the Clean Water Act, of knowingly filling wetlands without a permit. The defendant answered the charges by noting that his land had formerly been a dump, and his actions revolved around cleaning this old dump, activities that acted to improve rather than destroy the property. This line of argument was rejected. The court sentenced Pozsgai, who had received numerous warnings from the Army Corps about the need to obtain a federal permit before filling his property, and who was subject to a cease and desist order from the Corps, to three years in prison for each count against him (sentences running concurrently), one $200,000 fine, and one special $2,000 fine for the Crime Victim's Fund. This prison sentence is the longest jail term ever for an environmental crime. Additionally, he was ordered to restore the wetlands destroyed through his actions. Pozsgai's conviction was upheld by the 3rd Circuit. A motion by Pozsgai to reduce or correct his sentence was denied by the District Court for the Eastern District of Pennsylvania in 1991.[158]

An interesting addendum to this case appeared in 1990. In an article in *Legal Times*, the Justice Department was quoted as admitting that some of its legal work in the Pozsgai case was "shoddy."[159] It appears that the prosecutor who tried the case "misrepresented key evidence . . . against Pozsgai."[160] The problem centered on whether Pozsgai's property was subject to federal protection under the Clean Water Act. Although the government claimed the property was an adjacent wetland, it never presented proof of this claim. Pozsgai hoped this new evidence of prosecutorial foul-up might help his chances on appeal, but his convictions were allowed to stand.

The Pozsgai case highlights the opposing interests in the wetlands debate. Pozsgai became a kind of hero to property rights advocates, a victim of the draconian regulatory state. For the environmental lobby, Pozsgai was evil incarnate, bent on wanton destruction. The truth, no doubt, lies somewhere in between. But note what a senior attorney at the Natural Resources Defense Council said in 1992 regarding the case: "Filling in wetlands is not a victimless crime. They provide critical flood protection for adjacent property owners. You fill in your wetland at their *[sic]* peril."[161] Putting aside the question of whether Pozsgai recklessly disregarded the law, this statement points out the inherently illogical position of the government and the environmental lobby: they admit that wetlands are extremely valuable resources (especially for adjacent property owners) that must be protected by the criminal justice system, but yet, wetlands are not so valuable that the government should pay just compensation for them in takings cases. It can't work both ways.

Cases Involving Commercial Developers

A series of cases involving criminal convictions under Section 404 involve commercial developers. In *United States v. Marathon Development Corp.* (1988),[162] Marathon Development Corporation attempted to construct a shopping mall on wetlands without obtaining the proper federal permits. The development site contained over 20 acres of federally protected wetlands. In February 1986, the corporation was notified by the Army Corps that it would need a permit to dredge or fill this land. Marathon did not obtain a permit, and between June and September 1986 the corporation bulldozed in excess of five acres of wetlands.[163]

At trial, the defendants (both the president of the corporation and the corporation itself) conditionally pled guilty to a single charge of failing to obtain a Section 404 permit as needed. The president of the corporation was sentenced to a six month's suspended sentence, one year of probation, and a fine of $10,000. The company received a $100,000 fine. The case was appealed and the 3rd Circuit had to decide an issue left open at the trial level: were the defendants' actions exempt from Army Corps jurisdiction as a result of the nationwide permitting program? The corporation and its president argued that the Army Corps did not have jurisdiction over their actions because the land they bulldozed was a "headwater" subject to the provisions of the nationwide general permitting system.[164] The court rejected this argument, finding that the nationwide permitting program was not in force in Massachusetts at the time of the defendants' activities, so they could not claim an exemption from the Section 404 individual permit process.

In *United States v. Bill L. Walters Co.* (1989),[165] a development firm was charged with violating the Clean Water Act by illegally filling three acres of wetlands without a permit. The company was the developer of a large shopping mall in Denver. Bill L. Walters Co. pled guilty to a single count of willfully discharging fill materials into a wetland without a permit, and was fined $15,000, plus a small special assessment.

In *United States v. Phil Lambert, Inc.* (1990),[166] a development company operating out of Colebrook, New Hampshire, and its president, were accused of illegally filling seven acres of wetlands it owned. Both were also charged with illegally discharging pollutants into a stream and into adjacent wetlands. Both the company and its president pled guilty. The president was sentenced to two years in prison and two years of probation. This prison sentence was suspended, conditioned on his restoration of the filled area. The company was fined $100,000 (used to restore the wetlands) and also placed on two years' probation. Finally, the company agreed to give the state of New Hampshire five acres of virgin property as "restitution."

Also in 1989, the Western District Court of Missouri found a developer guilty of illegally bulldozing and filling wetlands without a permit. In *United*

States v. Stephen L. Johnson & Country Estates Inc.,[167] the defendant argued that he engaged in the bulldozing and filling activity so that he could provide sewer services to mobile home owners living in a trailer park owned by his company. This case was the first wetlands prosecution conducted under the 1992 Federal Sentencing Guidelines. The plaintiff was found guilty and sentenced to five months in prison, one year of supervised release from prison which included five months in a halfway house, as well as a $2,500 fine.

In *United States v. Garcia International* (1992),[168] the defendant pled guilty to a misdemeanor charge of illegally filling a wetland in order to build a parking lot. As part of the plea agreement, the defendant agreed to restore the property to its former condition and to give the state a conservation easement, in perpetuity, to its property.

The criminal cases brought under Section 404 raise interesting questions. Should private property owners be subject to criminal sanctions for filling or dredging *their* land? Should the Army Corps have the power to initiate such prosecutions? Both questions should be answered in the negative. Civil sanctions alone should be the tool government uses to "punish" those property owners who have the misfortune to want to develop their land.

In Section 404 cases, the property owners seek only to use their land in a productive fashion. Twenty years ago they would have been applauded; today their property is taken, and they are ostracized, fined, and jailed. Property owners wishing to develop wetlands should not be compared to persons who assault, maim, or kill others, or who wantonly destroy the property *of others*. Under the law, it is no crime to destroy what you own. Why are the standards different when it comes to wetlands? The answer, of course, is that wetlands have been assigned a higher status than ordinary property. In recent years they have been taken without compensation. The issue of criminal sanctions and much of the wetlands controversy would be resolved if government paid compensation to property owners when sensitive land is desired for public purposes.

5. Policy Implications and Final Thoughts

The scope of the Section 404 program has expanded dramatically since its inception in 1972. The program has engendered much controversy and will continue to do so as Army Corps jurisdiction spreads across "waters" with a questionable connection to interstate commerce. But while the purpose of Section 404 may be praiseworthy, the means adopted for achieving its ends are flawed.

The major problem with the current system of federal wetlands protection is not, as some commentators argue, that wetlands are being underprotected. Rather, it is that wetlands are being overprotected in inefficient and inequitable ways. The Section 404 program too often leads to partial or complete takings of private property for which the government, and therefore society at large, pays too little. Private landowners are forced to bear the costs of providing the public with valuable water-filtration systems, flood-protection zones, nature preserves, and aesthetically pleasing landscapes. Private property rights are taken for public purposes without compensation.

A first suggestion for resolving these inequities is to (1) return to a system that recognizes the value of a property rights system and (2) fund further purchases of private wetlands out of the general revenue. Recognition of property rights forces government to recognize opportunity costs, which in turn addresses the inefficiencies created by the current system. To say that taxpayers cannot afford to pay for wetlands protection is to argue that the value of wetlands has been overstated. When scarce tax dollars are allocated to wetlands purchases, agencies charged with protection of wetlands will be far more efficient when embarking on regulatory actions.

Adopting market discipline is not far-fetched. Indeed, the proposal could be implemented by expanding the scope of the current Wetlands Reserve Program, operated by the U.S. Department of Agriculture. This program pays farmers to restore agricultural land to wetlands and to protect the restored property. Crippled by insufficient funding, the program has met with limited success. In part, this might be explained by bureaucratic red tape. However, the price paid to farmers is also part of the problem. If farmers receive more money from the sale of crops, or if they receive greater federal subsidies for leaving land fallow than they do from the wetlands program, they will continue their current practices. The price paid for wetlands conservation must be competitive.

The Wetlands Reserve Program could be expanded to include all wetlands owners. A property owner facing a Section 404 permit denial could apply for federal funds to preserve her wetlands. If the government pays competitive prices to ensure dedication, wetlands owners will take advantage of the program. Indeed, in many cases the program would offer an attractive alternative for property owners who otherwise face costly, time-consuming litigation against the government, or who might be left with no legal recourse owing to a lack of funds.

Going further, criminal enforcement activities under Section 404 should be eliminated. Consider what the response would have been twenty years ago if someone had suggested that a neighbor be thrown in jail for cleaning up a dumpsite on his property. The suggestion would most likely have been laughed off as foolish at best, or feared as a menacing threat to personal liberty. Yet, this is the system under which we currently live. People who repeatedly violate Army Corps or EPA warnings about illegally dredging or filling their wetlands should be subject to civil fines, perhaps civil contempt of court charges, but no more.

During the past three decades, U.S. citizens have become ever more concerned with preserving the integrity of the environment. Efforts to protect the physical environment have led to a massive but needless expansion of federal regulatory interference with the rights of individuals and their property. Much personal liberty has been lost to this cause. Indeed, we might view our actions as a kind of Hobbesian exchange: environmental protection for personal freedom. One critic of the current command-and-control approach to environmental protection has stated: "We are in danger of strangling ourselves on government regulation and choking out the flame of that very right (property rights) which is at the heart of our system of liberties."[169]

Loss of freedom goes hand-in-hand with loss of property rights. Unfortunately, in the case of wetlands, the people most subject to Leviathan's burdens, property owners, have little voice in crafting the terms of the contract. A policy determination must be made concerning the future protection of wetlands. Will these resources be protected by a "steadily increasing stringency [in] the section 404 permit program" (as the environmental lobby suggests), or will traditional private property rights provide the basis for such protection? This chapter argues that the current system, which subjects wetlands owners to unfair burdens, is inequitable as well as economically inefficient. Wetlands owners should not be forced to bear disproportionate burdens of wetlands protection. Their property should not be subject to partial or complete regulatory taking without just compensation. They should not be sent to jail or face enormous fines because they choose to use their land in productive manners. Property rights enforcement will protect environmental rights just as surely as it will protect the rights of individuals to use property in beneficial ways. It is time to protect wetlands and other environmental assets by a return to the rule of law, based on common law property rules and contracts, and to abandon the rule of politics with its responsiveness to pressures by special interest groups.

Notes

1. A wetlands is defined by the government as "those areas that are inundated or saturated by surface or ground water at a frequency and duration sufficient to support and that under normal circumstances do support a prevalence of vegetation typically adapted for life in saturated soil conditions. Wetlands generally include swamps, marshes, bogs, and similar areas." See 33 C.F.R. 328.3 (b) (1993). Privately owned wetlands currently amount to 75 percent of the total number of wetlands in the U.S. See "Government, Keep Out," *The Economist*, July 2, 1994 at 26.

2. 33 U.S.C. §1251 et. seq. (1988).

3. 33 U.S.C. §1344 (1988).

4. See H.R. Rep. No. 92-911, 92d. Cong., 2d Sess. (1972)(March 11, 1972) reprinted in *Legal Compilation*, Supp. 1, vol. 1, Water (1973).

5. See S. Rep. No. 414, 92d Cong., 2d. Sess. 144 (1972), reprinted in 1972 U.S.C.C.A.N. 3668, 3882, discussing Congress's intention that "waters of the United States" be defined broadly. See also, *Hoffman Homes, Inc. v. EPA*, (7th Cir. 1992), rejecting overly broad jurisdictional claims by the EPA and the Army Corps.

6. A recent example of this sentiment is found in the October 1991 issue of *South Carolina Lawyer*, where C. C. Harness III notes that "a growing consensus has developed that unbridled wetlands destruction must end and an era of protection and restoration must begin." Harness further notes that the unbridled destruction of wetlands is a function of the "utilitarian mentality [that] continues today, as evidenced by well-intentioned public and private efforts to alter wetlands for flood protection, urban development, agricultural production and other uses" 33 *South Carolina Lawyer* 3 (1991).

7. See, Al Gore, *Earth in the Balance* (1992), who equates the current environmental "struggle" to "an environmental holocaust without precedent," and who argues that environmental protection must become "the central organizing principle for civilization" (p. 269).

8. "Wetlands can be protected by government purchase, but in an era of fiscal restraint it is impractical to purchase more than a fraction of wetlands threatened by development. . . . Currently, regulation is the principal source of wetlands protection, and the chief regulatory program is a federal one, authorized by section 404 of the Clean Water Act" (Blumm and Zaleha, "Federal Wetlands Protection Under the Clean Water Act: Regulatory Ambivalence, Intergovernmental Tension, and a Call for Reform," 60 *U. Colo. L. Rev.* 695, 697-8 (1989)). The implication here its that while it is "impractical" for the government to purchase wetlands, it is wholly practical to regulate wetlands to the point of nonuse. And, in a way, this is exactly right: by shifting the burdens of wetlands preservation to the private property owner, the government saves itself millions of dollars.

9. The fact that wetlands provide significant benefits is not disputed. Among the commonly cited benefits provided by wetlands are habitat for various mammals and marsh birds; food sources for migratory birds; study and sanctuary areas; shields from wave action, erosion, and storm damage; storage areas for storms and flood waters; recharge areas for ground water; spawning grounds; and large, efficient natural water filtration plants. See Ablard and O'Neill, "Wetland Protection and Section 404 of the Federal Water Pollution Control Act Amendments of 1972: A Corps of Engineers Renaissance," 1 *Vt. L. Rev.* 51, 51-52 (1976); Bianucci and Goodenow, "The Impact of Section 404 of the Clean Water Act on Agricultural Land Use," 10 *UCLA J. Envt'l. L. & Pol'y.* 41 (1991); Tripp and Herz, "Wetland Preservation and Restoration: Changing Federal Priorities," 7 *Va. J. Nat'l Res. Law* 221, 221-22 (1988).

10. See Tripp and Herz, *supra* note 9 at 250, fn. 118: "Of course, the most protective step is for the federal government to purchase wetlands outright. Though an extremely important tool of preservation, government acquisition will never reach all the wetlands worth saving." If this argument is correct, why not let those groups that most value the resource purchase what they desire, rather than forcing private property owners to provide a public benefit without compensation?

11. Rose-Ackerman, "Regulatory Takings: Policy Analysis and Democratic Principles," in *Taking Property and Just Compensation*, 30-31, Nicholas Mercuro, ed. (1992).

12. Pollot, *Grand Theft and Petit Larceny: Property Rights in America,* 36 (1993).

13. Coyle, *Property Rights and the Constitution: Shaping Society Through Land Use Regulation* 214 (1993).

14. Ibid. at 228.

15. Act of March 16, 1802, ch. 9, §26, 2 Stat. 132, 137.

16. Act of May 10, 1824, ch. 48, s 1, 2 Stat. 66, 67 (providing the Corps with limited authority to make site-specific harbor improvements). The definition of the term "navigable waters of the United States" has evolved over time. The term originally applied to waters that were "navigable in fact." See 33 C.F.R. §209.120(d)(1) (1975) for the Army Corps' earlier restricted view of its jurisdiction. Currently, the term has a much broader meaning and includes "all bodies of water within the United States, regardless of navigability, including territorial seas." Harris, Marshall and Cavanaugh, 1 *Environmental Crimes* §2.87 (1992). "All bodies of water" includes such things as intrastate lakes, potholes, wet meadows, saltflats and wetlands. See 33 U.S.C. §1362 (7) (1988); 33 C.F.R. §328.3 (a)(3) (1993).

17. U.S. Constitution. art 1, §8, cl. 3.

18. *Gibbons v. Ogden,* 22 U.S. (9 Wheat.) 1 (1824).

19. 125 U.S. 1 (1888).

20. Rivers and Harbors Act of 1890, ch. 907, §10, 26 Stat. 426.

21. Rivers and Harbors Appropriation Act of 1899, ch. 425, 30 Stat. 1121 (codified as amended at 33 U.S.C. §§401, 403 (1988) (hereinafter, Rivers and Harbors Act).

22. Ibid.

23. 32 Cong. Rec. 2297 (1899).

24. Rivers and Harbor Act, *supra* note 21 at § 10.

25. Ablard and O'Neill, *supra* note 9 at 56. See also 33 C.F.R. §209.120 (e) (1) (i), (g) (11) (1975).

26. Ibid. at 51.

27. *United States v. Republic Steel Corp.,* 362 U.S. 482 (1960).

28. Compare, *United States v. Standard Oil,* 384 U.S. 224 (1966) (discharge of gasoline prohibited by § 13 of the Rivers and Harbors Act); Blumm and Zaleha, *supra* note 8 at 701.

29. 33 C.F.R. §290.120 (d) (11) (1969).

30. Memorandum of Agreement between Secretary of the army Stanley Resor and Secretary of the Interior Stewart Udall (July 13, 1967), reprinted in 33 Fed. Reg. 18,672-73 (1968).

31. 16 U.S.C. §661-66 (c) (1988).

32. 33 C.F.R. §320.4 (a) (1993).

33. See Ablard and O'Neill, *supra* note 9 at 57, n. 35.

34. 42 U.S.C. §4321 et. seq. (1988).

35. 33 U.S.C. §1251 et. seq. (1988).

36. Ibid. at §1251 (a).

37. Ibid. at §1344 (a).

38. Ibid. at §1362 (6).

39. 33 U.S.C. §1342 (1988).

40. 33 U.S.C. §1344 (c), (i) (1988).

41. Addison and Burns, "The Army Corps of Engineers and Nationwide Permit 26: Wetlands Protection or Swamp Reclamation?" 18 *Ecology L. Q.*, 619, 625 (1991). For a different explanation of the Army Corps' reluctance to accept a wider jurisdiction, relying on "early constitutional history," see Power, "The Fox in The Chicken Coop: The Regulatory Program of the U.S. Army Corps of Engineers," 63 *Va. L. Rev.* 503, 513 (1977).

42. 40 C.F.R. §104 et. seq. (1993).

43. 392 F.Supp 685 (D.D.C. 1975).

44. Ibid. at 686.

45. 33 C.F.R. §328.3 (a) (3) (1993).

46. Federal Water Pollution Control Act Amendment of 1977, Pub. L. No. 95-217, 91 Stat. 1566, codified as amended at 33 U.S.C. §§1251-1387 (1988). Note that some congressional opposition to expansion of the Section 404 program did exist. Senator Lloyd Bentsen of Texas, a state with a large agricultural sector, led the efforts to reduce the scope of the section (to no avail). 123 Cong. Rec. S26710-S26729, reprinted in 4 Senate Committee on the Environment and Public Works, A Legislative History of the Clean Water Act of 1977: A Continuation of the Legislative History of the Federal Water Pollution Control Act, at 901-50.

47. Addision and Burns, *supra* note 41 at 631.

48. A notable exception to the general bureaucratic and environmentalist dissatisfaction with Army Corps use of nationwide permits was expressed by President Reagan's Task Force on Regulatory Reform. The task force called for the expanded use of nationwide permits to help reduce delay and uncertainty in the permit process.

49. No. 82-3632 (D.D.C. 1982).

50. See Want, *Law of Wetlands Regulation* at §4.05(2) (1989). See also, *National Wildlife Fed'n v. Laubscher*, 662 F.Supp 548 (S.D. Tex. 1987), holding that the presence of migratory birds at a pond was sufficient to find Army Corps jurisdiction over the pond. Compare with *Hoffman Homes, Inc. v. EPA* (7th Cir. 1992), rejecting this same basis for finding Army Corps jurisdiction.

51. 474 U.S. 121 (1985). See also 40 C.F.R. §230.3 (s) (7) (1993).

52. Tripp and Herz, *supra* note 9 at 230-35.

53. Marzulla, "A Wetland That Not Even a Glancing Goose Could Save," *Land Rights Letter* 6 (June 1992).

54. *Hoffman Homes, supra* note 5.

55. Ibid. at 20.

56. 33 C.F.R. §330.2 (e) (1993).

57. 33 U.S.C. §1344 (e) (1988); 33 C.F.R. §330.1-330.4 (1993). For a general review of the Army Corps' nationwide permit system see, Addison and Burns, *supra* note 41.

58. 33 U.S.C. §1344 (f) (1) (A) - (E) (1988).

59. 33 U.S.C. §1344 (f) (2) (1988). See also Bianucci and Goodenow, *supra* note 9 at 53-54.

60. See 40 C.F.R. §233.30 (1993). The Army Corps has three levels of operations: 36 district offices, run by a colonel or lieutenant colonel; 9 division offices, run by a brigadier general or major general; and the main office (Chief of Engineers Office) located in Washington, D.C. Want, *supra* note 50 at §3.02(2).

61. *Environmental Crimes, supra* note 16 at §2.38.

62. 40 C.F.R. §233.34 (1993).

63. 33 U.S.C. §1344 (c), (i) (1988). Such vetos are, in fact, rare.

64. See Addison and Burns, *supra* note 41 at 628; 33 U.S.C. §1344 (c) (1988).

65. Want, *supra* note 50 at §3.01.

66. Ibid. at §3.03.

67. 28 U.S.C. §1491 (1988).

68. The Supreme Court has not accepted certiorari for any of the Section 404 cases that have, to this date, been decided by the Claims Court and the federal Circuit.

69. See, Butler, "Regulatory Takings after *Lucas*," in 3 *Regulation* 76 (1993).

70. See generally CLEAN WATER ACT: Private Property Takings Claims as a Result of the Section 404 Program, GAO Report, GAO/RCED-93-176FS August 1993.

71. Ibid., p. 1.

72. 657 F.2d 1184 (Ct. Cl. 1981), certiorari denied, 455 U.S. 1017 (1982).

73. Ibid. at 1188.

74. Ibid.

75. Ibid. These conditions included an "understand[ing] that all permits applications are independent of each other and that the granting of this permit does not necessarily mean that future applications for a permit or permits in the general area of the proposed work by Marco Island Development Corporation or other will be similarly granted." Also included was an agreement by Deltona not to "advertise or offer for sale as suitable building lots parcels of land which (1) are in whole or in part seaward of the mean high water line and which (2) could not be made suitable for the erection of residences or other structures in the absence of a Department of Army fill permit that has not yet been issued." Ibid.

76. Ibid. at 1192.

77. *Agins v. City of Tiburon*, 447 U.S. 255 (1980).

78. Ibid. at 260.

79. 438 U.S. 104 (1978).

80. *Deltona v. United States, supra* note 72 at 1189.

81. Ibid. at 1192.

82. Ibid.

83. The court characterized this case in the following terms: "Reduced to its essentials, this case merely presents an instance of some diminution in value. The Supreme Court, however, has squarely held that mere diminution, standing alone, is insufficient to establish a taking." Ibid. at 1192-93.

84. Ibid. at 1192.

85. Ibid. at 1193.

86. Ibid.

87. *Lucas v. South Carolina Coastal Council*, 112 S.Ct. 2886 (1992). In *Lucas*, the plaintiff purchased two beachfront parcels of land on a barrier island off Charleston, South Carolina, in 1986. When, pursuant to the Beachfront Management Act of 1988 (South Carolina), Lucas was prohibited from building on his land, he sued the state, alleging that application of the Act to his property constituted a compensable taking of his property. Lucas won at the trial level, the decision was reversed by the South Carolina supreme court, and the case went to the U.S. Supreme Court. Justice Scalia wrote a landmark decision, holding the case ripe for review, finding the application of

the "prevention of public harm" principle to the case was error, and remanding the case to the South Carolina supreme court. *Lucas* is not a sweeping victory for property rights advocates, because Justice Scalia's holding is rather narrow (the case still relies on the concept that all economically viable uses of property must be taken by government regulation before compensation will be due. Richard Epstein's arguments for compensating partial takings have not been accepted by the Court). However, dicta in the case points to an important shift in the Court's willingness to tolerate what it views as excessive government regulation of private property.

88. *Deltona v. United States, supra* note 72 at 1192.

89. 364 U.S. 40 (1960), where the Supreme Court stated that the Fifth Amendment "was designed to bar Government from forcing some people alone to bear public burdens which, in all fairness and justice, should be borne by the public as a whole."

90. 657 F.2d. 1210 (1981).

91. *Penn Central v. City of New York, supra* note 79.

92. *Jentgen v. United States, supra* note 90, at 1214.

93. 18 Cl. Ct. 548 (1989). Note: a typographical error occurred in recording the title of this case. The correct spelling of the plaintiff's surname is "Ciampitti."

94. Ibid. at 552.

95. Ibid. at 554.

96. Ibid. at 556. The nuisance exception says that government regulations prohibiting land uses that are nuisances under the common law do not take property and, hence, do not require compensation under the Fifth Amendment.

97. Ibid. at 557 *quoting Keystone Bituminous Coal Association v. DeBenidictis,* 480 U.S. 470, 492 (1987).

98. Ibid.

99. Ibid. at 559.

100. 22 Cl. Ct. 310 (1991).

101. *Tabb Lakes, Ltd. v. United States,* 10 Fed.3d 796 (1993).

102. *Tabb Lakes, Ltd. v. United States,* 26 Cl. Ct. 1334 (1992).

103. *Tabb Lakes, Ltd. v. United States,* 715 F.Supp. 726 (E.D. Va. 1988), affirmed 885 F.2d 866 (4th Cir. 1989).

104. *Tabb Lakes, supra* note 101 at 799.

105. Ibid.

106. See *First English Evangelical Lutheran Church of Glendale v. County of Los Angeles,* 107 S. Ct. 2378 (1987).

107. *Tabb Lakes, supra* note 101 at 800.

108. 30 Cl. Ct. 63 (1993).

109. Ibid. at 65.

110. *Beure-Co. v. United States,* 16 Cl. Ct. 42 (1988).

111. Ibid. at 49.

112. 791 F.2d 893 (Fed. Cir. 1986) *certiorari denied,* 479 U.S. 1054 (1987), on remand 21 Cl. Ct. 161 (1990).

113. *Florida Rock v. United States,* 21 Cl. Ct. 161, 169 (1990).

114. The total figure awarded by the Claims Court represents: $1,029,000 in just compensation, $1,778,554 in interest (as of the decision date July 23, 1990), and $808,785 in plaintiff's litigation costs.

115. 21 Cl. Ct. 153 (1990).

116. State permission to undertake the dredge and fill activity on 11 of the 51 acres still held by Loveladies was based on the company's agreement to develop a new wetlands area on a different 11 acres. See *Loveladies Harbor v. United States, supra* note 115 at 154 (1990), and Marzulla and Marzulla, "Regulatory Takings in the United States Claims Court," 40 *Catholic Univ. L. Rev.* 549, 560 (1991).

117. *Loveladies Harbor v. United States, supra* note 115 at 158.

118. 18 Cl. Ct. 783 (1989).

119. Ibid. at 786.

120. Ibid. at 787.

121. See 33 C.F.R. 320.4 (b) (4) (1993).

122. *Formanek v. United States, supra* note 118 at 789.

123. Ibid. at 793.

124. Ibid. at 794.

125. Ibid.

126. Ibid. at 796.

127. Ibid. quoting *Loveladies Harbor, Inc. v. United States*, 15 Cl. Ct. 381, 396 (1988).

128. Ibid. at 797.

129. Ibid. at 798.

130. *First English Evangelical Church, supra* note 106; *Nollan v. California Coastal Commission*, 107 S.Ct. 3141 (1987).

131. See Blumm and Zaleha, *supra* note 8 at 754-59; Hanley, "A Developer's Dream: The United States Claims Court's New Analysis of Section 404 Takings Challenges," 19 *Environmental Affairs* 317, 346-50 (1991).

132. Hanley, *supra* note 130, at 348.

133. Ibid. at 351.

134. Blumm and Zaleha, *supra* note 8 at 756.

135. Ibid. at 697.

136. Another critic of the Supreme Court takings jurisprudence in *Lucas* argues that private property rights should not be allowed to trump government regulation of wetlands development because "the protection of wetland and coastal ecosystems can be *crucial* to public safety and welfare." Goldman-Carter, "Protecting Wetlands and Reasonable Investment-Backed Expectations in the Wake of *Lucas v. South Carolina Coastal Council*, 28 *Land and Water Review*, 425, 428 (1993).

137. See, Blumm and Zahela, *supra* note 8 at 758, who state: "Given the high social costs associated with ongoing wetlands losses, it ought to be too late in the day to recognize a fundamental right to fill a wetland over government objection."

138. McMurry and Ramsey, "Environmental Crime: The Use of Criminal Sanctions in Enforcing Environmental Laws," 19 Loyola L.A. L. Rev. 1133, 1134-35 (1986).

139. *Environmental Crimes, supra* note 16 at §1.02.

140. 33 U.S.C. §1319 (c) (4) (1988).

141. *Environmental Crimes, supra* note 16 at §2.35.

142. 33 U.S.C. §1319 (c) (1988).

143. CR 83-891 (S.D. Fla. 1988).

144. 87-CR-20030-BC (E.D. Mich. 1987).

145. CR 88-03100-WEA (N.D. Fla. 1988), affirmed 904 F.2d 713 (11th Cir. 1990).
146. "Trials and Tribulations of Landowners," *Los Angeles Times,* October 18, 1992, K2.
147. Ibid. *Anderson Independent-Mail,* March 1994, James Kirkpatrick, p. C1.
148. S-90-0216 (D Md May 31, 1990).
149. *Environmental Crimes, supra* note 16 at §2.54.
150. CR 2-90-02 (D Md 1991) upheld, Nos 91-5032, -5033 (4th Cir 1992).
151. "Do You Sleep Better Now That Ellen's in Jail?" *Washington Times,* January 19, 1993, F2.
152. "Look who's being jailed for pollution," *Star Tribune,* September 9, 1992, 17A.
153. Ibid.
154. The MacNeil/Lehrer NewsHour, interview with William Ellen, Jan. 1, 1993.
155. *Washington Times, supra* note 151.
156. The MacNeil/Lehrer News Hour, *supra* note 154.
157. 757 F. Supp. 21 (E.D. Pa. 1991), certiorari denied, 111 S.Ct. 48 (1990), affirmed in part, reversed in part by *United States v. Pozsgai,* 947 F.2d 938 (3rd Cir. 1991).
158. *United States v. Pozsgai,* 757 F.Supp. 21 (E.D.Pa. 1991).
159. "Starr Conceded Missteps in Wetlands Case," *Legal Times,* July 23, 1990, 6.
160. Ibid.
161. *Los Angeles Times,* "Trials and Tribulations of Landowners," October 18, 1992, Real Estate; K2.
162. CR No 87-129MC (D. Mass. May 4, 1988), affirmed 867 F.2d 96 (1st Cir. 1989).
163. *United States v. Marathon Development Corp.,* 867 F.2d. 96, 97 (1st Cir. 1989).
164. See 33 C.F.R. §330.2 (d) (1993).
165. 88-CR-375 (D. Colo. 1989).
166. CR 89-53-01/02-L (D. N.H. Jan 22, 1990).
167. 88-03495-01/02 CR (W.D. Mo. 1989).
168. (S.D. Cal 1992), *Environmental Crimes, supra* note 16 at §2.54.
169. John Moore, "Taking on 'Takings.'" *National Journal* 582 (March 7, 1992).

References

Ablard, Charles, and Brian O'Neill. "Wetland Protection and Section 404 of the Federal Water Pollution Control Act Amendments of 1972: A Corps of Engineers Renaissance." *Vermont Law Review* 1 No. 1 (1976): 51-115.
Addison, Thomas, and Timothy Burns. "The Army Corps of Engineers and Nationwide Permit 26: Wetlands Protection or Swamp Reclamation?" *Ecology Law Quarterly* 18, (1991): 619-69.
Bianucci, Larry, and Rew Goodenow. "The Impact of Section 404 of the Clean Water Act on Agricultural Land Use." *UCLA Journal of Environmental Law and Policy* 10, No. 1 (1991): 41-65.

Blumm, Michael, and D. Bernard Zaleha. "Federal Wetlands Protection Under the Clean Water Act: Regulatory Ambivalence, Intergovernmental Tension, and a Call for Reform." *University of Colorado Law Review* 60, No. 4 (1989): 695-772.

Butler, Henry. "Regulatory Takings After *Lucas*." *Regulation* 76, No. 3 (1993): 76-81.

Clean Water Act: Private Property Takings Claims as a Result of the Section 404 Program. Washington: General Accounting Office, 1993.

Coyle, Dennis J. *Property Rights and the Constitution.* Albany: SUNY, 1993.

"Do You Sleep Better Now That Ellen's in Jail?" *Washington Times* (January 19, 1993): F2.

Epstein, Richard. *Takings.* Cambridge, MA.: Harvard University Press, 1985.

Goldman-Carter, Jan. "Protecting Wetlands and Reasonable Investment-Backed Expectation in the Wake of *Lucas v. South Carolina Coastal Council*," *Land and Water Law Review* 28, No. 2, (1993): 425-66.

Hanley, Thomas. "A Developer's Dream: The United States Claims Court's New Analysis of Section 404 Takings Challenges." *Boston College Environmental Affairs Law Review* 19, No. 2 (1991): 317-53.

Harris, Christopher, Raymond Marshall, and Patrick Cavanaugh. *Environmental Crimes.* Colorado Springs: Shepard's/McGraw-Hill, 1992.

Harness, C.C.. "The Future of Freshwater Wetlands." *South Carolina Lawyer* 33, No. (1991): 3-10.

Houck, Oliver. "Hard Choices: The Analysis of Alternatives Under Section 404 of the Clean Water Act and Similar Environmental Laws." *University of Colorado Law Review* 60, No. 4 (1989): 773-840.

Interview with William Ellen. *The MacNeil/Lehrer NewsHour* (January 1, 1993).

Kirkpatrick, James. *Anderson Independent-Mail* (March, 1994): C1. "Look Who's Being Jailed for Pollution." *Star Tribune* (September 9, 1992): 17A.

Marzulla, Roger. "The New 'Takings' Executive Order and Environmental Regulation—Collision or Cooperation." *Environmental Law Reporter* 18, No. 7 (July, 1988): 10254-60.

Marzulla, Roger, and Nancie Marzulla. "Regulatory Takings in the United States Claims Court." *Catholic University Law Review*, 40, No. 3, (1991): 549-69.

McMurry, Robert, and Stephen Ramsey. "Environmental Crimes: The Use of Criminal Sanctions in Enforcing Environmental Laws." *Loyola of Los Angeles Law Review* 19, No. 4 (1986): 1133-69.

Memorandum of Agreement Between Secretary of the Army Stanley Resor and Secretary of the Interior Stewart Udall. Washington: July 13, 1967.

Pollot, Mark L. *Grand Theft and Petit Larceny: Property Rights in America.* San Francisco: Pacific Research Institute for Public Policy, 1993.

Power, Garret. "The Fox in the Chicken Coop: The Regulatory Program of the U.S. Army Corps of Engineers." *Virginia Law Review* 63, no.4 (1977): 503-59.

Rose-Ackerman, Susan. "Regulatory Takings: Policy Analysis and Democratic Principles." In *Taking Property and Just Compensation*, ed. by Nicholas Mercuro. Boston: Kluwer, 1992: 30-44.

"Starr Conceded Missteps in Wetlands Case." *Legal Times* (July 23, 1990): 6.

"Trials and Tribulations of Landowners." *Los Angeles Times* (October 18, 1992): 2.

Tripp, James, and Herz, Michael. "Wetland Preservation and Restoration: Changing Federal Priorities." *Virginia Journal of Natural Resources Law* 7, No. 2 (1988): 221-75.

Want, William. *Law of Wetlands Regulation*. New York: Clark Boardman, 1989.

Zuckerman, Seth. *"Loveladies Harbor, Inc. v. United States: The Claims Court Takes a Wrong Turn—Toward a Higher Standard of Review."* *Catholic University Law Review* 40, No. 3 (1991): 753-86.

Chapter 5

Property Rights Conflicts Under the Endangered Species Act: Protection of the Red-Cockaded Woodpecker

Lee Ann Welch[1]

In the early 1990s, people in the timber and other land-based industries could hardly think of endangered species protection without immediately conjuring up images of regulatory takings.   Highly publicized court actions involving protection of the threatened northern spotted owl placed millions of acres of forest lands off limits to loggers in the Pacific Northwest.   At the same time, timber firms in the southeastern United States began to encounter severe restrictions that stemmed from efforts to protect the red-cockaded woodpecker.

Reared in a property rights regime that protected the rights of private land-owners, timber owners understandably desired to manage their land and harvest timber in response to market forces. If land rights were taken, the owners expected to be paid. Following the evolving mandates of the Endangered Species Act (ESA), which ultimately empowered federal agencies to restrict land rights without owner compensation, the U.S. Fish and Wildlife Service set out to implement the law. As it read the statute, in order to protect and recover resident endangered species on the land, the Fish and Wildlife Service could prevent landowners from developing, harvesting timber, farming, or any other such activity. As private landowners saw the situation, such regulation by the

Fish and Wildlife Service was nothing less than a constitutional taking of their land rights without providing just compensation.[2]

The property rights stance taken by federal agencies in the 1990s, which relied on command-and-control regulation, stood in sharp contrast with the government's earlier free market position when the agencies drew on taxpayer funds to purchase sensitive habitat occupied by a threatened species. For a combination of reasons, a regime shift occurred that replaced property rights protection with a system of feudal land rights managed by politicians and their appointees. Owners of timberland, as well as other landowners, struggled to protect the natural resources they managed as they encountered a regulatory process designed to protect the new, superior rights of endangered species. Similarly, a shift occurred in the interpretation of endangered species protection. No longer was the emphasis on saving individual species, but rather on preserving entire ecosystems and habitats.

This chapter examines the ESA, its evolving interpretation, and the resulting land rights controversy that has emerged. The chapter discusses the background of the ESA and then provides a detailed case study involving a major North Carolina timber operation, the Cone land controversy, which involves protection of the red-cockaded woodpecker.

Part 1 of the chapter reviews some history of earlier wildlife preservation acts and explains how land was previously purchased for endangered species protection and recovery. This section describes the possible forces that caused the federal government to supplement its purchase of sensitive lands with regulatory takings of land rights.

To gain an understanding of the law's effects, one must understand the law's key provisions. Part 2 of the chapter gives an overview of pertinent sections of the Endangered Species Act (ESA), identifies difficult legislative language found in the statute and explains how the law affects private landowners. The section ends with a series of cases that illustrate the conflicts that can arise when perceived regulatory "takings" interfere with landowner rights.   T h e red-cockaded woodpecker (RCW) plays a key role in the Cone land controversy. The bird's biology, ecology, and protection form the focus of Part 3, which carries the story to the southeastern United States. Along with details on Ben Cone's timber operation and his encounter with the RCW, this section discusses Cone's alternatives and their implications. Finally, part 3 outlines strategies proposed by the Fish and Wildlife Service and the Environmental Defense Fund for resolving conflicts over protection of the red-cockaded woodpecker. Part 4 discusses alternatives that have been proposed for dealing with the land rights conflicts, and part 5 ends the chapter with a discussion of policy changes that might be adopted to reform the Endangered Species Act.

1. The Endangered Species Act and Land Purchase

Few people know that federal statutes protecting endangered species have been on the books for almost thirty years, for the simple reason that until fairly recently there was no control of private land use for endangered species preservation. The language of the first Endangered Species Act of 1966 and later versions of the law emphasized government purchase of sensitive lands, which were then set aside as habitat for the targeted species. Somewhere around the mid-1980s, however, a new property rights regime emerged. In addition to acquiring land through the market, the federal government began to use its regulatory powers to acquire land rights. A system of feudal land-use rights replaced private property rights. Under the new regime, government assumed the position of superior owner and dictated a system of actions to be followed by the citizen-tenant. The bundle of private property rights held previously by landowners was sharply reduced.

The purchase of habitat for the preservation of native endangered species began with the 1964 Land and Water Conservation Fund Act (LWCFA), which created the Land and Water Conservation Fund (LWCF). This fund was established "for the acquisition of land, waters, or interests in land or waters . . . for any national area which may be authorized for the preservation of species of fish and wildlife that are threatened with extinction."[3] This was the first time that the Department of the Interior was granted the authority to purchase habitat for endangered species on other than a species-by-species basis (Yaffee, 1982).

The Land and Water Conservation Fund laid the groundwork for the 1966 Endangered Species Preservation Act, which empowered the secretary of interior to purchase land for the preservation of domestic wildlife threatened with extinction. The main purpose of the 1966 Act was the acquisition of habitat for wildlife refuges (Yaffee, 1982). The Act appropriated $15 million from the Land and Water Conservation Fund for such purchases but limited the amount spent per year to $5 million and the amount spent per project to $750,000. Under this Act only native species could be listed as endangered and only on the basis of technical factors. The "taking" of listed species was prohibited only on federal lands that were designated as wildlife refuges.[4]

The Endangered Species Preservation Act was replaced in 1969 by the more stringent Endangered Species Conservation Act. This Act extended protection to endangered subspecies and prohibited interstate commerce in unlawfully taken reptiles, amphibians, mollusks, and crustaceans. The Act required the secretary of interior to list species threatened with worldwide extinction and to prohibit their importation into the United States (Bean, 1983). It also increased the amount of money that could be allocated from the Land and Water Conservation Fund to $2.5 million dollars per project.[5]

Finally, the 1973 Endangered Species Act, still in effect today, was adopted. Unlike the earlier acts, the language of this Endangered Species Act was restrictive and comprehensive at the same time. It extended its coverage and protection to all endangered animals and plants worldwide, not just in the United States. It limited both government and private actions when dealing with land designated as habitat for endangered species. Most importantly though, the ESA removed all restrictions on the use of the Land and Water Conservation Fund for the purchase of land.[6]

Activities under the Land and Water Conservation Fund

The Land and Water Conservation Fund is the source of funds for purchase of land by the Fish and Wildlife Service, as well as the Forest Service, the Bureau of Land Management, and the National Park Service. Since its establishment in 1964, the LWCF has provided approximately $3.6 billion to these federal agencies to acquire lands, and another $3.2 billion has been allocated as matching funds for states to purchase land (National Research Council, 1993). Currently, these four federal agencies control 626 million acres, 28 percent of the U. S. land surface. More to the point, the Fish and Wildlife Service maintains 89 million acres of this total land base in its 472 wildlife refuges (National Research Council, 1993).

As the environmental movement shifted into high gear during the 1960s and 1970s, these four land management agencies steadily increased their land base. When private land was desired for public purposes, the land management agencies purchased it. From 1965 to 1979, the total purchases under the fund increased from an average of 729 acres per year to 258,270 acres per year (National Research Council, 1993). By the mid-1970s, the wildlife refuge system had grown to more than 30 million acres. The system continued to grow in the late 1970s under President Carter, who added 12 million acres by Executive Order in 1978. In 1980, the Alaska National Interest Lands Act designated another 42.9 million acres of Alaskan territory as refuge lands. By 1980, the Fish and Wildlife Service's land base stood at 87 million acres (Shanks, 1984).

The potential for property rights takings began to emerge at the end of the Carter administration in 1980 when Congress cut appropriations to the LWCF. Land purchases fell to an annual average of 145,000 acres, down by almost 100,000 acres from the 1979 level (National Research Council, 1993). Several factors seemed to influence this strategic change. First, in 1979, the General Accounting Office stated that the previous land-purchase practices overlooked less expensive alternatives and did not take into account the high maintenance costs associated with a large land base. Second, inholder protests against federal land acquisition began to surface (National Research Council, 1993).

The End of the Land Purchase Regime

In the late 1970s and early 1980s a movement known as the Sagebrush Rebellion emerged among cattlemen, ranchers, miners, and other groups that opposed expansion of public lands. There was also an increasing interest in expanding the sale of public land rights for energy production, resulting from the Arab oil boycott of 1973 and the 1979 OPEC product cutbacks. The most productive known energy reserves were located on public lands (Shanks, 1984). As a result, the Reagan administration began to sell public land, and a moratorium was placed on LWCF appropriations (National Research Council, 1993). Secretary of the Interior James Watt requested no funds for ESA land acquisition. Environmental groups, not federal agencies, made the acquisition recommendations to Congress during this time period (Hellman, 1991).

Over the past twelve years, LWCF budget requests have fluctuated depending on the president in office at the time. The Reagan administration asked that no funds be appropriated, with the exception of 1984 when a small amount was requested. Following the Reagan years requests from the LWCF reached a peak of $365 million in fiscal year 1993 under Bush and then diminished under Clinton to $209 million for fiscal year 1994 (Wilderness Society, 1994).

However, a president's budget request does not necessarily dictate congressional action. Despite efforts exerted by sitting presidents to reduce land purchases, Congress continued to appropriate significant amounts to acquire private land for endangered species based on the recommendations of environmental groups. These trends are reflected in Figures 5.1 and 5.2, which focus solely on land acquisitions for endangered species protection by the Fish and Wildlife Service. The sharp expansion of land purchases of species habitat for the years 1968 to 1993 is shown clearly in Figure 5.1. Most of the increase begins in 1984 and accelerates after 1987.[7] Figure 5.2 presents the fiscal side of the land-purchase activities. Expenditures rise sharply in 1985 and continue at a high level from that point forward. With increased funds for acquiring habitat and expanding authority to take land by regulation, the Fish and Wildlife Service became a formidable land-control agency.

Given two methods for gaining control of land, one market-based and the other based on political control, the Fish and Wildlife Service could make choices.[8] Some species have received the benefits of large expenditures, while habitat for others has been taken by regulation. As of 1993 only 24 percent of the listed species were found on National Wildlife Refuges (Young, 1993). The service has generously used Conservation dollars to acquire land for a selected few species like the key deer and American crocodile. In contrast, the service has chosen to take land from private landowners for species like the red-cockaded woodpecker. Curiously, efforts to maintain and expand public landownership for some species have been coupled with a feudal land rights system for others. While some private landowners become parties to voluntary exchanges

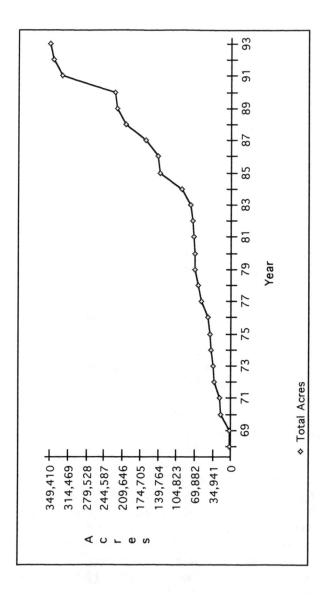

Source:
Fish and Wildlife Service Land and Water Conservation Fund
Summary of Land Obligations for 1968-1993. Division of Realty,
Fish and Wildlife Service. 1994.

Figure 5.1 Acres of land purchased from 1968 to 1993 with Land and Water Conservation Fund monies by the
Fish and Wildlife Service for endangered species

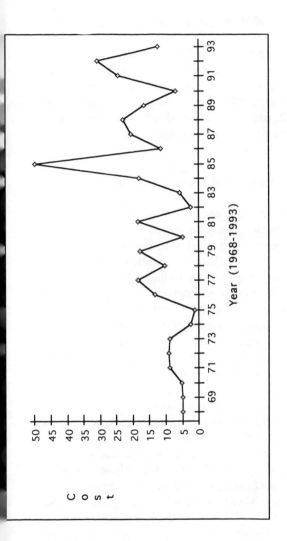

Source:
Fish and Wildlife Service Land and Water Conservation Fund
Summary of Land Obligations for 1968-1993. Division of Realty,
Fish and Wildlife Service. 1994.

Figure 5.2 Land and Water Conservation Fund monies used annually by the Fish and Wildlife Service to purchase land for endangered species from 1968-1993 (in millions of dollars)

in certain cases, other landowners become victims of a heavy-handed effort to take the use of their land without compensation.

2. The Endangered Species Act and Its Major Elements

As it turns out, the Endangered Species Act of 1973 (ESA) has emerged as one of the most powerful environmental laws ever written. The Act was adopted to extend protection to endangered and threatened plant and animal species and to assure their recovery. Since passed in 1973, it has been amended and renewed in 1976, 1977, 1978, 1980, 1982, and 1988. It was due for reauthorization in 1992, but in early 1995 reauthorization had yet to come.

Listing, Designation of Critical Habitat, and Recovery Planning

Section 4 of the act provides for listing of endangered species, designation of critical habitat, and recovery planning actions that are the responsibility of the secretary of the interior. The secretary can list a species by any of three methods: listing on the secretary's initiative, listing by petition, and emergency listing.[9] Listing by petition is the most common method and involves some interested party, which has typically been an environmental group, petitioning for the listing of a particular species. An interested party can petition to have any biological species listed as well as "any subspecies of fish or wildlife or plants, and any distinct population segment of any species of vertebrate fish or wildlife which interbreeds when mature."[10] On reviewing a petition, the secretary is required by section 4 to list "based solely on the basis of the best scientific and commercial information on a species' status, without reference to possible economic or other impacts of such determination."[11]

The secretary of the interior is required, with some exceptions, to designate critical habitat when making a new listing. Critical habitat is defined as "the specific area within the geographical area occupied by the species, at the time it is listed in accordance with the provisions of section 4 of this act, on which are found those physical or biological features essential to the conservation of the species."[12] Despite the general requirement for habitat designation, critical habitat is frequently not assigned. Only 12 percent of the domestic listed species have designated critical habitat.[13] The secretary may make exception in cases where the designation would pose a threat to the species or where sufficient biological data are lacking.[14] Unlike the listing process, which disregards economic impact, the secretary is required to consider economic impacts and any other impacts when designating critical habitat.[15]

The development of a recovery plan forms the third requirement in the process. The secretary is not required, however, to develop and implement a recovery plan if it will not promote the conservation of the species. The secretary may procure the services of any other private or public agencies when developing such a plan.[16] The agencies that write the recovery plans are the Fish and Wildlife Service and the National Marine Fisheries Service (Gordon and Streeter, 1994).

Jeopardy Prohibition: Federal Lands

Section 7 of the Endangered Species Act provides for protection of endangered and threatened species on federal lands. According to this section federal agencies cannot authorize, fund, or carry out any action that may "jeopardize the continued existence of any endangered species or threatened species or result in the destruction or adverse modification of habitat of such species."[17]

In order to meet this requirement, federal agencies must consult with and provide a biological assessment statement (similar to an environmental impact statement) to the Fish and Wildlife Service (FWS) or the National Marine Fisheries Service (NMFS) on any proposed action (O'Laughlin, 1992). Then the FWS or NMFS can issue either a "jeopardy opinion" if the action will potentially harm the species or a "no jeopardy opinion" if it will not (Littell, 1992). A jeopardy opinion denies and halts the proposed activity until it is modified and no longer harms the species (O'Laughlin, 1992). Jeopardy opinions can even extend to federal actions on privately owned lands, like land assistance programs (Heissenbuttel and Murray, 1992).

When the ESA was amended in 1978, Congress created the Endangered Species Committee, nicknamed the God Squad, that could grant exemptions to federally proposed actions receiving a jeopardy opinion under section 7. The committee consists of six members of the president's cabinet and subcabinet, and a representative from each affected state. An exemption is granted only if there is no other reasonable or prudent alternative and the project is of great public interest or significance (Littell, 1992).

The provision for exemption provides some flexibility to the ESA, but it has rarely been used since 1978. It was created to resolve the Tellico Dam/snail darter controversy in 1978, but the God Squad did not grant an exemption. Since then the committee has granted an exemption for the Graylocks Dam and Reservoir involving the whooping crane (General Accounting Office, 1992). More recently the Bureau of Land Management filed for an exemption for forty-four timber sales in 1991 that jeopardized the northern spotted owl, but the committee granted only thirteen of those sales (Heissenbutell and Murray, 1992).

Takings on Private Lands

Section 9 of the ESA has the most application to private landowners; it prohibits "takings" of listed species by any person, public or private. The term "take" is defined in section 3 as "to harass, harm, pursue, hunt, shoot, wound, kill, trap, capture, collect, or to attempt to engage in any such conduct."[18] As defined by the Fish and Wildlife Service, the terms "harm" and "harass" include any land action that adversely modifies habitat, therefore harming or injuring just one member of a listed species.[19] Frequently, it is the "harm and harass" provision that prohibits private landowners from using their land in cases involving listed species. This provision converts an environmental statute into a land-use control law.

Any person who does "take" an endangered species is subject to enforcement under section 11 of the ESA. A person violating Section 9 may be subject to a civil penalty up to $25,000 for each violation and a criminal penalty up to $50,000 and/or imprisonment up to one year.[20]

Incidental Takings

In 1982, the Endangered Species Act was amended to allow for "incidental takings" of listed species. This exemption was added to permit development of land inhabited by the mission blue butterfly on San Bruno Mountain near San Francisco. The incidental take provision allowed for an exemption to section 9 of the Act if the developers agreed to create other permanent open space as undisturbed habitat (Littell, 1992).

Incidental takes are takings of endangered or threatened species that are authorized in conjunction with an otherwise lawful action, and if permitted by the secretary of the interior, are not in violation of sections 7 or 9 of the ESA. Permits for an exemption can be obtained by federal or private parties. Nonfederal parties must write a Habitat Conservation Plan (HCP) that outlines the measures that will be implemented to conserve the given species (Sugg, 1993-94). Section 10 allows for permits to be granted to private parties in "any taking otherwise prohibited by section 9 if such taking is incidental to, and not the purpose of, the carrying out of an otherwise lawful activity."[21]

Section 10 has been praised as a flexible alternative to the otherwise prohibitory language of the ESA; however, it has not been as widely successful as expected. Many HCPs have been initiated, but only twenty-five have been approved. The development and approval of a plan is a slow, drawn-out process that most private landowners are not willing to undergo (Thornton, 1993).

Furthermore, Section 10 does not provide any funding for the development and implementation of Habitat Conservation Plans. The burden of paying for such a plan rests solely on the shoulders of the private landowner and can be costly to carry. For example, a landowner at San Bruno Mountain contributed over $1 million for biological studies for an HCP involving the mission blue, callippe silverspot, and bay checkerspot butterflies. Landowners in Riverside County, California have already paid $25 million for a HCP concerning the Stephens' kangaroo rat (Thornton, 1993). Currently, the HCP provision of section 10 is the only vehicle that private interests can utilize to avoid endangered species conflicts, but this provision, like so many others in the ESA, imposes the cost of conservation on private landowners.

A Review of the Endangered Species Act in Operation

Statutory language is one thing; the operation of a law is something else. In the case of the ESA, most would agree that success means protection of endangered species to the point that they again flourish. As it turns out, the ESA in practice has not accomplished this goal. As noted earlier, implementation of the ESA requires several actions. The first is to list and then take actions to protect endangered and threatened plants and animals. The second is to recover these species.

As of July 1, 1994, the FWS and the NMFS had listed 1,427 species, with 895 native to the United States. Beyond the 1,427 listed species, the Fish and Wildlife service has identified 295 category 1 species (species for which FWS has adequate information to support proposals to list as endangered or threatened but has not listed). In addition, the FWS has identified 3,497 category 2 species (species that may be listed based on available data).[22]

A larger number of listed species does not necessarily mean that more species are being recovered. In fact, the General Accounting Office in 1990 found that over 80 percent of the species on the list were declining despite protection afforded them by the ESA.[23] The ever-increasing number of listed and candidate species combined with the stationary funding received has created a tremendous backlog of uncompleted recovery plans at the FWS and the NMFS. As more species are added, the number of consultations with other federal agencies increases, reducing the number of staff and resources for other activities like recovery planning. Less money is available per species for recovery plan preparation and implementation (General Accounting Office, 1988).

While listing has been a burgeoning activity, little has been done with recovery. Only 53.7 percent of the listed species are covered by approved recovery plans.[24] In 1992, the General Accounting Office found that 65 percent of the approved recovery plans took three years or more to produce from the date of listing (GAO, 1992). The recovery planning process is slow in part because the ESA does not provide time frames for achieving recovery.

Furthermore, the ESA does not require the FWS/NMFS to keep up-to-date trend information on species movement away from or toward recovery. If the agencies did compile and maintain this information, they could determine the relative success of the endangered species program. Approved recovery plans are rarely updated. Each plan identifies and prioritizes tasks in order to initiate the tasks most required to prevent extinctions or irreversible declines. This priority system is frequently not followed, because recovery plans contain too many high priority tasks making it impossible to complete them all (GAO, 1988).

With successful recovery, ESA listing will ultimately lead to delisting. Only nineteen species have been delisted. Seven species were taken off because they were extinct and eight because of errors in original data. (In fact, they were not endangered.) The remaining four, three bird species in Palua in the Western Pacific and the Rydberg milk-vetch plant, have recovered on their own with almost no assistance from the FWS (Lambert and Smith, 1994).[25] Unfortunately, there is no incentive for the FWS to recover and delist species. The agency receives money for species listed, not for those delisted.

Funding

The way that funding is allocated and used has been the fundamental problem underlying the ineffectiveness of the ESA. The Act, more than any other federal environmental law, is underfunded for the goals it was created to accomplish. This is evidenced by the fact that Congress appropriates less than $50 million annually to the FWS and NMFS for endangered species protection and recovery (Gibbons, 1992). This is an amount equivalent to that spent on a couple of miles of the Interstate Highway System (Thornton, 1993).

With little funding, subsequent problems result. Less money is available for scientific studies to develop critical habitat designations or to write recovery plans. The FWS and the NMFS never have the money to spend for implementing creative solutions to endangered species conflicts.

In its 1988 report, the General Accounting Office stressed that the stationary funding received by the FWS and the NMFS "makes it essential that available funds are optimally used" (GAO, 1988). Nonetheless, the funding received by the FWS and the NMFS for wildlife protection is inaccurately budgeted and inefficiently used. In 1988, the General Accounting Office found that the FWS was not accurately tracking or reporting expenditures among subcategories such as listing, consultation, research, law enforcement, and recovery. In addition, funds at FWS regional offices that were allocated for one subcategory were shifted to other subcategories without being submitted to the House and Senate Committees on Appropriations or FWS budget officials (GAO, 1988).

Most of the funds allocated by Congress for the endangered species program are used on only a few high-profile species, even though the 1973 Endangered Species Act mandates protection and recovery of all those listed. The FWS has a priority system under which species are given a numerical ranking so that those most likely to go extinct will receive the most funds (GAO, 1988). The General Accounting Office found, however, that this system is rarely followed.

The competitive process of allocating funds on a species-by-species basis is determined more by politics than by biology and priority. According to Don Coursey, economist at the Harris School of Public Policy Studies at the University of Chicago, "This process may be complicated, disjointed, subjected to manipulation by special interest groups, bundled with other issues, and plagued by other side effects of the U.S. democratic process" (Coursey, 1994). In a study examining endangered species expenditure patterns, Coursey found that larger, more popular endangered species such as the bald eagle, grizzly bear, Florida panther, and California condor received more money than did lizards, small rodents, insects, and snails (Campbell, 1994).

In a similar study done at Harvard University entitled "Patterns of Behavior in Biodiversity Preservation," Andrew Metrick and Martin Weitzman found that 54 percent of the endangered species funds were spent on just ten of the 554 listed species in November 1990 (Barro, 1994). A few of the top ten, the bald eagle, grizzly bear, and Florida scrub jay, have large viable breeding populations and do not seem to be threatened with extinction. Six of the top ten are listed as subspecies and have very closely related sister species that are not endangered. Meanwhile true monotypic species like the red hills salamander and the Choctawahatchee beach mouse, which are objectively much closer to extinction, receive less than $10,000 a year each (Barro, 1994).

As revealed by spending priorities, the ESA might be viewed as an ineffective piece of legislation because it says one thing but, in practice, does another. For example, on the one hand, the Act mandates protection for each and every listed species no matter the cost, including costs borne by private property owners who have their land taken without compensation. On the other hand, the government's spending patterns suggest that the cutest and most popular species receive more funding and a higher priority than those that are truly threatened with extinction (Barro, 1994).

Program Costs

Recovery efforts have been expensive so far. Over the past fifteen years, the government has spent over $4 million airlifting 18,000 sea turtle eggs from northeastern Mexico to the United States for release (Taubes, 1992). The FWS spent over $23 million between 1989 and 1991 on recovery for the Stephens' kangaroo rat in California (National Wilderness Institute, 1992). The Department of the Interior estimates that the cost of tearing down two dams to recover the sockeye salmon in Washington would be between $154 million and $314 million (Lambert and Smith, 1994). The Interior Department's inspector general estimates future recovery costs for all listed and candidate species at $4.6 billion (Office of Inspector General, Department of Interior, 1990).

We must recall that neglect of cost is mandated in section 4 of the ESA. To illustrate the consequences, consider the northern spotted owl in the Pacific Northwest. Protection of this subspecies has resulted in the designation of 6.9 million acres of land as critical habitat. There has been an increase in the affected communities in unemployment, alcoholism, suicide, battered spouses, and troubled children. The University of Oregon has reported that local taxes must increase by more than tenfold in five Oregon counties to replace the federal payments they once received from timber sales (Heissenbuttel and Murray, 1992).

The protection of the northern spotted owl limited the harvest of old-growth timber in the Pacific Northwest, contributing to a reduction in the harvest from a 1989 high of 12 billion board feet to 1.2 billion board feet, consequently driving the price of lumber to its highest ever. This translates into an estimated increase of $4,000 in the construction cost of an average home (Woods, 1994). While these factors combined indicate high cost and might alter a decision to list if considered, the ESA moves forward without the burden of justifying benefits somehow measured against costs.

The Use of Science

The ESA says that a listing is to be based on the best scientific and commercial data, but a review of some ESA experiences suggests that listing is based more on political factors. Section 3 of the Act defines species as an entire biological species as well as "any subspecies of fish or wildlife or plants, and any distinct population segment of any species of vertebrate fish or wildlife which interbreeds when mature."[26] This can also include hybrid species.

Genetic and molecular evidence is not taken into account when defining subspecies or distinct populations. Genetic differences between a subspecies and a species are not necessarily reflected in physical differences. For instance, race differences like hair and skin color and size exist among the human species, even though genetically no real differences exist (Felten, 1990). Biological scientists insist that subspecies are not considered distinct, because they can interbreed with members from other populations and produce viable offspring. Yet as of July 1991, thirty-three of the fifty-one native mammal species listed were subspecies as were thirty-one of the sixty native bird species (Oliver, 1992).

It was the subspecies definition that provided the basis for listing the northern spotted owl. The northern spotted owl is considered a subspecies of the spotted owl, which is quite abundant along the Pacific Coast in California. Where the ranges of the two meet, it is difficult to physically distinguish the spotted owl from the northern spotted owl (Oliver, 1992). Even blood tests show no genetic difference between the species and its subspecies (Rice, 1992).

The listing of the northern spotted owl was driven more by politics than by science. Mainstream environmental groups pushed to have the subspecies listed as threatened to protect the entire old-growth forest ecosystem rather than the bird. Andy Stahl, a resource analyst for the Sierra Club Legal Defense Fund, has admitted, "Until legislation is adopted to protect these forests, we need at least one surrogate—if you will—that will provide protection for the forests. . . . As the strategy for protecting old growth matured, it appeared that wildlife would offer the most fruitful hunting grounds. . . . Thank goodness the spotted owl evolved in the Northwest, for if it hadn't, we'd have to genetically engineer it" (Sugg, 1993).

In fact, reputable scientific evidence has demonstrated that the northern spotted owl's numbers are larger than first believed. In 1986, an Audubon Society study found that 1,500 pairs of owls should be preserved. In 1990, the government's recovery team issued a plan to protect 2,320 pairs. Today, 3,500 pairs exist. In addition, recent studies show that the owl can thrive in second-growth forest. Even with this evidence, the owl has not been delisted. Just in case, mainstream environmentalists have found another forestpreserving species in the marbled murrelet should the spotted owl fail them. Environmentalists and the FWS are manipulating the ESA to "protect" millions of forested acres nationwide (Sugg, 1993).

Geography also matters in listing, since a species can be endangered in one region or state, yet be abundant in another. In fact, every state has its own endangered, rare, and threatened animal and plant list. For instance, the bald eagle is not on the endangered species list in Alaska but is listed as threatened in Minnesota, Michigan, Wisconsin, Washington, and Oregon, and is listed as endangered in the other states.[27] Frequently, a species is listed because it occurs naturally in limited numbers and could be eliminated by a one-time catastrophe. The inspector general for the Department of the Interior found in 1990 that 60 percent of listed species and 70 percent of candidate species are endemic to one particular state (Office of the Inspector General, Department of Interior, 1990).

Species are often listed that are not even endangered in the first place. The Tumamoc globeberry was listed as endangered in 1986 because the population size was estimated at less than 2,400 and at risk of extinction. The species was delisted in 1993 because further study showed that the original survey had investigated only one percent of the globeberry's potential habitat. In actuality the species is quite abundant. Numerous agencies spent a total of $1.43 million to protect the species before it was delisted (National Wilderness Institute, 1993a). Bad science can be quite expensive.

Failure to consider science can lead to destruction instead of protection. A good example is the Stephens' kangaroo rat in Riverside County, California. FWS officials warned residents that disking on their land to create firebreaks would destroy kangaroo rat habitat and would be subject to prosecution under the ESA. No firebreaks were created. The result: fire damaged most of the kangaroo rat habitat in the area as well as many human homes (Rohrabacher, 1994).

Regulatory Takings of Private Lands

Regulation of land by the ESA has led inevitably to confrontations with owners of private land. Section 9 of the ESA prohibits any person, public or private, from taking a listed species. Take is defined in section 4 as harass, harm, pursue, hunt, shoot, wound, kill, trap, capture, and collect. Harm is defined by FWS guidelines as "an act which actually kills or injures wildlife. Such activities may include significant habitat modification or degradation where it actually kills or injures wildlife by significantly impairing essential behavior patterns, including breeding, feeding or sheltering."[28]

Land-use restrictions stem directly from section 9. If landowners destroy habitat in the course of their operations, then they are subject to fines and/or imprisonment under Section 11 of the ESA. Regulation of normal land use, which would not have created a cause of action under nuisance or trespass law, is considered by some private landowners to be a taking of private property for public use.

For example, in Riverside County, California, Andy and Cindy Domenigoni have been prohibited from farming 800 acres since 1988 because it is Stephens' kangaroo rat habitat, imposing a cost on them of $400,000 (Lambert and Smith, 1994). Brandt and Venice Child purchased 500 acres in Utah for development into a campground and resort, but their plans were halted when the Kanab ambersnail was found on their land. The land-use restrictions imposed a cost of $2.5 million in diminished property value.

Another action that could be termed a regulatory taking occurred on the Off property in the San Joaquin Valley of central California, which supposedly housed the endangered blunt-nosed lizard. The Offs faced criminal charges when, according to FWS officials, they destroyed lizard habitat by plowing part of their farm to plant barley for cattle feed. Even though no lizards were found at the time by the FWS on the land, the Offs were prevented from further plowing of their land. In order to avoid an expensive legal fight, they gave up 60 acres of their land to the FWS (Fitzgerald, 1993).

The land of Beth Morian, an environmentalist and member of the Zoological Society of Houston's board of directors, has also been taken under the ESA. Thirty-four pairs of the now-endangered black-capped vireo were found on her family's Davenport Ranch west of Austin, Texas. Morian donated 62 acres of the land to the city of Austin for a nature preserve to help protect the declining bird even before it was placed on the endangered species list (Fitzgerald, 1993).

Soon after, the vireo was listed and Morian's family were prohibited from proceeding with a $2 million development project to sell sixty-six home sites. Now nearly half of their property sits idle because it is designated as black-capped vireo habitat (Fitzgerald, 1993). Morian had these comments: "They have taken our land. We want to see species preserved, but people should have a place too" (Fitzgerald, 1993).

Margaret Rector, a 73-year-old retiree also from Austin, Texas, has had her 15 acres "taken" because of the ESA-listed black-capped vireo and the golden-cheeked warbler. She purchased the land in 1973 as an investment to finance her retirement. Rector has been unable to sell the land because it is essentially worthless with its resident endangered species, but she is still required to pay property taxes on the land (Litvan, 1994).

These individuals not only lost the value of their land, but they have also incurred great costs in legal and consulting fees. Should they decide to take court actions, the property owners will bear the cost of having their land appraised to determine the loss in value, and other necessary legal expenses. They have to pay wildlife biologists to determine what land is available for use. None of these costs and the cost of time forgone are reimbursed by the government.

Perhaps mainstream environmentalists support the ESA not for its ability to preserve species diversity but because of its ability to regulate private land use as in the cases mentioned above. Edward O. Wilson and Paul R. Ehrlich, biologists and environmentalists, have asked the government "to reduce the scale of human activities" and "to cease 'developing' any more relatively undisturbed land." According to them, "Every new shopping center built in the California chapparal, every hectare of tropical forest cut and burned, every swamp converted into a rice paddy or shrimp farm means less biodiversity."[29] Angered by recent property rights victories in Congress and the courts, environmentalists are pushing for a provision in the Marine Mammal Protection Act that explicitly regulates private land use and would legally allow the taking of property rights.

Incentives

There are perverse incentives built into the ESA. Because the Act has the potential to take property, it provides incentives for landowners to prevent endangered species from locating on their property. Landowners nationwide understandably fear they will be penalized if endangered species chose their land for habitat.

If a landowner suspects that an endangered species has located on his land, he may not report its presence to the government. He might even go as far as killing the species or forcing it from his property before it is found by someone else. Some landowners have preemptively destroyed potential habitat and accelerated development in order to avoid ESA restrictions.

These negative incentives are evidenced in stories about the red-cockaded woodpecker of the southeastern United States and the northern spotted owl of the Pacific Northwest. Instead of allowing trees to become old-growth and prime habitat for these two species, landowners are cutting timber at a faster rate and on shorter rotation schedules. In the Pacific Northwest there are fewer old-growth Douglas-fir plantations because they are being cut at young ages for chips and paper products (Lambert and Smith, 1994).

The perverse incentives in Section 7 of the ESA were illustrated in a severe case involving red-cockaded woodpeckers and a development company in Ocala, Florida. The president and vice president of Development and Construction Corporation of America Inc. killed two red-cockaded woodpeckers and ordered that their employees cut down 90 to 150 cavity trees. This cost the developers a maximum penalty of $100,000 per charge (DiSilvestro, 1987).

The ESA overall has not been effective in accomplishing its goal: protecting and recovering endangered species. So far, few species have been recovered and delisted. Even though the taxpayer costs of recovering species is large, mistakes are still made when making scientific evaluations. The costs borne are also large for private landowners who face the regulatory taking of property should they practice good land stewardship that provides habitat for endangered species. Perhaps newly developed policies that focus on property rights protection will ensure that species, like the red-cockaded woodpecker, will continue and recover.

3. The Red-Cockaded Woodpecker *(Picoides borealis)*

The red-cockaded woodpecker (RCW) was listed as an endangered species in 1970. Prior to its decline, the bird was abundant in the old-growth pine savannahs, particularly longleaf, of the Southeastern Piedmont and Coastal Plain ranging from New Jersey to Texas, and inland to Kentucky, Tennessee, and Missouri. It has been listed as endangered because of loss and alteration of its habitat. In pre-Columbian times, longleaf was the dominant species on 56 million acres and a significant component on 36 million acres of forests, providing 92 million acres of suitable RCW habitat (Smathers et al., in preparation). It has been estimated that 2 million acres of this ecosystem type now remain. The RCW's range is now confined to the southeastern states, with the northern reaches ending in North Carolina. Most of the remaining populations are small, fragmented, and genetically isolated (Walters, 1991).

The total number of RCWs is not known with much accuracy. The FWS estimates, however, that 4,400 groups remain (3,100 on federal lands, 340 on state lands, and 960 on private lands). It is believed that 500,000 groups could have been supported by the once vast 92-million-acre longleaf pine ecosystem (Smathers et al., in preparation).

The red-cockaded woodpecker excavates cavities in live, old-growth pine trees that usually have the red-heart fungus. They use these trees for roosting and nesting. Excavation of live pines is an unusual habit because it takes such a long time to build the necessary cavity, anywhere from ten months to several years. Older trees (80-120 years) have a smaller heartwood core that is easier to excavate. Red-heart fungus softens the heartwood core by decay, thereby making excavation easier.

Fire is also an integral part of the woodpecker's habitat. Fire prevents the hardwood midstory and understory from growing up and encroaching upon the cavity. If this happens, the woodpecker will abandon the cavity because predators have better access to the cavities by the hardwood encroachment. Thus, typical woodpecker habitat consists of pine trees in an open, parklike situation.

The woodpecker is nonmigratory and territorial. Territories are large (50-150 Ha), because an extensive area is required for foraging. The birds forage for invertebrates by scaling bark and pecking. RCWs live in social units known as groups or colonies. Each group consists of a breeding pair and up to four male helpers that assist in incubation, feeding, and protection. The territory of a group consists of an aggregate of cavity trees, known as a cluster, in close proximity to other trees used for foraging (Walters, 1991).

Current experiments have focused on ways to recover the RCW by establishing large, genetically viable populations. Carole Copeyon has developed a technique for artificially constructing cavities for the RCW, because ecological studies have shown that cavities are a limiting resource (Walters, 1991). There is now a method to construct completed cavities and starter holes. The woodpeckers were receptive in Copeyon's North Carolina Sandhills study area (Copeyon, 1990).

Copeyon's technique has also been used successfully to recover the large population of RCWs in Francis Marion National Forest in South Carolina after the destruction by Hurricane Hugo. As of January 1993, 1,000 artificial cavities and starter holes had been constructed in Francis Marion National Forest. In the 1992 nesting season 63 percent of the Francis Marion woodpecker nests were found in artificial cavities (Nickens, 1993, 29). Artificial cavities have also been placed in recruitment stands on Francis Marion National Forest, where no RCWs previously resided. In the 1992 nesting season, six of the seven established "recruitment stands" had active colonies, and five of these six colonies had successfully nested (Nickens, 1993, 29).

Copeyon's technique also has made establishment of new colonies of RCWs by relocation a possibility. Rudolph and others with the USDA Forest Service have conducted two translocation and reintroduction experiments in Davy Crockett National Forest, Angelina National Forest, and Sabine National Forest

in Texas (Rudolph et al., 1992). The first experiment involved introduction of
an adult male and female. The adult male eventually left the introduction site
and was replaced by translocating a juvenile male. The two birds eventually
produced two offspring. Another experiment involved the introduction of a
juvenile male and female. The researchers were unable to tell if this pair was
breeding but the two birds did remain on the site (Rudolph et al., 1992).

These experiments show that there is hope for the recovery of the RCW.
The studies suggest that the birds can be moved from private lands to federally
owned lands, where they have a much better chance of reproductive viability
and long-term survivability. Movement of individual birds may provide a
solution to the conflicts that have resulted from the protection of the RCW on
private lands under the Endangered Species Act.

The Red-Cockaded Woodpecker Conflict

The RCW's protection under the Endangered Species Act has a substantial
effect on the timber industry in the Southeast. The estimated 4,400 colonies of
woodpeckers known to exist would require a minimum of 2.2 million acres of
federal, state, and private timberland.[30] The woodpecker's requirement for large
stands of mature pine conflicts with normal timber harvesting activities on these
lands. The mature timber stand that is so valuable as habitat to the woodpecker's survival is also the most valuable in terms of dollars to the timber industry.
This conflict has been felt on both federal and private lands, as normal land-use
activities have been halted or delayed in order to provide habitat for the bird.

The four large remaining populations of RCWs are located on southeastern
public lands in the Apalachicola National Forest in northern Florida, the Francis
Marion National Forest in South Carolina, the Kisatchie National Forest in
Louisiana, and the Sandhills of North Carolina, where the birds are located on
various state lands and the Army's Fort Bragg (Nickens, 1993). The management and protection of these large populations have created conflicts between
different federal agencies and the FWS.

In the precedent case of *Sierra Club v. Yeutter,* U.S. District Judge Robert
Parker ruled that the Forest Service's even-aged harvesting practices in eastern
Texas were "harming" the red-cockaded woodpecker, and therefore were in
violation of Sections 7 and 9 of the Endangered Species Act.[31] Parker ordered
the Forest Service to halt its clear-cutting practices within 1,200 meters of the
RCW colonies, preventing the harvesting of a third, or 200,000 acres, of
national forestland in Texas (Larmer, 1989). This ruling also had an adverse
effect on the local timber industry in Texas, which obtains much of its timber
from the national forests. Robert Birch of the Angelina County Farm Bureau
speculated that the timber left uncut would be enough to operate five sawmills
(Larmer, 1989).

At Fort Bragg in North Carolina, normal training and maneuvering activites have been altered significantly because of the presence of a large population of RCWs. Four hundred no-traffic areas have been marked off with red tape or distinctive signs on trees, indicating that a RCW tree is 60 meters away. In 1991, $20 million firing range was shut down because RCW cavity trees had been destroyed (Charles, 1991).

Effects of the woodpecker's protection have also been felt by the private timberland owner, with 90 percent of the 89 million acres of pine forest in the region being privately owned. Indeed, it is possible that 75 percent of the RCW's nesting habitat is located on these private lands (Society of American Foresters, 1992).

The private landowner is especially susceptible to the effects of the ESA because the lands held are usually small acreages with less than 10 acres per tract. Designation of these small acreages as habitat can lead to complete loss of economic value. This can be devastating to the small, private landowner who is depending on money from his timberland.

Since the listing of the RCW as an endangered species, two recovery plans have been written by the FWS, one in 1979 and another in 1985. The 1985 recovery plan has set a recovery goal of fifteen viable populations or 4,500 to 7,500 groups total. A viable population is defined as 250 groups that reproduce and successfully fledge young annually. The FWS states in its recovery plan objectives that recovery should occur on federal lands since the populations on privately owned lands are small and isolated (RCW Recovery Plan, 1985).

Formerly, the FWS used Henry's 1989 guidelines or the "Blue Book" to provide standards for timber management practices in RCW habitat on federal and private lands (Henry, 1989). Currently, the FWS is implementing draft guidelines for the private landowner included in the Red-cockaded Woodpecker Procedures Manual for Private Lands (Costa, 1992). These guidelines appear to be more lenient than Henry's guidelines. If followed by landowners, the guidelines will avoid a Section 9 "taking" situation. Under these new guidelines a private landowner who has an RCW colony cannot harvest timber within a half-mile radius from the center of the colony unless the residual habitat following the harvest contains four key requirements.[32] In addition, the manual addresses such subjects as (1) habitat conservation planning and incidental take guidelines, (2) comprehensive habitat management and conservation program guidelines, and (3) formal consultation for federal actions involving private lands (Costa, 1993).

Protection of the endangered RCW has been a top priority for federal and state agencies. According to the National Wilderness Institute, more money was spent by the states in 1992 on the RCW than on any other endangered species. Almost 50 percent or $64 million of all reported state endangered species funds were spent on this one bird (National Wilderness Institute, 1993a).

The money being spent for the RCW is not on purchase of habitat for the bird. No Land and Water Conservation Fund monies have been appropriated or budgeted for the acquisition of land for the protection and recovery of this woodpecker.[33] The FWS has listed the bird and mandates its protection, but has not paid for its habitat. Mainstream environmental groups petition for preservation of habitats and old-growth ecosystems inhabited by surrogate species, but neither have they paid for land rights.[34] Consequently, the burden of payment for RCW habitat falls on the shoulders of a few unlucky landowners.

There have been many cases involving private landowners and the RCW. One of the most notable so far has been that of Benjamin Cone Jr., which involves 1,600 acres in Pender County, North Carolina, a case to be discussed in depth later.

Another noted case involves the Sumner property in Georgia. The timber on this property was sold in May 1991 on sealed bid for $270,000. FWS officials inspected this property and reported that it supported an active woodpecker colony. Timber harvest was halted until the findings were further investigated. In November 1991, the supposed colony was discovered to be inactive. The Sumners had to pay consulting and legal fees that were never reimbursed by the government, and they were prevented from harvesting timber on the land for a period of months (Wood, 1994).

Local problems resulting from reduced timber harvest on private lands and public lands can lead to even larger global problems. The RCW has been called the northern spotted owl of the South because like the owl it has the potential to make for a "train wreck" significantly decreasing timber harvest and shutting down parts of the timber industry.[35] This is especially true since the timber industry has shifted its efforts from the Pacific Northwest to the Southeast (National Wilderness Institute, 1993b). Unlike in the Pacific Northwest where most of the timber comes from federal lands, in the Southeast most of the timber is harvested from small private landholdings.

When enough private landowners are prohibited by the Endangered Species Act from harvesting timber, then supply is decreased, pushing up forest products prices, already high because of Clean Water Act issues and the disposition of the public lands in the Northwest (Suwyn, 1993). Since October 1992, lumber prices have increased by some 90 percent, and a major part of this is directly attributable to the protection of the northern spotted owl (Suwyn, 1993). This 90 percent increase translates into a $10-$12 billion extra burden imposed on home builders and others seeking to remodel their homes (Sugg, 1993). While burdensome in their own right, the cutting restrictions generated by the ESA are compounded by limitations posed by the Clean Water Act. As yet, the lumber price effects of protecting the RCW have not been identified, but the potential for further reductions in supply is clear.

The Cone Land Controversy

Protection of the RCW under the Endangered Species Act has had significant impacts on timberland owners in the southeastern United States. The story of Cone's Folly, a large tract of land in Pender County, North Carolina, owned by Benjamin Cone Jr., illustrates the difficulties posed to all parties when private property rights are threatened by commandand-control regulation (Deterling, 23).

Benjamin Cone Sr., who lived in Greensboro, North Carolina, and made a large amount of money during the Depression, purchased the land in Pender County. After purchasing the first tract, he acquired various other parcels, to bring the entire Cone ownership to its current 7,200 acres. The land was jokingly referred to as Cone's Folly because people in Greensboro thought it silly that Cone was using his money to purchase seemingly worthless land in rural Pender County.

In 1982, Benjamin Cone Jr. inherited the 7,200 acres of land from his father. He was required by the government to pay over $1 million in estate taxes based on an appraisal of the value of the timber on the land. Protection of the RCW was not an issue then. It was assumed that Benjamin Cone Jr. owned his timberland free and clear and could manage and harvest timber as he saw fit.

Pender County is located in the southeastern part of the North Carolina coastal plain. The Cone property is located in the western section of the county near Atkinson and borders the Black River. The county is fairly rural and sparsely populated, with most of the land being utilized for agriculture and silviculture. The land has been managed for wildlife primarily and timber production secondarily. Ben Cone Jr. devotes a great deal of time and money to maintain this property as a hunting preserve. He lives in Greensboro and pays a caretaker to live on the property.

Dirt roads on the land are well maintained, and the sides of the roads are planted with chuffa and rye for wild turkey. The wild turkey has made a comeback in North Carolina partly because of Cone's efforts. The FWS in North Carolina, with cooperation and help from Cone, relocated wild turkeys to establish a viable population at Cone's Folly. The property is burned frequently to provide habitat for quail and deer. Food plots are grown and maintained. Cone spends money for tractors, gasoline, machinery, and helpers to provide habitat for wildlife on his land.

In the past Cone has clear-cut his land infrequently. He shows an aversion to cutting any tree, unless prompted to do so by good forestry practices. He describes the timber on his land as a low-yield, tax-deferred savings account.

Cone has canoed the Black River frequently and allows other groups such as the Sierra Club to put canoes on his property. He considers this river to be one of the most valued assets on his property, and he strongly supports its protection. The Black River is recognized as one of the cleanest and most undisturbed rivers in the United States and is currently being considered as a historic and scenic site. Several extremely old bald cypress trees, dating back 1,000 years, have been located on the Black River.

The Discovery of the Red-Cockaded Woodpecker

Ben Cone and his caretaker note that in the 1970s there were a couple of red-cockaded woodpeckers on Cone's Folly (Conversation with Cone, March 19, 1994). However, the birds posed little problem because Cone did not wish to cut the tree habitat at that time. In short, there was no competition for the land rights. Cone believes there was an increase in the number of birds and cavity holes in the early 1990s. He speculates that after Hurricane Hugo hit the Francis Marion National Forest in South Carolina, the birds from the large population there abandoned their homes and moved to North Carolina.

In 1991, Cone tried to sell some timber from his land. According to normal procedure he had Dan Gelbert, a professional forester, cruise the tract. It was then that the presence of the birds was actually discovered and recorded. Soon after Gelbert noted the woodpeckers, Cone hired a wildlife biologist, Dave Dumond, to determine the number of birds. The population was large. Dumond has since discovered that there are twenty-nine birds and twelve colonies. These clusters of trees have been marked and are located in two tracts on the property, the House-to-Barn Tract and the Sandridge Tract. The House-to-Barn Tract consists of mostly loblolly pine and adjoins a highway. The Sandridge Tract is mostly longleaf pine and is more central to the property. Both tracts have been managed for quail hunting in the past. These management practices have provided a cleared understory that ironically has made the land attractive for RCW. The Sandridge Tract is raked for valuable longleaf pine straw. Both tracts are still being managed and used for hunting.

Assessment of the woodpecker habitat has determined that 1,560.8 acres have been affected by the bird's presence. According to the FWS's 1989 Henry Guidelines, applied first to the Cone property, a half-mile radius must be drawn around each colony within which no timber can be harvested. If timber is harvested, Cone is subject to a severe fine and/or imprisonment under the Endangered Species Act. Essentially, 1,560.8 acres of Cone's land is worthless for its timber, but he is still required by law to pay taxes on its previous value.

Changes in Land Management Practices

In order to accommodate the RCW, Cone has made several changes in the way he manages the wildlife and the timber on the affected and adjoining acreages. First, he has begun to clear-cut frequently on the lands adjoining the affected acreages. In the past Cone clearcut a 50-acre block every five to ten years. Since the woodpeckers have been found on his land, he has clearcut 300 to 500 acres every year on the rest of his land. Cone has these comments on his harvesting practices, "I cannot afford to let those woodpeckers take over the rest of the property. I'm going to start massive clearcutting. I'm going to a 40-year rotation instead of a 75- to 80-year rotation" (Sugg, 1993).³⁶

In fact, Cone sent a registered letter to Federal Paper Board, which has land adjoining his property to inform them of their possible liabilities regarding protection of the bird. Cone never heard back from them, but they immediately began clear-cutting all the timber adjacent to Cone's Folly. Apparently, they did not want the woodpeckers on their land either.

Cone has had to change his burning practices in the House-to-Barn and the Sandridge tracts. Even though not required by law to do so, he continues to burn to improve the habitat for quail. He plows and bushhogs a 10-to-20-yard circle around each cavity tree and rakes the straw away from each tree. Habitat trees must be protected from high flames. If a tree ignited and was destroyed, this would result in a taking under Section 9. Cone described this different practice as "not easy," and he estimates it adds five days of labor each time he prescribes burns.

Finally, Cone can no longer cut timber on the affected acreage, which is the largest change in his timber operation. Thinning is common in timbered forests, but now, permission to thin must be granted by the FWS.

The Economic Impact of Species Protection

Cone had an appraisal made by Charles Moody III of Realty Services of Eastern Carolina in January 1993 to determine the loss in value of the affected acreage. Moody determined that without the woodpeckers the value of the 1,560.8 acres with hunting leases, timber production, and straw raking is $2,230,000 (Moody, 1993). With the woodpeckers the 1,560.8 acres are worth only $86,500, with the only residual values being straw and hunting leases. This is a 96 percent reduction in value.

In addition, Cone has incurred other costs. He must pay to accommodate the woodpeckers in his burning practices. He has had to pay a wildlife biologist, a forester, an appraiser, and a lawyer to provide assistance and consultation on this legal and economic problem. He has not been reimbursed by the government for these costs, nor for the loss in value of his land.

When one considers the twenty-nine woodpeckers and the loss in value of land it is possible to calculate the cost of each bird in dollars. Each bird costs approximately $73,914 and their total habitat is worth $2,143,500. Ben Cone, not the federal government or the general public, who bears the costs of caring for the RCWs on his land.

What Are the Options?

Cone faces five options as he ponders his situation. As might be expected, some are more attractive than others.

Option 1: Continue with current practices. Under this option, Cone would maintain the status quo by burning to maintain habitat for the woodpeckers and clear-cutting all the timber adjacent to the affected acreage. This is the least feasible option for both the birds and Cone. Cone cannot recover the added operating costs. The RCW population will stabilize and eventually the birds will begin to inbreed, leading to low genetic variability. The woodpecker population on Cone's land would eventually die out.

Option 2: Sell to the children. Cone has two sons in their twenties. He is fearful that on this death his sons will inherit the woodpecker problem. The sons will be required by law to pay inheritance taxes of 55 percent of the land value, since the value of the property exceeds $1 million. The affected acreage is really worth only $85,600 with the woodpeckers present, but according to the government and the IRS the land will be appraised for $2.2 million for tax purposes. Cone proposes to sell the 1,560 acres to his sons now for the $86,500 value so that they will not have to pay high inheritance taxes on worthless land.

Cone considers this option to be the most attractive. If he sells the land, it is up to his sons to manage it, and they will likely allow midstory trees to grow up. In this event, Cone estimates that in twenty years the woodpeckers will abandon the nesting sites. The woodpecker also loses in this option.

Option 3: Sue the government. This option would involve Cone filing suit against the federal government on the grounds that his Fifth Amendment property rights have been violated. He would argue that his land has been taken for a public purpose without just compensation. Cone's lawyer, Marion Follin, believes there is a fifty-fifty chance of winning the case.

Cone wants to take this case to court to prove a point. He has the resources and the time to undertake such an option if he chooses. However, he fears that a court battle would bring even more exposure to his case. He fears possible threats from environmental groups similar to the tree spiking incidents in the Pacific Northwest. He also recognizes that the government has a deep pocket and can extend a legal battle for a long time through the appeal process. If Cone loses in court, he also fears a later backlash from the government.

Attorney Follin has estimated court costs to be approximately $100,000. This figure does not include consulting fees for witnesses, bringing the total costs to $200,000 or more. This cost must be weighed against the loss Cone will incur if he does nothing. If he does nothing, he will never recover the value from the current timber on his land. The trees will continue to mature until they all acquire heart rot fungus and die, and Cone will have to wait another twenty years to gain any value from replanted trees.

There are not many precedent cases on which Cone can rely. *Lucas v. South Carolina Coastal Council* seems a likely candidate, but in that case the Supreme Court ruled that where the government "seeks to sustain regulation that deprives land of *all* economically beneficial use, we think it may resist compensation only if the logically antecedent inquiry into the nature of the owner's estate shows that the prescribed use interests were not part of his title to begin with."[37] The 1,560 acres that are affected in Cone's case are only part of the 7,200 total acres he owns; Cone is still acquiring value from the other acreage. The land that he owns has continually been used for timber harvesting, and it has been appraised based on the value of the timber.

There are some possible legal precedents in the U.S. Court of Claims. The first is *Loveladies Harbor, Inc. v. United States.*[38] In this case the government proposed under Section 404 of the Clean Water Act that the landowner use the land for hunting, birdwatching, and harvesting salt hay instead of residential development. This proposal constituted a 99 percent loss in value; compensation was awarded.

In the second example, *Whitney Benefits, Inc. v. United States,* the rights to mine coal were taken away from the landowner.[39] The government argued that the land could be used to ranch and farm instead. Compensation was also awarded in this case because the court held that the statute denied the plaintiffs the right to all of the viable use of their coal property.

Cone stands to lose a great deal of time and money if he goes to court. Of course, this loss must be weighed against the possible recovery of his rights. He will also be setting a precedent for future cases involving the violation of property rights by environmental regulations.

Option 4: Negotiate with the Fish and Wildlife Service. Ralph Costa, the the FWS recovery coordinator for the red-cockaded woodpecker, has suggested that Cone apply for an incidental take permit for the rest of the 7,200 acres (Conversation with Ben Cone, March 19, 1994). This would involve following section 10 of the Endangered Species Act and developing a Habitat Conservation Plan (HCP). As another alternative, Cone could devise a Memorandum of Agreement (MOA) similar to Georgia Pacific's "no-take" plan.

Cone sees this option as a "no win" for him; the FWS is giving him nothing in exchange for his loss. He believes that this option is still placing the full responsibility of the woodpeckers on him. He will not be compensated for his land or other costs incurred, such as expenditures for lawyers, consultants, and appraisers.

Option 5: Do nothing. With this option, Cone would leave the land alone and would allow nature to take its course. There would be no burning; his best quail and deer hunting acreage would be ruined. The trees will eventually die or rot and will not be merchantable. The midstory will grow up and eventually the birds will abandon the colonies to find other appropriate nesting habitat. Cone would lose the $2.2 million of current timber value, and the best hunting on his land; the woodpeckers lose their homes. Neither the woodpeckers nor the landowner would win.

Current Status of the Story

Costa recently issued new guidelines for the management of the redcockaded woodpecker on private lands. These guidelines are not as strict as Henry's 1989 guidelines, known as the Blue Book. Cone has hired a private wildlife biologist, Dave Dumond, to survey the land to determine if any timber exists within the specified RCW habitat that can be safely harvested under the new guidelines. After this determination is made, Cone will attempt to sell this timber to companies that will bid. However, he will attach the liability of the woodpeckers to the sale. Cone is assuming that no timber company will bid on such timber, considering the consequences that would result should they destroy woodpecker habitat. He is probably correct in his assumption.

After Cone has demonstrated that the complete parcel of land, the entire 1,560 acres, is worthless, he will have more evidence to support his case in federal court should he sue the government. Cone is still trying to decide between options 2 and 3. Selling the land now to his children seems to be the more practical solution. No matter the outcome, the whole experience has been an emotional one for Cone. In the past year he has become a great advocate for private property rights in the local area, talking to many groups and appearing frequently in the media. Cone feels he has an obligation to take this to court, to uphold the Constitution and private property rights.

Some Thoughts on the Situation

Stories like Benjamin Cone's are becoming more and more common as environmental statutes become land-use regulations. Cone is not a poor man, he owns a great deal of land, and many people find it hard to feel sorry for him in his predicament. If he owned only 60 acres, and all 60 had been taken under the Endangered Species Act for protection of the woodpecker, it would be easier to draw sympathy to his cause. But the principles involved in this case are the same no matter how wealthy the landowner or how much land is involved.

Cone says he has been criticized for being "just another greedy landowner," according to one letter to the editor (Conversation with Ben Cone, March 19, 1994). He is clear-cutting the land around the designated woodpecker habitat as fast as he can, and he is making approximately $300,000 per clear-cut. On top of that he is asking to be compensated $2.2 million for 1,560 acres by the government.

Cone may also be criticized for being antienvironment. He is seen as trying to destroy the habitat of a valuable endangered species by arguing against the Endangered Species Act. He has said many times that he truly believes that the red-cockaded woodpecker is an endangered species that needs to be protected. He continues to prescribe-burn the forest floor of the RCW habitat to improve hunting for quail when it would serve him better to let the midstory trees encroach, forcing the bird to leave.

In the past he has proved that he is an environmental steward. He supports the protection of the Black River as a valuable resource. He helped with the comeback of the wild turkey in North Carolina. He spends thousands of dollars a year on food plots, burning, and other maintenance for wildlife.

Cone feels he is being punished for taking care of his land and the wildlife on it. He burned to establish habitat for quail and deer. He did not clear-cut, instead preserving an old-growth forest. These practices have also created prime habitat for twenty-nine red-cockaded woodpeckers.

At this point, the woodpecker is also losing. Cone has been clear-cutting, isolating these woodpecker colonies. The population size will continue to grow, and then the numbers will stabilize. Genetic isolation and inbreeding will occur, and eventually biology tells us that this population will die out and thus will not contribute to the overall recovery of the species.

In this case the Endangered Species Act is accomplishing the opposite of its intended goal. The government is not protecting species but is instead contributing to their destruction by angering and alienating the private landowner with the perverse incentives contained in the Endangered Species Act. Similarly, environmental groups petition the government not for actions that will save more species, but for actions that will save endangered ecosystems and habitats. To these groups, the endangered species is not the red-cockaded woodpecker, but rather the ancient forests it inhabits. A compromise can be reached in this situation so that both Cone and the red-cockaded woodpeckers on his land will benefit. If Cone is compensated, rights to habitat for the red-cockaded woodpecker will transfer to the new owner, and the woodpecker may be allowed to recover as a viable population.

4. Alternative Approaches to the Land Rights Conflict

Because of concern over potential takings of private land rights in order to protect the red-cockaded woodpecker, several parties have proposed alternatives. Both the Fish and Wildlife Service and the Environmental Defense Fund have suggested possible solutions to the conflict.

Ralph Costa, the FWS recovery coordinator for the red-cockaded woodpecker, has been working with individuals in the private sector to formulate a private lands strategy that will benefit both the private landowner and the bird. The objectives of this plan according to Costa are as follows:

(1) Minimize loss of genetic diversity at the species level.
(2) Increase RCW populations on public lands, particularly in lations, and on appropriate non-federal lands.
(3) Foster and develop cooperative relationships between and among federal, state, and private parties, with the goal of maintaining and/or establishing additional, relatively large populations beyond those targeted as recovery populations.
(4) Minimize the economic impacts of RCW habitat retention to small property private landowners.

The strategy has three components: (1) the already discussed RCW private lands manual, (2) statewide Habitat Conservation Plans (HCP), and (3) Memoranda of Agreement (MOA) (Costa, 1993).

The Emerging Memorandum of Agreement

As currently construed, the Memorandum of Agreement (MOA) is drafted as a contract between a private party, like a corporation, and the FWS. When employed with RCW habitat, the private party agrees to provide and actively manage RCW habitat, a task not required by corporate landowners in either the Henry's 1989 guidelines or the new RCW procedures manual for private lands. In exchange, the private landowner receives more flexibility when harvesting timber in these areas. This strategy can also be used in cases involving large tracts of nonindustrial private timberland (Costa, 1993; Smathers et al., in preparation).

The first and most notable of these MOAs has been the "no-take" plan developed by Georgia Pacific Corporation (GP). GP has agreed to no net loss of approximately 115 to 120 active colonies of woodpeckers on its timberlands in Arkansas, North Carolina, South Carolina, Louisiana, and Mississippi, the largest number of colonies known to exist on a single private ownership (Wood, 1994). This particular MOA specifies that GP will stop cutting timber on 10 acres that immediately surround each of the colonies on its land holdings. The company will establish a 510-acre buffer zone around each RCW colony within which it will "log more carefully" (Schneider, 1993). In addition, more than four hundred GP foresters will be trained to better identify colonies, locate new ones, and monitor habitat (Vongs, 1993).

According to Gene Wood, a forest wildlife ecologist for the company, GP had an incentive to develop a MOA because of the strict 1989 RCW guidelines that were incompatible with its commercial timber management. GP stood to lose more than any other southern timber company since it has so many RCW colonies. The MOA allowed GP to continue its forty-year sawtimber rotation and harvesting practices while protecting and actively managing for the woodpecker at the same time. In addition, the FWS guaranteed GP that it will not be prosecuted under Section 9 of the Endangered Species Act should woodpeckers abandon cavity trees (Conversation with Gene Wood, August 1, 1994). The MOA allowed GP to enter into some type of agreement with the FWS with more flexibility than a Habitat Conservation Plan.[40] An HCP would have been expensive, would have opened the company's land to public inspection, and would have involved deed covenants on affected lands (Wood, 1994).

As of January 1994, GP had protected 112 colonies and 50,000 acres of habitat (Woods, 1994). Furthermore, since signing the agreement, GP has received beneficial publicity promoting the company as more environmentally conscious. Hancock Timber Resource Group has signed a similar MOA with the FWS and four others are currently being negotiated (Smathers et al., in preparation).

An MOA implicitly assigns land rights to the U.S. government. A new feudal-like property rights regime emerges when an agreement is struck. By agreeing to accept regulatory restrictions on some of his property, the private landowner is given an opportunity to continue profitable operations on other portions of his land. Even under the best of circumstances, an MOA falls far short of a freely negotiated contract between similarly situated buyers and sellers. The heavy hand of the government poses a threat: either the landowner signs or else.

When accepted by a private landowner, an MOA can be effective in protecting large RCW populations located primarily on private industrial land. Indeed, a modified MOA, with payments for all costs imposed, could become the basis for transactions that recognize private property rights.

Statewide Habitat Conservation Plan

The statewide Habitat Conservation Plan is a component of the strategy designed to deal with the small private landowner and the smaller demographically isolated red-cockaded woodpecker population (Smathers et al., in preparation). Section 10 of the Endangered Species Act provides for the development of Habitat Conservation Plans to help resolve problems when the activities of private landowners are in conflict with endangered species protection. Like an MOA, the Habitat Conservation Plan represents a transfer of land-use rights from the private owner to the U.S. government. Essentially, a private landowner can be given an incidental take permit from the FWS if he submits and prepares an appropriate conservation plan.[41] Also, it must be determined that the purpose of the activity is not to take the species or to jeopardize the survival and recovery of the species elsewhere (Quarles et al., 1991).

The HCP has provided some flexibility to the often stringent Endangered Species Act; however, such an individual plan can be quite expensive for a private landowner in terms of time and money for environmental and legal consultation. Sometimes the costs for an individual HCP can reach into the millions of dollars (Thornton, 1993). In the case of the proposed statewide Habitat Conservation Plan for the red-cockaded woodpecker, all affected parties in a particular state will collaborate and pay to develop an umbrella plan. This will spread the transaction costs of HCP establishment among many private landowners and alleviate the burden associated with individual plans (Smathers et al., in preparation).

Going Beyond MOAs and HCPs: Endangered Species Certificates

Kennedy and Smathers, two researchers at Clemson University, in cooperation with the FWS have proposed a marketable Transferable Endangered Species Certificate (TESC) program to supplement the statewide HCP. This program would allow private landowners who participate in the statewide Habitat Conservation Plan to earn TESCs or credits for juvenile fledglings produced by breeding pairs on their land. These juvenile red-cockaded woodpeckers would then be translocated to federal lands where they would be added to larger populations. Each certificate will have an attached economic value and can be traded or sold with other landowners. Ownership of a TESC would allow a timberland owner to log or take other action to destroy RCW habitat (Gutfield, 1993).

These Transferable Endangered Species Certificates improve the economic position of the private landowner by allowing him or her to cut timber and derive some value from RCW-designated habitat. The newly recognized property rights that lie behind the certificates will also help the long-range recovery of the bird by adding juvenile birds to large populations on federal lands, ending the problem of demographic isolation. The certificate program converts an endangered species into an asset that generates value to landowners now constrained by the ESA statute.

Comments on the Private Land Strategy

The problems that have stemmed from the protection of the red-cockaded woodpecker on private timberlands in the South seem to be resolvable. The private lands strategy proposed by Ralph Costa does not completely address the problem, but it is one of the first attempts to compromise with, rather than alienate, the private landowner. Costa realizes that emerging conflicts with private landowners can create legal problems for the FWS and biological problems for the woodpecker. He has been the main force behind establishing a comprehensive private lands strategy to stifle the controversy surrounding the protection of RCWs on private lands.

The strategy's statewide Habitat Conservation Plan and Transferable Endangered Species Certificate program have been criticized for a number of reasons. The TESC program still places a considerable cost on the private landowner and does not provide enough incentives for creating RCW habitat. Under the TESC program land rights can still be taken. Small private landowners often liquidate their timber on rather short notice for a variety of reasons, but under the stateside HCP they will be prevented from doing so until they accumulate enough endangered species certificates (Wood, 1994).

In addition, the private lands strategy would not be applicable to all private landowners. Private parties like Ben Cone, who own large tracts of private nonindustrial land, are not eligible for the new programs, even if they wish to be. Costa states that one of the objectives of the private lands strategy is to "minimize the economic impacts of RCW habitat retention to small property landowners" (Costa, 1993). A small landowner is defined as owning less than 1,000 acres (Costa, 1993). Cone does not qualify because his holdings total 7,200 acres.

The proposed statewide Habitat Conservation Plan would be available only to small, private landowners (<1,000 acres) or to individuals or corporations owning more than 1,000 acres but harboring small groups (<5) isolated (>5 miles) from other RCW groups. According to Costa, the statewide HCP is not appropriate for large landowners, like Cone, who harbor relatively large RCW populations (>10). He states that these types of situations can best be remedied through individual Habitat Conservation Plans or Memoranda of Agreement (Costa, 1993).

As stated in the previous section, Cone does not consider an individual Habitat Conservation Plan or Memorandum of Agreement a reasonable solution to his conflict with the FWS. He would have to incur the costs of writing and implementing the plan, and even then he would still not be able to use the 1,560 acres of woodpecker habitat. He would only have incidental take on the rest of Cone's Folly Plantation, not on the affected acreage. In short, individuals like Cone will not readily accept a feudal rights system.

Environmental Defense Fund Proposal

Michael Bean, chairman of the Environmental Defense Fund's wildlife program, has proposed two incentive-based approaches to resolve red-cockaded woodpecker conflicts in the Sandhills of North Carolina. The first of these is the Tradeable Credit Approach, similar in theory to the Transferable Endangered Species Certificate program. This approach was created to give landowners an incentive to rehabilitate abandoned RCW colonies on their property. Landowners must provide rehabilitated colonies on their land, before they can take other active colonies. At first a two-for-one mitigation (two colonies rehabilitated for every one taken) will be required. After a certain goal number of colonies is reached in the population, a one-for-one mitigation will go into effect (Bean, 1993).

Under this approach landowners could also take active colonies if they pay another landowner to rehabilitate colonies on that other owner's land. In this way valuable mitigation credits could be earned by landowners for later use or sale to others. There would be an incentive to rehabilitate abandoned RCW colonies even before others are taken (Bean, 1993).

Second, Bean has proposed a Voluntary Land Enrollment Approach. In this approach landowners would be encouraged to voluntarily enroll their lands into a state program that would require them to manage their property for RCW habitat. According to Bean, specified management practices would include longer rotation cycles, prescribed burning of understory, pine straw harvest, cavity augmentation, and reforestation. In return, landowners would receive compensation. Bean suggests compensation in the form of direct annual payments from a trust fund (to which federal, state, or private landowners that have adversely impacted red-cockaded woodpeckers and their habitat must contribute), tax credits, or further benefits under state-supported stewardship programs (Bean, 1993).

The Environmental Defense Fund approaches have more application to Cone and the private landowner in general. They are more applicable to all landowners, large and small, as there is no mention of landowner size. Bean's proposal emphasizes management for RCW habitat rather than for juvenile birds. Creating appropriate habitat may provide homes for other endangered or threatened wildlife endemic to the longleaf savannah. Bean's approach gets to the root of the problem, the destruction of RCW habitat.

However, there are some drawbacks. Bean's proposal does not address the FWS's objective of establishing viable populations on federal lands, because his approach does not provide for translocation of birds from private to federal lands. Under EDF's proposal there may be demographic isolation, as private lands with appropriate RCW habitat are frequently separated from each other.

The Real Story?

On the surface, the red-cockaded woodpecker/private landowner conflict appears simple. The FWS is using the Endangered Species Act to take land from private landowners without just compensation. A deeper analysis leads to a richer picture with more players, one involving special interests like timber companies and mainstream environmental groups.

The first player, the FWS, has no incentive to recover and delist the red-cockaded woodpecker. The FWS gets funded only when a species is listed as endangered. Costa has included the proposed Transferable Endangered Species Certificate program in his private lands strategy, which is a better solution than regulatory taking. However, it is not clear whether the TESC program is truly a marketable approach or merely a political attempt to quiet the small private landowner in the South. Clearly, if this program is implemented, the FWS will save itself from future takings cases and from compensating landowners.

Second players, large timber companies, appear to be losing a great deal to the Endangered Species Act. They could lose thousands of acres of timberland because of protection of endangered species like the red-cockaded woodpecker. However, large timber companies in the South have not vocally fought the regulation, as evidenced by their refusal to aid Cone financially in a possible court battle with the government. Instead, Georgia Pacific and other large timber companies have written Memoranda of Agreement with the FWS that increase their role in managing habitat for RCWs. What is the true motivation behind writing such plans? Are large timber companies gaining from regulations protecting RCW habitat and take land from the noncorporate private landowner?

Mainstream environmental groups are third players. Their primary goal appears to be protecting and recovering the red-cockaded woodpecker. For example, they continue to petition to have species listed; yet listing is not in fact promoting recovery. As it is, the Endangered Species Act is not recovering species; yet environmental groups are pushing Congress to strengthen the prohibitive language of the statute upon reauthorization. If environmental groups truly wanted to save species, their expected behavior would be different. Perhaps preserving species like the red-cockaded woodpecker is not their objective at all. Perhaps their objective, as it appears to be in the case of the northern spotted owl, is preservation of the ecosystem inhabited by the endangered animal. Perhaps environmental groups strongly support the Endangered Species Act not for its ability to protect and recover species, but rather for its ability to control land and stop development.

The fourth and least powerful players in this picture are the private land-owners. Cone and other private landowners do not have the money or the political clout of the FWS, the timber companies, or the environmental groups. Yet they have been put at the center of the conflict. They (along with the endangered species) are the only group that truly loses under the Endangered Species Act. To them the solution to this conflict can be found in the Fifth Amendment to the Constitution. When the government wants land for red-cockaded woodpeckers, it should justly compensate those who own the land.

5. Implications for Policy and Final Thoughts

This chapter has described the background of the Endangered Species Act of 1973, discussed its implementaton, and identified serious property rights issues that have emerged since the mid-1980s. While the objectives of the ESA are noble, the implementation of the act leaves significant room for improvement. There are clear opportunities to modify the statute and provide legislation that protects private property rights and assists in the recovery of endangered species.

Simple Compensation for Land Rights

First off, the ESA should be reformed to explicitly authorize compensation to property owners for the lost use of their land. The Land and Water Conservation Fund of the pre-1980s should be reauthorized and funded.

Robert Smith, the director of environmental studies at the Cato Institute, suggests that the language of the Act return to the 1966 and 1969 Acts that authorized the federal government to purchase easements or full title to land. In this way the government would make efficient, cost-effective choices as to which species and habitats to protect (Smith, 1992).

The federal government could learn about efficient land acquisition from private groups such as the Nature Conservancy and Ducks Unlimited. The Nature Conservancy has purchased over 5.5 million acres since 1951. They economize by buying only the ownership rights that they really want and selling land that has no special natural value. Ducks Unlimited has improved over 6 million acres of wetlands habitat worldwide by purchasing conservation easements, a guarantee that an owner will not destroy the habitat (Kaufman, 1993).

To purchase land for species protection, John Baden, chairman of the Foundation for Research on Economics and the Environment, and Randal O'Toole, forest economist, have proposed a "biodiversity trust fund." This fund would be similar to the Land and Water Conservation Fund of the 1966 and 1969 Acts and would be funded with revenues generated from public land activities, such as logging, mining, oil and gas development, grazing, and recreation.

The fund would be used to purchase private lands or conservation easements for identified endangered species habitat. A board of trustees including economic and business leaders, environmental activists, and conservation biologists would manage the biodiversity trust fund. Baden believes that selling 10 percent of the public lands would generate $500 million to $1 billion a year for the purchase of habitat (Barker, 1993).

More Use of Federal Lands

According to Richard Stroup, PERC senior associate, the government should rely on public lands to preserve and reintroduce endangered species (Fitzgerald, 1993). The government is the largest holder of land in this country, owning 720 million acres of land or some 32 percent of the total land (Bast, Hill, and Rue, 1994). Increased use of public lands for endangered species habitat would serve a public interest and not interfere with private land rights. The FWS would better manage and monitor larger, viable populations of endangered species if they were in a localized, protected area instead of spread over small tracts of privately owned land.

Along these lines, in 1992 the Center for Plant Conservation at the Missouri Botanical Garden signed a contract with the U.S. Forest Service to collect seeds, propagate rare plants, and redistribute them onto public lands (Fitzgerald, 1993). A similar program is the proposed private lands strategy for the red-cockaded woodpecker. Juvenile birds will be translocated from private lands to cavity trees on federal lands in order to establish viable populations (Smathers et al., in preparation).

Focusing on Positive Incentives

Recognition of the fee simple property rights of landowners can eliminate the perverse incentives of Sections 7 and 9, which must be modified to encourage landowners to manage for habitat of listed species rather than destroying it. If landowners are rewarded when they discover endangered species, then property rights will increase in value, and habitat will be expanded. By placing a marketable value on wildlife, endangered species can become assets rather than liabilities, and more species can be protected, recovered, and eventually delisted (Sugg, 1993-94).

Recently, Defenders of Wildlife, a national conservation organization, attempted to provide incentives to ranchers in Montana and Wyoming to help the wolf make a comeback. Ranchers fear that wolves will prey on their livestock and have strongly opposed the proposed federal reintroduction program. Defenders has created a private insurance program to compensate ranchers for any loss of livestock to wolf predation. The organization has raised $100,000 for their compensation fund and has paid $12,000 to ten ranchers since 1987 for livestock lost to wolves. They have also created a wolf reward program by offering $5,000 to any rancher who allows a pair of wolves to breed and produce a litter of pups on his land. This program removes the negative incentives for the preservation of the wolf by offering "a carrot rather than a stick" (Anderson, 1993).

The Endangered Species Certificate program mentioned in the private lands strategy for the red-cockaded woodpecker is a way to provide positive incentives to the private landowner. A similar market-based system has been suggested in California to alleviate some of the endangered species conflicts there (e.g., Stephens' kangaroo rat). The proposal would allow landowners to earn conservation credits for enhancing or preserving habitat. These credits could be sold to developers or other interested parties as mitigation for impacts on wildlife habitat (Thornton, 1993).

A market-based approach to endangered species protection would rely on the efficiency and creativity of the marketplace. Placing a value on wildlife that can be sold or bought rather than taking property through regulation would enable both land rights and species to be better protected and restored.

Prioritize Protection with Improved Use of Science

The FWS should focus on protecting and recovering "keystone" species, rather than every subspecies and distinct population.[42] If only full-fledged, biological species were listed, there would be more money to spend on each species. Biologist David Ehrenfield admits in the book *Biodiversity*:

> the species whose members are fewest in number, the rarest, the most narrowly distributed—in short, the ones most likely to become extinct—are obviously the ones least likely to be missed by the biosphere. Many of these species were never common or ecologically influential; by no stretch of the imagination can we make them vital cogs in the ecological machine. (Simon and Wildavsky, 1993)

Perhaps protection of these very rare, narrowly distributed populations could be accomplished by environmental groups through voluntary action (Lambert and Smith, 1994).

Similarly, the FWS should prioritize habitats that need to be protected. A new technology known as gap analysis that can graphically display information from satellites on a map can determine areas that are the richest in animals and plants. Those that are the richest in diversity could be acquired and preserved by the government to promote efficient recovery of the most species (Sansonetti, 1992).

Privatization of Wildlife

One of the most radical policy suggestions calls for privatization of endangered species. But the idea may not be so far-fetched. Zimbabwe has increased the population of the elephant by rejecting Western-type state control and protectionism. According to Dr. Graham Child, the former director of

Zimbabwe's Department of National Parks and Wildlife Management, Zimbabwe has adopted a policy that allows for the "devolution of rights to use wildlife outside protected areas to the people with it on their land" (Sugg, 1993-94).

South Africa has also privatized endangered wildlife through game ranching. Game ranchers own and manage their animals for hunting, tourism, and consumption. While struggling on the rest of the continent, the white rhinoceros is prospering in South Africa mostly because of game ranching. By receiving an estimated $15,000 per head, ranchers have a great incentive to raise rhino and manage for their habitat (Weaver, 1991).

Game ranching could also prove to be successful in protecting endangered species in the United States. This type of privatization would increase the numbers in wildlife populations as well as giving wildlife habitat economic value, providing the private landowner with an incentive to leave it intact. Even portions of the ecosphere that do not have currently marketable value could benefit. Don Ashley, a consultant for the Florida Alligator Farmers Association, argues that the commercialization of alligators could help protect Florida's remaining wetlands. Giving alligators a market value would also give their wetlands habitat a value (Sugg, 1993-94).

Similarly, game ranching has been used by David Bamberger in Texas to increase the numbers of the scimitar-horned oryx, a species that is almost extinct in its native sub-Saharan range. He has preserved twenty-nine of the thirty-one remaining bloodlines. In addition, the Exotic Wildlife Association, the game ranching organization to which Bamberger belongs, owns over 125 species and 200,000 animals, 19,000 of which are threatened or endangered (Sugg, 1992).

Final Thoughts

The goals of protection and recovery of wildlife outlined in the Endangered Species Act are important. When a threatened species is protected in the name of biodiversity, the benefits accrue to a large number of interested citizens who look to government to act in their behalf. Constitutional protection of property rights is also important, and landowners understandably count on government to provide this fundamental service. Abuse of property rights on either side of the problem undermines the interests of all citizens. Property rights provide security to endangered species habitat on private and public land, just as they provide protection to the activities of farmers, ranchers and owners of timberland. The solution to ESA controversies must include property rights protection for all parties. The interests of those who seek increased species protection must be balanced against the interests of those who call for secure property rights. Just compensation for private property is one sure way to generate balance between competing users of land.

As currently implemented, the Endangered Species Act is unduly burdensome and one-sided. Private landowners, like Ben Cone, are expected to bear the cost of providing species habitat that presumably serves a broad public interest. Environmentalists and naturalists who want more habitat protection pay no price for landowner services. The services of the Ben Cones of the world seem free. As a consequence, ESA proponents understandably demand continuous expansion of species protection on private land. Since the mid-1980s, taxpayers have also escaped much of the burden of habitat expansion. As a result, regulatory takings are unconstrained. There are no strong incentives to search for and resolve the most serious problems or to find least-cost ways for protecting a targeted species.

By taking land rights from private parties, the government has alienated and angered the one group that could help the most in providing species protection. Instead of strengthening conservation tendencies, the ESA gives incentives for landowners to destroy potential habitat rather than preserve it. Species like the red-cockaded woodpecker simply will not recover if the government continues to infringe on private landowner rights. A return to taxpayer-funded habitat acquisition would go a long way toward resolving the problem for all parties.

The backlash of landowner outrage generated by regulatory takings seems to have sent a message to the regulators. As indicated in this chapter, the FWS is offering a more sensible approach when dealing with private land. The Environmental Defense Fund's proposal and others discussed in the chapter offer property rights approaches for resolving some of the conflicts. The use of markets offers a way to protect species while also protecting landowner rights. But there is more fundamental work to be done on ESA enforcement. Merely stating that endangered species must be protected is not enough. Well-defined species targets must replace the broader and more nebulous definitions that emerged when land rights were taken with impunity. Science must be brought to bear in this task and in determining just how much habitat and how many locations are necessary.

Two recent actions suggest that major ESA revisions are in the works. If upheld, a March 11, 1994 decision of the U.S. Circuit Court of Appeals (D.C.) may end regulatory takings of private property rights. In *Sweet Home Chapter of Communities for a Greater Oregon v. Bruce Babbitt, Secretary of the Interior,* the D.C. Circuit Court ruled that habitat modification on private property does not constitute a taking of a listed species and should not be prohibited under the ESA." The court invalidated the FWS's definition of "harm," which previously included habitat modification, citing that it "was neither clearly authorized by Congress nor a 'reasonable interpretation' of the statute" (Sugg, 1994a). Individuals like Ben Cone may have recovered their Fifth Amendment protection.

On June 14, 1994, Secretary of the Interior Bruce Babbitt announced new directives and policies that will make ESA enforcement more flexible (Forest Resource Group, 1994). Under his proposal, the FWS and the National Marine

Fisheries Service will issue joint directives requiring the use of sound science. Science-based decisions will include peer review by independent experts. The new directives also require 30-day completion of recovery plans upon the listing of a species, with specific attention paid to economic impact. The listing and plans must identify activities that are exempt from activities that otherwise constitute a species taking.

Along with court and agency actions, the U.S. Congress in 1995 was debating changes in the ESA and property rights legislation that could dramatically affect ESA procedures. In all this, one thing seems clear: Property rights protection will be strengthened, which means that endangered species will be more secure in the future than in the past.

Notes

1. The author would like to express appreciation to the Political Economy Research Center for their funding and guidance, Mr. Ben Cone for allowing the author to tell his story, and her family and friends for their continued support. Gratitude is extended to the countless other individuals who assisted in this project.

2. The legal meaning of the term "taking" is unclear and has yet to be completely defined for cases involving the Endangered Species Act. The term is being used here and throughout the rest of the chapter in the popular sense. The "taking" used here in the context of property rights is not to be confused with a "taking" of a species under Section 9 of the Endangered Species Act.

3. Land and Water Conservation Fund of 1964, 78 Stat. 897.

4. Endangered Species Preservation Act of 1966, P.L. No. 89-669, 80 Stat. 926.

5. Endangered Species Conservation Act of 1969, P.L. No. 91-135, 83 Stat. 275.

6. Endangered Species Act of 1973, P.L. No. 93-205, 87 Stat. 884.

7. This increase in acreage for endangered species habitat averages only 15,000 acres per year. This trend is small when compared with the millions of acres that are acquired for other areas like national parks and wilderness areas each year (see Bast, Hill, and Rue's *Eco-Sanity*, p. 203). Perhaps the comparatively small land base for endangered species explains why the FWS and its environmentalist supporters push for takings.

8. The FWS has a priority system for acquisition on which it bases its recommendations to Congress. Environmental groups also have acquisition agendas that they submit to Congress (see Wilderness Society, Wild Land and Open Spaces: Priorities for the Land and Water Conservation Fund—FY '95). Because of the two agendas, funding is often not appropriated as the FWS had planned. In these cases the FWS might choose to "take" land through regulation. Further research could determine if this is indeed a factor.

9. 50 C.F.R. § 424 (1992).

10. Endangered Species Act of 1973, 16 U.S.C. § 1532 (1988).

11. 50 C.F.R. § 424 (1992).

12. Endangered Species Act of 1973, 16 U.S.C. § 1532 (1988).

13. Telephone conversation with an official from the Branch of Information Management, U.S. Fish and Wildlife Service Endangered Species Program, July 25, 1994.

14. 50 C.F.R. § 424 (1992).

15. Endangered Species Act of 1973, 16 U.S.C. § 1533 (1988).

16. Ibid.

17. Endangered Species Act of 1973, 16 U.S.C. § 1536 (1988).

18. Endangered Species Act of 1973, 16 U.S.C. § 1532 (1988).

19. 50 C.F.R. § 17.3 (1992).

20. Endangered Species Act of 1973, 16 U.S.C. § 1540 (1988).

21. Endangered Species Act of 1973, 16 U.S.C. § 1539 (1988).

22. Telephone conversation with an official from the Branch of Information Management, U.S. Fish and Wildlife Service Endangered Species Program, July 14, 1994.

23. World Wildlife Fund, "Reasons to avoid amending the Endangered Species Act," Fact Sheet.

24. Telephone Conversation with an official from the Branch of Information Management, U.S. Fish and Wildlife Service Endangered Species Program, July 25, 1994.

25. Ibid.

26. Endangered Species Act of 1973, 16 U.S.C. § 1532 (1988).

27. 50 CFR § 17.11 (1992). As interpreted by Lambert and Smith in *The Endangered Species Act: Time for a Change,* 1994.

28. 50 CFR § 17.3 (1992).

29. Erlich and Wilson, "Biodiversity Studies: Science and Policy" (as cited in Simon and Wildavsky, 1993).

30. This figure was calculated using the half-mile radius requirement for each group and a conversion factor of 640 acres per square mile. There are approximately 502 acres required for every colony and 2.2 million acres required in all for the 4,400 colonies that exist in the South.

31. *Sierra Club v. Yeutter,* 926 F.2d 429 (5th Cir. 1991).

32. According to the 1992 RCW Procedures Manual for Private Lands these four elements include (a) minimally between 50 sq. ft. basal area of pine timber on 60 acres and 10 sq. ft. of basal area on 300 acres for foraging habitat; (b) a minimum of 10 acres stocked at 50 sq. ft. per acre preserved for the colony area; (c) foraging habitat stands at least 25 years old with stems averaging at least 10 in. diameter at breast height; and (d) no separations with foraging habitat stands in excess of 300 ft. As cited by Gene Wood, The Red-Cockaded Woodpecker—Private Lands Issue, Presentation at the National Association of Conservation Districts 48th Annual Convention, February 2, 1994, p. 3.

33. Fish and Wildlife Service, Land and Water Conservation Fund Summary of Land Obligations and Summary of Appropriations, 1968-93.

34. Exceptions include Ducks Unlimited and the Nature Conservancy Fund as described in Part 5 entitled "Implications for Policy and Final Thoughts."

35. Secretary of the Interior Bruce Babbitt has used the term "train wreck" to describe the northern spotted owl situation in the Pacific Northwest.

36. Cone says that his massive clear-cutting practices are due to the presence of the red-cockaded woodpecker. Some might argue that Cone is clear-cutting his land not because of the woodpeckers but because of the increasing prices of timber. The sawtimber on Cone's land has increased in value in the past two years because of the decreased sup-

ply from the Pacific Northwest due to spotted owl protection and because of the increased housing market. More data would have to be gathered to refute Cone's claim.

37. *Lucas v. South Carolina Coastal Council,* 112 S. Ct. 436 (1991).

38. *Loveladies Harbor, Inc. v. United States,* 21 Cl Ct 153 (1990).

39. *Whitney Benefits, Inc. v. United States,* 18 Cl. Ct. 354 (1989).

40. For more information on Habitat Conservation Plans refer to Part 3 of this chapter entitled "The Endangered Species Act and its Major Elements."

41. For more information on incidental take permits refer to Part 3 of this chapter entitled "The Endangered Species Act and its Major Elements."

42. "A 'keystone' species serves as a critical link in the interconnected chain of life within a community." See Kunich, "The Fallacy of Deathbed Conservation under the Endangered Species Act," p. 557.

43. See Bast, Hill, and Rue, *Eco-Sanity,* p. 203.

44. *Sweet Home Chapter of Communities for a Great Oregon v. Babbitt,* No. 92-5255 (D.C. Cir., March 11, 1994).

References

Anderson, Terry. 1993. A carrot to save the wolf. *The Margin.* Spring: 28.

_____. 1993. A snail retreat. *Wall Street Journal.* December 27: 6.

_____. 1994. Enraging Species Act. *Wall Street Journal.* April 19: A20.

Barker, Rocky. 1993. *Saving All the Parts: Reconciling Economics and the Endangered Species Act.* Washington: Island Press.

Barro, Robert J. 1994. Federal protection—only cute critters need apply. *Wall Street Journal.* August 4: A14.

Bast, Joseph L., Peter J. Hill, and Richard C. Rue. 1994. *Eco-Sanity.* Madison Books: Lanham, Md.

Bean, Michael J. 1983. *The Evolution of National Wildlife Law.* Praeger: New York.

Bean, Michael J. 1993. Incentive-based approaches to conserving red-cockaded woodpeckers in the sandhills of North Carolina. In *Building Incentives into the Endangered Species Act* (ed. Wendy E. Hudson).

Campbell, Andrew. 1994. Survival of the richest. *University of Chicago Magazine.* April: 17.

Charles, Dan. 1991. Wee woodpecker halts the tanks. *New Scientist.* 132 (December 14): 9.

Cone, Benjamin. Conversation. March 19, 1994.

Copeyon, Carole K. 1990. A technique for constructing cavities for the red-cockaded woodpecker. *Wildlife Society Bulletin.* 18: 303-11.

Costa, Ralph. 1992. Red-cockaded Woodpecker Procedures Manual for Private Lands (Draft). U.S. Fish and Wildlife Service, Southeast Region. Atlanta, Ga. 56pp.

Costa, Ralph. 1993. The Issue of Red-Cockaded Woodpeckers on Private Lands. U.S. Fish and Wildlife Service. 17pp.

Coursey, Don. 1994. The revealed demand for a public good: evidence from endangered and threatened species. Harris School of Public Policy Studies Working Paper 94-2.

Deterling, Del. 1994. A Broken Law That Needs Fixing. *Progressive Farmer*. March: 20-23.

DiSilvestro, Roger L. 1987. Endangered species? Load the shotgun. *Audubon*. September: 12.

Dumond, David. Conversation. March 18, 1994.

Dunlap, Thomas R. 1988. *Saving America's Wildlife*. Princeton: Princeton University Press.

Ehrlich, Paul, and Edward O. Wilson. 1991. Biodiversity studies: science and policy. *Science*. 253 (August 16): 758-762.

Endangered Species Act of 1973, P.L. No. 93-205, 87 Stat. 884 (1973).

Endangered Species Act of 1973, 16 U.S.C. § 1531-1540 (1988).

Endangered Species Conservation Act of 1969, P.L. No. 91-135, 83 Stat. 275 (1969).

Endangered Species Preservation Act of 1966, Pub. L. No. 89-669, 80 Stat. 926 (1966).

Felten, Eric. 1990. Species listing a can of worms. *Insight*. August 27: 24-25.

Fitzgerald, Randy. 1993. When a Law Goes Haywire. *Reader's Digest*. September: 49-53.

Follin, Marion G. Letter to Steve Parker, Southeastern Legal Foundation. January 13, 1993.

Forest Resources Group of the American Forest and Paper Association. 1994. Babbitt announces new ESA policies. *Forest Resources*. June 20: 1.

Gibbons, Ann. 1992. Mission impossible: Saving all endangered species. *Science*. 256: 1386.

Gordon, Robert, and Jim Streeter. 1994. Going broke?: Costs of the Endangered Species Act as revealed in endangered species recovery plans. National Wilderness Institute: Washington, DC.

Gutfield, Rose. 1993. New Schemes Are Tried to Assist Woodpecker. *Wall Street Journal*. April 15: B1.

Heissenbuttel, John, and William R. Murray. 1992. A Troubled Law in need of Revision. *Journal of Forestry*. 90(8): 13-16.

Hellman, Donald J. 1991. Statement before the National Academy of Sciences Committee on Federal Acquisition of Lands for Conservation. The Wilderness Society. March 1.

Henry, V. G. 1989. Guidelines for Preparation of Biological Assessments and Evaluations for the Red-cockaded Woodpecker. U.S. Fish and Wildlife Service, Southeastern Region, Atlanta, Ga.

Kaufman, Wallace. 1993. The cost of "saving": You take it, you pay for it. *American Forests*. 99(11-12): 17-19, 58-59.

Kunich, John Charles. 1994. The fallacy of deathbed conservation under the Endangered Species Act. *Northwestern School of Law of Lewis and Clark College Environmental Law*. 24: 501-79.

Lambert, Thomas, and Robert J. Smith. March 1994. The Endangered Species Act: Time for a Change. Center for the Study of American Business. Policy Study No. 119.

The Land and Water Conservation Fund Act of 1964, 78 Stat. 897 (1964).

Larmer, Paul. 1989. A clearcutting ban for the birds. *Sierra*. 74 (March/April): 28-30.

Littell, Richard. 1992. *Endangered and Other Protected Species: Federal Law and Regulation*. Washington, D.C.: The Bureau of National Affairs.

Litvan, Laura M. 1994. A clash over property rights. *Nation's Business*. 82(4): 57 59.

McKay, Nicole. 1994. Species Conservation: At Whose Cost. (Unpublished.)

Moody, Charles. Real Estate Appraisal for a Portion of the Cone's Folly Tract containing 1560.8 acres, Caswell Township, Pender County, NC. August 19, 1992.

National Research Council. 1993. *Setting Priorities for Land Conservation*. Washington, D.C.: National Academy Press.

National Wilderness Institute. 1992. An endangered species blueprint. *NWI Resource*. 3(3): 1-21.

National Wilderness Institute. 1993a. State expenditures on red-cockaded woodpecker expose possible fear of a "spotted owl" for the South. *Fresh Tracks*. April.

National Wilderness Institute. 1993b. *Fresh Tracks*. August.

Nickens, Eddie. 1993. Woodpecker wars. *American Forests*. 99(172): 29-32, 54-55.

Office of Inspector General, U.S. Department of Interior. 1990. Final Audit Report on the Endangered Species Program, U.S. Fish and Wildlife Service (No. 90-98). September.

O'Laughlin, Jay. 1992. What the law is and what it might become. *Journal of Forestry*. 90: 6-12.

Oliver, Charles. 1992. All creatures great and small. *Reason*. April: 24-27.

Quarles, Steven, John A. McLeod, and Thomas R. Lundquist. 1991. The Endangered Species Act and its application to private lands. American Forest Resource Alliance. Technical Bulletin No. 91-06.

Rice, James Owen. 1992. Where many an owl is spotted. *National Review*. March 2: 41-3.

Rohrabacher, Dana. 1994. A bird in the brush. *American Spectator*. March: 86.

Rudolph, D. Craig, Richard Connor, Dawn Carrie, and Richard R. Schaefer. 1992. Experimental Reintroduction of Red-cockaded Woodpeckers. *Auk*. 109: 914-16.

Sansonetti, Thomas L. 1992. Economic Impacts of the Endangered Species Act. Remarks at Institute on Public Land Law (September 24): Paper 10.

Schneider, Keith. 1993. Babbitt Gets Between a Bird and a Logging Company. *New York Times*. April 18: E2.

Shanks, Bernard. 1984. *This Land Is Your Land*. San Francisco: Sierra Club Books.

Simon, Julian L., and Aaron Wildavsky. 1993. Assessing the empirical basis of the "biodiversity crisis." Competitive Enterprise Institute. May.

Smathers, W. M. Jr., R. Costa, and E. T. Kennedy. (Draft in preparation). Marketable Endangered Species Certificate Incentives for Private Landowners: the Red Cockaded Woodpecker.

Smith, Robert. 1992. The Endangered Species Act: saving species or stopping growth. *Regulation*. Winter: 83-87.

Society of American Foresters. 1992. White Paper and Position Statement on Red-cockaded Woodpecker Protection and Habitat Management on Private Lands.

Sugg, Ike C. 1992. To save an endangered species, own one. *Wall Street Journal*. April 31: A10.

Sugg, Ike C. 1993-94. Caught in the Act: Evaluating the Endangered Species Act, Its Effects on Man and Prospects for Reform. *Cumberland Law Review.* 24(1): 1-78.

Sugg, Ike C. 1993. Ecosystem Babbitt-Babble. *Wall Street Journal.* April 2: A12.

Sugg, Ike C. 1994a. Worried about that owl on your land? Here's good news. *Wall Street Journal.* April 6: A21.

Sugg, Ike C. 1994b. Defining "harm" to wildlife. *National Law Journal.* June 24: C1-C3.

Suwyn, Mark. 1993. We saved the salamander but it wasn't easy. *Wall Street Journal.* November 29: A14.

Taubes, Gary. 1992. A dubious battle to save the Kemp's Ridley Sea Turtle. *Science.* 256 (May 1): 614-16.

Thornton, Robert D. 1993. The search for a conservation planning paradigm: Section 10 of the ESA. *Natural Resources and Environment.* 8(1): 21-22, 65-67.

U.S. Fish and Wildlife Service. 1985. Red-cockaded Woodpecker Recovery Plan. U.S. Fish and Wildlife Service, Atlanta, Ga. 85pp.

U.S. Fish and Wildlife Service Division of Endangered Species. Telephone conversation with an official from the Branch of Information Management, July 14, 1994.

U.S. Fish and Wildlife Service Division of Endangered Species. Telephone conversation with an official from the Branch of Information Management, July 25, 1994.

U.S. Fish and Wildlife Service Division of Realty. 1994. Land and Water Conservation Fund Summary of Land Obligations for 1968-93.

U.S. Fish and Wildlife Service Division of Realty. 1994. Land and Water Conservation Fund Summary of Appropriations for 1968-1993.

U.S. General Accounting Office. 1988. Endangered species: Management improvements could enhance recovery program: Report to the Chairman, Subcommittee on Fisheries and Wildlife Conservation and the Environment, Committee on Merchant Marine and Fisheries, House of Representatives. December. GAO/ RCED-89-5.

U.S. General Accounting Office. 1992. Endangered Species Act: Types and numbers of implementing actions: Briefing report to the Chairman, Committee on Science, Space, and Technology, House of Representatives. May. GAO/RCED 92-131BR.

Vongs, Pueng. 1993. The real woodpecker deal. *Audubon.* 95 (September/October): 28-29.

Walters, Jeffrey, R. 1991. Application of Ecological Principles to the Management of Endangered Species: The case of the red-cockaded woodpecker. *Annu. Rev. Ecol. Syst.* 22: 505-23.

Weaver, Stephen M. 1991. The elephant's best friend. *National Review.* August 12:42-43.

Wilderness Society. 1994. Wild Land and Open Spaces: Priorities for the Land and Water Conservation Fund—FY '95.

Wood, Gene W. 1993. Endangered Species Act policy and red-cockaded woodpecker protection. Presentation at the American Pulpwood Association Convention, Asheville, N.C. November. (Unpublished.)

Wood, Gene W. 1994. The red-cockaded woodpecker—private lands issue. Presentation at the National Association of Conservation Districts 48th Annual Convention, Phoenix, Ariz., February 2. (Unpublished.)

Wood, Gene W. Telephone conversation. August 1, 1994.

Woods, Walter. 1994. Supply crisis drives price of lumber to new heights. *Greenville News Upstate Business*. January 30: 8(3).

World Wildlife Fund. "Reasons to Avoid Amending the Endangered Species Act." Fact Sheet.

Yaffee, Steven L. 1982. *Prohibitive Policy*. MIT Press: Cambridge, Mass.

Young, Mary Anne. 1993. The role of the National Wildlife Refuge System in endangered species management. *Endangered Species Update*. 10(7): 1-4.

Chapter 6

The Property Rights Movement and State Legislation

Hertha L. Lund

As noted in previous chapters, many frustrated landowners have turned to the U.S. Claims Court for redress for property losses or, like David Lucas and Mrs. Dolan, appealed their cases to the Supreme Court. Hoping to limit future regulatory takings by local and state governments, many others have joined coalitions and focused their energies on state legislatures.

The movement to obtain protective state legislation is truly a populist movement, twentieth-century style. By some counts, more than five hundred property rights organizations have formed across the nation, and these ordinary citizens are making their presence felt in their home states. They are joined by a diverse array of farmer and rancher organizations, labor unions, developers, and in some cases, local government officials who have focused their attention on state capitals. Legislative bodies nationwide have felt the pressures of this populist movement, which has one overriding goal: To uphold the counterpart of Fifth Amendment protection at the state level.

By August 1994, more than a hundred related bills had been introduced in forty-four states. (See Appendix A.) In August, some twelve legislative bodies had passed laws and the debate continued in the remaining legislative bodies.

(See Appendix B for sample legislation.) Anyone who thinks the property rights movement is something concocted in Washington by a few trade associations and politicians who seek to stymie the environmental movement are either sorely misinformed or simply don't understand what is going on. Yes, there is plenty going on in Washington, but the real action is in the fifty states.

This chapter looks closely at state legislative actions that are responding to to the property rights movement. The first part of the chapter describes the property rights movement, what it is not and what it is, and how the movement centered on efforts to obtain state legislation. The section discusses the political forces that converged and battled in the legislative process and describes efforts that were successful for property rights advocates and some where those efforts failed. Section three, which follows, examines pending legislation, identifies common elements found in the bills and refers to a state-by-state listing of legislative content and activity included as Appendix A. The last section offers some concluding thoughts. The chapter is also close companion to Chapter 7, which provides background for a theoretical treatment and an empirical analysis of the state legislation movement.

1. The State Legislative Effort: What It Is Not and What It Is

What It Is Not

Some commentators erroneously think that the current effort to reassert property rights protection is antienvironmentalism in disguise. For example, the lead editorial in the July 31, 1994, *Atlanta Journal/Constitution* focuses on Washington and says:

> To hear people in Washington talk, Americans are angrily demanding a wholesale gutting of the nation's environmental laws. And Congress is frighteningly close to succumbing to that demand. "It's almost tea party time in America," predicts an ebullient U.S. Rep. Billy Tauzin of Louisiana, one of the leaders of the anti-environmental crusade. "Clearly, the teapot's boiling here. It's steaming and the lid's about to blow."[1]

Then the editorial writer talks about efforts to "gut" the Endangered Species Act, the Clean Water Act, the Safe Drinking Water Act, and Superfund, indicating that a group of sold-out politicians are responding to pressures from the mining industry, oil industry, "Western ranchers, big-time farmers and real estate developers," who have "financed a highly successful yet very quiet public relations campaign aimed directly at Congress."[2] The editorial tells us "they succeeded in creating an illusion of a rebellion where none exists."[3]

In a widely distributed media mailing, fifteen major environmental organizations joined ranks, for the first time ever, in a call for action.⁴ The letter says that "polluters have blocked virtually all our efforts to strengthen environmental laws." Going on, the message refers to a grassroots movement, but indicates that the real pressure is from polluters—big industry, large farms, and others that simply want to make more money by polluting. According to the letter, the new antienvironmental message has three simple parts. The first is regulatory takings, which is described as a call from industry to "pay them *not* to pollute our air and water and *not* to destroy our wildlife and public lands." The other two arguments involve calls for cost-benefit and comparative risk analyses and an end to unfunded federal mandates that require state and local governments to meet new costly environmental rules without federal funding. This grand statement from the environmental establishment mischaracterizes the property rights issues. Property owners are not asking to be paid for not polluting. They want to be paid when their property is taken.

What It Is

The property rights movement gives the appearance of being anti-environmental for one straightforward reason. Practically all the grievances raised about land rights spring from the way environmental statutes have been enforced. Increasingly, particularly since the mid-1980s, regulators have chosen to enforce rules that effectively deny private landowners the right to use their land. Surely, there are some property owners who oppose certain environmental statutes, but by and large, the majority are simply seeking to have a voice in the matter and then to be paid when specific parcels of land are taken out of owner control. As pointed out in Chapter 5 on the Endangered Species Act, prior to the mid-1980s, Congress appropriated funds for the purpose of purchasing sensitive habitat. With funds to buy land, the Fish and Wildlife Service had less reason to engage in regulatory takings. Later, regulatory takings became the rule; purchase was the default position. Government efforts to control wetlands followed a similar pattern. Chapter 4 on wetlands describes how funds were appropriated to the U.S. Department of Agriculture to purchase wetland easements from farmers. Then the agency moved to regulation. As regulation expanded, and purchases took a back seat, more and more property owners became incensed.

Few people heard about widespread dissatisfaction with the Endangered Species Act (ESA) or wetlands control during the early 1980s. Of course, there were highly publicized incidents like the snail darter and Tellico Dam, but by and large, the legislative goals of the ESA and other environmental statutes were accepted by rank-and-file Americans. It is the means of attaining the goals, the effort to provide public benefits at the expense of private landowners, that has created the property rights movement. In short, the galvanizing issue is stated clearly and elegantly in the Fifth Amendment: "[N]or shall private property be taken for public use without just compensation."

Property rights legislation is seen by its proponents as a way to introduce balance into legislative decisions and government regulations. Federal regulations and related state laws typically require rigorous analysis to identify environmental risk, but there are no requirements for an analysis of risk to the nation's fundamental property rights system, the system that protects wetlands when they are defined and ensures that sensitive habitat remains off-limits to disturbing activities, once habitat property rights are defined.

Today, wetlands are defined using extreme assumptions about potential sensitivity and the possibility that migratory birds might light in a seasonally wet field. With disregard for property rights effects, species that may be abundant in one state are listed as endangered in a neighboring state, when in fact, the range of the species includes major parts of the two states.

Property owners recognize that caution is exercised by regulators who seek to carry out their mandate. They also know that regulators will be less cautious when making decisions if land can be taken without compensation and if there are no requirements for systematically weighing the costs of regulatory actions against the benefits.

While property rights legislation that requires analysis and a balancing of costs against benefits is viewed as beneficial to property owners, it is also likely that taxpayers and government will benefit as well. Indeed, legislation requiring state regulators to consider the property rights implications of their actions, before taking action, can preclude future legal suits that impose high costs.

The State Action: Where Bills Passed

As of August 1994, Arizona, Delaware, Idaho, Indiana, Mississippi, Missouri, North Carolina, Tennessee, Utah, Virginia, Washington, and West Virginia have passed measures to ensure protection of private property rights. The process used to pass these measures and the legislation varies from state to state.

Prior to 1993, three states—Washington, Delaware, and Arizona—had passed some type of property rights legislation. Washington was one of the first states to pass a property rights measure at the state level. The Washington property rights measure, signed into law in 1992, was not a stand-alone property rights bill. It was added as an amendment to the 1991 Growth Management Act and requires the attorney general to establish a checklist that enables state agencies and local governments to evaluate proposed regulatory or administrative actions. The Growth Management Act was a state land-use planning bill that was strongly opposed by private property rights advocates.

The Arizona story is a particularly interesting one, for on June 1, 1992, Arizona Governor Fife Symington signed into law the first stand-alone property rights bill that had real teeth. The legislation was an effort to "protect private property rights of Arizonians against state regulatory conduct which may amount to prohibited 'takings' under the U.S. and Arizona Constitutions," according to a news release by Governor Symington.[5] Attempts were made to portray the measure as hostile to the environment. In reply to such claims, Governor Symington asked this question, "Is it their position that environmentalism requires its adherents to denigrate the principle of private property as it has been known in America from the very dawn of our national existence? If so, then they have embraced an environmentalism which is foreign to me, and I would gladly place my environmental record against that of any holder of high office anywhere in the country." Governor Symington further stated:

Private property rights lie near the source of the liberty under which Americans are free to enjoy the God-given beauty of the Earth. It is the nature of government constantly to close in upon that liberty, to diminish it, to consume it. It is no coincidence, I think, that the most filthy environmental conditions in the history of the world are found today in the former Soviet Union and in Eastern Europe. A clean environment is a commodity like any other, and it cannot be had without cost. Paying that cost requires capital; accumulation of capital requires markets; and markets require eternal vigilance in the protection of private property.[6]

A governor who understood economics and the environment was most likely the strongest asset in getting the bill passed in Arizona. In addition to a wise governor, there was a strong coalition supporting the bill. Coalition members included:

Agri-Business Council of Arizona; American Desert Racing Association; Amigos; Arizona Aquaculture Association; Arizona Association of Realtors; Arizona Automobile Dealers Association; Arizona Cattle Feeders' Association; Arizona Cattle Growers' Association; Arizona Cattlemen's Association; Arizona Chamber of Commerce; Arizona Citizens Coalition on Resource Decisions; Arizona Cotton Growers Association; Arizona Farm Bureau Federation; Arizona Mining Association; Arizona Multi-House Association; Arizona/New Mexico Coalition of Counties; Arizona Nursery Association; Arizona State AFL-CIO; Arizona Trail Riders, Inc.; Arizona Vegetable Growers Association; Arizona Wool Producers Association; Associated General Contractors; Cactus & Pine Golf Course Superintendent Association; County Supervisors Associations of Arizona; Graham County Chamber of Commerce; Grand Canyon State Electric Cooperative Association; Home Builders Association of Central Arizona; International Brotherhood of Teamsters, Local Union #104; International Council of Shopping Centers; Irrigation and Electrical Districts Association of Arizona; National Federation of Independent Business of Arizona; Retail Grocers of Arizona; Stone Forest Industries; and others not listed.[7]

Such a wide array of groups in the coalition provided enough support to pass the legislation over the outcry of environmental groups. However, opponents of the legislation were able to get enough signatures to require the measure to go to a referendum vote in November 1994.

The bill that passed, but was later defeated in the referendum, required the attorney general to adopt guidelines to assist state agencies in identifying government actions that may be constitutional takings. The bill required state agencies to analyze (1) the likelihood of an action resulting in a taking, (2) other alternatives to the action, and (3) an estimate of the state's cost of compensation. This was a "look before you leap" type of bill.

Delaware was also one of the first states to pass a property rights measure. In 1992, Delaware passed a version of the "look before you leap" type of bill that requires the attorney general to review the promulgation of rules and regulations by state agencies to determine the effect on private property rights. G. Wallace Caulk, administrator of the Delaware Farm Bureau Federation, said the bill was opposed by environmental groups; however, the coalition supporting the bill had a working relationship with the environmental groups, which softened the opposition. Apparently, a strong agriculture coalition that fully supported the bill was a key element to its successful passage. And the fact that the governor and attorney general were supportive certainly helped. Also, the bill did not have a fiscal note attached.[8]

According to Caulk, the law is working well so far and the environmental group rhetoric has died down. The law has saved the state from taking challenges that could have resulted from 150 new regulations.

In 1993 Florida, North Carolina, Virginia, and Utah passed property rights legislation. Both Florida's and North Carolina's bills do not have much impact on property rights. The Florida bill that passed was a study bill that established a committee to study the issue. North Carolina's law is limited to compensation for land under navigable waters.

Virginia also passed weak property rights measures in 1993. The legislature adopted a bill that established a joint subcommittee to study Virginia governmental actions that may result in a taking of private property. Since the passage of the study bill, the subcommittee has been fairly inactive on the issue. However, supporters of property rights took another tack and assisted the passage of administrative rules that require an economic impact analysis of any proposed regulation. This measure was supported by the governor and was enacted through internal rules and legislation. The governor also signed an executive order requiring all agencies to review all previous rules under the economic impact analysis. John Johnson, assistant director for public affairs of the Virginia Farm Bureau, said the advocates used different language, avoided the inflammatory buzz words, and accomplished the same goal as property rights legislation through passage of the economic impact analysis requirement.[9]

Supporters of property rights legislation in Utah also faced strong opposition from environmental groups; however, they were successful in passing a strong property rights measure. Tom Bingham, of the Utah Farm Bureau Federation, said the environmental groups shoot themselves in the foot because of their lack of credibility after venting rhetoric against property rights that simply was not accurate.[10] Besides the environmental groups rendering themselves ineffective, Bingham said there was a strong coalition supporting the legislation. The coalition included realtors, manufacturers, taxpayers, mining and petroleum interests, the Chamber of Commerce, and agriculture groups.

Aiding the bill in passage was a low fiscal note, with support from the governor and an attorney general who agreed to be neutral. Initially the Utah bill was saddled with a high fiscal note; however, the sponsor of the bill got all parties involved and the fiscal note disappeared after studies and evaluations that indicated the law would not be expensive to implement. In fact, Bingham said many government officials admitted that they should be doing the property rights assessment regardless of whether the legislation passed.

The biggest obstacle was convincing the urban legislators that the legislation would not create new property rights, according to Bingham. He said supporters of legislation had to convince many legislators that the bill would only safeguard existing property rights instead of creating new property rights.

So far the bill has not had that much impact on government regulations, Bingham said, "It hasn't hamstrung the agencies although they may be a little more cautious and be paying more attention to private property rights."[11]

In 1994 Indiana, Idaho, West Virginia, Utah, Mississippi, Tennessee, and Missouri passed property rights legislation. In Indiana, property rights legislation encountered little or no resistance. Indeed, environmental groups never really opposed the legislation. The main emphasis was on saving the state's treasury by reviewing takings implications before there was a compensable takings as in the Lucas case.

The Indiana bill requires the attorney general to consider the impact of every proposed rule on property rights. The bill also requires the attorney general to alert the governor and the head of the agency proposing the rule if the rule could result in a takings. The measure started in the Senate where it passed out of the Agriculture Committee by a vote of ten to zero. There was some opposition to the bill from the Hoosier Environmental Committee at this hearing, and the bill died in committee because of time constraints.

However, the Indiana House had already passed a bill that would establish an Administrative Rules Oversight Committee, a standing joint legislative committee, with the power to receive complaints from citizens regarding administrative rules and procedures. This bill became the vehicle for a private property rights protection initiative advanced by the Indiana Farm Bureau.[12]

Robert Kraft, legislative director of the Indiana Farm Bureau, described the action this way: "In the process of lobbying for the bill in committee we not only secured support but generated so much interest in the bill that it wound up with a total of sixteen of Indiana's fifty senators signing on as cosponsors."[13] The bill passed the Senate by a vote of forty-nine to zero. The governor of Indiana signed the bill into law on May 7, 1993.

Success was a result of several key approaches, Kraft said. Proponents always emphasized that the bill was pro-private property rights; never did they allow the rhetoric to portray the bill as antienvironmental. They emphasized the Lucas case and the reduction of a state's potential liability if the takings ramifications were evaluated. "This argument was especially persuasive because of the budget battle which was raging concurrently and the desire of all legislators to appear to be fiscally aware and sensitive," Kraft said.[14] Also contributing to Indiana's success was the broad coalition that supported the bill, which included the Indiana Manufacturer's Association and the Indiana Chamber of Commerce.

In contrast to the low-profile, relatively easy process of passing legislation in Indiana, it took four years and a high-profile campaign before Idaho passed a property rights measure. In the struggle the governor vetoed property rights legislation several times.

Sixteen organizations formed the Idaho Private Property Coalition in 1992. The spokesman for the coalition said its mission was "to preserve and protect the property rights guarantees of the Fifth Amendment to the United States Constitution, and of . . . the Constitution of Idaho, which require just compensation be paid any citizen whose property is taken by government for public use."[15] Coalition members in Idaho included:

Idaho Wool Growers Association; Idaho Mining Association; National Federation of Independent Business; Idaho Cattle Association; Idaho Association of Realtors; Idaho Farm Bureau Federation; Idaho Innkeepers Association; Idaho Women for Ag; Idaho Association of Commerce and Industry; Idaho Sugarbeet Growers Association; Intermountain Forest Industry Association; Idaho Dairymen's Association; Potato Growers of Idaho; Associated Taxpayers of Idaho; Idaho State Grange; and American Agriculture Movement of Idaho.[16]

Again, there was major opposition from environmental groups, Bill Brown, executive vice president of the Idaho Farm Bureau, said. When the legislation finally passed in 1994, the governor did not veto the bill. The Idaho bill was also a "look before you leap" bill and places the burden of action on the attorney general.

In West Virginia the takings issue surfaced as a result of mandated buffer zones on certain streams. The West Virginia Department of Environmental Protection (DEP) at first was unwilling to discuss the takings implications of mandated buffer zones. As a result of increased awareness of takings liability on a national level, many citizens were still concerned about takings. The West

Virginia Farm Bureau was asked to intervene and began to research the issue with a delegate of the state legislature, who assigned a staff attorney to draft a proposal. The proposal developed into The Private Property Protection Act.

Marc Harman writing about the bill in the West Virginia Farm Bureau News said:

> In drafting a meaningful bill several considerations were repeatedly discussed. First and foremost, state law could neither expand nor contract what the courts have already ruled regarding takings. Secondly, the biggest problem associated with the takings issue is the lack of ability—financial, time, etc.—of the average citizen to take on big government and challenge an alleged taking. Because of the . . . general complexity of takings issues, research alone could cost thousands of dollars, not counting actual court time. For example, David Lucas in his landmark takings case spent five years and $500,000 to win.[17]

West Virginia's bill requires the DEP to evaluate or assess the possible effect on private property of certain agency actions that are "reasonably likely" to require compensation. The DEP acknowledged that it could handle the assessment requirement without hiring new staff, resulting in little financial impact on the agency to implement the law.

According to Harman, the property rights issue was the most complex and most controversial issue to confront the West Virginia Farm Bureau Federation.[18] "Opponents included the UMWA, AFL-CIO, West Virginia Environmental Council and the West Virginia Wildlife Federation," he said. "These groups waged absolute war on the West Virginia Farm Bureau and supporters of the Private Property Protection Act utilizing gross intellectual dishonesty and alleging the bill would create a variety of ills to the state."[19] Harman said success in passing the bill was in large part due to the effort of certain members of the House and Senate, who took the time and effort to become educated on the issue.

Mississippi passed legislation that was really not what property rights supporters wanted. The law applies only to forestry and requires compensation for any government action that takes 40 percent or more of the property's value. Supporters of property rights are expected to introduce another, all-encompassing bill in the next session.

Tennessee also passed a bill that was less than what property rights advocates had desired. Julius Johnson, of the Tennessee Farm Bureau Federation, explained that the final version was a negotiated agreement with environmental groups, who had actively opposed the property rights measure.[20] The bill that passed requires the attorney general to review current court decisions and to publish what he thinks would be a takings. The law provides property tax relief for property that has been diminished in value due to regulations. Also, the law requires the government to pay attorney fees and expenses in a takings case, if the property owner is successful. The measure was "foot in the door legislation," according to Johnson, who said they would be introducing stronger property rights measures in the future.[21]

Missouri was the latest state to pass property rights legislation. That state passed a "look before you leap" bill in May 1994. A bill had passed in 1993; however, the governor vetoed the first bill. This time he signed the bill into law with a three-year sunset provision, meaning the law will expire in three years.

Other State Action

Besides the thirteen states that have enacted property rights related legislation, almost a hundred property rights bills have been introduced in forty-two states in 1993-94. (See Appendix A.) Bills have passed at least one house in eleven states. States that were not successful in passing property rights legislation report opposition from environmental groups, suspected interference with local zoning, and high fiscal notes. Fiscal notes are the projected cost to implement legislation. Opponents of property rights legislation often attacked the legislation with a high fiscal note, knowing that legislators would be wary to pass any costly legislation.

In Nevada, proponents of property rights legislation encountered major opposition from local government and state agencies. State agencies attached major fiscal notes, which slowed the bills down. In Montana, the same problem occurred. The Nevada supporters of property rights legislation went to the association of counties and asked what the association would support.

The result was a resolution that directs the attorney general and local government to develop a checklist to evaluate government actions for possible impacts on private property. The resolution, which passed, requires the attorney general's office to train themselves and hold workshops for agency people in order to understand the checklist. In reaching agreement about the resolution, property rights proponents and county officials learned from each other and found useful middle ground.

In Florida, the property rights advocates started out with a bill that quantified a taking, which means that if a regulation reduced a property owner's land value by 40 percent, the property owner would be entitled to automatic compensation. As the law stands, there is no sure measurement of a taking that is less than a 100 percent diminution in property value. The outcome was not popular with the cities and counties. The bill that specified a bright line for takings passed the House. Environmental groups would have killed the bill in the Senate; however, proponents established a private property study commission to study the issue before the bill was killed in the Senate.

Opposition by environmental groups was so strong that Florida's governor vetoed the legislation that created a study commission. The governor received so many phone calls and letters about his veto, he made up his own study commission to study property rights implications.

New Mexico also suffered strong opposition to property rights legislation from the state government. New Mexico's bill dealt only with the executive agencies. The state agencies came up with million-dollar estimates for the cost of administering and complying with the bill.

Jeff Witte, director of governmental affairs of the New Mexico Farm and Livestock Bureau, said they tried to turn the high-cost arguments against the state agencies.[22] He explained that if the cost to do impact assessments was supposedly so high, the state must be open to many takings cases for taking private property. Even though this argument was somewhat successful, Witte said that the environmental community's opposition in addition to state agency opposition was too great to get the bill passed.[23]

In Maine, the major obstacles to passing legislation were again environmental organizations, state regulatory agencies, and municipal associations. Their major opposition was based on the objection to the financial obligations they would incur when their actions took away property rights, according to Jon Olson of the Maine Farm Bureau Association.[24]

A review of state political action suggests the following: in states where property rights legislation has passed, the issue of fiscal impact was seen as negligible. In addition, opposition from environmental groups was weak; where it was strong it was offset by the populist movement that supported the legislation. Understandably, opposition from environmental groups strengthened after passage of the first property rights bills. As more state legislative bodies took up the issue, environmental groups sounded the battle call.

Groups found frequently opposing legislation include the Sierra Club, the Bar Association, the state wildlife and parks agencies, the Nature Conservancy, the Conservation Voter's Alliance, and the Wildlife Federation. At the national level a strong coalition of environmental lobby groups banded together and sent out a call to action to oppose property rights. These groups include:

American Oceans Campaign; Center for Marine Conservation; Defenders of Wildlife; Environmental Action Foundation; Friends of the Earth; Greenpeace, USA, Inc.; League of Conservation Voters; National Audubon Society; National Parks and Conservation Association; National Wildlife Federation; Natural Resources Defense Council; Sierra Club; Sierra Club Legal Defense Fund; Wilderness Society; and Zero Population Growth.[25]

2. A Closer Look at the Legislation

There are basically two kinds of statutes: "Look before you leap (LBYL)," which was referred to earlier, and statutes that seek to define a bright line to indicate when a regulatory taking occurs, whether 100 percent, 90 percent, or some lesser loss of economic value is to be the defining mark. Appendix B contains three model statutes that are frequently considered by state legislators when writing proposed bills. These were drafted by Defenders of Property Rights, the American Farm Bureau Federation, and the Legislative Exchange Council. A review of these shows common elements that relate to the two categories of laws just mentioned. LBYL is by far the more popular legislative proposal.

Look Before You Leap

If property rights legislation requiring a takings analysis had been on the books in South Carolina, it is possible that citizens in the state could have avoided paying out $3.1 million in litigation and settlement costs in the Lucas case. A takings liability analysis would be easier and cheaper than current NEPA rules that require an environmental impact statement of all governmentally sponsored actions that may impose environmental costs. This LBYL legislation is one of the two common types being introduced across the United States.

LBYL is patterned after Executive Order 12630, which was signed by President Reagan in 1988. Executive Order 12630 was modeled after the environmental impact analysis required by the National Environmental Policy Act of 1970. The Executive Order required executive branch agencies to review their actions to prevent unnecessary takings and to budget money to pay for necessary takings.[26] Unfortunately, Executive Order 12630 has been ignored and per se repealed by the Clinton administration.

LBYL legislation at the state level requires state agencies to assess the takings implications of state regulations before the regulations are adopted. For example: most bills require the attorney general to develop guidelines—based on principles enumerated in the statute—for agencies to use in determining whether their actions have constitutional takings implications. The guidelines are usually updated annually. Using the guidelines, state agencies must assess the takings implications of their proposed actions. The assessment must include (1) an analysis of the likelihood that the action may result in a constitutional taking, (2) alternatives that would reduce the impact on private property and reduce the risk of a taking, and (3) an estimate of the financial cost for compensation if the action is determined to be a taking.

LBYL legislation is purely procedural and does not alter or expand the standards governing when compensation is due under the U.S. or state Constitution. The legislation seeks to ensure—by increasing awareness of potential takings implications—that government policies do not inadvertently effect takings of private property, with the resultant cost to taxpayers of having to pay compensation.

According to Nancie Marzulla, chief legal counsel of Defenders of Property Rights, "This healthy approach to government decision making . . . will reduce the likelihood of state citizens having to pay for the taking of private property by avoiding adopting regulations for which the Constitution requires the payment of just compensation. In short, this legislation will save money."[27]

Government has been hit with big takings bills in the last few years. In *Whitney Benefits, Inc. v. United States*,[28] a property owner in Wyoming was awarded close to $120 million in damages and interest for the taking of private property rights. In this case the chief judge of the U.S. Claims Court, Loren A. Smith, held that the enactment of the Surface Mining and Reclamation Act of 1977 totally eliminated the economic value of the plaintiff's coal, which constituted a taking under the Fifth Amendment. The government denied the plaintiff's access to mine coal because the coal was located under an alluvial valley floor.

The previously mentioned case of *Lucas v. South Carolina Coastal Council* was an instance where a state ended up having to pay for a taking; in that case, $1.5 million. The trend in takings case law indicates that a state is wise to assess regulations for takings implications. Had South Carolina realized that it would be liable for such costs, the South Carolina Coastal Council might have made a different decision in the Lucas case and perhaps budgeted the money to condemn the property for public use. A prior assessment could also save the cost of a lawsuit for the taxpayers and the individual landowner.

States that have passed the LBYL type of legislation are Arizona, Delaware, Idaho, Indiana, Missouri, Tennessee, Utah, Washington, and West Virginia. Others are considering this provision in pending legislation. (See Figure 6.1.)

LBYL bills do have a weakness. These bills often require a takings analysis that depends on the judge hearing the case. There is no set formula to determine what is a taking. There are several categorical takings.[29] However, most takings analysis is done on an ad hoc basis.[30] This ad hoc analysis can make it hard to conclusively determine whether a government action would be a taking.

Although LBYL bills have a weakness with ad hoc case-by-case analysis, there is enough established takings law to undertake an useful assessment of regulation. While magic numbers are hard to develop, at the very least an analysis can outline the possible ramifications of regulatory action and can identify the groups, sectors, and individuals who will likely bear the brunt of the cost.

State-by-State Legislative Update

12 states have passed property rights legislation.
44 states have introduced property rights bills.

updated 10/6/94

■ **property rights bill passed**   ▨ **property rights bill introduced**

States that have enacted property rights legislation

Arizona[1]	Delaware	Idaho	Indiana
Mississippi[2]	Missouri	N. Carolina[3]	Tennessee
Utah	Virginia[4]	Washington	West Virginia

1) Opposition circulated and successfully gathered signatures for a referendum to repeal the law. A vote will occur in the 1994 General Election in November. The law does not go into effect unless it is approved in the referendum.
2) Compensation act that applies only to private forest land.
3) Applies to claims to land under navigable waters only.
4) Study bill establishing a joint subcommittee to study state governmental actions which may result in a taking of private property and determine whether current laws or procedures should be changed.

Figure 6.1 State-by-state legislative update

Takings Quantification Bills

Takings quantification bills establish the definition of a taking by statutorily creating a trigger point at which a regulatory taking and inverse condemnation are presumed to have occurred. These bills entitle any property owner to automatic compensation if the property owner proves that the government regulation reduced the property value by a certain percentage.

Defenders of Property Rights drafted model legislation that would establish the definition of a taking as a diminution in value of 50 percent or more. (See Appendix B.) This compensation bill would *not* preclude property owners who suffer a takings of less than 50 percent from challenging the regulatory action in court.[31]

Quantification bills have been introduced in Delaware, Idaho, Maine, New York, Oregon, Pennsylvania, South Carolina, Texas, and Washington. The most common trigger point has been 50 percent as established in the Defenders of Property Rights model legislation. Delaware introduced this type of legislation during the 1994 legislative session and succeeded in getting it passed in the Senate, which supporters perceived as their biggest obstacle. The legislation is scheduled to surface in the House when the legislature reconvenes in 1995. One reason it was fairly easy to pass was a result of the LBYL legislation that had been on the books in Delaware for several years, according to G. Wallace Caulk, administrator of the Delaware Farm Bureau Federation. The LBYL legislation had not created the havoc that opponents had suggested that such a measure would cause.[32]

A combination of quantification and "look before you leap" has been introduced in four states: California, Mississippi, New Hampshire, and Washington. Again, the most common trigger point is a 50 percent diminution in value.

3. Some Final Thoughts on the Legislative Movement

The land rights movement that has blossomed across the nation is a peculiarly American phenomenon, a grassroots effort led in many cases by ordinary citizens who have grievances to be redressed by their government. No matter how one might feel about the issue, most would likely agree with a process that reveals the ability of ordinary people to petition government and obtain what they perceive to be relief.

The stories recounted in this chapter tell us that the state property rights movement has to do with environmental rules and regulations, but that the contest is not so much about the environment and whether or not it should be protected. The issue is about property rights and a time-honored system that allows a person to exclude others who refuse to pay for highly desirable land rights.

As indicated here, property rights legislation has passed in states where broadly based coalitions saw a common need to protect property. Diverse groups, which seldom come together to seek political action, find the property rights issue to be crucial to their interests. Politicians understandably respond to intense and broadly based demands. In some cases, environmental groups were not so active; in yet other cases, environmentalists deflected the property rights threat.

Just what might explain the outcomes will not likely be known, no matter how much one might research the question. However, a public choice analysis of property rights legislation, when and where it was introduced, may shed considerable light on the subject. That is discussed in Chapter 7.

Notes

1. "Come back to earth," *Atlanta Journal/Constitution,* July 31, 1994, R4.
2. Ibid.
3. Ibid.
4. Press release by combined leadership of the nation's largest environmental groups, signed by Ted Danson, president of the American Oceans Campaign, et al. (undated, 1994).
5. News Release by Governor Fife Symington: Symington Signs Into Law S.B. 1053 Relating To Private Property Rights (June 1, 1992). However, this was defeated in a referendum.
6. Ibid.
7. Coalition letter from Cecil Miller, president of the Arizona Farm Bureau Federation, to Fife Symington, governor of Arizona (May 26, 1992).
8. A fiscal note is the estimated cost to implement the legislation. Opponents of legislation often try to create a high fiscal note because legislators are so wary of spending taxpayers' money.
9. Telephone interview with John Johnson, assistant director for public affairs of the Virginia Farm Bureau Federation (September 7, 1994).
10. Telephone interview with Tom Bingham of the Utah Farm Bureau Federation (August 11, 1994).
11. Ibid.
12. Letter from Robert D. Kraft, legislative director of the Indiana Farm Bureau, to Lorna Frank, legislative director of the Montana Farm Bureau Federation (August 9, 1993).
13. Ibid.
14. Ibid.
15. Idaho Organizations Form Private Property Coalition, *Eastern Idaho,* November 13, 1992 at 21.
16. Ibid.

17. Marc Harman, Private Property Protection in West Virginia, West Virginia Farm Bureau News (June 1994).

18. Telephone interview with Marc Harman of the West Virginia Farm Bureau Federation (August 3, 1994).

19. Ibid.

20. Telephone interview with Julius Johnson of the Tennessee Farm Bureau Federation (September 7, 1994).

21. Ibid.

22. Memo from Jeff Witte, director of governmental affairs of the New Mexico Farm and Livestock Bureau, to Lorna Frank, legislative director of the Montana Farm Bureau Federation (August 16, 1993).

23. Ibid.

24. Memo from Jon Olson of the Maine Farm Bureau Federation to the author (August 17, 1993).

25. Environmental group press release, *supra* note 4.

26. Roger J. Marzulla, *Environmental Law Reporter,* 18 ELR 10254, July 1988.

27. Nancie Marzulla, *Land Rights Letter.*

28. *Whitney Benefits, Inc. v. United States,* 18 Cl.Ct. 394 (1989).

29. *Lucas v. South Carolina Coastal Council,* 112 S.Ct. 2886, 2893-94 (1992).

30. *Penn Central Transportation v. New York City,* 98 S.Ct. 2646, 2659 (1978).

31. See Chapter 1 by Nancie Marzulla.

32. Telephone interview with G. Wallace Caulk, administrator of the Delaware Farm Bureau Federation (September 7, 1994).

Appendix A
Status of State Property Rights Legislation, September 1994[1]

Bill No.	Year	Type	Status and Date of Last Action or Instruction to Committee
Alabama			
H. 413	1994	Compensation	Reported favorably from House Cmte on Commerce, Transporation, & Utilities 1/20/94. Withdrawn 4/18/94.
S. 349	1994	Compensation	Senate Cmte on Agriculture, Conservation and Forestry 1/18/94. Reported favorably 2/2/94. Died.
Arizona			
(S. 1151) Ariz. Rev. Ann. §§ 9-462.02, 11-830	1994	Compensation	Signed into law in 1994. Authorizes a city to acquire by purchase or condemnation, private property for the removal of nonconforming uses and structures. Effective 7/17/94.
(S. 1053) Ariz. Rev. Ann. § 37-220, 221, 222	1992	Planning	The assistant attorney general is charged with determining when proposed government action has takings implications. Signed into law in 1992. Public interest groups have circulated a petition to repeal the law. Law will go before the voters in the 1994 election. Not effective unless approved in referendum.
(H. 2589) Ariz. Rev. Stat. § 17-41-192	1994	Appoints Ombudsman	Creates ombudsman office in the office of the Arizona Legislative Council to represent the interests of private property owners in proceedings involving government action.
H. 2460	1994	Condemnation Procedure	House Cmte on Ways and Means 1/7/94. Never heard in Cmte. Died 5/17/94.
California			
A. 145	1994	Planning	Failed passage in Senate Judiciary Cmte. Reconsideration was granted 6/14/94. Set for a committee hearing on 6/21/94; however, meeting was canceled.

1. This appendix is provided by Defenders of Property Rights, Washington, D.C.

Bill No.	Year	Type	Status and Date of Last Action or Instruction to Committee
California			
A. 2629	1994	Compensation	To Senate Cmte on Judiciary 5/24/94. Failed passage in cmte 8/16/94.
S.R. 57	1994	Special	Establishes "Private Property Rights Week." Introduced and sent to Senate Rules Committee 8/25/94.
A. 2328	1993	Planning	Failed passage in Assembly Cmte on Local Government 1/12/94.
A. 2322	1993	Planning	Died in assembly.
Colorado			
S. 165	1994	Planning	From Sen. Cmte on State, Veteran and Military Affairs: Postponed indefinitely 5/03/94.
S. 194	1994	Planning	Passed Senate on third reading 4/20/94. Postponed indefinitely in House Cmte on Appropriations: 5/03/94.
Connecticut			
H. 5583	1994	Special	Establishes cause of action for owner to recoup lost value due to water company structure abutting property. Passed House 5/4/94. To Senate.
H. 5598	1994	Study	Passed Senate Cmte on Environment 3/14/94. In Joint Cmte on Appropriations 4/14/94.
Delaware			
Del. Code Ann. tit. § 605	1992	Planning	Requires that no rule or regulation by any state agency become effective until the Attorney General has 29, reviewed it to determine any possible implications.
H. 513	1994	Compensation	Introduced to House Cmte on Env. and Nat. Resources 5/18/94.
S. 56	1993	Compensation	Died in Senate Cmte on Community and County Affairs 3/18/93.
S. 49	1993	Compensation	Passed Senate; 3/24/94. Died in House Cmte on Transportation and Infrastructure 3/29/94.

Bill No.	Year	Type	Status and Date of Last Action or Instruction to Committee

Florida

H. 1437	1994	Study	Introduced 2/8/94. Governmental Accountability Sub-Cmte 2/18/94. Died in Governmental Operations Cmte 4/15/94.
H. 485	1994	Compensation	Withdrawn from House Cmte on Appropriations 4/4/94.
S. 2262	1994	Special	Directs Dept. of Highway Safety and Motor Vehicles to issue license plates commemorating property rights. To Cmte on Transportation 2/21/94.
S. 630	1994	Compensation	Senate Cmte on Community Affairs 2/08/94. Died.

Georgia

| H. 1343 | 1994 | Compensation | House Cmte on Judiciary 1/14/94. Read only two times in the House. Died in Committee. |
| H. 1706 | 1994 | Planning | House Cmte on Judiciary 2/08/94. Read only two times in the House. Died in Committee. |

Hawaii

H. 1724	1993	Planning	House Cmte on Judiciary 1/28/93. Carried over to 1994 session.
H. 2128	1993	Planning	House Cmte on Judiciary, and House Cmte on Consumer Protection and Commerce 1/29/93. Died in Consumer Protection and Commerce. Carried over to 1994 session.
H.C.R. 401	1993	Planning	Died in Finance Cmte 3/23/93.
H. 3349	1994	Planning	House Cmte on Judiciary, and House Cmte on Finance 1/28/94. Died in Finance.
S. 1645	1993	Planning	Senate Cmte on Judiciary, and Senate Cmte on Planning, Land Use and Water Use Management 1/29/93. Died in Cmte.
S. 3123	1994	Planning	Senate Cmte on Judiciary, and Senate Cmte on Ways and Means 2/1/94. Died in Ways and Means.

Bill No.	Year	Type	Status and Date of Last Action or Instruction to Committee

Idaho

| (H. 659) Idaho Code § 67-8003 | 1994 | Planning | Signed into law 3/21/94. Requires the Attorney General to establish a process and a checklist to better enable state agencies to evaluate regulatory actions to assure that such actions do not result in takings. Effective 7/1/94. |

Illinois

| H. 1135 | 1993 | Compensation | Died in House Cmte on Agriculture and Conservation 3/5/93. |

Indiana

| (H. 1646) Ind. Code § 4-22-2-32 | 1993 | Planning | Passed as part of the 1993 Administrative Oversight Act. |

Iowa

H. 350	1993	Planning	Died in House Cmte on Agriculture 4/12/93.
H. 2166	1994	Compensation	Died in House Cmte on Agriculture 2/15/94.
S. 2148	1994	Compensation	Referred to Senate Cmte on Agriculture 3/28/94. Died in Cmte.

Kansas

| S. 293 | 1993 | Planning | Passed both Houses; Governor veto 4/22/94; Failed Senate override vote 4/30/94; (25/14). Died |

Kentucky

| H. 821 | 1994 | Compensation | Recommitted from House Rules Cmte to House Cmte on Judiciary 3/22/94. Died in Cmte. |
| H. 732 | 1994 | Planning | Withdrawn 3/10/94. |

Louisiana

| H. 1748 | 1993 | Planning | Passed House (100/0). Died in Senate 5/2/93. |

Bill No.	Year	Type	Status and Date of Last Action or Instruction to Committee

Maine

| L.D. 672 | 1993 | Compensation | Died between Houses 6/15/93. |

Maryland

| S. 34 | 1992 | Planning | Passed Senate (26/20). Received unfavorable report from House Env. Matters Cmte (14/10). Died in Cmte 4/12/93. |

Massachusetts

| H. 3851 | 1994 | Planning | Passed Joint Cmte on State Administration; to House Cmte on Ways and Means 4/21/94. |
| S. 1212 | 1993 | Planning | From Joint Cmte on State Administration 1/31/94. To Senate Cmte on Ways & Means 1/31/94. Consigned to study order and no action taken 6/9/94. |

Minnesota

| H. 2335 | 1994 | Planning | House Cmte on Environment and Natural Resources 3/03/94. Died in Cmte. |

Mississippi

(S. 2464) Miss. Code Ann. §§ 17-1-3, 95-3-29.	1994	Compensation (forest land only)	Signed by Governor 4/08/94. Effective 10/1/94.
S. 2487	1994	Planning and Compensation	Died in Senate Cmte on Judiciary 1/11/94.
S. 2005	1994	Compensation	Passed Senate 2/10/94. Reported out of House Cmte on Judiciary with amendment 3/1/94.

Missouri

| (H. 1099/ S. 558) Mo. Rev. Stat. §§ 536.017 536.018 | 1994 | Planning | Passed House and Senate. Singed into law 6/3/94. Effective 8/28/94. |

Bill No.	Year	Type	Status and Date of Last Action or Instruction to Committee

Missouri

| H. 1585 | 1994 | Planning | House Cmte on Judiciary and Ethics 2/08/94. Died in Cmte. |

Montana

| H. 570 | 1993 | Planning | Passed full house on first reading (59-40), 3/23/93. Passed second reading (55-44), 3/23/93. Sent to Senate 4/14/93. Died in Cmte 4/14/93. |

Nebraska

| L. 1100 | 1994 | Planning | Passed Legislative Cmte on Government, Military and Veterans' Affairs 3/02/94. Died in Cmte 4/15/94. |

Nevada

A. 542	1993	Planning	Died in Govt. Affairs Cmte 4/28/93.
S. 142	1993	Compensation	Died in Govt. Affairs Cmte 1/27/93.
S. 285	1993	Planning	Died in Govt. Affairs Cmte 3/15/93.
S. 384	1993	Planning	Died in Govt. Affairs Cmte 4/93/93.

New Hampshire

H. 608	1993	Compensation	Died in House upon unfavorable report by Muni & County Govt. Cmte 3/16/93.
H. 1200	1994	Compensation	House Cmte on Judiciary 1/05/94. Died in Cmte 4/26/94.
H. 1486	1994	Planning	House Cmte on Judiciary 3/04/94. Died in House vote 3/10/94.

New Jersey

| A. 2106 | 1994 | Planning | To Assembly Committee on State Government 9/12/94. |

Bill No.	Year	Type	Status and Date of Last Action or Instruction to Committee

New Mexico

| H. 536 | 1993 | Planning | Action postponed indefinitely. House Appropriations & Finance 2/17/94. |
| H. 684 | 1993 | Planning | Action postponed indefinitely in House Appropriations & Finance Cmte 2/17/94. Died. |

New York

| A. 5641 | 1993 | Compensation | Assembly Cmte on Judiciary 3/02/93. |
| S. 2832 | 1993 | Compensation | Senate Cmte on Judiciary 1/05/94. |

North Carolina

| (S. 1437) N.C. Gen Stat. §113-206 | 1994 | Compensation (claims to land under navigable waters only) | Ratified 7/7/94. |

Oklahoma

H. 1812	1993	Planning	Passed House; to Senate Cmte on Judiciary 3/15/93. Died in Cmte.
H. 2506	1994	Planning	To House Judiciary Cmte 2/7/94.
H. 1495	1991	Compensation	Died in House Judiciary Cmte 3/11/92.

Oregon

H. 2408	1993	Compensation	Died in House Judiciary Cmte 8/05/93.
H. 2899	1993	Compensation	Died in Sub-Cmte on Agriculture 8/05/93.
H. 2935	1993	Planning	Died in Sub-Cmte on Agriculture 8/05/93.
H. 3087	1993	Compensation	Died in Judiciary Cmte 8/05/93.
H. 3128	1993	Compensation	Died in Commerce Cmte 8/05/93.
S. 829	1993	Compensation	Companion Bill to H. 3128. Introduced to Senate Cmte on Agriculture & Nat. Res. Cmte on Judiciary, and Cmte on Ways and Means. 3/22/93. Died in Ways & Means 8/05/93.

Bill No.	Year	Type	Status and Date of Last Action or Instruction to Committee

Pennsylvania

H. 803	1993	Compensation	Died in House Cmte on Local Government 3/22/93.
H. 1890	1993	Compensation	Died in House Cmte on Local Government 6/23/93.

South Carolina

H. 3785	1993	Condemnation procedure	Died House Cmte on Judiciary 3/30/93.
S. 125	1993	Compensation	Died Senate Cmte on Judiciary 1/12/93.
S. 385	1993	Condemnation procedure	Died in Senate Cmte on Judiciary 2/09/93.
S. 816	1993	Planning	Died Senate Cmte on Judiciary 6/01/93.
S. 1254	1992	Planning	Died in Senate Cmte on Judiciary 2/4/92.
S. 1230	1992	Planning	Died in Senate Cmte on Judiciary 1/28/92.

South Dakota

H. 1263	1994	Planning	Died in House Cmte on Agriculture and Natural Resources 2/16/94.

Tennessee

(S. 2643/ H. 2647) Tenn. Code Ann. § 12-1-201 et seq.	1994	Planning	Signed by Governor 5/09/94. Effective 7/01/94.

Texas

H. 485	1993	Planning/ Compensation	Died in State Affairs Cmte 3/15/93.
S. 1225	1993	Planning	Companion Bill to H. 485.

Bill No.	Year	Type	Status and Date of Last Action or Instruction to Committee

Utah

(H. 163) Utah Code Ann. §§ 63-90a-1-63-90a-4	1994	Planning	Signed by Governor 3/16/94. Effective 5/2/94.
Utah Code Ann. §78-34a-1 to 78-34a-4	1994	Planning	Enacted in 1993.

Vermont

H. 421	1993	Planning	House Cmte on Government Operations 2/25/93. Died in Cmte 6/12/94.
S. 110	1993	Planning	Senate Cmte on Judiciary 2/11/93. Died in Cmte 6/12/94.
P. 14	1992	Compensation	Died in Senate Judiciary Cmte.

Virginia

(H. J.R. 624) 1993 Va. Acts 624.	1993	Study	Passed House. Passed Senate 2/23/93.
H.J.R. 74	1994	Study	Continued study bill passed in 1993. Passed House and Senate 2/15/94. Study Cmte members appointed 6/13/94.
H. 2369	1993	Planning	House Cmte on General Laws 1/28/93. Died in Gen. Laws House Cmte 2/9/93.

Washington

Wash Rev Code § 36.70A.370	1992	Planning	Requires the Attoney General to establish a checklist that enables state agencies and local governments to evaluate proposed regulatory or administrative actions to ensure that such actions do not result in the taking of private property.

Bill No.	Year	Type	Status and Date of Last Action or Instruction to Committee
Washington			
H. 1381	1993	Permit	Died in House Cmte on Judiciary 3/11/93.
H. 1487	1993	Notice (Wetlands)	Died in House Cmte on Natural Resources and Parks 3/11/93.
H. 1843	1993	Compensation	Died in House Cmte on Judiciary 3/11/94.
H. 1932	1993	Planning	Died in House Cmte on Judiciary 2/11/94.
H. 1933	1993	Planning	Died in House Cmte on Judiciary 3/11/94.
H. 1934	1993	Wetlands	Died in House Cmte on Judiciary 3/11/94.
H. 2379	1994	Permit and Compensation	Died in House Cmte on Judiciary 3/11/94.
H. 2470	1994	Planning	Died in House Cmte on Judiciary 3/11/94.
H. 2500	1994	Planning and compensation	Died in House Cmte on Judiciary 3/11/94.
S. 5081	1993	Notice (Wetlands)	Died in Senate Cmte on Governmental Operations 3/11/94.
S. 5369	1993	Condemnation procedure	Died in Senate Cmte on Governmental Operations 3/11/94.
S. 5431	1993	Compensation	Passed Senate Cmte on Natural Resources; to Senate Cmte on Ways and Means 3/03/93. Referred to Natural Resources 3/11/94.
S. 5475	1993	Compensation	Died in Senate Cmte on Natural Resources 3/22/94.
H. 1488	1993	Compensation	Died in House Cmte on Judiciary 1/29/93.
S. 5136	1993	Vested Rights	Died in Senate Cmte on Governmental Operations.
S. 6167	1994	Planning and condemnation procedure	Senate Cmte on Natural Resources 1/14/94. Died in Senate Cmte on Natural Resources 3/11/94.

Bill No.	Year	Type	Status and Date of Last Action or Instruction to Committee

West Virginia

(H. 4065) West Va. Code §§ 22-1a-1 - 22-1a-6	1994	Planning (Part of the West VA DEP reorganization)	Introduced 1/20/94. Passed 3/12/94. Signed into law 3/30/94. Effective 6/12/94.
H. 4165	1994	Planning	Passed House Cmte on Government Organizations 2/28/94. Died in House Judiciary Cmte 2/28/94.
S. 249	1994	Planning	Companion Bill to H. 4165. Died in Senate Judiciary Cmte 2/2/94.

Wisconsin

| A. 1185 | 1994 | Planning | Died in Assembly Cmte on Elections and Constitutional Laws 3/31/94. |
| S. 757 | 1994 | Planning | Companion Bill to A. 1185. Died in Senate Cmte on State Govt. Operations and Corrections 3/30/94. |

Wyoming

| S. 60 | 1994 | Planning | Failed 2/23/94. |

Glossary of Types of Bills

Compensation: Provides a private property owner with the right to invoke inverse condemnation once the threshold reduction in market value (usually 50%) due to a government action has been reached. The owner, in other words, may require the government agency to either purchase the property or pay compensation for the full value of the property. These laws do not prevent an owner from seeking compensation for a reduction in value lower than the threshold.

Condemnation procedure: Mandates specific procedures for the condemnation of private property for public use.

Notice: Requires local governments to give notice to private property owners of any proposed actions that will affect their property.

Permit: Provides damages to private property owners who are unlawfully denied a permit that is required for a use of their property.

Special: These bills are unusual in nature and do not fit into any of the other categories. Brief explanations are given in the column entitled "Status and date of last action or instruction to committee".

Study: Provides a mechanism for the government to study the issue of takings and decide how best to address it.

Vested Rights: Provides that an owner's right to develop his land vests at a certain point in the application process, usually after a permit has been granted.

Wetlands: Prevents wetland designation from reducing the value of private property.

Appendix B
Sample Legislative Language[1]

Model Bill
Property Rights Preservation Bill

Section 1. <u>Preamble</u>.
a. It is the policy of this state that no private property may be taken for public use by governmental action without payment of just compensation, in accordance with the meaning ascribed to these concepts by the United State Supreme Court and the Supreme Court of this state.

b. The purpose of this Act is to require state agencies, guided and overseen by the Attorney General, to evaluate proposed government actions that may result in a constitutional taking of private property in order to avoid unnecessary burdens on the public treasury and unwarranted interference with private property rights. It is not the purpose of this Act to affect the scope of private property protections afforded by the United States or state Constitutions.

Section 2. <u>Short Title</u>.

This Act shall be known as the "Property Rights Preservation Act."

Section 3. <u>Definitions</u>.

As used in this Act:
a. "State agency" means the state of _____ and any officer, agency, board, commission, department or similar body of the executive branch of state government, and any of the political subdivisions of the state or agencies thereof;
b. "Government action" means
   i. existing and proposed rules and regulations that if adopted or enforced may limit the use of private property;
   ii. existing or proposed licensing or permitting conditions, requirements or limitations on the use of private property;
   iii. required dedications or exactions of private property;

c. The term "government action" does not include:

   i. the formal exercise of the power of eminent domain;
   ii. the forfeiture or seizure of private property by law enforcement agencies as evidence of a crime or for violations of law;
   iii. orders issued by a state agency or court of law that result from a violation of law and that are authorized by statute;
   iv. the discontinuance of government programs;

1. The first item is provided by the American Farm Bureau Federation. Item two is from Defenders of Property Rights.

d. "Constitutional taking" or "taking" means the taking of private property by government action such that compensation to the owner of that property is required by either:

    i.   the Fifth or Fourteenth Amendment to the United States Constitution; or

    ii.   Article __, Section __ of the Constitution of the state of _____.

Section 4. Guidelines for Determining Takings.

a. The Attorney General shall develop and provide to state agencies guidelines to assist in the identification and evaluation of government actions that may result in a constitutional taking. The Attorney General shall base the guidelines on current law as articulated by the United States.

Section 5. Designation of Responsible Official.

The Attorney General shall designate an official within the office of the Attorney General who shall be responsible for ensuring compliance with this Act.

Section 6. Takings Assessment by State Agency.

Before a state agency takes any government action, the agency shall prepare a written assessment of the constitutional takings implications of such action, in compliance with the guidelines developed pursuant to Section 4 of this Act. The agency shall deliver copies of this assessment to the Governor, appropriate financial management authority, and Attorney General. The agency's assessment shall

a. assess the likelihood that the government action may result in a constitutional taking;

b. clearly and specifically identify the purpose of the government action;

c. explain why the government action is necessary substantially to advance that purpose, and who no alternative action is available that would achieve the agency's goals while reducing the impact on the private property owner;

d. estimate the potential cost to the government if a court determines that the action constitutes a constitutional taking;

e. identify the source of payment within the agency's budget for any compensation that may be ordered; and

f. certify that the benefits of the government action exceed the estimated compensation costs.

Section 7. Emergency Action.

If there is an immediate threat to public health and safety that constitutes an emergency and requires an immediate response, the takings assessment required by section 6 of this Act may be made when the response is completed.

Section 8. Source of Compensation.

Any award made to an owner of private property from a government agency for a constitutional taking, including any award of attorneys' fees and costs, shall come from the agency's existing budget unless the agency has previously disclosed an estimate of the costs of the appropriate financial management authority and funds were included in the budget for that purpose.

Section 9. <u>Attorneys' Fees and Costs</u>.

An owner of private property who successfully establishes that a government action is a constitutional taking of such owner's property requiring payment of just compensation shall be awarded reasonable attorney's fees and costs incurred in reestablishing that claim, in addition to other remedies provided by law.

Section 10. <u>Causes of Action</u>.

a. An aggrieved property owner shall have a legal cause of action against a state agency that violates this Act for compensatory damages, writs of mandamus or prohibition, or other appropriate legal or equitable relief.

b. The Attorney General may bring an action to enforce compliance with this Act.

Section 11. <u>Valuation of Property</u>.

The effect of government action that is a constitutional taking on the fair market value of private property shall be reflected in the assessed valuation of such property for taxes, levies and similar purposes.

Section 12. <u>Effective Date</u>.

This Act is effective January 1, 1994.

A BILL

To ensure that the state establish a reasonably objective standard for the impact of regulations on the value of property, and to afford a method of relief for an owner whose value has been diminished as a result of government regulation.

Section 1. SHORT TITLE.

This Act may be cited as the "Regulatory Impacts Act of 1993."

Section 2. DEFINITIONS.

(A) "Diminution in value of fifty per cent or more" means a fifty per cent reduction in the fair market value of the property subject to the statute, regulation ,rule guideline or policy; or, to the denial of any permit, license, authorization or governmental permission.

(B) "Inverse condemnation" means a suit against the government to recover money damages equal to the diminution in the fair market value of the property.

(C) "Owner" means the owner of property at the time the statute, regulation, rule, guideline or policy was passed, or owner at the time that the permit, license, authorization or governmental permission was denied.

Section 3. DIMINUTION IN VALUE.

(A) **Cause of action.** The owner of any property may sue the government whenever the application of a statute, regulation, rule guideline or policy to a parcel of property, or the denial of any permit, license, authorization or governmental permission of any kind by the government causes a diminution in value of the property of fifty per cent or more.

(B) **Jurisdiction.** This suit may be filed in the state court which shall have exclusive jurisdiction of the claim, and the owner shall be entitled to a trial by jury. In such suit, the owner may either recover: (1) a sum equal to the diminution in value of the property, and retain title thereto; or to (2) recover the entire fair market value of the property prior to the diminution in value of fifty per cent or more, and transfer title to the government upon payment of the fair market value. If the statute, regulation, rule, guideline or policy is rescinded, or if the permit, license, authorization or governmental permission is granted, prior to final judgment, then the owner shall be entitled to recover in the pending action reasonable and necessary costs of suit incurred to date, together with any economic losses sustained by reason of the acts giving rise to the diminution in value.

(C) **Public Nuisance Exception.** No compensation shall be required by virtue of this Act if the owner's use or proposed use of the property amounts to a public nuisance as commonly understood and defined by background principles of nuisance and property law. The government bears the burden of proof with respect to this affirmative defense.

Section 4. INVALIDATION.

(A) **Cause of Action.** Any person may commence a civil action on his own behalf against the government to invalidate any statute, regulation, rule, guideline or policy, or to invalidate any provision or condition of any permit, authorization or governmental permission, which does not substantially advance its stated governmental purpose. The state court shall have exclusive jurisdiction over such actions and such action may be pleaded in the alternative in a complaint containing a cause of action contained in Section 3.

(B) "Person" for purposes of this section means a person or persons having an interest which is or may be adversely affected by the statute, regulation, rule, guidelines or policy or by the provision or condition of any permit, authorization or governmental permission.

(C) A suit for invalidation shall be ripe for adjudication upon the enactment of the statute, regulation, rule, guideline or policy or the imposition of any provision or condition of any permit, authorization of governmental permission to any parcel of property.

Section 5. APPLICATION; STATUTE OF LIMITATIONS.

(A) **Retroactive application.** The Act shall apply to statutes, regulations, rules, guidelines or policies as well as to any provision or condition of any permit, authorization or governmental permission, in effect at the time of enactment of this Act or hereinafter enacted.

(B) **Statute of limitations.** The statute of limitations for actions brought pursuant to this Act shall be six years from the enactment of any statute, regulation, rule, guideline or policy, or the denial of any permit, license, authorization or governmental permission by the government.

Section 6. AWARD OF COSTS; LITIGATION COSTS.

The court, in issuing any final order in any action brought pursuant to this Act, shall award costs of litigation (including reasonable attorney and expert witness fees) to any prevailing or substantially prevailing plaintiff.

Section 7. CONSTITUTIONAL OR STATUTORY RIGHTS NOT RESTRICTED.

Nothing in this Act shall restrict any remedy or any right which any person (or class of persons) may have under any provision of the state or federal Constitution, statute or laws of the state or United States.

Chapter 7

The Political Economy of State Takings Legislation

Jody Lipford and Donald J. Boudreaux

The U.S. Constitution guarantees each citizen freedom from uncompensated expropriation of private property by government. Specifically, the Fifth Amendment states that "private property [shall not] be taken for public use, without just compensation."

This protection of private property is extended to the states by the Fourteenth Amendment, which says that "any State [shall not] deprive any person of . . . property, without due process of law." Indeed, protection of private property from state-government takings is buttressed by state constitutions, forty-eight of which contain takings clauses similar to that in the Constitution's Fifth Amendment.[1] In addition, twenty-four state constitutions extend protection to property that is "damaged" by government action, even if it is not "taken."[2]

Despite these constitutional protections, legislation to reaffirm private property rights had been introduced in forty-two state legislatures by August 1994, and some form of property rights protection legislation has passed in eleven states. Although the content and effect of the legislation varies across the states, the introduction and passage of this legislation reflects a grassroots movement at the state level to protect private property from government intrusions.

The introduction and enactment of property rights legislation at the state level raise a number of questions. What kinds of state and local government regulations constitute "takings" of private property? What interests are supporting this "takings" legislation? What is the content of the proposed and enacted legislation? Why, in light of the constitutional constraints, is protection being sought at the state level in statutes? This chapter answers these and other questions about the growing property rights movement.

To begin, the chapter examines government regulations that have threatened the rights of private landowners. To illustrate some of these regulatory actions, court cases that have challenged these regulations are also briefly reviewed. The next section of the chapter addresses the question of why state legislation is being pursued as a means of protecting private property rights. The third section reviews the development of state legislation, focusing on the states of Arizona and Washington as case studies of the land rights movement. The salient features of the legislation passed in these two states are also presented and discussed. To explain legislative decision making, Public Choice theory used by economists and political scientists is explained in the fourth section of the chapter. The fifth section draws on the Public Choice theory developed in section four to present an empirical analysis of the legislative decision-making process. Interests supporting and opposing property rights legislation are identified, and predictions are offered about which states are likely to introduce or pass such legislation in the future. Some final thoughts are offered in the conclusion.

1. The Issue: Regulatory Takings

It is clear that the Fifth Amendment of the U.S. Constitution protects private property holders from outright—i.e., physical—seizure.[3] What is not clear is what protection is afforded property owners when government *regulations* devalue private property without explicitly taking the property (i.e., without formally stripping the owner of title to the property). Devaluations of private property resulting from government regulation are referred to as "regulatory takings," and it is these takings with which the land rights movement is concerned.

The majority of laws and regulations that take private property emanate from the federal government. These laws and regulations, including the Endangered Species Act, wetlands regulations (as set forth in the Clean Water Act), and regulations limiting the use of public land, have had a significant impact on the values of land belonging to farmers, developers, and inholders,[4] and this impact has been an impetus to the land rights movement.

The Endangered Species Act, for example, has come under fire from landowners across the country because of its paralyzing effect on development.

The Act's rules and regulations have been described as "so inflexible and rigid that almost any improvement to private property where an endangered-species habitat is located can subject the property owner to substantial civil and criminal fines and penalties" (Marzulla, 1992a). The stringency of the Endangered Species Act is amply evident to Ben Cone, a North Carolina landowner who has lost approximately $1.8 million dollars in timber sales because the endangered red-cockaded woodpecker inhabits his land.[5] Similarly, the *possibility* that the golden-cheeked warbler or the black-capped vireo may inhabit a tract of land in Travis County, Texas, has forced the delay of construction for a potential homeowner (Camia, 1994, 1060).

Wetlands protection regulations have also played havoc with landowners' investment opportunities and land values. In Illinois, development of 43 acres was challenged by the Environmental Protection Agency because 0.8 acre of the property was classified as an "isolated wetland."[6] Farming is also inhibited by wetlands regulations. In Louisiana, a farmer has been prevented from raising crawfish and harvesting cyprus trees for over four years because his property is considered a wetland by federal regulations. The landowner estimates that "lost crawfish sales are costing him $24,000 a year, and uncut timber, even more" (Camia, 1994, 1061).[7]

Owners of land near or surrounded by federally owned land, such as national parks and forests, may suffer diminution of property value when public land-use regulations and policies are restricted or altered. For example, restrictions on grazing have raised the ire of ranchers,[8] as has the reintroduction of wolves into Yellowstone National Park. Even bison and elk can reduce agricultural property values: these grazing animals do not respect property boundaries and may destroy crops on adjacent private land.

These and other federal land-use regulations have created controversy and helped to galvanize the land rights movement into a viable and growing political force. Industry and individuals have joined forces in an effort to retard or stop the number of federal regulatory takings. Nevertheless, the land rights movement has directed much of its efforts toward passage of state legislation because, as explained in the following major section, the prospects for federal legislation that protects private property rights are small. Although legislation at the state level cannot override federal statutes, it can protect landowners from state and local government statutes and regulations, many of which are fashioned after federal laws and regulations.

These state and local government land-use regulations, which may assume many forms, pose a serious threat to property values. To illustrate some forms of state and local government regulatory takings and their consequences for landowners, three kinds of regulations are considered in this section: urban land-use regulations, environmental regulations, and historic preservation regulations. This list does not exhaust all forms of regulatory takings, nor are the distinctions between these regulations always clear—these categories may be somewhat artificial—but these regulations provide a framework for considering state and local government actions that devalue private property.

Urban Land-Use Regulations

State and local government statutes and regulations often take private property through restrictions on the use of urban land.[9] For example, zoning laws and growth management acts may limit or prohibit development. The rationale for these laws rests on the premise that growth spawns problems such as crowding, congestion, and demands for public services that may be difficult to meet.

Nevertheless, these regulations effectively take private property by denying landowners the right to transfer their properties to alternative, more highly valued uses. The result has been denied or delayed development, often followed by lawsuits. For example, the city of Tigard, Oregon, granted a permit to landowners wishing to expand their plumbing supply business. But the permit was conditioned upon the landowners agreeing to set aside part of their property for a public bike path and storm drain. The property owners argued that the city's actions constituted a taking of property for which compensation was due. The property owners filed suit, and although they lost in the state courts, the U.S. Supreme Court ruled in their favor in June 1994 (Barrett, 1994; *The Economist*, July 2, 1994).

Other examples include a landowner in Lee County, Florida, who sued when he was denied the right to develop 35 acres of his property because of a growth management act, as well as a Minnesota landowner who sued a municipality that imposed a two-year moratorium on development (Weaver and Solov, 1992).[10] In each case, landowners were denied development rights because of urban land-use regulations. And note that even though the courts may eventually provide recourse from uncompensated takings, delays in obtaining building permits may be costly to property owners who are temporarily denied use of their properties.[11]

Urban land-use regulations may be used not only to restrict development, but also to redistribute income. For example, in 1980, and again in 1985, Seattle passed housing preservation ordinances designed to preserve the city's low-income housing. The 1980 ordinance

contained a housing replacement fee provision that imposed a license fee on owners who demolished low-income housing and a tenant relocation provision that required owners to pay for relocation assistance to tenants displaced by development. (Marshall, 1993, 873)

The 1985 ordinance was similar in content: it, too, contained a tenant relocation requirement and "required owners to replace a percentage of the destroyed housing by either paying the City or building replacement housing" (Marshall, 1993, 873). Though successfully challenged in the Washington Supreme Court, these ordinances vividly illustrate how far-reaching land-use regulations can go.[12]

Environmental Regulations

Environmental regulations are perhaps the most controversial of all state regulations. The protection of wetlands or wildlife evokes ardent criticism from many landowners because of its significant impact on property values. For example, many Utah residents were upset when their state Division of Wildlife Resources "opted . . . to protect from development 20,000 more acres . . . to preserve the habitat of the desert tortoise and the region's unique plant life" (Lavelle, 1993). Similarly, Florida's Department of Environmental Regulation denied a landowner a permit to dredge and fill property on which the landowner had planned to build two houses.[13]

The preservation of habitat and wetlands may be worthy objectives, but when preservation is achieved through restrictions on the use of private property, a regulatory taking has occurred and compensation is due. The propriety of compensation is especially evident when, as in the Florida case cited above, the restrictions on property use are implemented *after* the landowner has purchased the property.[14]

Another important species of environmental directives are beachfront protection regulations. Many coastal states have passed laws designed to protect their beaches from erosion. Ironically, these laws may run afoul of landowners' private efforts to develop their properties as well as to protect them from erosion. In Chatham, Massachusetts, a storm in 1987 overwhelmed a section of beach that had previously provided natural protection for residents' property. Residents then sought to construct revetments to retard further beach erosion, but their request for permits to build the revetments was denied because of the Massachusetts Wetlands Protection Regulations.[15] These citizens' beachfront properties are now more subject to erosion than they would have been had the regulations not interfered with their private actions.

Perhaps the most famous land rights case in recent history, *Lucas vs. South Carolina Coastal Council* (1992),[16] resulted from state regulations of beachfront property. In 1977, South Carolina enacted the Coastal Zone Management Act requiring owners of land in designated "critical areas" (beaches and lands adjacent to sand dunes) to secure permits from the newly created South Carolina Coastal Council before using the land in ways "other than the use the critical area was devoted to on [September 28, 1977]."[17] Then, in 1988 the South

Carolina legislature enacted the Beachfront Management Act. This statute extended the definition of "critical area" substantially landward. (The only kinds of construction permitted under the Act on the newly designated critical areas were of temporary, nonhabitable structures.)

In 1986, with the intention of building single-family homes, David Lucas purchased two residential lots on the Isle of Palms, a barrier island off the coast in Charleston, for $975,000. The purchased property was on an area of the island that two years later was to be encompassed by the newly expanded legislative definition of critical areas. At the time of Lucas's purchase, however, his plans for developing the lots were fully within the law. The state refused to compensate Lucas for his property-value loss occasioned by the 1988 statute.

Lucas sued for compensation under the takings clause. He lost in the South Carolina supreme court. South Carolina's high court held that the Beachfront Management Act was intended by the legislature to eliminate "noxious uses" of private property—which the building of permanent homes on this barrier island were presumably determined to be by the legislature. And elimination of noxious uses is a legitimate exercise of the state's police power that does not require compensation. The U.S. Supreme Court reversed the South Carolina court, holding that the 1988 statute took all value away from Lucas's property. When property is rendered valueless by government regulation, a compensable taking has occurred.[18]

Historic Preservation Regulations

Regulations that preserve historic sites can also impose severe restrictions on land use, and the burdens imposed on landowners may be onerous. For example, in Philadelphia the City Historical Commission designated the Boyd Theater a historic site because of its allegedly unique architecture.[19] The designation as a historical site gave the City Historical Commission great latitude to control the theater (thereby, of course, taking power to control the theater from its owner). The owner was required to maintain the property with personal funds, faced criminal sanctions if the property was not maintained, and was prohibited from altering the property in nearly any way without prior approval from the commission. The expectations of the owner, who had plans for future development of the property, were clearly denied. Upon challenge in the courts, the Pennsylvania supreme court ruled in favor of the landowner.[20]

In Virginia, preservation of Civil War battle sites has sparked controversies over land use. In Culpeper County, development of a 5,266-acre "edge city" was halted when the Virginia Department of Historical Resources and the National Park Service declared the property to be developed as "'eligible' for listing in the National Register" (*Richmond Times-Dispatch*, August 4, 1991, H-7). The historical significance of the site, which is dubious, stems from a series of skirmishes in 1863 known as the Battle of Brandy Station. Although the battle ranked "91st in casualties, and 72nd in troop involvement," the Virginia Department of Historical Resources wanted to "set aside an area three times the size of Manassas, five times the area of Antietam and four times the size of Gettysburg" (*Richmond Times-Dispatch*, August 4, 1991, H-7). A review of the historical significance of the site was undertaken and the historical designation was ultimately dropped "because of an uproar from property owners" (*Richmond Times-Dispatch*, December 1, 1993, B-4).

Summary

Laws and regulations enacted by federal, state, and local governments often have a significant impact on landowners' development opportunities and property values. The goals of these regulations are often noble and worthwhile. Species preservation, environmental and beachfront protection, historical preservation, and controlled and managed growth and development are all rooted in ideals with which few would disagree. Nevertheless, when government regulation reduces the value of private property, a regulatory taking has occurred, and compensation is due. Uncompensated regulatory takings, such as those cited above, have been the impetus of state legislation designed to protect private property rights.

2. Why Pursue State Legislation?

The previous section reviewed a number of federal, state, and local government regulations and their consequences for landowners. A remaining question is why the land rights movement is seeking recourse through state statutes. In this section, two explanations are explored: the uncertainty of judicial rulings and the lack of federal protection from regulatory takings.

The Uncertainty of Judicial Decisions

Landowners' challenges to physical takings will certainly be upheld by the courts. However, the outcome is less certain when the taking is regulatory. The courts have long been plagued by questions of what government actions constitute a taking, and the circumstances under which a taking is compensable. The 1887 case of *Mugler v. Kansas* upheld the power of states to close via prohibition legislation existing and heretofore law-abiding breweries. The brewery owner in *Mugler* argued that he was entitled to compensation under the takings clause of the Fifth Amendment because this regulation took property value from him even though he formally retained title to the brewery and the real property on which it rested. Disagreeing with the owner, the U.S. Supreme Court denied compensation because "a prohibition simply upon the use of property for purposes that are declared, by valid legislation, to be injurious to public health, morals or safety of the community, cannot in any sense, be deemed a taking . . ."[21] Thus, even though the owner's property value was dramatically diminished by the regulation, and even though the general public was admitted to benefit from this regulation, the general public was not required to pay for its benefits by compensating with tax dollars the brewery owner for the disproportionate loss he suffered because of the regulation. The brewery owner was consequently compelled to personally pay for—in the form of great property-value loss—the public benefits believed to emerge from the regulation.

In contrast to *Mugler*, however, is the famous 1922 case of *Pennsylvania Coal v. Mahon*.[22] Here, speaking through Justice Oliver Wendell Holmes, the Court ruled that government could regulate private property without compensation only if the regulation's costs to property owners are not excessive; if the regulation "goes too far" then compensation is due to property owners even if they retain title to affected properties.[23] The *Mahon* Court, unfortunately, offered no guidance on how to determine when a regulation goes so far as to become a compensable taking of private property.

The Supreme Court attempted to establish criteria for determining when a compensable taking has occurred in its 1978 ruling in *Penn Central Transportation Co. v. New York*.[24] The criteria to be considered when evaluating the takings implications of a government action are

(1)   the character of the governmental action,

(2)   the economic impact of the action on the claimant, and

(3)   the extent to which the regulation has interfered with the distinct, investment-backed expectations of the owner (Marzulla 1988, 10255).

Nevertheless, these criteria are subject to a case-by-case, ad hoc analysis, and fail to provide a consistent application of the takings clause to regulatory takings. Commenting on the takings cases addressed by the Supreme Court, Buck (1993, 1285) writes that "(w)ithout a set formula, Supreme Court opinions reveal an admitted array of inconsistent and arbitrary results" and that the Court has never determined "when a diminution [of property value] of less than one hundred percent constitutes a taking" (1297).

Consistent application of the takings clause may be just as elusive at the state level. Toth (1991, 508-14) provides a detailed historical account of the Utah court system's application of the state's takings clause. From 1890 to 1935, the courts generally ruled in favor of landowners, whether property was taken outright or only damaged by government action. However, from the mid-1930s to the mid-1960s, the courts used sovereign immunity "to preclude all just compensation claims against the state" (511). Since the mid-1960s, however, the courts have not consistently applied sovereign immunity to takings cases and have sided more often with landowners.

Uncertainty about judicial attitudes regarding regulatory takings is costly to landowners and regulators alike. Landowners are left wondering about property usage and value, and whether they have legal recourse when a regulation proscribes specific land uses. Regulators must contemplate whether their actions will result in lawsuits holding state and local governments liable for the diminution of property values (Arrensen, 1988, 654). The latitude for judicial discretion is wide. How much has land been devalued and, more importantly, will the diminution of value in any given case be sufficient for the court to find that a compensable taking has occurred? Will the court consider the relative magnitudes of public benefits and private harm and, if so, how will benefits and costs be weighed and measured? These questions and others plague those who rely on a slowly evolving common law, and the court's interpretation of that law, to determine the outcome of cases involving regulatory takings.

Legislation offers a potential solution to the problem of uncertain judicial rulings. State laws governing application of the takings clause may provide clearer guidelines and criteria for determining when a compensable taking has occurred. Because landowners would benefit from more predictable rules governing regulatory takings,[25] it is hardly surprising that they and other advocates of private property rights have sought to preempt the common law of takings with state statutes.[26]

Lack of Federal Protection

Given that judicial enforcement of the takings clause has been inconsistent, legislation may be a preferred alternative for protection of private property rights. The preference for statutory certainty over judicial uncertainty does not, however, explain why legislation is being sought at the *state* level. The reason, not surprisingly, is that the prospects for passage of federal legislation protecting private property rights are not promising.

Some protection of private property rights was granted by the federal government when, in March 1988, President Reagan signed Executive Order 12630. The objectives of this Executive Order are to force federal agencies to consider the takings implications of their regulations and to estimate the costs of compensating landowners whose properties have been ruled as taken by the courts. To achieve these objectives, the Executive Order requires a takings impact analysis of regulations implemented by executive departments and agencies, and guidelines "for the risk and the avoidance of unanticipated takings" to be set up by the attorney general (Marzulla, 1988, 10258).

Despite the protection afforded property owners by Executive Order 12630, the order suffers from two problems. First, it applies only to executive departments and agencies, and not to state and local government regulatory agencies. Second, and perhaps more importantly, the Clinton administration is not enforcing this order (*Christian Science Monitor*, September 22, 1993, 1).

Past efforts in Congress to enact legislation protecting private property rights have been unsuccessful. One notable bill, the Private Property Rights Protection Act of 1991, would have effectively codified Executive Order 12630. Congress did not pass this bill. But even if property rights legislation is now passed, as seems more likely, given the Republican majorities in both houses after the 1994 elections, the legislation would face a certain veto by President Clinton.[27]

3. The Land Rights Movement at the State Level

To this point, we have shown that numerous state and local government regulations may take private property without compensation to the owner. Whatever the content and intent of these regulations, landowners recognize that these takings pose a credible threat to their rights and wealth, and that judicial rulings and federal legislation are unlikely sources of protection. Given these judicial and national statutory shortcomings, the land rights movement has turned to state legislatures across the country in efforts to obtain statutory protection of private property rights. By August 1994, more than a hundred bills had been introduced in forty-two state legislatures, and 11 states had passed some form of property rights legislation.[28] The states that have introduced or passed property rights legislation, as well as the form that legislation has taken, are shown in Table 7.1.

This section addresses several questions about the land rights movement and the legislation it has championed. What is the content of the legislation? How much protection is provided by the legislation? Which interest groups support —and which oppose—this legislation? Finally, to capture the flavor of the land rights debate, case studies of the land rights movement in Arizona and Washington are documented.

Table 7.1. The Status of State Property Rights Legislation: August 1994

States with Private Property Rights Legislation[1]

Arizona	Indiana	North Carolina	Virginia
Delaware	Mississippi	Tennessee	Washington
Idaho	Missouri	Utah	

States in Which Planning Legislation Has Been Introduced

Alabama	Louisiana	New Mexico	Vermont
California	Massachusetts	Oklahoma	Virginia
Colorado	Minnesota	Oregon	West Virginia
Georgia	Montana	Rhode Island	Wisconsin
Hawaii	Nebraska	South Carolina	Wyoming
Iowa	Nevada	South Dakota	
Kansas (Vetoed)	New Hampshire	Texas	

States in Which Defined-Takings Legislation Has Been Introduced

California	Iowa	New Hampshire	Rhode Island
Delaware	Kentucky	New York	South Carolina
Florida	Maine	North Carolina	Texas
Georgia	Maryland	Oregon	Washington
Idaho (Vetoed)	Nevada	Pennsylvania	

[1] All passed bills are planning bills, except those of Florida, Mississippi, North Carolina, and Virginia. The Virginia law establishes a committee to study regulations that may take private property and to possibly recommend changes in the law. The Mississippi and North Carolina laws are defined takings laws; however, they are restricted to forest land and land under navigable waters, respectively.
Source: Defenders of Property Rights.

The Forms of Property Rights Legislation

The legislation introduced at the state level assumes primarily two forms. One form is "planning" laws (often referred to as "look before you leap" laws) that, like Executive Order 12630, require the establishment of guidelines obligating state agencies to evaluate the takings implications of their regulations. Delaware enacted such a law in 1992, the aims of which are made clear by its contents:

> No rule or regulation promulgated by any state agency shall become effective until the Attorney General has reviewed the rule or regulation and has informed the issuing agency in writing as to the potential of the rule or regulation to result in a taking of private property (Amendment to Chapter 6, Title 29, Delaware Code, §605)

As this example shows, the purpose of "planning" or "look before you leap" laws is largely precautionary. However, as indicated by the Lucas episode, giving careful consideration to a potential takings can help avoid costly future litigation.

The second form of legislation, referred to as "defined takings" (or "compensation") legislation, explicitly requires state governments to compensate individuals whose land has suffered diminished value because of government regulation. Although the proposed bills may exempt regulations that require the exercise of police power or the protection of public safety and health, they commonly promulgate a "50 percent rule" that mandates compensation whenever a government regulation devalues property by 50 percent or more. Although only two defined-takings laws of limited scope have been passed,[29] they have been introduced in nineteen states, including South Carolina. South Carolina's proposed bill states:

> Whenever implementation by the State or any of its political subdivisions of any regulatory program or law operates to reduce the fair market value of real property to less than fifty percent of its fair market value for the uses permitted at the time the owner acquired the title . . . the property is deemed to have been taken for the use of the public (South Carolina Private Property Protection Act)

In addition, the state would give owners "the right to require condemnation . . . or to receive compensation for the reduction in value caused by the government action." The Act does allow exemptions for the "exercise of police power" and the regulation of a "public nuisance" (South Carolina Private Property Protection Act).[30] These exemptions address a common concern about the ability of local governments to use zoning as a tool for reducing costly spillover effects.

Proponents and Opponents of Property Rights Legislation

The proponents of property rights legislation include a variety of landowners and users who fear that government regulations may proscribe current land uses or deny future development opportunities. The real estate and home building industries, apprehensive about regulations such as growth management acts and zoning laws, strongly support legislation protecting land rights, as do farmers who are threatened by environmental and other development regulations.

In western states, where job opportunities and economic welfare are highly and visibly dependent on natural resources, the land rights movement has expanded beyond the interests of realtors, developers, and farmers to include the interests of miners, loggers, ranchers and other land-intensive industries. These industries and their supporters argue that government regulations, especially environmental regulations, compromise private property rights and threaten future economic growth. This "wise use" movement (as the western land rights movement is often called) is generally considered more extreme than the property rights movement in the eastern states. Despite its extremism, the "wise use" movement has broad appeal to rural landowners as well as political conservatives and libertarians (Kriz, 1993).

Opponents of the land rights movement include advocates of historical preservation, environmental protection, and controlled urban growth and development. Environmental interest groups, such as the Audubon Society, Sierra Club, and Wilderness Society, ardently oppose the land rights movement. These groups argue that the purpose of the land rights movement is to cripple governments' regulatory capacity, thereby compromising public safety and health, and the environment. Indeed, they accuse the advocates of the land rights movement of deceiving the public of their true intentions by supporting legislation with "difficult-to-bash titles like 'The Private Property Rights Protection Act'" (Kriz, 1993; Lavelle, 1993).

Both sides attempt to appeal to taxpayers by making predictions about the fiscal impact of land rights legislation. Opponents of land rights legislation argue that state and local governments cannot afford to pay the compensation that would inevitably result from the passage of land rights legislation. Proponents, in contrast, argue that a growing number of costly claims against state and local governments will result from *failure* to pass legislation governing regulatory takings. Land rights advocates argue that costly litigation can be avoided by forcing state agencies to consider the takings implications of regulations *before* they are implemented.

Land rights advocates also point out that compensation for takings does not, in fact, increase the social costs of regulations; it merely spreads these costs more equitably over all taxpayers. When government regulation slashes the market value of a piece of property, the costs of the regulation are borne disproportionately by the uncompensated property owner, even though the benefits of the regulation are enjoyed by citizens as a whole. Thus, requiring compensation for such regulations forces taxpayers generally to share in the costs of whatever benefits they secure from government regulation.

Proponents of stronger property rights protection also note another advantage of requiring compensation whenever government action significantly diminishes property values. Requiring that voters at large—through general tax revenues—pay for the costs of government regulations helps ensure that legislators will avoid those regulations whose full social costs exceed the benefits. When voters have to pay fully for what government does, voters' representatives will seek regulation only when the full benefits exceed the full costs.

Arizona: A Case Study of Environmentalist Opposition to Land Rights Legislation

The conflict over property rights legislation is perhaps nowhere better illustrated than in Arizona, where a bitter legislative battle pitted property rights advocates against environmentalists. The struggle for land rights legislation in Arizona began in 1991 and early 1992 when several property rights protection bills were introduced in the state legislature. These bills, fashioned after President Reagan's Executive Order, required economic analyses of the takings implications of state government regulations. They received strong support from agricultural, ranching, and mining interests, who believed government regulations threatened their use of private property, their rights to use public land, and the state's opportunities for economic growth and development (*Arizona Republic*, February 23, 1992, D14). One bill, referred to as the Arizona Community Stability Act, would have "benefit[ted] the state's cattle ranchers, timber companies, mining firms and other . . . 'extractive' industries" by requiring "Arizona's resources . . . to be 'managed so as to avoid creating instability in resource-dependent communities.'" "Instability" might be better translated as "job loss," as shown by Arizona timber companies' opposition to the state's Game and Fish Department's efforts to protect the northern goshawk (*Phoenix Gazette*, February 28, 1992, A1).

These bills immediately sparked the ire of environmentalists and state government agencies. The Outdoor Editor of the *Arizona Republic* expressed outrage over legislation that he believed would thwart state environmental regulations and require compensation for wildlife-induced damages to private and public lands. In particular, environmentalists feared the legislation would require costly studies of takings impacts, and that compensation for takings would be paid from the state's Heritage Fund, which is supported by the state's lottery "for the benefit of wildlife and for cultural, historical and recreational nourishment" (*Arizona Republic*, February 23, 1992, D14).[31]

Property rights proponents countered that the intent of the bills was only to reestablish and secure private property rights. The House majority leader stated that the legislation was meant to show that "private property rights are basic civil rights." Another state representative said that the intent of the legislation was merely to put "humans first" (*Phoenix Gazette*, February 28, 1992, A1).

With strong support from rural legislators, the Private Property Rights Act passed with large majorities in both houses, and on June 1, 1992, Governor Fife Symington signed the bill into law. The law requires the attorney general to "adopt guidelines to assist state agencies in the identification of governmental actions that have constitutional takings implications" and ensures that

> [b]efore the state agency implements a governmental action that has constitutional takings implications, the state agency shall submit a copy of the assessment of constitutional takings implications to the governor and the joint legislative budget committee. (State Land-Private Property Rights Protection, Chapter 107, S.B. 1053, § 37-221 and § 37-222)

Nevertheless, the controversy did not end with the governor's signature. Environmentalists—many of whom expected Symington to veto the bill—gathered approximately 70,500 signatures to force the bill to be placed on the November 1994 ballot for consideration as a citizens' referendum (*Phoenix Gazette*, September 30, 1992, B2). Ultimately the environmentalists won; the bill did not pass the referendum vote.

Washington: A Case Study of the Reaction of Property Rights Proponents to Growth Management Legislation

In 1991, Washington State passed a growth management act designed to give county and city governments more control over local land use. Specifically, the bill requires counties and cities "to assure the conservation of agricultural, forest, and mineral resource lands" and to "adopt development regulations that protect critical areas" (Growth Management—Revised Provisions, Chapter 32, Sec. 21, 1991), such as wetlands, "fish and wildlife habitat conservation areas, frequently flooded areas, and geographically hazardous areas" (Final Bill Report, ESHB 1025, 1). In addition, the Act requires counties to designate urban growth areas "within which urban growth shall be encouraged and outside of which growth can occur only if it is not urban in nature" (Growth Management —Revised Provisions, Chapter 32, Sec. 29, 1991).

The Act does, however, contain a provision for the protection of private property. Section 18 of the Act requires the state attorney general to establish "an orderly, consistent process . . . that better enables state agencies and local governments to evaluate proposed regulatory or administrative actions to assure that such actions do not result in an unconstitutional taking of private property." Washington's bill, like Arizona's bill, is a "planning" bill.

Despite the potential protection afforded property owners by Section 18 of Washington's Growth Management Act, property rights advocates have rallied against the Act's restrictions on land use.   By early 1992, a plethora of property rights protection bills had been introduced in the Washington State legislature. These bills, among other things, would have required compensation for regulatory taking, redefined wetlands, and exempted counties with populations under 200,000 from growth management regulations. Support from developers, farmers, and other property owners was strong (*Seattle Post-Intelligencer*, February 21, 1992, B1).

Near the close of Washington's 1992 legislative session, popular sentiment was turning against the Growth Management Act.   Interest groups opposing environmental regulations and supporting property rights, including the Center for Defense of Free Enterprise, the National Inholders Association, and the Pacific Legal Foundation, helped to organize and promote popular protest against land-use regulations.   Although required-compensation and wetlands-mapping bills failed, the legislature did cut "more than $4.5 million from growth management programs" and repealed "a central tenant of the Growth Management Act—confining development within urban areas" (*Seattle Post-Intelligencer*, March 18, 1992, A1).   Additional property rights legislation, including defined-takings bills, continues to be introduced in state legislature, but has yet to pass (*Seattle Post-Intelligencer*, January 15, 1994, A6).

The Future of Property Rights Legislation at the State Level

The examples of Arizona and Washington show how heated the battle for (and against) land rights legislation can be. Assessing future prospects for land rights is difficult, but as government constraints on land use become more burdensome, the property rights movement will likely gain momentum. The passage of widely encompassing defined-takings legislation would be an especially powerful sign of the movement's success. As shown in the following sections, Public Choice analysis and econometric methods can help determine if and where property rights legislation is likely to be introduced and passed.

4. The Public Choice Theory of Legislative Decision Making

Public Choice is the use of economics to understand and explain government activities and political outcomes. The fundamental premises of Public Choice are few and very commonsensical. First, politicians are just as self-interested as private citizens; the typical politician is no more likely than anyone else to wake up mornings and regularly ask him or herself "What can I do today— regardless of what it costs me—to help my fellow citizens?" Being self-interested, politicians are exceedingly concerned with getting elected and reelected. And electoral strength is positively affected by support from interest groups and negatively affected by taxes as well as by reductions in programs valued by constituents.

Second, voters also are self-interested. Voters support candidates whom they expect to generate for them the largest net increase in wealth. Tobacco farmers in the Carolinas vote for candidates that zealously champion government subsidies for tobacco, just as federal government employees in Maryland and Virginia consistently vote for candidates promising generous federal pay raises and pension benefits, and just as farmers in California vote for candidates who support government-subsidized water supply. In general, any time a group of voters can garner benefits through the political process and not have to pay fully for these benefits—i.e., any time a group of voters can push all or part of the costs of their benefits onto someone else—they are prone to do so. (Why pay full cost for something if you can have the bulk of the tab picked up by others?) Politicians typically are willing to help such groups in return for the groups' campaign contributions and political backing.

Third, special interest groups enjoy a hefty advantage within legislative and executive corridors over the general, public interest. The nature of special interest groups makes possible political outcomes in which groups of organized voters extract benefits from less organized voters.[32]

Special interest groups are comprised of people with significant stakes in legislation designed to transfer income from the public as a whole to members of interest groups. Louisiana sugar farmers are a classic special interest group. The government annually bestows millions of dollars of benefits on a relatively small number of American sugar farmers. High tariffs and import restrictions on imported sugar, as well as other price-support mechanisms, ensure that each American pays two to three times more for sugar than he or she would pay if government were uninvolved in the sugar market. Each American is damaged a small amount by the sugar program, while each of the small number of sugar farmers is benefited enormously. Thus, the typical American has little incentive to lobby against the sugar program, while each sugar farmer has robust incentives to lobby in support of it. With the costs of a government program spread out literally over millions of people, but with the benefits of the program concentrated on a handful of beneficiaries, *each* of the beneficiaries has more to gain by maintenance of the program than *each* of the losers has to gain by its repeal. This is true even if the total social costs of the program vastly exceed its total benefits. Thus, the beneficiaries lobby hard for the program's maintenance (or even extension), while the losers—citizens at large—have inadequate incentives to organize and push for repeal.

Fourth, voters are rationally uninformed about government. This means that government is not monitored closely by citizens. Consequently, government is able to do things that it could not do if people were better informed.

People are uninformed for understandable ("rational") reasons. Knowledge and information are costly; their acquisition requires effort, time, and, often, money. But citizens' time and resources are limited. People have jobs to do, households to tend, children to raise, and a multitude of other important chores to perform. Becoming better informed means doing fewer of our other worthwhile daily tasks. And because *individually* we each have approximately a zero chance of affecting public policy outcomes (when was the last time your vote determined the outcome of an election?), it does not pay us to invest much in acquiring information about the vast bulk of what government does.

In contrast, it *does* pay members of special interest groups to stay informed about what government is doing—or could do—to their industries. Sugar farmers are quite aware of the current status in Congress of sugar price supports. A sugar farmer uninformed about, say, an effort to eliminate price supports stands to lose hundreds of thousands of dollars. Each sugar farmer, then, has powerful incentives to keep abreast of all programs affecting sugar farmers. But because each special interest program costs the typical taxpayer only a few dollars annually, taxpayers in general have weak incentives to stay informed about all that government does.

The conclusion of Public Choice scholarship is that, despite its many advantages, democracy is far from flawless. Democracy is prone to unduly benefiting politically well-organized and powerful groups while unloading the costs of these programs onto politically weak groups. However, Public Choice does offer some hope to members of currently unorganized—and, hence, currently politically disadvantaged—groups: as the exactions of other political coalitions rise, members of presently disadvantaged (i.e., politically unorganized) groups have increasingly strong incentives to organize themselves into more effective political lobbies. That is, as the exactions of more organized interest groups increase, there comes a point when those who bear disproportionate shares of these exactions find it worthwhile to form and maintain their own lobbying groups and political movements to defend themselves from other interest groups. We believe that the recently emergent land rights movement is precisely of this character. The frequency and the size of property rights deprivations have grown to such an extent that it is no longer worthwhile for property owners merely to suffer property-value losses without fighting back.

5. Which States Will Introduce Land Rights Legislation? An Empirical Test

Employing the Public Choice Model

The preceding section described the thrust of Public Choice, which assumes quite reasonably that legislators respond to constituent and interest group pressures when proposing and voting on legislation. In this section, the Public Choice theory as it applies to legislation protecting land rights will be tested. That is, constituents and interest groups who may have an interest in the passage of land rights legislation—or an interest in preventing the passage of land-rights legislation—are identified, and their effects on the likelihood of such legislation being introduced (and possibly passed) are estimated.

The Relevant Interest Groups

To summarize the discussion of the land rights movement and to set the stage for the empirical test, we identify the interest groups who are believed to affect the introduction and passage of land rights legislation. Supporters of land rights legislation are many and broadly based: builders and realtors who develop and sell property converted from other uses; farmers, ranchers, and miners who seek to maintain rights over their land or rights to use public land; and ordinary individuals who are denied building permits because of various land-use regulations. Clearly, the land rights movement is supported not only by land-intensive industries, large corporate farms, and developers, but also by ordinary citizens who believe their rights, livelihood, and property are threatened by government regulations. The movement is "grassroots" and "populist," deriving support from many sources.

The primary opponents of the land rights movement are environmentalists who seek control over sensitive land such as wetlands, beachfront property, and wildlife habitat. They have denounced the land rights movement as a threat to environmental preservation and public safety and health. Joining environmentalists in their opposition to the land rights movement are historic preservationists, advocates of controlled urban growth, and taxpayers who fear property rights legislation would result in higher taxes, reduced services, or both.

The Empirical Model

As the discussion to this point has shown, many interests may promote or oppose land rights legislation. The diversity and broad base of interest groups that support and oppose land rights legislation complicates the empirical modeling. For example, conflicts between the development and preservation of coastal property are irrelevant in over half the states. Similarly, growth management acts do not threaten the development opportunities of landowners in states with low population densities and slow (or negative) rates of population growth. In addition, conflicts over the use of federal land are often heated in western states, but aren't an issue in most eastern states.

The empirical model is further complicated because forty-two states have introduced legislation. Estimating the effects of exogenous variables on an endogenous variable is not feasible when the value of the endogenous variable is nearly the same for every observation. In this case, estimating the effects of interest groups or other factors on the probability that property rights legislation will be introduced (or passed) in a state legislature is not feasible because nearly all states have introduced some form of the legislation.

To circumvent this problem, the empirical estimates are carried out with data from November 1993. These data are shown in Table 7.2 (in the same format as presented in Table 7.1), and reveal that thirty-three states had introduced or passed property rights legislation by November 1993. Using the November 1993 data not only permits empirical estimation, but also offers the advantage of assessing which interests yielded influence early in the legislative process.

The empirical model captures many of the diverse interests that may support or oppose passage of land rights legislation. The model is expressed in functional form as:

$$LAW = F(DCLAUSE, POPGROWTH, LEGISLATORS, LCV/USCC,$$
$$PCDEBT, SHORE, FEDLAND, LANDGSP)$$

where LAW is the variable that designates whether or not a state has introduced of a property rights protection bill. Mathematically, LAW is assigned a value of zero for states that have not introduced a property rights protection bill and a value of one for states that have introduced such a bill.

Nine independent variables are used in the estimates. The first, DCLAUSE, indicates the presence of a "damages clause" found in twenty-four state constitutions. All else equal, the presence of a damages clause may afford landowners additional protection from regulatory takings and lessen the demand for statutory protection. If so, we expect that the presence of a damages clause in a state constitution reduces the likelihood that a land rights protection bill will be introduced in that state.

Table 7.2. The Status of State Property Rights Legislation: November 1993

States with Private Property Rights Legislation[1]

Arizona	Indiana	Virginia
Delaware	Utah	Washington

States in Which Planning Legislation Has Been Introduced

California	Maryland	North Carolina
Colorado	Massachusetts	Oklahoma
Florida	Mississippi	Oregon
Hawaii	Missouri	Rhode Island
Iowa	Montana	South Carolina
Kansas	Nevada	Vermont
Louisiana	New Hampshire	Washington
Maine	New Mexico	Wyoming

States in Which Defined-Takings Legislation Has Been Introduced

California	New York	South Carolina
Delaware	Oregon	Texas
Idaho	Pennsylvania	Washington
Maine		

[1] All passed bills are planning bills except the Virginia bill, which establishes a committee to study regulations that may take private property and to possibly recommend changes in the law.

Source: Defenders of Property Rights.

The second variable listed is POPGROWTH, which designates the population growth of a state from 1980 to 1990. Population pressures increase the demands for land development, potentially resulting in more conflicts over land usage. Realtors, developers, and ordinary landowners, who have increased opportunities to profitably develop their land because of population growth, should lobby legislators for protection of their property and increase the likelihood that land rights legislation will be introduced.

The ratio of state legislators to voting-age population (expressed in hundreds of thousands) (LEGISLATORS) is included in the model because a high ratio of legislators to voting-age population (or a low ratio of voting-age population to legislators) reduces the transactions costs of informing legislators of constituents' interests and concerns. The ratio of legislators to potential voters is, of course, the same for both advocates and opponents of legislation within any given legislature. Nevertheless, proponents of property rights legislation have often initiated contact with legislators before opponents realized the importance of the issue.[33] For this reason, we expect a high ratio of legislators to voting-age population to increase the probability that land rights legislation will be introduced.

The fourth and fifth variables listed, LCV and USCC, are the average ratings given to a state's senators by the League of Conservation Voters, a pro-environmental interest group, and by the U.S. Chamber of Commerce, a pro-business interest group.[34] These variables are included to account for voters' tastes and preferences that may not be directly tied to identifiable economic interests, the inference being that citizens with a strong desire for environmental preservation will elect senators whose votes will earn them a high rating from the League of Conservation Voters, and that citizens who strongly desire economic development will elect senators whose votes will earn them a high rating from the U.S. Chamber of Commerce. A high average LCV rating should reduce the likelihood of a property rights protection bill being introduced in the state, while a high average USCC rating should increase the likelihood that such a bill will be introduced.

Because compensation paid to landowners could have a significant impact on the fiscal condition of state governments, the per capita debt of each state (PCDEBT) is included in the model. The effect of a takings law on government finance is unclear. As discussed above, opponents of property rights legislation argue that the passage of statutes granting additional protections to landowners would result in a plethora of lawsuits that, if lost by the state, could result in higher taxes and a divergence of funds away from other state priorities—such as education and public welfare—to landowners. In addition, economists and political scientists have long recognized that regulation is a substitute for taxation.[35] Consequently, regulation that is constrained by takings implications could force governments to raise taxes or to reduce services. On the other hand, proponents of property rights legislation point out that the means for legal recourse against takings are already present, and that planning legislation may save revenues by forcing state governments to consider the takings implications of their actions and avoid the implementation of those regulations that might result in lawsuits.[36]

Per capita debt is a measure of the fiscal soundness of a state, and should influence legislators' votes on property rights laws. If legislators believe that property rights legislation will result in higher taxes and reduced services, states with high debt levels will be less likely to introduce property rights legislation. On the other hand, if legislators believe that property rights legislation will help to diminish the number or complexity of costly lawsuits, then states with high debt levels will be more likely to introduce property rights legislation.

To capture the interests of landowners who own valuable coastal property and adjoining wetlands, each state's shoreline (SHORE), scaled by total land area and expressed in percentage terms, is included in the model.[37] Because of population growth along U.S. coasts, beachfront property is becoming increasingly valuable and subject to development pressure. At odds with this development pressure are a variety of regulations to prevent shoreline erosion and preserve wetlands. This combination of development pressure and land-use regulation points to intense conflicts over coastal land use. For this reason, we expect a lengthy shoreline (scaled by land area) to increase the probability that land rights legislation will be introduced.

The model also includes the percentage of state land owned by the federal government (FEDLAND). Although federal land falls under the jurisdiction of the federal government, conflicts over its use are many, especially when the government restricts mining or grazing rights. Landowners in states in which the federal government owns a substantial portion of total land area are likely to strongly support the land rights movement at the state level, even if federal regulations pose their biggest immediate problem. For this reason, constituents in states with a large percentage of publicly owned land are more likely to support land rights legislation than are constituencies in states with relatively small federal holdings.

Finally, we include in the model the share of gross state product accounted for by farming, agricultural services, forestry, fisheries, and mining (LAND-GSP). Legislators in states where land-intensive industries provide a large share of state income and jobs should be sympathetic to landowners' interests and support the introduction of land rights legislation.[38]

The Estimates

The results of the empirical tests are shown in Table 7.3. Because the dependent variable is qualitative, a logit procedure is used to estimate the model. Two estimates are shown, the first using LCV as a preference variable and the second using USCC as a preference variable. Estimating separate equations is

Table 7.3. Results of the Empirical Tests

Dependent Variable: Introduction of Property-Rights Protection Law

Independent Variable	Estimated Coeff.	T-Ratio	Partial Effect	Estimated Coeff.	T-Ratio	Partial Effect
Constant	4.238	2.177**		-3.094	-1.795	
DCLAUSE	-1.481	-1.259	-0.205	-1.184	-0.872	-0.139
POPGROWTH	0.028	0.444	0.004	-0.025	-0.347	-0.003
LEGISLATORS	0.100	1.810*	0.014	0.098	1.593	0.012
LCV	-0.063	-2.400**	-0.009			
USCC				0.108	2.675**	0.013
PCDEBT	-0.917E-03	-1.871*	-0.127E-03	-0.770E-03	-1.357	-0.904E-04
SHORE	0.195	2.266**	0.027	0.182	2.092**	0.021
FEDLAND	0.120	2.300**	0.017	0.101	1.537	0.012
LANDGSP	-0.194	-1.568	-0.027	-0.173	-1.275	-0.20
Likelihood Ratio Test	27.125***			34.921***		
R-Square	0.423			0.544		
No. of Right Predictions	42			45		

* Significant at the 10 percent level for a two-tail test.
** Significant at the 5 percent level for a two-tail test.
*** Significant at the 1 percent level for a one-tail test.

necessary because these variables are highly inversely correlated; that is, senators with high LCV ratings tend to have low USCC rating, and senators with high USCC ratings tend to have low LCV ratings.[39] If both variables are estimated in the same equation, the separate effects of the variables on the dependent variable cannot be accurately estimated. For each variable, three statistics are given: the estimated coefficient, the t-ratio, and the partial effect. Because the estimated coefficients in logit regressions do not provide a measure of the effect of a change in an independent variable on the dependent variable, the partial effects (or derivatives) must be calculated and reported separately.[40]

Turning first to the estimate using LCV as the preference variable, we find that the model performs well. The likelihood ratio test reveals that the explanatory power of the model is significant; the R-square statistic indicates a good fit;[41] and the model predicts whether or not a state has introduced a property rights protection bill with 84 percent accuracy.[42]

Most of the model's independent variables are of expected sign and significance. A high ratio of legislators to voting-age population increases the probability that legislation will be introduced. The calculated partial effect indicates that the probability of introducing property rights legislation increases by .014 with the increase of one state legislator per 100,000 of population. On the other hand, a strong environmental sentiment, as evidenced by the LCV rating, reduces the likelihood that property rights legislation will be introduced. The partial effect suggests that a one-point rise in the LCV rating reduces the probability that property rights legislation will be introduced by .009.

The per capita debt variable indicates that state legislators believe that property rights legislation would result in increased takings lawsuits and a reduction in regulatory authority. Because increased lawsuits and reduced regulatory authority would place increased demands on state revenues, legislators are less likely to introduce property rights legislation where debt levels are already high.[43] Specifically, a $100 increase in a state's per capita debt level reduces the probability of introducing land rights legislation by .0127.

A high share of coastal or federally owned land increases the likelihood that property rights legislation will be introduced. The positive sign on the SHORE variable indicates that owners of coastal property will support legislators' efforts to protect their property from erosion and wetlands regulations. A one percentage point increase in shoreline area increases the likelihood of property rights legislation being introduced by .027. Similarly, the positive sign on FEDLAND suggests that conflicts over the use of public lands heighten landowners' interest in protecting their property; a one percentage point increase in the share of state land that is federally owned increases the likelihood that property rights legislation will be introduced by .017.

Three variables are statistically insignificant: DCLAUSE, POPGROWTH, and LANDGSP. DCLAUSE is negative, as expected, but its insignificance may indicate that a constitutional damages clause does not result in differential judicial interpretation and application of the takings clauses found in state constitutions.

The insignificance of POPGROWTH is perplexing because it seems to imply that population growth does not result in development pressure that, in turn, increases the demand for property rights legislation by realtors, developers, and ordinary citizens. Nevertheless, this conclusion is probably inaccurate. The insignificance of POPGROWTH can be explained by its relatively high correlation with FEDLAND. Western states, which have experienced much faster population growth than the country as a whole, are also the states where the majority of federal land is held." For this reason, the empirical model is unable to reveal the importance of population growth when both variables are estimated in the same equation.

When the model is estimated with FEDLAND omitted, the coefficient on POPGROWTH is positive and significant (at the 5 percent level), indicating that population growth does result in development pressure that increases the likelihood that a state will introduce land rights legislation. The partial effect is .028; that is, an increase in a state's population growth rate of one percentage point raises the probability that land rights legislation will be introduced by .028. Because the results of these estimates are essentially the same as those reported in Table 7.3 (except for the significance of POPGROWTH), they are not reported in Table 7.3 or discussed in the text.

The sign on LANDGSP is unexpectedly negative, the coefficient is nearly significant at conventional levels, and the partial effect indicates that a one percentage point increase in the share of gross state product accounted for by land-intensive industries reduces the likelihood that land rights legislation will be introduced by 0.027." We note that some heavily agricultural states, such as Nebraska, North Dakota, and South Dakota, had not introduced property-rights legislation by November 1993. In addition, Alaska, which is heavily dependent on mining, has yet to introduce property rights legislation. The negative and insignificant coefficient on this variable is difficult to explain, but may suggest that farmers, loggers, and miners are not as effective at lobbying for their interests as expected. Alternatively, the positive and significant coefficients found on SHORE and POPGROWTH (when FEDLAND is omitted from the model) suggest that development pressure rather than the presence of land-intensive industries—as argued by many environmentalists—may be what drives the land rights movement.

The results of the second estimate are similar. Again, the explanatory power is significant, the fit is good, and the predictive power is high (90 percent). The substitution of the Chamber of Commerce rating for the League of Conservation Voters rating shows that a pro-business, pro-development attitude among voters (expressed by the senators they elect) is highly instrumental in promoting property rights legislation. A one percentage point increase in the USCC rating raises the probability of introducing property rights legislation by .012. Coastal property is also found to significantly increase the probability that property rights legislation will be introduced into the state legislature; the partial effect of the SHORE variable is .021.

The signs on DCLAUSE and LANDGSP remain negative and insignificant in this specification of the model, casting further doubt on the significance of these factors as determinants of whether a state will introduce land rights legislation. The coefficient on PCDEBT is also negative, suggesting that legislators are concerned about the impact of property rights legislation on state finances and services, but it is insignificant in this estimate. POPGROWTH is also negative and insignificant in this estimate, however, the coefficient on POPGROWTH is positive and significant (at the 10 percent level), with a partial effect of .012, if FEDLAND is omitted from the model. (See Table 7.4.) This finding provides further evidence that population growth spurs the introduction of land rights legislation.

LEGISLATORS and FEDLAND are again positive and nearly significant at conventional levels in this estimate. The sign on LEGISLATORS again suggests that proponents of property rights legislation promoted their interests in legislatures where transactions costs were low, and the sign on FEDLAND supports the argument that a high share of federal land in a state is an impetus to the property rights movement.

To summarize, the empirical estimates suggest that a pro-development attitude among voters, low-cost access to state legislators, high rates of population growth, and the presence of coastal and publicly owned lands increase the probability that a state legislature will seriously consider property rights legislation. On the other hand, a pro-environment sentiment and high levels of per capita debt reduce the probability that a state legislature will consider legislation to protect private property rights. The presence of a damage clause in a state constitution and strong land-intensive industries in a state may also reduce the probability that a state will consider property rights legislation, but the effects of these factors are not statistically significant in either estimate.

Additional Inferences from the Empirical Model

Insights into the expansion of the land rights movement can be gained by examining some of the predictions made by the empirical estimates. The first estimate, using LCV, predicts that Alabama, Georgia, Kentucky, Michigan, and New Jersey should introduce property rights legislation. The second estimate, using USCC, predicts that New Jersey and Wisconsin should introduce property rights legislation. Using the August 1994 data, we find that these predictions have already been upheld for four of the six states: Alabama, Georgia, Kentucky, and Wisconsin. The future will verify whether the models'

Table 7.4. Results of the Empirical Tests with FEDLAND Omitted

Dependent Variable: Introduction of Property-Rights Protection Law

Independent Variable	Estimated Coeff.	T-Ratio	Partial Effect	Estimated Coeff.	T-Ratio	Partial Effect
Constant	2.583	-1.757*		-3.068	-1.911*	
DCLAUSE	-1.168	-1.200	-0.269	-1.429	-1.107	-0.219
POPGROWTH	0.119	2.322**	0.028	0.076	1.840*	0.012
LEGISLATORS	0.064	1.378	0.015	0.083	1.491	0.013
LCV	-0.035	-1.891*	-0.008			
USCC				0.102	2.873***	0.016
PCDEBT	-0.850E-03	-1.941*	-0.195E-03	-0.785E-03	-1.510	-0.120E-03
SHORE	0.140	1.973*	0.032	0.173	2.031**	0.027
LANDGSP	-0.010	-0.123	-0.023	-0.052	-0.509	-0.008
Likelihood Ratio Test			18.695****		31.375****	
R-Square			0.291		0.489	
No. of Right Predictions			40		42	

* Significant at the 10 percent level for a two-tail test.
** Significant at the 5 percent level for a two-tail test.
*** Significant at the 1 percent level for a two-tail test.
**** Significant at the 1 percent level for a one-tail test.

predictions for Michigan and New Jersey are upheld. The only states that have yet to introduce property rights legislation and are not predicted to do so by either estimate are Alaska, Arkansas, Connecticut, Illinois, North Dakota, and Ohio. The current status of the land rights movement, in conjunction with the models' predictions, reveals how broadly based and rapidly growing the movement is.

It is also interesting to note that both models predict that Iowa, New York, and Pennsylvania should not have introduced property rights legislation. An explanation of why these states have introduced property rights legislation is difficult. One explanation may be that relevant interests supporting property rights legislation are not accounted for by the empirical model. Alternatively, the explanation may lie with the rapid growth of the land rights movement and the near ubiquitous presence of property rights legislation. (All contiguous states are bordered by at least one state that has introduced or passed some form of property rights legislation.) Although the empirical models have not perfectly forecast which states will and will not introduce property rights legislation, the current and future status of the land rights movement is and will be affected by many of the factors identified in the empirical model.

6. Some Final Thoughts on the Land Rights Movement

The land rights movement has risen in response to scores of federal, state, and local regulations that, in part or in whole, restrict development opportunities and reduce property values. Unlike physical takings, regulatory takings do not guarantee compensation to landowners who have suffered diminution of property values as a consequence of government regulation. Further, judicial rulings are often uncertain and costly to pursue. An important response to these regulatory takings is a growing movement to protect private property rights at the state level. As of August 1994, forty-two states had introduced property rights legislation, and eleven had passed some form of the legislation. Further, the empirical model estimated in this chapter predicts that Michigan and New Jersey will consider property rights legislation in the future. Nevertheless, introduction of legislation does not ensure passage, as evidenced by the relatively small number of states that have passed property rights legislation, nor does passage ensure enactment, as evidenced by the legislation that has been vetoed in Idaho and Kansas or, as in the case of Arizona, defeated in public referendum.

The combination of a growing land rights movement and increased government regulation promises continued conflicts over land use that may intensify during the middle and late 1990s. If the land rights movement is successful, its supporters will have done much to preserve the constitutional protections of private property and individual liberty into the twenty-first century.

Notes

1. See Ivy (1988) for discussion. Only New Hampshire and North Carolina do not have takings clauses in their constitutions. Nevertheless, Ivy reports that "the courts in those states have required just compensation for government takings" (p. 332).

2. Ivy (1988) and Toth (1991) briefly discuss this point. Toth lists the states with a "damages" clause. They are Alabama, Arizona, Arkansas, California, Colorado, Georgia, Illinois, Kentucky, Louisiana, Minnesota, Missouri, Montana, Nebraska, New Mexico, North Dakota, Oklahoma, Pennsylvania, South Dakota, Texas, Utah, Virginia, Washington, West Virginia, and Wyoming.

3. In *Loretto v. Teleprompter Manhattan CATV Corp.*, 458 U.S. 419 (1982), the Court ruled that any time the government physically and permanently takes even a small amount of private property, a compensable taking has occurred under the Fifth Amendment.

4. Inholders are landowners whose property, in whole or in part, is surrounded by publicly owned land.

5. See Henderson (1994). Ironically, the Endangered Species Act may be having an adverse impact on the woodpecker population because some landowners are cutting their timber at accelerated rates to avoid future woodpecker inhabitation.

6. Isolated wetlands are not connected to other bodies of water. The landowner won the suit against the EPA because the court ruled that the EPA does not have jurisdiction over isolated wetlands. See Marzulla 1992b for details.

7. Other examples of property that has been "taken" by wetlands regulations can be found in Marzulla and Marzulla (1991), 558-61.

8. See *The Economist*, March 6, 1993.

9. This discussion draws heavily upon Arrensen (1988), 664-65.

10. In the Florida case, the landowner filed suit against the county and won in the trial court. When the case was appealed, however, the Circuit Court remanded the case for further consideration of the facts in the case. See *Reahard v. Lee County*, Case No. 91-3593, 11th Cir. 1992. In the Minnesota case, the courts ruled in favor of the landowner. See *Woodbury Place Partners v. City of Woodbury*, Case No. CO-88-3249, 10th Judicial District, Minn., 1991.

11. The Oregon case cited above was settled only after a five-year dispute between the landowners and the city.

12. The details of two 1992 challenges to these ordinances are explained in Marshall (1993). In both cases, the Washington supreme court ruled that the city of Seattle denied substantive due process to the plaintiffs. The consideration of due process took precedence over takings considerations in both cases, takings claims being remanded in one case and denied in the other. Interestingly, the revised provisions of Washington's 1990 Growth Management Act allow cities and counties to assess impact fees on development and impose housing relocation fees, if development destroys low-income housing.

13. See Weaver and Solov (1992). The Court of Appeals ruled in favor of the landowner. See *Vatalaro v. Dept. of Environmental Regulation*, Florida, 5th DCA, 1992.

14. For ethical arguments in favor of compensating landowners whose property has been devalued by changes in the law, see Heyne (1993).

15. Chatham residents did suffer property damage. They lost a suit for damages. See Skelton (1990) for details.

16. 112 S.Ct. 2886 (1992).

17. Ibid., at 2889.

18. Although *Lucas* was a welcome victory for property owners, it is a narrow one. Crucial to the majority's reasoning in *Lucas* was a lower-court factual finding that the regulation rendered Lucas's property valueless. Had the regulation taken only a portion—even a substantial portion—of Lucas's property value, Lucas may not have prevailed. Note also that bureaucracies respond to profit-making incentives with no less vigor than do private landowners. The state of South Carolina was eventually ordered to buy the land from Lucas if it wished to prevent building on the sites. After purchasing Lucas's property, the state then resold the land to a developer!

19. This section draws heavily upon a November 16, 1993, release by Defenders of Property Rights and Marzulla 1991.

20. *United Artists Theater Circuit, Inc. v. City of Philadelphia* (1993).

21. 123 U.S. 623, 668-69 (1887).

22. 260 U.S. 393 (1922) (holding that a coal company could not be prohibited without compensation from exploiting its mineral estate by a regulation designed to protect the surface owner).

23. Ibid., at 414-15.

24. 438 U.S. 104 (1978).

25. A desire for predictability may, in part, explain why many industries favor statutes (such as the Clean Water Act) to the common law for environmental regulation.

26. Some landowners may also favor state statutes because they provide protection at a lower cost than litigation. William R. Frazier, a property owner in Culpeper County, Virginia, the site of the Battle of Brandy Station, made this point when he argued that litigation is "great if you can afford $200,000 to $300,000. That might even get you to the Supreme Court" (*Richmond Times-Dispatch*, December 1, 1993, B-4).

27. In October 1993, Louisiana congressman W. J. Tauzin attempted to amend a bill authorizing a National Biological Survey to require compensation to landowners whose property was devalued by federal regulations. The amendment was denied, however, because it was not considered relevant to the bill under consideration (Camia, 1994).

28. For details of these property rights bills, see Appendix A in Chapter 6 in this book.

29. Mississippi and North Carolina have passed defined takings laws, however, the laws are applicable only to timber land and land under navigable water, respectively.

30. As noted in Table 7.1, a third type of bill, requiring only that a committee study the takings issue, has been introduced and passed in Virginia. This is the only state to introduce this form of property rights legislation.

31. The costs of the legislation were estimated at $2 million initially for the Arizona Game and Fish Department and between $60 million and $100 million annually for all other affected agencies (*Arizona Republic*, May 17, 1992, D11).

32. See McCormick and Tollison (1981).

33. See Lavelle (1993, 34) for an admission by environmentalists that they did not anticipate the land rights movement.

34. Both ratings are scaled from 0 to 100.

35. See Posner (1971) and Buck (1993, 1284).

36. For a discussion of the view that property-rights legislation will save taxpayers money, see Marzulla (1993).

37. Although we use the terms *coastline* and *shoreline* interchangeably in the text, the measures of coastline and shoreline are different. Coastline is a measure of the "general outline of seacoast," while shoreline is a measure of the "outer coast, offshore islands, sounds, bays, rivers, and creeks . . . to the head of a tidewater or to a point where tidal waters narrow to a width of 100 feet" (*The World Almanac and Book of Facts, 1992*, p. 385). The shoreline measure is employed in the empirical estimates.

38. Data on the independent variables are from 1990, except for the U.S. Chamber of Commerce ratings, which are from 1991, and the voting-age population, which is from 1992.

39. The simple correlation coefficient between LCV and USCC is -.675.

40. The partial effect or derivative is calculated as $\beta\rho(1-\rho)$ where β is the estimated coefficient and ρ is the predicted probability that the dependent variable equals one. Because the predicted probability differs for each observation, the partial effect also differs for each observation. To facilitate the discussion, the partial effects reported in Table 7.3 have been calculated using values of ρ that are calculated using the mean values of the independent variables.

41. The R-square statistic reported is the McFadden R-square. It is calculated in the following way: $R^2 = 1 - [L(\beta)/L(0)]$ where $L(\beta)$ is the value of the likelihood function from the estimated model and $L(0)$ is the value of the likelihood function when the model contains only the intercept.

42. The prediction criterion uses .5 as a cut off point. That is, the model predicts correctly when it assigns a state that has not introduced a property rights protection bill a probability of introduction less than 0.5, and when it assigns a state that has introduced a property rights protection bill a probability of introduction of .5 or greater.

43. Similar results are found when per capita taxes are substituted for per capita debt.

44. The Bureau of Census defines western states as Alaska, Arizona, California, Colorado, Hawaii, Idaho, Montana, Nevada, New Mexico, Oregon, Utah, Washington, and Wyoming. Collectively, 54.5 percent of the land area of these states is owned by the federal government, compared with 29.2 percent for the country as a whole. These states also experienced more rapid population growth than any other region of the country from 1980 to 1990. The population of these states grew 22.3 percent over the decade, compared to a 9.8 percent increase for the country as a whole. The simple correlation coefficient between POPGROWTH and FEDLAND is .578.

45. In alternate regressions, we included the per capita membership of state farm bureaus; however, this variable is also insignificant and other results are essentially unchanged. We also disaggregated LANDGSP into its separate components (farms; agricultural services, forestry, and fisheries; and mining), but these variables are also insignificant and the other results essentially unchanged.

References

Arrensen, David A. 1988. "Compensation for Regulatory Takings: Finality of Local Decisionmaking and the Measure of Compensation." *Indiana Law Journal* 63 (Summer): 649-68.

Barrett, Paul M. 1994. "A Store Owner's Squabble with a City Tests Government's Right to Private Land." *Wall Street Journal.* (March 23): B1. Brookes, Warren T. 1991. Civil War Against Property Owners? *Richmond Times-Dispatch* (August 4): H-7.

Buck, David C. 1993. "'Property' in the Fifth Amendment: A Quest for Common Ground in the Maze of Regulatory Takings." *Vanderbilt Law Review* 46 (October): 1283-332.

Burkhart, Barry. 1992. "Bills Proposed by House, Senate Derived from less-than-pure Motives." *Arizona Republic* (February 23): D14.

Burkhart, Barry. 1992. "Symington May Face 2 Bills Best Scrapped." *Arizona Republic* (May 17): D11.

Camia, Catalina. 1994. "Legislators Draw in the Reins on Environmental Rules." *Congressional Quarterly Weekly Report.* (April 30): 1060-1064.

Defenders of Property Rights. 1993. Pennsylvania Supreme Court Strikes Down Over-reaching by Philadelphia Historical Commission. Washington, D.C.: Defenders of Property Rights.

"Government, Keep Out." 1994. *The Economist* (July 2): 26.

Henderson, Bruce. 1994. "Property Rights Debate Could Shape Environmental Law." *The State.* (April 18): B5.

Heyne, Paul. 1993. "Economics, Ethics, and Ecology." In *Taking the Environment Seriously,* ed. by Roger E. Meiners and Bruce Yandle. Lanham, Md: Rowman & Littlefield.

Hoye, David. 1992. "Environmental Interests Put on Defensive: Legislation Feared Tip of Iceberg." *Phoenix Gazette* (February 28): A1.

"Is Taking Stealing?" 1993. *The Economist* (March 6): 24.

Ivy, Lee. 1988. "The 1986 Term 'Takings' Clause Cases: A Unified Approach to Regulatory Takings?" *Oklahoma City University Law Review* 13 (Summer): 325-56.

Knickerbocker, Brad. 1993. "Property-Rights Movement Gains Ground in Congress." *Christian Science Monitor* (September 22): 1.

Kriz, Margaret. 1993. "Land Mine." *National Journal* (October 23): 2531-34.

Kull, Randy. 1992. "Petitions Submitted to Halt Property Law: Measure May Go to Arizona Voters." *Phoenix Gazette* (September 30): B2.

Lavelle, Marianne. 1993. "The 'Property Rights' Revolt: Environmentalists Fret as States Pass Reagan-Style Takings Laws." *National Law Journal* 15 (May 10): 1.

Marshall, Stephanie E. 1993. "Property as a Civil Right: The Expansion of Washington State Regulatory Takings Law." *Willamette Law Review* 29 (Fall): 867-92.

Marzulla, Nancie G. 1991. "Pennsylvania Court Strikes a Blow Against Unduly Burdensome Historic Designation of Private Property." *Land Rights Letter* (December): 6.

Marzulla, Nancie G. 1992a. "A Two-Front Battle for Property Rights." *Christian Science Monitor* (September 18): 19.

Marzulla, Nancie G. 1992b. "A Wetland That Not Even a Glancing Goose Could Save." *Land Rights Letter* (June): 6.

Marzulla, Nancie G. 1993. "Who Benefits from the State Private Property Legislation? You, the Taxpayer." *Land Rights Letter* (June): 4.

Marzulla, Roger J. 1988. "The New 'Takings' Executive Order and Environmental Regulation—Collision or Cooperation?" *Environmental Law Reporter* (July): 10254-60.

Marzulla, Roger J., and Nancie G. Marzulla. 1991. "Regulatory Takings in the United States Claims Courts: Adjusting the Burdens That in Fairness and Equity Ought to be Borne by Society as a Whole." *Catholic University Law Review* 40 (Spring): 549-69.

McCormick, Robert E., and Robert D. Tollison. 1981. *Politicians, Legislation, and the Economy: An Inquiry into the Interest-Group Theory of Government*. Leiden: Martinus Nijoff.

Penhale, Ed. 1992. "Developers Chip at Growth Control: Attack on the State's Law Is Paying Off in Senate." *Seattle Post-Intelligencer* (February 21): B1.

Posner, Richard A. 1971. "Taxation by Regulation." *Bell Journal of Economics and Management Science* 2 (Spring): 22-50.

Skelton, Harold N. 1990. "Houses on the Sand: Takings Issues Surrounding Statutory Restrictions on the Use of Oceanfront Property." *Boston College Environmental Affairs Law Review* 18 (Fall): 125-58.

Springston, Rex. 1993. "Merit of Land Regulation: Debated Measure to Limit Governmental 'Takings' Has More Foes than Friends at Session Here." *Richmond Times-Dispatch* (December 1): B-4.

Staff Report. 1994. "Property Owner Compensation Backed." *Seattle Post-Intelligencer* (January 15): A6.

Toth, Justine T. 1991. *"Coleman v. Utah State Land Board*: Searching for a Balanced Approach to "Takings" Under the Utah Constitution." *Utah Law Review* (Spring): 505-29.

Wallace, James, and Scott Maier. 1992. "Putting on Pressure for Property Rights: Anti-Environmentalists Gain Headway in Olympia." *Seattle Post-Intelligencer* (March 18): A1.

Weaver, Ronald W., and Mark D. Solov. 1992. "New Standards, If Not Greater Protection, Against Land Use Regulations." *The Florida Bar Journal* 66 (December):58-61.

Data Sources

LAW: Defenders of Property Rights.

DCLAUSE: States are listed in Toth (1991).

POPGROWTH: U.S. Bureau of Census, *Statistical Abstract of the United States: 1992* (112th edition). Washington, D.C., 1992, Table 25, pp. 22-23.

LEGISLATORS: Voting-age population is from U.S. Bureau of Census, *Statistical Abstract of the United States: 1993* (113th edition). Washington, D.C., 1993, Table 453, p. 282.

The number of state legislators is from U.S. Bureau of Census, *Statistical Abstract of the United States: 1992* (112th edition). Washington, D.C., 1992, Table 430, p. 266.

LCV Ratings: Barone, Michael, and Grant Ujifusa. 1991. *The Almanac of American Politics 1992*. Washington, D.C.: National Journal, various pages.

USCC Ratings: Congressional Quarterly, Inc., *Congressional Quarterly Almanac 1992*. Vol. XLVIII, Washington, D.C., 1993, p. 12-F.

PCDEBT: The Council of State Governments, *The Book of the States*. 1992-92 Edition. Lexington, Ky, 1992, Table 6.18, p. 389.

SHORE: Shoreline mileage is obtained from *The World Almanac and Book of Facts, 1992*. New York: Pharos Books, 1991, p.385.

Land area is obtained from *The World Almanac and Book of Facts, 1992*. New York: Pharos Books, 1991, p. 386.

FEDLAND: U.S. Bureau of Census, *Statistical Abstract of the United States: 1992* (112th edition). Washington, D.C., 1992, Table 343, p. 207.

LANDGSP: U.S. Department of Commerce, *Survey of Current Business*, Vol. 73, No. 12, Washington, D.C., 1993, pp. 42-49.

Chapter 8

Elements of Property Rights:
The Common Law Alternative

Roger E. Meiners

Today, farmers are told that if they wish to cut hardwood on their own bottom
land, they should first obtain a Corps of Engineers 404 permit, particularly if
any soil, roots, or stumps are to be relocated (CLE International, 1993). The
problem? The activity may take place on what is defined to be a wetland.
Movement of soil to another location can be interpreted as unregulated discharge
into national waters, and that is a criminal offense.

We hear a lot about government-sponsored heritage and national landmark
programs. Zoning and other land-use restrictions can follow automatically.
Unrelated or adjacent private land can be affected, and permission of the owner
is not required. Marty and Bill Mowry, who own and operate a 300-acre bison
ranch in Hawaii, learned the hard way when they received a letter from their
local zoning board (Miniter, 1992). They say: 'We can't operate our ranch if
we are down-zoned to conservation.'

Before a person builds a house on a newly purchased lot, Mike Elkins,
director of enforcement for the U.S. Fish and Wildlife Service, recommends
first getting an assessment of flora and fauna from the state fish and wildlife
service (*U.S. News & World Report,* 1992). If the lot contains habitat for an
endangered species—and there are more than eight hundred on the list and

petitions to list an additional eight thousand—the plans for a new house may be put on hold, or altered to fit a regulatory constraint.

Endangered species have been given an unspecified but superior claim to habitat. Ocie and Carie Mills of Navarre, Florida, should know. In 1989, they were convicted and sentenced to twenty-one months in federal prison for placing nineteen loads of builder's sand on a small lot where they were building a home. The ditch where the sand was placed was declared to be a sensitive wetland and potential species habitat (Bethell, 1994).

Beware of operating a farm too close to a national park. You should check on land ownership patterns around you. Ann Corcoran, of Antietam, Maryland, and former Audubon Society lobbyist, and her husband, Howard, a U.S. EPA attorney, own a 300-acre cattle farm near the Antietam National Park and have restored an 1832 farmhouse located there (Spencer, 1993). The purchase of land surrounding the Corcorans' farm by conservation organizations and its transfer to the U.S. Park Service, if continued, will leave the Corcoran's land as an inholding, subject to government's power of eminent domain. They could lose their farm or the ability to operate the farm and raise cattle. Ann Corcoran is now publisher of the *Land Rights Letter*.

Each of these episodes relates to property rights. And each of the individuals involved in the noted struggles no doubt felt confident that their fee simple ownership of land entitled them to engage in the activities later found to be proscribed by regulation.

Traditionally, the importance of private property was not questioned. Not only has private property been understood to be key to economic prosperity, but it has been assumed to be the primary foundation of individual freedom.[1] "The private ownership of any valuable resource . . . can confer the economic independence that permits genuine political and social choice."[2]

Contemporary discussions about property rights have become convoluted. Most self-declared environmentalists are hostile to private property.[3] When Al Gore states, in reference to private property, that public policy has gone "so far toward individual rights"[4] (when the opposite is clearly happening) and no eyebrows are raised, there is no doubt that traditional rights are under siege. This is contrary to the key elements required to have a society of free and responsible individuals as intended by the founders of the nation.

Earlier chapters in this book tell about the numerous federal environmental statutes passed in the 1970s and how they restricted traditional private property rights in favor of central government control of property. Whether for wetlands, water quality, or endangered species protection, personal rights have been restricted in favor of government command-and-control. Other chapters relate the details of how citizen contests have been playing out in the courts and how a popular backlash has erupted as citizens see their rights to private property being restricted. This chapter recounts how the enforcement of property rights by citizens and communities provided environmental protection in the absence of federal interference. That is, before the days of federal control of land and environmental use, what did citizens do to protect themselves and their property?

The first section of this chapter discusses the meaning given to *rights* in a natural law context. After tracing the development of property rights in a constitutional context, the section then discusses common law, the legal framework used for centuries to protect individual rights, and the rules that evolved to protect land rights. Section two presents capsule summaries of a series of common law cases to illustrate how common law rules dealt with water, land, and air pollution.

1. What Are Rights and How Did They Evolve?

The English Roots and Natural Law

The basis of much of American law is English law. When the nation was founded, much English law, especially the common law, and the rights and duties it provides for all citizens, was incorporated into the new legal regime functioning under the federal Constitution. It is a modern myth that our rights were created by the Constitution (the "supreme law of the land"); the writers of the Constitution presumed *inalienable rights* that we hold simply by virtue of being free people in a free nation. As one great British legal scholar expressed over a century ago, "personal freedom does not really depend upon or originate in any general proposition contained in any written document."[5]

The Constitution created the basic framework of government, expressly limited the powers of government, and provided specific safeguards against invasions of certain rights. But the Constitution did not *grant* us all rights we have as citizens. We are presumed to have a host of individual rights, often called *natural law*. Some natural law is expressed through the common law, but the elements of natural law were simply presumed to be understood by the judiciary. "Thus the Framers [of the Constitution] believed that liberty and personal security are the ultimate purposes of society; they favored limited government and dispersal of power, feared the tyranny of political majorities, and . . . subscribed to the belief that individuals have fundamental and inalienable rights with which government may not interfere."[6] A free people established the government of the United States. This is unlike most governments in the history of the world, which grant some rights to their citizens; the state is presumed to be the source of all law. The United States is one of the few governments created by a free people who understood that they possess inalienable rights.

This simple point has been lost in political and judicial talk about citizens having "rights" to assorted public benefits, such as a "right" to medical care or a "right" to Social Security. The use of the word *right* in such contexts has confused understanding of what rights are in a historical legal context. No doubt the legislature has the power to collect taxes to spend on things such as medical care and Social Security, but to presume that the "right" to receive benefits granted by the legislature is similar to the inalienable rights understood by the framers of the Constitution is a serious perversion of the basis of liberty. The rights that make us a free people are *natural rights*; they are not granted by a legislature that was created by a free people.

That is why the modern debate over property rights is a key constitutional issue. If traditional property rights are lost in favor of legislated control of property, a major cornerstone of all liberty has been lost. We come closer to being like most peoples in the world—granted certain favors (called "rights") at the pleasure of the legislature, but having few rights that may not be invaded by the legislature and the agencies it creates to execute its wishes. There is a large volume of scholarly work on this topic, but the property rights movement discussed by Nancie Marzulla in Chapter 1 is motivated by a common sense understanding that the natural rights we have by virtue of living in the United States are being seriously eroded in favor of state control.

Common Law Property Rights

The basis of American property law is the common law. Traditionally, governments played limited roles in property, primarily by having local offices provide places to register documents related to property and, through the courts, by resolving disputes under the common law of real property. Such rights in America are strong, unlike in much of the world where individual rights to control and dispose of property are sharply limited by governments that will not provide secure protection for private property. Thanks to our English heritage, we have a long common law basis for private control of property.

The primary alternative to private property is collective control of property. There is a rich history of different forms of property control from around the world. There is general agreement that private ownership leads to the most efficient use of land. Private ownership reduces the problems we witness when there is communal access to land—such as overuse, lack of investment to improve its quality over time, and little incentive to work hard to improve the land. Indeed, "the key to land conservation is to bestow upon living persons property rights that extend perpetually into the future. . . . Throughout history, many close-knit groups have recognized that perpetual private ownership makes for better land stewardship."[7]

Private property rights in America, usually in the form of fee simple title, provide strong presumptions in favor of property use and control by the legally recognized owner. This system has evolved over hundreds of years and is closely tied to our economic prosperity and personal liberty. While those who support restrictions on private property through environmental regulation usually pay homage to the notion of private property, it is routinely asserted that governmental controls on private property are needed to protect public health and the health of the environment, because individual abuses of property produce environmental destruction that others in society cannot protect themselves from. That is, if not constrained by regulators, private property owners will pollute and impose costs on others in society. Most proponents of command-and-control regulation argue that the common law of property fails to protect the environment adequately. In many cases, the proponents of regulation are ignorant of how common law worked to deal with environmental issues.

Nuisance as a Common Law Cause of Action

How did common law work to protect ordinary people from unwanted pollution? At common law, owners of rights to land have the right to exclude from their land unwanted people and pollution. The laws of trespass and nuisance provide causes of action, and common law courts provide remedies that include injunctions and damages. The notion that landowners can call the sheriff to chase unwanted people from their land is hardly controversial, since the common law basis for doing so is still more or less intact. However, the idea that landowners could and did protect their property from pollution is hardly recognized; many people believe sincerely that we would all succumb to pollution were it not for federal regulation and the Environmental Protection Agency.

For centuries before EPA existed, the *nuisance* cause of action provided the basis of common law environmental protection. For example, people owning land along rivers had the right to beneficial use of the water that passed their property. If an upstream user discharged damaging waste into the stream, without first obtaining permission from the downstream owner, then the downstream party had a cause of action against the polluter based on the tort of nuisance. When convinced by scientific evidence that the polluter had damaged the party downstream, the court moved against the polluter. The offending party was generally ordered to cease polluting and to pay damages.

While sometimes difficult to apply, since scientific evidence of harm is required, the concept of nuisance is generally commonsensical. As Justice Sutherland said, "Nuisance may be merely a right thing in a wrong place like a pig in the parlor instead of the barnyard" (*Village of Euclid*, 1926). Causes of action for nuisance claims can be either public or private, but nuisances may be combined public and private nuisances (*Capurro,* 1972).

A *public nuisance* is an action that causes inconvenience or damage to the public health or public order, or an act that constitutes an obstruction of public rights (*Stoughton,* 1948). For example, a firm that discharges emissions that damage the health of citizens in a city could be charged with public nuisance. Normally, only public officers (attorneys general or district attorneys) have standing to sue to abate public nuisances. However, individuals who show they suffer harm distinctly different from that suffered by the general public may also be granted standing to sue to abate a public nuisance.

Public nuisances are not limited to protecting interests in land. Claims of nuisance may arise from conducting certain businesses. For example, the court in *Ballenger v. City of Grand Saline,*[8] heard a suit in which residents living near a "chicken house" complained of offensive odors. *Ballenger* involved the city seeking a permanent injunction to abate the operation of a wholesale chicken business. There, the city alleged various nuisances, including noise and odor.[9] The Court of Appeals upheld the lower court's decision that the operation was "in fact and in law" a public nuisance, and that the city was entitled to permanently abate the activity.

In cases like *Ballenger,* the defendant could argue that the complaining party had "come to the nuisance" and sometimes prevail. That is, common law rules provide safeguards against individuals buying polluted land at bargain basement prices and then suing the polluter in the hopes of obtaining a windfall.

While public nuisance provides a basis for protecting the general rights held by a community of people, private nuisance applies to harmful actions that damage individual landowners. *Private nuisance* is defined as a *substantial and unreasonable interference* with the use and enjoyment of an interest in land (*Ryan,* 1955). The interference may be intentional *or* reckless. In pollution law, the typical case involves a defendant that is operating in a way that is offensive or harmful to the plaintiffs. The legal issue posed in such cases is whether the "act" of the defendant is an intrusion that is "sufficiently noxious" to give rise to a finding of nuisance.

While private nuisance claims have been traditionally limited to protecting the interest to land, modern courts have been more generous, holding that the action protects all pleasures, comforts, etc., normally associated with occupancy of land. Current case law also allows for consequential damages to the "possessor of land interest" to allow recovery for injuries to his own health (*Vann,* 1936) and for loss of services of family members (*U.S. Smelting,* 1911).

Cases based on common law private nuisance claims generally discuss the "weighing process," of various factors involved. Generally speaking, the actor's conduct will be condemned as "unreasonable" if the gravity of the harm outweighs the utility of the conduct (*Restatement, Second, Torts,* 1972). This weighing process is used by courts in both public and private nuisance actions.

Today, federal environmental statutes have largely displaced the protections previously afforded by common law rules. Actions that might have been considered nuisances in the past are now permitted under various environmental regulations. For example, acid mine drainage that damaged marine life was held immune from a public nuisance claim because the discharges were administratively sanctioned under state law.[10] Under clean air and clean water statutes, polluters are given permits that allow them to discharge specified amounts of pollutants. In some cases, what had been a common law nuisance is allowed to become respectable business.

The Move to Central Control

The modern environmental movement is thought to have started in the 1960s with the publication of books such as Rachael Carson's *Silent Spring,* which concerned problems such as the destruction of bird eggs from overuse of chemicals such as the pesticide DDT.[11] Media and the public attention to assorted pollution issues helped produce general support for a host of major federal controls beginning with the Clean Air Act of 1970 and the Clean Water Act of 1972. Within ten years there was a regime shift in favor of federal control of environmental matters that now means substantial restrictions on the use of private property subject to a host of federal regulations. Major attributes of private property, including air quality, water quality, land use, and habitat control, have been taken from private property owners and placed under federal regulation.

At the time the property controls called environmental regulations were imposed, little attention was devoted to two key questions: (1) are governments better stewards of the environment than private property owners, and (2) are there major environmental problems that the common law cannot solve? The focus here is on the second question. With respect to the first question, it has long been understood that governmental control of property generally yields lower economic productivity than does private control, and more to the point here, there is good evidence that governments are poor stewards of the environmental quality. "The sorry environmental records of federal land agencies and Communist regimes are a sharp reminder that governments are often particularly inept managers of large tracts [of land]."[12] So one puzzle in the environmental saga is why the government, given its dismal record on environmental protection, was looked to as the preferred protector of the environment. That issue is not addressed here.

2. How the World Used to Work

The story to be told in the rest of this chapter is how the common law worked to provide environmental protection before the advent of federal regulatory control that largely replaced common law protection for the environment. The common law of environmental protection occurred by the application of various parts of the common law to violations of personal rights. This happened before modern environmental law was invented, so we look to the record of common law cases that occurred over the years. We now call this environmental protection, but at the time, most of these thousands of cases were simply seen as individuals or communities protecting their rights to healthy air, water, and land.

We now move to a review of some common law cases concerning water, air, and land protection. Cases will be summarized to give a flavor of the general state of the law. The cases come from courts around the country, which indicates that while common law details varied from state to state, the essence of the rules were much the same in all states.[13]

Water Pollution

In 1987 "The Final Report of the National Groundwater Policy Forum" stated that "the federal government must have primary responsibility for groundwater quality, with state assumption of implementation under federal oversight."[14] That policy recommendation simply summarizes the law since passage of the Clean Water Act in 1972 and other statutes since then. The federal government controls how much of what may be dumped into waters and requires the states to enforce its policies.

We have become so used to centralized control that we cannot remember that a generation ago the federal government played little role in water quality. Instead, citizens and communities protected their own waters, through enforcement of common law rights and through various local water-quality regulations. The primary common law rights that were enforced were the right, under tort law, not to suffer a nuisance or a trespass. Most states also enforced riparian law, which provides that all who have property that abuts a waterway or body of water have the right to normal use of the water, but may not reduce the use and enjoyment of the water by other and downstream users. Cases during the past hundred years indicate how the common law enforced water rights. These cases are not unusual; they only illustrate the process that was at work.[15]

Carmichael v. City of Texarkana (94 F. 561, W.D. Ark., 1899)

The Carmichaels owned a 45-acre farm in Texas, with a stream running through it, that bordered on the state of Arkansas. The city of Texarkana, Arkansas, built a sewage system for the city, to which were connected numerous residences and businesses. The sewage collected in the city was deposited "immediately opposite plaintiffs' homestead, about eight feet from the state line, on the Arkansas side." The Carmichaels sued the city in federal court in Arkansas.

The court found that the "cesspool is a great nuisance because it fouls, pollutes, corrupts, contaminates, and poisons the water of [the creek], depositing the foul and offensive matter . . . in the bed of said creek on plaintiffs' land and homestead continuously . . ." thereby "depriving them of the use and benefit of said creek running through their land and premises in a pure and natural state as it was before the creation of said cesspool." The Carmichaels were forced to connect their property to a water system to obtain water for "their family, dairy cattle, and other domestic animals, fowls, and fish." The cost of the water hookup and use was $700; they claim the value of their property was reduced $5,000, the reduced enjoyment of their homestead over the previous two years was valued at $2,000, and the dread of disease was valued at $2,000. Besides the claim for damages, the Carmichaels also sued in equity for a permanent injunction against "said open sewer, cesspool, and nuisance."

Judge Rogers found that the city was operating properly under state law to build a sewer system, but that there was no excuse for fouling the water used by the Carmichaels, regardless of how many city residences benefited from the sewer system. Citing other cases, the court found that the action at law for damages was proper as was the request for an injunction. The court cited 2. Add.Torts, 1085: "If a riparian proprietor has a right to enjoy a river so far unpolluted that fish can live in it and cattle drink of it and the town council of a neighboring borough, professing to act under statutory powers, pour their house drainage and the filth from water-closets into the river in such quantities that the water becomes corrupt and stinks, and fish will no longer live in it, nor cattle drink it, the court will grant an injunction to prevent the continued defilement of the stream, and to relieve the riparian proprietor from the necessity of bringing a series of actions for the daily annoyance. In deciding the right of a single proprietor to an injunction, the court cannot take into consideration the circumstance that a vast population will suffer by reason of its interference." Judge Rogers held: "I have failed to find a single well-considered case where the American courts have not granted relief under circumstances such as are alleged in this bill against the city."

Norton v. Colusa Parrot Mining & Smelting Co. et al. (168 F. 202, D. Mont., 1908)

Several ranchers who owned land along the Deer Lodge River in Montana sued three mining companies for polluting the river. The court addressed the issue of action at law and action in equity. The court held that the farmers had a common law right to sue for an injunction, an action in equity, and could request a jury trial for that action, but that equity actions had to be kept separate from action in law (request for damages). The ranchers could join together in bringing the equity action, they did not have to sue individually, and the mining companies could be joined together as defendants, rather than suing each individually.

Whalen v. Union Bag & Paper Co. (208 N.Y. 1, 101 N.E. 805, 1913)

A New York case illustrates how strictly riparian rights could protect water quality. A new pulp mill polluted a creek. A downstream farmer, Whalen, sued the mill for making the water unfit for agricultural use. The trial court awarded damages of $312 per year and granted an injunction against the mill to end harmful pollution within one year. The appellate division denied the injunction and reduced the damages to $100. The court noted that the mill was an important economic asset to the area. It cost over $1 million and employed 500 people, which was worth far more than the water was to the plaintiff. The Court of Appeals (New York's highest court) reinstated the injunction:

> Although the damage to the plaintiff may be slight as compared with the defendant's expense of abating the condition, that is not a good reason for refusing an injunction. Neither courts of equity nor law can be guided by such a rule, for if followed to its logical conclusion it would deprive the poor litigant of his little property by giving it to those already rich.[16]

To make clear that its decision went beyond a case involving serious destruction of water quality, the court cited an earlier Indiana holding:

> The fact that the appellant has expended a large sum of money in the construction of its plant, and that it conducts its business in a careful manner and without malice, can make no difference in its rights to the stream. Before locating the plant the owners were bound to know that every riparian proprietor is entitled to have the waters of the stream that washes his land come to it without obstruction, diversion, or corruption, subject only to the reasonable use of the water, by those similarly entitled, for such domestic purposes as are inseparable for and necessary for the free use of their land; they were bound also to know the character of their proposed business, and to take themselves at their own peril whether they should be able to conduct their business upon a stream . . . without injury to their neighbors; and the magnitude of their

investment and their freedom from malice furnish no reason why they should escape the consequences of their own folly."

This holding does not mean that there could be no pollution. It meant that there was no excuse for uninvited pollution. To avoid water rights litigation, the mill owner could have contracted for riparian rights from downstream landowners or bought the land along the stream."

Kirwin v. Mexican Petroleum Co. (267 F. 460, D. R. I., 1920)

The plaintiff ran a shore resort called "Kirwin's Beach." The defendant "did discharge and suffer to escape from its plants, steamers, barges, etc., into the waters of the Providence river, large quantities of oil and kindred products, which were carried by the winds, currents and tides of the Providence river upon plaintiff's beach, fouling and polluting the beach and waters, and rendering the same wholly unfit for bathing, whereby the value of plaintiff's property and business is destroyed."

Judge Brown upheld the right of the action. "Land located on the shores of the Providence river and Narragansett Bay have a special value, owing to the riparian rights of access to the waters. This right of access is a private right, incidental to ownership of the upland. The general public does not have the right to cross or occupy private lands to gain access to the shores below the high-water mark, at which private ownership terminates."

Kirwin could sue for the value of the lost business, under an action of private nuisance, in compensation for the loss of use of the beach. The public, through the state attorney general or local public prosecutor, would have a right to sue for the public nuisance that was caused by the fouling of the water and of the beach to the high tide line.

The oil company claimed that it could not be held responsible because there was no negligence (carelessness) shown on its part. The judge held that to be irrelevant. "A nuisance may be created by the conduct of a business with all the care and caution which is possible, and with appliances in perfect order and most carefully operated. . . . It is the general rule that negligence is not an element in an action for a nuisance, and need not be alleged. 'Actions for nuisance, properly speaking, stand irrespective of negligence.' Bigelows's Leading Cases on Torts, p. 473."

Missouri v. Illinois (200 U.S. 496, 26 S.Ct. 268, 1906), Justice Holmes.

The city of Chicago pumped its sewage into a canal originally built in 1848, under an 1822 act of Congress that allowed it to cross federal lands. The canal was greatly expanded in 1900, reversing the flow of the Chicago river—away from Lake Michigan toward the Mississippi—and, as the city grew, drawing more water from the lake. Flushed with water from Lake Michigan, the canal carried the sewage, "1,500 tons of poisonous filth daily into the Mississippi," via the Desplaines and then the Illinois rivers. Other cities similarly dumped sewage into the Mississippi.

The state of Missouri asserted that the Chicago sewage was the cause of typhoid in St. Louis. The Court noted that enough water from Lake Michigan was mixed in the sewage that, where the canal dumped into the Illinois River, "it is a comparatively clear stream to which edible fish have returned. Its water is drunk by the fishermen, it is said without evil results." The Court accepted that sewage could cause typhoid, of which as many as four hundred people per year died in St. Louis between 1890 and 1903. The court reviewed a test of the ability of bacilli to live in water that flows long distances (it being over 350 miles from Chicago to St. Louis); scientists testified that it was unlikely that the bacilli could survive in the river for that long. Second, because other towns closer to St. Louis dumped sewage into the river, there were multiple sources of filth that could be the source of the bacillus. There was no reason to single out Chicago for the expense that St. Louis must incur to filtrate the water it draws from the river. Case dismissed.

Sanitary Distict of Chicago v. United States (266 U.S. 405, 45 S.Ct. 176, 1925), Justice Holmes.

The U. S. government, at request of the secretary of war, sued Chicago for diverting water from Lake Michigan in excess of 250,000 cubic feet per minute (about double that rate), as had been authorized by the secretary. The higher diversion rate, used to flush sewage from Chicago into a canal, which eventually flows to the Mississippi, lowered the water level, and would lower it further over time, in Lakes Michigan, Huron, Erie, Ontario, and St. Clair, and the rivers connecting them, which was creating an obstruction to the navigable capacity of said waters. Chicago defended the water diversion as needed to flush the sewage to protect public health.[19]

The Court held there was no question but that the federal government regulates navigable waters; hence the secretary, as ordered by Congress, can decide such matters as proper levels of diversions of such water bodies. The secretary gave Chicago its first permit in 1899. Subsequently the limit of 250,000 cubic feet per minute was established. Chicago complained also that it would have to spend $100 million if not allowed to increase its flow. The Court dismissed Chicago's defense, granting the secretary an injunction to stop the excess flow in sixty days.

Wisconsin et al. v. Illinois et al. (278 U.S. 367, 49 S.Ct. 163, 1929), Chief Justice Taft

Wisconsin and other states sued Illinois and Chicago for Chicago's continued draw of water at 8,500 cubic feet of water per second (510,000 cubic feet per minute) from Lake Michigan, despite the 1925 Court decision. When the case was filed, the Court appointed a special master, Charles Evans Hughes, with authority to take evidence and report to the Court with his findings of fact, his conclusions of law, and his recommendations. After the previous ruling by the Court, Chicago asked the secretary for a new permit to draw water at an annual average rate of 8,500 cubic feet per second, subject to certain conditions. The permit required the Chicago to begin constructing some primary treatment plants to reduce the strain on the canal.

The plaintiffs here contend that the water draw has lowered the Great Lakes and connecting rivers by six inches, causing serious harm to navigation. Further, they note that Chicago has requested that the water draw be increased to 10,000 cubic feet per second, which would drop the lake and river levels another inch.

The Court reviewed the federal legislation giving the secretary the power to control lakes and rivers for navigation purposes. The Court found such a delegation of power to be proper under the Constitution. "Though Congress, in the exercise of its power over navigation, may adopt any means having some positive relation to the control of navigation and not otherwise inconsistent with the Constitution, it may not arbitrarily destroy or impair the rights of riparian owners by legislation which has no real or substantial relation to the control of navigation or appropriateness to that end." The Court denied the right of the Secretary to allow Chicago to increase drainage to 8,500 for sanitary purposes. The secretary was authorized by Congress to consider navigation, which included navigation on the canal, but the increase in water draw was not related to navigation and so was improper.

To reduce future problems, Chicago must build new treatment plants to reduce their water need; the special master (Hughes) would oversee what happened to see that the city took care of its needs and would not increase its water draw. The city was ordered to return gradually to the old water draw level.

Wisconsin v. Illinois (289 U.S. 395, 53 S.Ct. 671, 1933), Chief Justice Hughes

Wisconsin and other states accused Chicago and Illinois of not getting busy building sewage treatment facilities that would allow it to reduce the water draw from Lake Michigan, as ordered by the Court in 1929. The special master appointed by the Court, now Edward McClennan since Hughes ended up on the Court, reported to the Court that indeed Chicago was footdragging, but the financial market for new bonds was wrecked by the Depression, so the city could not obtain financing. However, since the city and its sanitary districts are creatures of the state of Illinois, the state is bound by the prior Court order and so must assist the city in obtaining financing, which the special master thinks could be had with state assistance.

"In deciding this controversy between states, the authority of the court to enjoin the continued perpetration of the wrong inflicted upon complainants, necessarily embraces the authority to require measures to be taken to end conditions, within the control of defendant state, which may stand in the way of the execution of the decree." The state was specifically ordered "to take all necessary steps," including new appropriations, to get funding for the sewage treatment facility to be completed quickly so the water draw could be reduced.

International Paper Co. v. Maddox (105 F. Supp. 89, W.D. La., 1951)

International Paper (IP) had a plant on Bodcaw Bayou, built in the 1930s, that fouled the water. IP paid forty landowners along the bayou for "perpetual right to discharge . . . effluent" the cost of which was several hundred thousand dollars. Maddox made his living running a fishing camp in the bayou (at least 20 miles downstream); his livelihood was injured by the pollution. He sued for damages or, in the alternative, for an injunction against further pollution. Expert testimony was that, over the years, IP had improved its water treatment, so it was not killing as many fish as before, but the quality of fishing and quality of the bayou had been injured. The court awarded Maddox $8,000 damages for loss of value of business and reduction in property value because of loss of prior pristine waters.

International Paper Co. v. Maddox (203 F. 2d 88, 5th Cir., 1953)

The appeals court affirmed the decision. The pollution was a nuisance for which plaintiff could receive payment for temporary damages as well as for permanent damages. The fact that IP was making continuous improvements to pollution control, some of which had been hampered by inability to get certain equipment during the war, did not affect the right of plaintiff to be compensated for losses.

New Jersey Dept. of Environmental Protection v. Ventron Corp. (468 A.2d 150, S.Ct., N.J., 1983)

New Jersey sued various parties for mercury pollution of a waterway. The state's supreme court held: "We believe it is time to recognize expressly that the law of liability has evolved so that a landowner is strictly liable to others for harm caused by toxic wastes that are stored on his property and flow onto the property of others. Therefore, we overrule Marshall v. Welwood [N.J. S.Ct., 1876] and adopt the principle of liability originally declared in Rylands v. Fletcher [England, 1868]. The net result is that those who use, or permit others to use, land for the conduct of abnormally dangerous activities are strictly liable for resultant damages."

the Restatement (Second) of Torts reformulated the standard of landowner liability, substituting "abnormally dangerous" for "ultrahazardous" and providing a list of elements to consider in applying the new standard ... whether an activity is abnormally dangerous is to be determined on a case-by-case basis, taking all relevant circumstances into consideration.

As set forth in the Restatement:
In determining whether an activity is abnormally dangerous, the following factors are to be considered:

    (a) existence of a high degree of risk of some harm to the person, land or chattels of others;
    (b) likelihood that the harm that results from it will be great;
    (c) inability to eliminate the risk by the exercise of reasonable care;
    (d) extent to which the activity is not a matter of common usage;
    (e) inappropriateness of the activity to the place where it is carried on; and
    (f) extent to which its value to the community is outweighed by its dangerous attributes.

Land Pollution

The primary problem caused by land pollution is water pollution due to seepage from improperly disposed toxic wastes. Hence, there are very few cases that concern only the pollution of one's own land. After the famous Love Canal case in the late 1970s, Congress passed the Superfund law in 1980 to regulate the cleanup of toxic waste sites. How the common law might have dealt with this issue appears in a small number of cases that have occurred despite the Superfund law.

Village of Watsonville v. SCA Services (426 N.E.2d 824, S.Ct., Ill., 1981)

The Illinois EPA, backed by the U.S. EPA, supported the right of a chemical waste landfill, which was alleged to be causing damage to a nearby village, to remain in operation. The Illinois supreme court found that the landfill was causing groundwater contamination and that there could be a chemical explosion given the disposal technique used. The court held that the landfill was a public and a private nuisance; the village residents had been there first. The landfill was built with state and federal approval, which encouraged the landfill owner to ignore consequences to its neighbors. The court noted that toxic landfills were legitimate, but held that they had to be constructed so as not to impose costs on surrounding landowners who had not agreed to the intrusion. It issued a permanent injunction against the landfill and ordered that the toxic wastes be dug up and moved, and the land restored.

New York v. Schenectady Chemicals, Inc. (459 N.Y.S.2d 971, 1983)

Schenectady Chemicals (SC), during the 1950s and early 1960s hired an incompetent company to dispose of its toxic wastes. During those years, the hauler dumped 46,300 tons of chemical wastes in a swampy 13-acre site that drains into an aquifer serving thousands of people. Prior to this action, it became clear that there was some damage being done to some wells in the aquifer. Of the waste, 82.2 percent came from General Electric and Bendix (who had already agreed to pay up); SC contributed 17.8 percent. The state sued for SC to pay its share of the remediation costs, and asked for assorted penalties under New York's environmental conservation law (ECL).

The court held that the ECL did not apply; the dumping occurred before the permit system was established, so no penalties from that ECL were relevant. The cause of action that applies is public nuisance, which has been defined by the Court of Appeals of New York as "A public, or as sometimes termed a common, nuisance is an offense against the State and is subject to abatement or prosecution on application of the proper governmental agency." Further, this court noted, "One who creates a nuisance through an inherently dangerous activity or use of an unreasonably dangerous product is absolutely liable for resulting damages, irregardless of fault, and despite adhering to the highest standard of care."

SC was liable for its nuisance and was ordered to pay its pro-rata share of the cleanup expense. The fact that the ECL does not apply to this action does not preclude common law liability.

New York v. Monarch Chemicals et al. (456 N.Y.S.2d 867, App. Div., 1982)

The appellate court upheld liability based on nuisance for a landlord who leased land to Monarch Chemical, which allowed chemicals to seep into groundwater while occupying the premises: "the legal concepts governing a landlord's liability for its tenant's activities have been expanded to the point that a landlord may now be held responsible for negligence in the selection of a tenant and also for the wrongdoing of the tenant when the landlord continues to exercise control over the premises. " The landlord knew the tenant was using the property for toxic chemicals, was informed by an engineer that there were seepage problems, but ignored it.

The court held the landlord to be responsible, like Monarch Chemical, to help pay for the cleanup. The fact that the ECL does not apply does not absolve liability since common law liability applies.

New York v. Shore Realty Corp. (759 F.2d 1032, 2nd Cir., 1985)

Several acres had been used for chemical storage. About 700,000 gallons in assorted tanks, some of which leaked, had been placed on the land. Shore agreed to buy the land to use for a real estate development, knowing that there would have to be a cleanup, which one company estimated would cost about $1 million (the company reported groundwater contamination). Using the cleanup company's report, Shore asked the New York State Department of Environmental Conservation (DEC) for a waiver of liability if the cleanup were performed. The waiver was denied, but Shore bought the property anyway and evicted the tenants (chemical dump operators).

After the purchase, Shore did a little fixing up, but the chemicals sat there, some leakage still occurring. New York operated under the state's mini-Superfund law and sued for its response costs. Under this law (and Superfund), Shore was liable along with all other parties involved for state mandated cleanup even though Shore did not operate the dump.

Shore argued that since EPA did not put the site on the Superfund's National Priority List of sites to be cleaned, it could not be liable. The court held that that was irrelevant to state action. The court of appeals upheld the district court's finding of liability based on public nuisance.

> "Shore, as a landowner, is subject to liability for either a public or private nuisance on its property upon learning of the nuisance and having a reasonable opportunity to abate it.

> "It is immaterial ... that other parties placed the chemicals on this site; Shore purchased it with knowledge of its condition—indeed of the approximate cost of cleaning it up—and with an opportunity to clean up the site ... Shore is liable for maintenance of a public nuisance irrespective of negligence or fault. Nor is there any requirement that the State prove actual, as opposed to threatened, harm from the nuisance in order to obtain abatement.

Such liability is irrespective of state superfund liability; it exists under common law.

Wood v. Picillo (433 A.2d 1244, S.Ct., R.I., 1982)

Neighbors sued a farmer who maintained a hazardous waste dump on his property. The plaintiffs claimed the dump emitted noxious fumes and polluted ground and surface waters. Holding for the plaintiffs, the Rhode Island supreme court overturned a 1934 decision that would have held for the defendant because groundwaters were "indefinite and obscure." The 1934 court had held that plaintiffs in pollution cases had to show that defendants should have "foreseen" the consequences of their action, that is, were negligent. The 1982 court held that since 1934

> the science of groundwater hydrology as well as societal concern for environmental protection has developed dramatically. As a matter of scientific fact the course of subterranean waters are no longer obscure and mysterious. . . . We now hold that negligence is not a necessary element of a nuisance case involving contamination of a public or private waters by pollutants percolating through the soil and traveling underground routes.

That is, a rule of strict liability was imposed on polluters who cause damage to ground and surface waters. This standard of care is consistent with old common law tort rules imposing strict liability in case of hazardous materials.[20] Liability is imposed if there is evidence of injury or of potential to cause injury. Advances in knowledge of the effects of toxic substances mean tougher standards today than in years past.

Air Pollution

Few common law air pollution cases are found compared to water pollution. One reason is because most air pollution comes from multiple sources, making it more difficult to identify the defendant. But these cases make clear that the courts long recognized liability for air pollution. Since passage of the Clean Air Act of 1970, the EPA has been the primary controller of air quality. The agency and various state pollution agencies operating under EPA supervision issue pollution permits to major pollution sources and determine pollution limits on vehicles and other emission sources. There have been almost no common law cases since 1970.

Georgia v. Tennessee Copper Co. (206 U.S. 230, 27 S.Ct. 618, 1907)

The state of Georgia, on behalf of its citizens, sued two companies that operated copper smelters in Tennessee near the Georgia border. Justice Holmes noted that a public nuisance had been created because the "sulphurous fumes cause and threaten damage on so considerable a scale to the forests and vegetable life, if not to health, within [Georgia]. " The plaintiffs argued that they had recently constructed new facilities that reduced the scope of the problem, but the Supreme Court held for Georgia.

The Court held that the companies would be given a reasonable time to build more emission control equipment, but that if such equipment did not adequately reduce emissions so as to protect plant life in Georgia, the state could ask the Court for an injunction to shut the plants down.

In 1915 the parties returned to the Supreme Court. Defendant companies showed that their new equipment, which was very expensive, reduced emissions by more than half. Georgia argued that this was not enough and demanded that the plants be closed. The chief justice appointed a scientist from Vanderbilt University to spend six months, at company expense, studying the emissions and the likely effect of new controls. In the meantime, the Court ordered the companies to cut back production so as to reduce emissions further. Based on the evidence presented by the scientist, the companies would either be allowed to continue operation with more emission control equipment in place, or, if that could not reduce emissions sufficiently, an order to shut the plants would be issued.

Gainey v. Folkman (114 F. Supp. 231, D. Az., 1953)

A cattle rancher sued an adjoining landowner for injunctive relief against further crop dusting of cotton, for damages to the plaintiff's cattle, and for injuries to the plaintiff's employees, allegedly caused when chemicals from dusting drifted over the plaintiff's ranch. Chemicals included DDT, Ben-Hex, and Parathion. These were applied properly by the crop duster, but some blew across the road onto employees, cattle, and cattle feed. The plaintiff claimed that an employee became ill and that the cattle lost weight, reducing their value.

Testimony from U.S. Department of Agriculture and University of Arizona Extension Service experts supported the defendant's position that the chemicals were properly applied and that there was no scientific evidence that the level of exposure was harmful to humans or cattle. A toxicologist reported that there was no evidence that the levels of exposure were harmful and that the levels found in a cow that was autopsied were below harmful levels.

The court noted that if the exposure had been shown to be harmful, the action would have been proper as a nuisance, but since evidence was to the contrary, judgment was for the defendant.

Fairview Farms, Inc. v. Reynolds Metals Co. (176 F. Supp. 178, D. Ore., 1959)

A Reynolds aluminum plant caused various acidic gases (fluorides) to settle on the plaintiff's adjoining farm, rendering parts of the forage on the farm unusable for the dairy cattle, causing some injury to the herd, and making some milk useless. Since Reynolds knew of the problem, which constitutes an intentional tort of trespass, it had installed improved fume control equipment over the years. The plant was built during World War II. Starting in the 1940s, Reynolds made payments to Fairview for the damages and some years paid Fairview to keep no dairy cattle in the fields. Reynolds told Fairview that it was constantly working to improve emission controls (emission levels did drop over the years) and that its scientists would take samples from Fairview property to constantly check for dangerous levels of contamination to the herd and its forage.   During the 1950s, Reynolds decided the emissions were no longer at a harmful level and ceased payments. Fairview sued in tort for damages; the court, reviewing procedural claims, held that Fairview could go forward with a claim for trespass for damages. The court held that Reynolds must take measures "to minimize the escape of fluorides from its plants . . . [to] the maximum possible consistent with practical operating requirements . . ."—that is, use the state of the art equipment. Reynolds would continue to be liable to Fairview for any damages, but an injunction against any emissions from Reynolds was denied, so long as Reynolds could show that it was meeting industry standards for emission controls.

R. L. Renken et al. v. Harvey Aluminum, Inc. (226 F. Supp. 169, D. Ore., 1963)

Landowners near an aluminum plant in The Dalles, Oregon, sued in trespass and nuisance for air pollution emitted by the plant (fluorine and other toxic gases). The plant was the largest employer in the town (550 employees). In the 1950s the plant had installed various emission control devices, including scrubbing towers and sprayers, which stopped over 90 percent of the emissions; nevertheless, about 1,300 pounds of fluoride escaped during daily operations. The company asserted that nothing more could be done. Experts testified that emission controls could be tightened, but only at substantial cost.

The court ordered the company to pay surrounding orchards for damages to their crops caused by the trespass of the damaging gases. The company was also ordered to install the new emission control equipment within one year, or an injunction against any further emissions (i.e., plant shutdown) would be issued, as requested by the plaintiffs.

Reynolds Metals Co. v. Martin (337 F.2d 780, 9th Cir., 1964)

The Martins owned a 1,500-acre cattle ranch that suffered from pollution emitted from the Reynolds plant. They sued for $1.4 million for actual damages and $1 million for punitive damages, and asked for an injunction if Reynolds did not install better emission control equipment. Reynolds moved for dismissal, which was denied by district court, so Reynolds appealed.

The court denied the appeal, holding there was a trespass, which the Oregon high court has defined as "any intrusion which invades the possessor's protected interest in exclusive possession, whether that intrusion is by visible or invisible pieces of matter or by energy which can be measured only the mathematical language of the physicist." There is also a nuisance here, but in Oregon the key action in such cases is trespass. The suit is to proceed.

Bradley v. American Smelting and Refining Co. (104 Wash.2d 677, 709 P.2d 782, S.Ct., Wash., 1985)

The Bradleys lived on Vashon Island, Washington, four miles from a copper refinery run by American Smelting (ASARCO). The Bradleys sued ASARCO, a New Jersey corporation, in federal court in Washington for damages in trespass and nuisance from the deposit on their property of airborne particles of heavy metals from ASARCO's smelter. The smelter had operated since 1905; it was regulated by state and federal air pollution laws and was in compliance with all regulations. The gases that passed over and landed on the Bradley's land could not be seen or smelled by humans; they required microscopic detection.

The federal court, which would use Washington common law to determine the case, was uncertain as to what that law was since there were so few cases in the area. The court asked the Washington supreme court to tell it the status of Washington common law of nuisance and trespass as applied to air pollution.

The court held that ASARCO "had the intent requisite to commit intentional trespass." Even though no harm was intended, and even though ASARCO did not know the Bradleys, the company knew particles were being emitted from its facilities. Second, the court held that "An intentional deposit of microscopic particulates, undetectable by the human senses, gives rise to a cause of action for trespass as well as a claim of nuisance." Hence, the ASARCO emissions created a nuisance and a trespass. The court noted that for a cause of action for nuisance or trespass to be successful, there must be "proof of actual and substantial damages." Under the statute of limitations, the plaintiffs had three years to file the action once the injury becomes known. And the court held that the case was not prohibited by the Washington Clean Air Act, the state equivalent of the federal Clean Air Act. Upon return to federal court, the case was dismissed for lack of evidence of damage to the plaintiffs or their property from the air pollution.

3. Final Thoughts

We cannot know how common law liability rules for pollution would have developed in the past few decades had their evolution not been largely precluded by statutes and regulatory controls. But other areas of law offer some clues. Recent advances in pollution control technology, advances in understanding the consequences of pollution, and changes in society's attitude about the acceptability of pollution would have led to a rule of strict liability under the common law for polluters, as has occurred in product defect law. Even in its limited role, the common law often sets standards far tougher than those set by statutes.[21]

The common law does not evolve the most economically efficient or even the most "just" rules. But the decisions of hundreds of independent judges, responding to thousands of cases filed independently by private parties seeking to protect their common law rights, are far more likely to produce sensible principles than are legislative bodies that produce rules greatly influenced by special interests, or rules that may reflect a crisis of the moment but make little sense for the long term.[22] The principled nature of the common law lies in its evolutionary and competitive nature. The weakness of statutes is in their being influenced by special interests and lack of competitiveness. Had individuals and states been allowed to pursue common law remedies, such as private and public nuisance actions against polluters, litigation would have resulted in a more considered approach of the consequences of alternative rules of law.

It is not clear that pollution regulations have produced "better" environmental protection than what may have emerged from the common law in the absence of congressional interference to "solve" an alleged crisis. Of even greater significance is the loss of a key part of American individual freedom, the control of private property, in favor of centralized control. It is not clear that the environment is better; it is clear that some freedom has been lost. The environment is more likely to be protected by individuals seeking to protect their rights than when such matters are determined by technologically driven standards established by legislators and regulators.

Notes

1. These vignettes are drawn from Bruce Yandle, "Property Rights, Bootleggers, Baptists and Spotted Owls," a presentation made to the South Carolina Agricultural Council, Cayce, S.C., April 23, 1993. Also, see Bruce Yandle, "Regulatory Takings,

Farmers, Ranchers and the Fifth Amendment," Clemson, S.C.: Center for Policy Studies, October 1994.

2. See Robert C. Ellickson, "Property in Land," 102 *Yale Law Journal* 1315 at 1352 (1993), for references to the views of Thomas Jefferson and more modern commentators.

3. See Charles T. Rubin, *The Green Crusade* (1994); Robert H. Nelson, "Environmental Calvinism: The Judeo-Christian Roots of Eco-Theology," in *Taking the Environment Seriously*, 233-55 (Roger Meiners and Bruce Yandle, eds., 1993); and James Bovard, *Lost Rights* (1994) for discussion of the hostility of environmentalists to private property. See Al Gore, *Earth in the Balance* (1992) and Senator George Mitchell, *World on Fire* (1991) for anti-private property views of two major political leaders.

4. Gore, note 3, at 278.

5. A. V. Dicey, *The Law of the Constitution* (1982; first edition, 1885) at 123.

6. Bernard Siegan, *Economic Liberties and the Constitution* (1971) at 12.

7. Ellickson, note 2, at 1369.

8. *Ballenger v. City of Grand Saline,* 276 S.W.2d 874 (Tex. Civ. App—Waco, 1955, no writ); see also *State of New York v. Shore Realty Corp.*, 759 F.2d 1032 (2d Cir., 1985) (owners of waste disposal site must cleanup); *National Sea Clammers Assn. v. City of New York*, 616 F.2d 1222; judgment vacated 453 U.S. 1, 101 S.Ct. 2615 (1981) (plaintiffs brought action against government officials alleging they had permitted discharge of sewage that resulted in damage to their industry); *Philadelphia Elec. Co. v. Hercules, Inc.*, 762 F.2d 303, 315, cert. denied 474 U.S. 980, 106 S.Ct. 384, 388 (1985); (property owner sued corporation alleging contamination of groundwater and river as a result of operation of chemical plant); *United States v. Solvents Recovery Serv. et al.*, 496 F. Supp. 1127, 1142 (D. Conn., 1980). (The United States brought action seeking injunctive relief against two corporations for allegedly polluting groundwater).

9. Specifically, the court in *Ballenger* noted the city's allegations: That the appellant was a wholesale dealer in chickens; that in the pursuit of his business he erected a chicken house within a residential section of the City, the house being a temporary structure consisting of "a big pen covered by a huge roof," this house or pen being adjacent to Green Street; that in the operation of his chicken house the appellant loads and unloads chickens at all hours of the night, permits refuse, offal and feathers to accumulate therein and allows dead chickens to lie around the premises to such extent as to become a breeding place for flies; that the noises and foul odors emanating from the chicken house are such as to disturb the residents of the entire neighborhood, the noises keeping them awake at night and the foul odors making it impossible for them to sit in comfort on their porches or to eat their food without closing the doors and windows of their homes; "that the dead chickens, the refuse from the chickens, the offal, and the decayed eggs together with the flies create a hazard which endangers the health of all the residents of this area."

10. See *People v. New Penn Mines, Inc.*, 212 Cal. App. 2d 667 (1963) (holding that the Attorney General's power to sue for public nuisance was pre-empted by establishment of administrative apparatus to deal with water pollution).

11. It is interesting that Carson failed to note that the federal government was largely responsible for the overdoses of DDT that caused many environmental problems. See Christopher Bosso, *Pesticides and Politics* (1987),

12. Ellickson, note 2, at 1335; also see Richard Stroup and Jane Shaw, "Environmental Harms from Federal Government Policy," in *Taking the Environment Seriously,* 51-72 (Roger Meiners and Bruce Yandle, eds., 1993).

13. Legalese is avoided as much as possible, but that is not difficult since judges used to write in clear English, unlike many judges and their clerks today who seem compelled to demonstrate their scholarly ability by writing difficult terms in large quantities.

14. *Groundwater Protection* (Washington, D.C.: The Conservation Foundation), at 36.

15. For a review of all cases in one state, see Peter Davis, "Theories of Water Pollution Litigation," 1971 *Wisconsin Law Review* 738.

16. 208 N.Y. 1 at 5.

17. Ibid., quoting *Weston Paper Co. v. Pope*, 155 Ind. 394, 57 NE 719.

18. For a discussion of such practices by paper mills, see Davis, *supra* note 15, at 777-80.

19. Baseball fans will be interested that this case went to the Supreme Court on appeal from the federal district court in Illinois, Judge Kennesaw Mountain Landis presiding. He had moved on to his more famous occupation prior to disposition by the Supreme Court.

20. *Rylands v. Fletcher*, L.R. 3 H.L. 330 (1868), is a principal case for the proposition, "So use your own property as not to injure your neighbor's property." This principle comes from Roman law. See 5 *Water and Water Rights*, Sec. 49.03(b) n. 43.

21. Business has lobbied hard for over a decade for statutory limits on common law liability for defective products. Industry associates actively supported passage of the pollution statutes in the early 1970s.

22. See Staaf and Yandle, "Common Law, Statute Law, and Liability Rules," in Meiners and Yandle, eds., *The Economic Consequences of Liability Rules*, 1991. Concerning the role of special interests, corporate and otherwise, in the making of regulations, see Meiners and Yandle, eds., *Regulation and the Reagan Era*, 1989.

References

Bethell, Tom. "Property and Tyranny," *The American Spectator*, August 1994, pp. 16-17.

Capurro v. Galaxy Chem. Co., 2 ELR 20386 (Md. Cir. Ct., 1972) (chemical plant emissions enjoinable as public nuisance and also constitute a private nuisance allowing damages for diminution in property values).

"Impact of the Federal Wetlands Act on Real Estate," Technical Report 964, Denver: CLE International, January 1993, p. 5.

Miniter, Richard. "Trouble in Paradise," *Reason*, August/September 1992, p. 48.

Restatement, Second, Torts § 826(a), at 3 (Tent. Draft No. 18, 1972).

Ryan v. City of Emmetsburg, 4 N.W.2d 435, 232 Iowa 600; *Hederman v. Cunningham*, 283 S.W.2d 108 (Tex. Civ. App.—Beaumont, 1955, no writ).

Spencer, Leslie. "Fighting Back," *Forbes*, July 19, 1993, pp. 43-44.

Stoughton v. Ft. Worth, 277 S.W.2d 150 (Tex. Ct. App.—Ft. Worth, 1955, no writ); *Enchave v. City of Grand Junction*, 193 P.2d 277, 118 Colo. 165 (1948).

U.S. Smelting Co. v. Sisam, 191 F. 293 (8th Cir., 1911); *Towaliga Falls Power Co. v. Sims*, 6 Ga. App. 749, 65 S.E. 844 (1909).

Vann v. Bowie Sewerage Co., 127 Tex. 97, 90 S.W.2d 561 (1936).

Village of Euclid v. Ambler Realty, 272 U.S. 365, 388 (1926).

"When Landowners Clash with the Law," *U.S. News & World Report*, April 6, 1992, p. 80.

Yandle, Bruce. "Regulatory Takings, Farmers, Ranchers and the Fifth Amendment," Clemson, S.C.: Center for Policy Studies, October 1994.

Chapter 9

Federal Zoning: The New Era in Environmental Policy

Robert H. Nelson

Previous chapters of this book document the arrival of a new era in environmental policy in the United States. From the Clean Air Act, to the Clean Water Act, to wetlands protection, to the Endangered Species Act, U.S. environmental policies increasingly are about the regulation of land use. And since these policies are driven by federal laws and regulations, whether Congress intended it or not, the result is the rise of a new system of federal land-use regulation. In the many areas that have come within the scope of this system, the federal government has the authority to decide which uses will be permitted and which will be excluded. As this authority is increasingly exercised, we are seeing, in effect, the emergence of a system of federal zoning.

Over the course of the twentieth century, the federal government has assumed greater and greater authority over all aspects of American life. Until the New Deal, the growing centralization of governing power had to overcome hurdles of Supreme Court resistence, accepted laissez-faire economic theories that prescribed a small government, and a long federalist tradition in the United States that said the federal government should be limited in its areas of responsibility relative to the states. Since the New Deal, however, little in the way of law, economics, or politics has stood in the way of the expansion of the federal role.

This chapter traces the development of the federal government as a national land-use planner. In describing the path that was traveled, the first section explains how federal land-use regulation emerged in the clothing of environmental statutes. Taken together, the statutes provide a dense land-use planning network. Eventually, the federal government became a highly visible and generally unwanted planner. Section two describes the reactions and adjustments that came as federal legislators attempted to maintain a grip on environmental control while escaping the land-use planner label.

Of course, land-use controls have a long history. Section three begins with a brief discussion of common law remedies that affected land use, moves to a discussion of community planning and zoning, and then explains how state governments and then the federal government became involved in the process. Following this evolutionary story, tracing a movement that eventually threatened property rights historically protected by government, the chapter concludes with some final thoughts on how federal land-use regulation might be redirected and how the federal government's role should be modified.

1. How the Federal Government Became a Land-Use Planner

Regulation of local land use was for many years one of the few exceptions to the federalization of American life.[1] Over the space of three years in the early 1970s, however, the key elements of a statutory foundation for federal land-use regulation were put in place. Many members of Congress may not have realized it, but the Clean Air Act of 1970, the federal Water Pollution Control Act Amendments of 1972 (Clean Water Act), and the Endangered Species Act of 1973 contained the authority for the federal government to regulate land use throughout much of the United States.

The Clean Air Act, for example, required in Section 110 that state implementation plans—subject to EPA review and approval—include such measures "as may be necessary to insure attainment and maintenance of . . . primary or secondary standards, including, but not limited to, land use and transportation controls."[2] A 1974 report of the Congressional Research Service noted that the Act authorized "the general use of land use controls to achieve the air quality standards." The CRS report further noted that "most of the authority to regulate land use rests with the States, but most States have delegated this authority to local governments. Although EPA has expressed a desire for State and local governments to assume responsibility for land use decisions required by the Act, the structure of the Act suggests that EPA may have to assume this responsibility in the absence of an adequate State or local response."[3]

Section 208 of the Water Pollution Control Act required areawide or regional water-quality and land-use planning that must include a process to regulate the "location, modification and construction of any facilities within the planning area which may result in a discharge of any effluent in the area."[4] By 1975, Fred Bosselman, a leading student of land-use regulation in the United States, would observe that "Congress has passed so many federal land-use regulations that in a few years only a rare development project of any size will get by without two and probably more federal approvals."[5]

The laws establishing federal authority to regulate land use were not enacted as such, but as elements considered necessary to protect clean air, clean water, endangered species, etc. An explicit proposal for federal zoning would undoubtedly have been voted down overwhelmingly in the Congress. Indeed, Congress did consider a mild form of national land-use legislation in the early 1970s. This bill proposed to offer financial incentives and other inducements to encourage a greater role for state governments in shaping land use. Proponents of the legislation went out of their way to declare that the federal government had no intention of trying to decide the substantive character of land use in each state. However, even in a political climate favorable to environmental legislation of all kinds, grassroots fears that a national land-use bill might prove to be the foot in the door for federal control over local land use were too much to overcome, and the legislation never passed.[6]

The full land-use consequences of the environmental legislation of the early 1970s, as subsequently amended, are only now coming to be more widely realized. For twenty years the Environmental Protection Agency and state environment departments were preoccupied with resolving the problem of pollution from power plants, steel mills, chemical factories and other large and conspicuous sources—the "stationary sources." When EPA made overtures about regulating farming activities, urban street runoff and other "nonpoint" sources, or suggested steps that would interfere in any great degree with the American love affair with the automobile, Congress generally uttered some menacing sounds. It was not long after enactment of the 1970s legislation that environmentalists were already complaining that "the agency has consistently defied the Congress and the courts in failing to move expeditiously in implementing land use controls."[7] This pattern continued for many years as EPA, even though it had the authority in existing law, often tread very lightly in matters of regulating local land use.

New Environmental Priorities

Two events have come together to bring about the recent moves toward a system of federal land-use regulation. First, EPA and state air and water regulators have exhausted most of the potential for cleaning up the large stationary sources.⁸ Yet Congress has mandated still further significant improvements in air and water quality, improvements that can now be achieved only by addressing the many individually small but cumulatively large sources of pollution that have been neglected in the past. Controlling these sources in considerable degree means controlling land use.

Second, the environmental movement and the federal government have shifted the goals of environmental policy toward "ecological" concerns. It is only in the past decade that protection of wetlands and endangered species have come to occupy center stage in environmental policy making. The Clinton administration's Budget Statement for Fiscal Year 1995 states that "nothing better characterizes the Administration's new approach to natural resource management than the emphasis on ecosystem management."⁹ To the extent that public lands are involved, as in almost 50 percent of the land area of the western United States, protection of ecosystems need not have major impacts on private land. However, in the East, South, and Midwest, and in half of the West, protection of an ecology means to a significant extent the management of the use of private land. Federal wetlands and endangered species laws have become in effect powerful forms of federal land-use regulation.

The goals of ecological management extend well beyond wetlands and endangered species. The new attention to ecological systems reflects a recognition that past environmental policies have been flawed because each law focused single-mindedly on one medium such as air or water, or on one object of concern such as wetlands or endangered species. However, it is the overall environmental result—the "state of the ecology"—that really matters. The condition of the ecology as a whole is a product of the complex interaction of many economic, biological, and other factors. Thus, environmental policy, in this view, must shift from looking at one piece at a time to studying the complex whole. As the Clinton administration's Budget Statement for 1995 indicated, the new government "emphasis on managing whole ecosystems replaces the piecemeal approach of the past wherein land, water, air, endangered species, and mineral and other resources were primarily dealt with one by one."¹⁰

Much the same idea was expressed earlier in this century by saying that housing policy must be coordinated with transportation policy, that sewer construction must be related to public school capacity, that planning must be "comprehensive" to achieve economically sound and aesthetically attractive land use in the United States. In short, the current demand for ecological management is a new and more fashionable way of stating the need for "comprehensive land use planning and control."¹¹ In the past, it was left to local government —with occasional state government involvement—to pursue the comprehensive management of land use. But as the federal government today asserts that it has the responsibility to ensure that ecological systems across the United States are protected, federal officials are in effect asserting the need for comprehensive federal planning and regulation of land use. Much in the way that zoning, subdivision, and other local regulations have traditionally been envisioned to provide the legal instruments to implement comprehensive local land-use plans, today existing federal environmental laws are to provide the regulatory authority to implement federal land-use plans.

No one told the American people that federal land-use regulation—federal zoning—was coming. The members of Congress, or at least many of them, did not know they were voting for it. Thus, the arrival in recent years of federal officials to tell many property owners across the United States that they may not use the land for this or that purpose has often come to these owners as a great surprise. Public anger has been fed by the clumsiness and rigidity that seems almost intrinsic to large central bureaucracies, and by the attempt to impose a "one size fits all" federal regulatory approach across the United States. Predictably, as described in earlier chapters of this book, stories of federal officials harassing and intimidating local property owners on minor matters have begun to be heard more and more frequently.

2. Reaction to the Unwanted Planner

The new federal regulatory role has, moreover, been asserted in a haphazard and uncoordinated way. The federal statutes establishing the authority for the federal regulation of local land use were not created with this purpose in mind. They were in most cases enacted to serve a narrower goal than improving land use or managing a whole ecology. (Indeed, if humans are included in the ecological frame of reference, "ecology" comes close to having the same meaning as "society.") Rather, the laws establish particular legal instruments for particular purposes—cleaning the air, cleaning the water, protecting a species, etc. The federal officials who administer these laws also are located in agencies and divisions that have their own historic missions. They reasonably enough approach their regulatory tasks from the one point of view of achieving the purposes of the particular law they administer.

Thus, they do not aim, indeed are sometimes legally prohibited from aiming, to achieve the best overall land-use result for society, all things considered. If it should happen that adequately protecting the black-capped vireo requires that other land-use goals be sacrificed, the Endangered Species Act declares that the needs of the vireo must trump other land-use concerns— in fact the whole range of other social and economic considerations. In short, the rise of environment law of the past quarter century has given the federal government the authority to regulate land use throughout the United States, but has parceled this authority out in pieces to agencies with absolute mandates to pursue narrowly defined regulatory objectives.

There are in effect not one by many federal systems of land-use regulation. They often overlap one another but nevertheless function without coordination among one another. In some cases the administrators of individual federal regulatory systems are directed by Congress not to take competing social considerations ("costs" an economist would say) into account.

In light of all this, it should come as no great surprise that the rise of federal land-use regulation has created some major problems. It is economically wasteful; it is administratively chaotic; it yields incoherent land-use policy; and often it does not serve the purpose of protecting the environment very well, when the full range of impacts on the environment is considered.[12]

Many members of the environmental movement thus far have resisted addressing these matters, for at least two reasons. First, major new legislation that opened up environmental law for wholesale revision might create openings for as many objectionable as desirable features. Second, many environmentalists have tended to address environmental law from an absolutist moral perspective. They have been able to sustain this outlook partly because they have focused their own interests and attentions on one particular area of environmental concern. Thus, any compromise of air quality, any acceptance of greater cancer risk, any loss of a species, is morally unacceptable and must not be allowed.

Environmentalism has deep religious roots in American culture. John McPhee once said of the man often considered the leading environmentalist of the past fifty years, David Brower, that "his approach is in some ways analogous to the Reverend Dr. Billy Graham's exhortations to sinners to come forward and be saved now."[13] Donald Worster, the distinguished environmental historian, recently commented that "the antidote for environmental destruction has been a movement called environmentalism and that movement has, in the United States, owed much of its program, temperament, and drive to the influence of Protestantism."[14] It has followed in the steps of other religiously inspired American reform movements such as abolitionism, women's suffrage, and temperance.[15] It has yielded at times environmental laws such as the Water Pollution Control Act of 1972, setting a national target to eliminate all pollution from the nation's waters by 1985, a provision of the law that follows in the spirit of the constitutional amendment of 1919 prohibiting all alcohol consumption in the United States.

The Political Fallout

Many practical criticisms of our current approach to developing and administering environmental law have been made by lawyers, economists, and other observers for quite some time, all to little avail.[16] What may prove more telling in stimulating a rethinking of U.S. environmental policy is that the rise of federal zoning is today creating a political crisis for the environmental movement. Federal environmental agencies are no longer dealing largely with impersonal corporate polluters who can be attacked as greedy "big business."

Instead, federal regulators increasingly are directing their commands and controls at millions of farmers, homeowners, automobile drivers, landowners, and other ordinary people—who also happen to be millions of voters.

Moreover, in the past, if truth be told, the big corporations themselves did not necessarily have much reason to object strongly to burdensome environmental regulations, as long as the costs were imposed uniformly throughout the industry, and could be passed on to consumers in a hidden fashion in higher prices. If environmental laws imposed differentially tighter requirements on new firms in an industry—as the "new source performance standards" of the Clean Air Act and a number of other environmental laws did—then all the better for existing industry. These laws could serve as anticompetitive protectionist devices blessed with the holy water of a high environmental purpose. Business lobbyists thus often could join happily with environmental groups in an "unholy alliance" to support the most stringent control requirements, as long as they were limited to new sources.[17]

The Clean Air Act Amendment of 1977 included strict sulfur control requirements with mandatory use of scrubbing technology for new power plants, enacted with the combined support of western environmentalists and eastern coal industry and union interests. These controls were designed specifically to limit the penetration of coal from new low-cost surface mines opening in the West and that had a low sulfur content that eliminated any real need for scrubbing, thereby threatening to capture portions of eastern utility markets.[18]

Millions of farmers and individual property owners, however, obtain no such protectionist benefits from the emergence of federal land-use regulation. Well represented in every congressional district, the groundswell of their complaints has begun to change the political landscape of environmental policy making. In Texas, for example, the prospect of the federal government enforcing the Endangered Species Act to zone large areas of the state was infuriating to many Texans. By the late summer of 1994 the Democratic governor of Texas, Ann Richards, regarded the Endangered Species Act as a potential danger to the entire Democratic party ticket in the fall elections (probably with good reason, based on the subsequent election results). Governor Richards appealed in September 1994 to Interior Secretary Bruce Babbitt to back off on the enforcement of the Act (which he did to some extent shortly thereafter):

The Fish and Wildlife Service's approach to implementing the [Endangered Species] Act in Texas has become so overreaching that it undermines public support for protecting our wildlife. During the past decade, the agency's efforts to enforce the law and protect wildlife have created *enormous* problems for landowners—most of whom are proud of their reputations for being good stewards of the land. In some cases the agency's inability to respond in a timely way has been merely inconvenient for the public; in other cases it has literally robbed people of their financial security. Some people have waited for months, if not years, for the Fish and Wildlife Service to give them a permit to proceed with their plans.[19]

The Antienvironmental Congress

Throughout the United States, public anger stirred by the rise of federal land-use regulation was so great by 1994 that the environmental movement, long one of the most politically popular groups and most effective lobbyists for its causes, suddenly found itself on the defensive. Indeed, by the end of the 1993-94 session, it was becoming clear that the environmental movement was suffering from an unprecedented erosion of political support in Congress. "The atmosphere for environmental issues in Congress is as bad as I've ever seen it."[20] "The Hill has become an environmental disaster area."[21] These were just two of many postmortems offered within environmental circles, shortly after the 103rd Congress went out of session.

A first sign of trouble had come as early as March 1993, when Congress forced President Clinton to back off on higher grazing fees on western public lands. By early 1994 the bill to raise EPA to cabinet status, expected to sail through, instead had to be pulled back, because influential congressmen kept insisting on adding requirements for benefit-cost analysis, risk assessments, and other unacceptable amendments. In late February a meeting of top environmental leaders with Congressmen George Miller and Henry Waxman decided that much of the pending environmental agenda would have to be scrapped. As described in a summary memorandum, widely circulated and commented on in Washington circles, an "unholy trinity" of congressional demands—(1) requirements for benefit-cost analysis and risk assessments, (2) limits on unfunded federal mandates, and (3) steps to avoid uncompensated takings of private property—was besetting all environmental legislation.[22]

The Clinton administration soon called off efforts to pass reauthorizations of the Endangered Species Act and the Resource Conservation and Recovery Act, and new legislation to create a National Biological Survey. Matters deteriorated still further in the closing days of Congress. Environmental priorities including the reauthorizations of Superfund, the Safe Drinking Water Act, the Clean Water Act, and a new public lands mining law all failed.

All this has created an unprecedented mood of soul searching in the environmental movement. Writing in the *Washington Post*, Jessica Mathews in October 1994 reiterated that "with respect to the environment, this Congress was pure scorched earth." She was of the opinion that "the legislative debacle may also be a sign that the first environmental era has just about played itself out while the next is not ready to be born." The future would have to give a new emphasis to the "small sources and individuals [that] have been largely ignored." There would also have to be a new "integration of environmental needs with broad policy setting in areas like energy, agriculture and transportation." All this would probably mean in practice "a shift from primary reliance on regulation to the use of economic signals"—which had the critical advantage that they could "be as easily applied to every consumer and small enterprise as to large businesses."[23]

The environmental movement, a quarter century after it first rose to national prominence, thus is reaching a crossroads. The old command-and-control regulatory strategies are no longer working, economically or politically. They have always been too rigid, tending to impose one technology standard, inhibiting the search for alternative and lower-cost protection strategies. They have always focused on one problem area at a time, neglecting the interactions with other types of environmental problems, to say nothing of the broader social consequences outside the environment. They have always neglected the individually small sources of pollution that cumulatively are sometimes the largest cause of the problem. But as environmental regulation becomes ever more costly, and is increasingly taking the form of land-use regulation, the existing form of environmental laws is becoming a political liability that the environmental movement itself can no longer afford. The rise of federal land-use regulation flies in the face of a longstanding American tradition of regarding land use as the most local of decisions, a matter where the involvement of state governments is barely tolerated, and where the federal government is warned strictly to "Keep Out."

More than anything else, the new political dynamic facing environmentalism may yield a basic rethinking of environmental protection strategies in the next few years. The election results of November 8, 1994, simply give further impetus to what had already seemed likely. The discussion will have to focus on a review of the character and problems of the system of federal land-use planning and regulation that has emerged since the 1970s. It will have to ask the question: what is the appropriate role for the federal government in regulating American land use?

3. From Common Law to Zoning
to Federal Control

In the original constitutional scheme, the federal government was given powers in limited areas, and the remaining areas were reserved for the states. The matters of state responsibility included the main object of land-use control until the early twentieth century, land uses creating smoke, noise, or other offensive impacts on their neighbors and which thus qualified as nuisances under the common law. The control of nuisances was handled through individual reviews of cases as their specific circumstances were brought before the courts. When zoning was introduced in the United States in New York City in 1916, and then spread rapidly thoughout the nation, it thus represented a major departure in land-use policy.[24] Instead of individual decisions by judges in response to the particulars of each case, zoning represented the establishment by the legislature of a set of permitting standards in advance of any particular application to build. Zoning advocates contended that this approach was superior to nuisance controls in that clear guidance was provided ahead of time to prospective developers. A common policy thus was substituted for the many decisions of individual judges. Case-by-case decision making, it was alleged, exhibited wide and unpredictably judicial variability in the determination of a nuisance.

Zoning was also said to be a necessary legal instrument that would enable municipalities to implement comprehensive land-use plans. There were high hopes in the progressive era early in the twentieth century that the introduction of comprehensive land-use planning would result in the building of more beautiful and more efficient American cities. It would be part of the scientific management of society that was at the heart of the progressive political philosophy for all areas of American life.[25] The Standard State Zoning Enabling Act, published by the Department of Commerce (under the direction of Secretary Herbert Hoover) in 1924, stated that "[Zoning] regulations shall be made in accordance with a comprehensive plan."[26] In 1928, the Standard City Planning Enabling Act, also issued by the Commerce Department, stated the rationale for planning:

> Every growing town or city with an agricultural or undeveloped belt around it not only needs good highway connection with the country, for example, but desires to forestall the strangling effect of ill-planned or unplanned suburbs. To some suburbs and towns the maintenance of clear roadways and good transit facilities which pass through other jurisdictions is of most vital importance. Inadequate approaches to an important bridge in one muncipality may become an intolerable burden to the citizens of others. Objectionable uses of land in one community may adversely affect another, as in the case of slaughter-houses with their offensive odors, or of factories set directly next to a city residence district.
>
> Orderly development from this point of view of the region as a whole must come eventually through comprehensive planning by regional commissions, which define and analyze regional problems, and devise practical measures for carrying them out.[27]

Although the planning and zoning theorists of the time considered that the metropolitan area or other large region was the appropriate jurisdiction for achieving coordinated land development, the tradition of local independence in land-use matters was too strong to overcome. Planning and zoning for the next forty years would be municipal. When planners pointed out that the actions of one municipality would often be inconsistent with those of another, and that regional planning could never be truly effective as long as each locality acted independently of others, their arguments were to no avail. In the event the development of metropolitan areas in the United States was never the result of a planning process in any sense that the early advocates of planning would have acknowledged as such.

The constitutionality of zoning was in great doubt for many years. The 1920s, after all, were a period when the Supreme Court was striking down many laws and government actions as unwarranted intrusions on private rights of contract and property ownership. However, to the surprise of many people, the Supreme Court in 1926 in the case of *Town of Euclid v. Ambler Realty* gave its blessing. Although there was much evidence to the contrary even then in the case before it, the Supreme Court accepted the argument that zoning represented an extension of nuisance law traditions; it was, as the Court said, a modern and more effective form of nuisance control. The Court also spoke approvingly of the constructive role that zoning could play as an instrument of implementing land-use plans developed by the professional experts in planning.[28]

The Supreme Court heard a second zoning case in 1928 but then did not accept another until the 1970s (resulting in the 1974 *Belle Terre* decision). The Court, reflecting a general American view, regarded the regulation of land as a state and local matter that should be addressed at that level. At the state level, legislatures and executive branches delegated almost all policy making and administrative authority for land-use regulation to local governments.

State judicial systems did, however, maintain a greater oversight role. The 1922 U.S. Supreme Court case *Pennsylvania Coal Co. v. Mahon* had established that a land-use regulation could be a taking, even through there was no literal physical confiscation of the property. State and local courts from time to time reversed municipal land-use regulations on the ground that they went "too far" and thus effectively took the land. More frequently, courts ruled that municipal zoning decisions were arbitrary and thus violated due process requirements of law. If one landowner was given permission to develop, for example, a court was not likely to allow a municipality to deny the same permission to an adjacent land owner, unless there was some clear and important difference in the circumstances of the two. On the whole, however, state and local courts were highly deferential toward the zoning enactments of local governments, reflecting a general judicial presumption of legislative deference that followed in the aftermath of the acquiescence of the Supreme Court in the late 1930s to the New Deal agenda of President Franklin Roosevelt.[29]

The Rise of State Land-Use Regulation

By the 1960s there was growing criticism of local land-use regulation and the beginning of efforts to assert a greater state role.[30] Critics of "exclusionary zoning" argued that local governments in the suburbs were keeping the poor and minorities bottled up in the inner cities, while middle- and upper-income groups lived on spacious lots in attractive suburban settings were protected by government regulation. The exclusionary zoning practices of suburban municipalities were a particular concern at a time when some of America's largest cities were exploding into riots. Two prestigious national groups, the National Commission on Urban Problems (Douglas commission) and the Kaiser committee on urban housing, both singled out the administration of local zoning as a principal source of the nation's alarming urban problems.

Other zoning critics contended that large projects such as a shopping center or power plant were having impacts well beyond the immediate municipality and thus should be subject to a regulatory process of wider jurisdiction. Such concerns led to the organization in 1964 by the American Law Institute of a working committee to produce a new "Model Land Development Code" for state and local land-use planning and regulation. After long discussion, and many drafts that were widely circulated and proved influential in ongoing policy debates, the final version of the Model Code was eventually published in 1976.

It proposed a major expansion of the state government role in land-use regulation. States should have regulatory oversight in designated "areas of critical state concern," that is, areas that had wetlands, wildlife, and other features of importance to the state as a whole. Within such "critical areas," local governments would retain the responsibility for preparing their own land-use plans and then administering local zoning and other controls in accordance with these plans. The state government thus would not be expected to regulate land directly. However, in a major departure from the traditional local zoning autonomy, in critical areas state authorities would have to approve the local plans and the regulatory regime for implementing them.

The Model Code also proposed a second new significant role for state government. States should assume the direct responsibility for the issuance of permits for large projects that represented "development of regional impact."

The thinking behind the Model Code was exerting a significant influence by the late 1960s, as a number of states reconsidered their traditional arrangements for regulation of land use.[31] In 1969, Massachusetts adopted a zoning appeals law to create a system of state review of local zoning decisions with respect to the siting of proposals submitted by nonprofit sponsors for low- and moderate-income housing projects. Between 1969 and 1975, more than twenty states adopted some form of legislation providing for a state role in the siting of energy facilities. In California, for example, the Energy Resources Conservation and Development Commission was established in 1974 with statewide authority to regulate the location of power plants.

States also moved to assert state authority to control land use in areas of particular environmental sensitivity. In 1973, New York established a new state system of land-use control over the 6 million acres (60 percent private land) of Adirondack Park. This vast acreage represents about 20 percent of the land area of New York. Vermont in essence made the entire state a critical area, thus leaving most important land-use decisions in the state potentially subject to state government determination. Florida followed closely the design of the Model Code, providing for state control over the siting of large projects with regional impacts and for the state to oversee land use in selected areas that had been designated as critical under the provisions of the Florida law. Oregon in 1973 adopted the Land Conservation and Development Act providing for state oversight of local planning and zoning.

Such moves by state governments to assume greater responsibility for land use were often bitterly resisted by local groups. In many states proposals to expand state regulatory authority were turned down by state legislators. Although wide federal authority to regulate local land use was contained in legislation such as the Clean Air Act of 1970 and the Water Pollution Control Act of 1972, these provisions were poorly understood outside the narrow community of experts on these laws. No one explicitly suggested in the heated land-use policy debates of the 1960s and 1970s that the federal government should itself enter into the zoning of America. The federal government had long protected what were in effect national "critical areas," the systems of national parks, wildlife refuges, wilderness areas, etc. However, if these systems were not found on public land, they were established through new direct acquisition of whatever private land was needed, rather than through a federal regulatory mechanism to control the use of the land.[32]

Congressional Action and Debate

Congress did, however, take some steps to encourage an increased role for state governments in managing and regulating land use. The Coastal Zone Management Act of 1972 offered financial incentives for states to establish planning and regulatory systems to oversee land use in their coastal areas. The incentives included not only funding for state coastal management programs but, in states with approved coastal programs, the law directed that the actions of federal agencies should be "consistent" with the state plan for the coastline, unless the federal government made a formal finding that a federal interest required otherwise. By 1994 only two coastal states, Georgia and Texas, were without federally approved coastal management plans.

In 1970 Senator Henry Jackson of Washington, chairman of the Senate Interior Committee, proposed the enactment of national land-use legislation that would have encouraged statewide planning and zoning. The Nixon administration was opposed to such an expansive state role but was willing to discuss a compromise. The result was an approach borrowing heavily from drafts of the Model Land Development Code and similar to the coastal zone management strategy enacted by Congress in 1972. National land-use legislation, which passed the Senate in 1973, proposed to offer federal funding to states for the development of statewide land-use programs. The state program would have to include mechanisms for state control over land use in areas of special environmental concern and control over development projects of greater than local significance. As the Senate report stated:

> The areas and uses are considered to be of State interest because decisions concerning them have impacts on citizens, the environment, and the economy totally out of proportion to the jurisdiction and the interests of the local decision-maker: the local zoning body or land use regulatory entity. Absent any form of regulatory control or oversight by the State, there may be no means of mitigating the adverse effects upon the regional, State, or national populace, economy, or environment which may result from decisions, made upon purely local considerations, concerning these areas and uses.[33]

The proponents of the legislation took pains to argue that the federal government was merely addressing matters of precedure: "The Committee has also carefully drawn [the proposed legislation] so as to avoid the transfer of any significant measure of authority over what have traditionally been local and State decisions." Instead of controlling the substance of land use, the purpose was "to move from an era of chaotic, *ad hoc*, short-term, case-by-case, crisis-by-crisis land use decisionmaking to an era of long-range planning and management." This step was required because of "the increasingly complex land use and resource allocation decisions faced by all levels of government" which in the future must "be made on a rational basis."[34]

After Senate passage in 1973, and with the support of leading members of Congress and the Nixon administration, national land-use legislation was widely expected to be enacted in the 1973-74 session of Congress. However, the House of Representatives refused on a 211-204 vote in June 1974 to bring the legislation to the floor and it failed again in 1975. When the bill died, it was one of the very few pieces of major environmental legislation not enacted in the 1970s. Its rejection was yet another indication of the longstanding fear of many Americans that a major federal land-use role would lead to an unwarranted intrusion of federal power into local affairs.

National land-use legislation as such has not been raised for serious discussion in Congress since the early 1970s. Instead, as described above, the goals of the legislation have been realized through legislation with other stated purposes. Indeed, the federal government has actually ended up with significantly greater powers and a much broader scope for control over state and local land use than the advocates of the 1970s legislation would have ever dared to propose explicitly.

The Federal Government and Land Use

The rise of federal regulation occurred in the context of a longer-run trend of federal land-use involvement that took place at first in other areas. Since the New Deal years, as the federal government has asserted its authority in many areas of American life, it was inevitable that federal actions would become a significant factor in shaping American land use. Indeed, the designs of federal transportation, housing, and many other policies have had significant impacts on the character of land use in the United States.

After World War II, the growing ownership of single-family homes was encouraged by federal policies such as the FHA system of home mortgage insurance, similar veterans insurance, and the federal tax deductability of interest payments on home mortgages. The construction of high-density public housing projects was a significant factor in keeping the poor and minorities clustered together and segregated in many inner cities, while the suburbs became the playground of the middle classes. Urban renewal was another federal policy with major consequences for American housing.

A landmark event for American land use was the the enactment in 1956 of the Interstate Highway Act. The federal provision of 90 percent funding spurred construction of expressways offering much faster access to the center city from distant suburbs, leading to the development of areas that had previously been farm or vacant land. The rapid travel on new beltways around the circumference of cities encouraged the movement of businesses into the suburbs and in general stimulated whole new patterns of metropolitan residential and commercial development.

Federal energy policy after World War II also had significant land-use impacts. The generous tax breaks offered the oil and gas industry helped to keep the price of gasoline low, encouraging the low-density and dispersed patterns of metropolitan development that would characterize Los Angeles, Houston, and other newer cities. In Europe, by contrast, governments looked to gasoline taxes as a major source of government revenue, and in this way actively intervened to promote higher densities of housing settlement. The price of natural gas for many years was also held by federal regulators at below-market rates, encouraging the building of larger single-family homes in suburban locations.

The Clean Air Act of 1970, the Water Pollution Control Act of 1972, and other environmental legislation of the 1970s thus were by no means the first instances in which the federal government took actions that could significantly influence land-use patterns across the United States. The 1970s were a major departure, however, in that the federal government now entered into areas where its land-use impacts were achieved through a direct regulatory and permitting mechanism.

Following enactment of the Clean Air Act in 1970, a host of questions with major implications for land use would have to be resolved. Would new land uses that emitted significant amounts of air pollution be permitted at all in areas where air quality fell below the national air-quality standards set by EPA? Would there be any limits on entry of new land uses into areas that were at present above the air-quality standards? If not, would this mean that industrial and residential growth would be channeled into areas with high existing air quality, until the air fell to the lowest acceptable levels? Would existing uses be subjected eventually to the same standards as new uses (the old zoning problem of nonconforming uses)?

Resolving all these matters, which has been taking place over the past two decades and is still evolving, amounted to the establishment of a comprehensive system of land-use regulation for the United States. The Clean Air Act in effect makes every state a federal "critical area," as this concept was formulated in the Model Code published by the American Law Institute. Also like the Model Code, the federal EPA assumes direct regulatory responsibility for certain particularly large and important facilities of regional impact—for example, power plants under the acid rain provisions of the 1990 Clean Air Act Amendments.

The federal Water Pollution Control Act of 1972, as noted above, has also had substantial impacts on local land use. The program for construction of municipal sewage treatment plants was in some ways analogous to the interstate highway program in that many billions per year of federal moneys were provided for instrastructure necessary to accommodate metropolitan growth. To date, the regulatory mechanisms of the Water Pollution Control Act have concentrated on limiting pollution from large stationary sources. These efforts have yielded significant improvements in some urban rivers and other water bodies, but on the whole, water quality in the United States is about the same as it was in 1972 (which may represent a real accomplishment to the degree that water quality would otherwise have deteriorated significantly).

The next reauthorization of the Clean Water Act is expected to take up the task of bringing nonpoint sources under tighter control. Yet regulation of farm operations, water runoff from residential streets, and other nonpoint sources will require in essence new controls over land use.

When it was enacted in 1973, the Endangered Species Act was hardly considered to be an opening wedge for federal land-use regulation. Yet the Fish and Wildlife Service soon interpreted the Act as prohibiting changes in private land use that would diminish the habitat available to a threatened or endangered species or in other ways reduce the likelihood of species survival. The resulting limitations on use of private land have been particularly resented by affected property owners because in many instances the uses permitted under the Act are tightly restricted. The creation of a National Biological Survey could give the Act still wider impact, because it could result in the discovery of many additional types of endangered species and of wide new areas of habitat not previously known to be occupied by existing endangered species. However, the federal Court of Appeals in Washington, D.C., ruled in 1994 that the manner of the Fish and Wildlife Service application of the Act to private land was not justified by the language of the Act—a matter what will no doubt require further resolution in the courts.

Under the Endangered Species Act, until a federal judge overturned the Interior Department listing of the gnatcatcher, the department was overseeing the development of habitat management plans for this bird species that covered significant undeveloped lands within the Los Angeles and San Diego metropolitican regions. The department was ostensibly concerned only with habitat conditions but there was no way to separate protection of habitat for an endangered species from decisions on the location of housing, open space, roads, and other land-use details. The habitat management plan for the gnatcatcher thus could not be just a plan to protect the gnatcatcher; it was in effect a plan for the pattern of land use over sections of extremely valuable metropolitan land.

The Interior Department went out of its way to enlist state and local participation. It attempted to delegate most of the responsibility for working up the details of habitat management plans to state and local groups. Yet, under the Endangered Species Act, the Interior Department had veto power over anything these groups devised. The plan in the end had to be an Interior Department plan to protect the gnatcatcher. Moreover, under the requirements of the Endangered Species Act, the Interior Department had to give first priority in resolving any land-use tradeoffs to the one imperative of the Act, that the particular species be maintained.

When wetlands protection, clean water, clean air, and other existing federal regulatory regimes are added to the Endangered Species Act, it may not be long before it is the exception rather than the rule to find a piece of land in the United States that is not within the scope of some federal system of land-use regulation.

4. Final Thoughts and Recommendations for Change

Since the key statutes were enacted in the early 1970s, the rise of federal land-use regulation has represented a sharp departure from previous traditions in the United States of local government responsibility for land use. Emerging in an unintended and unplanned fashion over the past quarter century, the current system of federal land-use regulation is economically and administratively irrational, and is probably not politically viable.

We can expect to hear many proposals to resolve the current administrative incoherence through greater federal planning and coordination. Since the federal land-use role is here to stay, it will be said, the next step must be to rationalize and improve it. Not less but more federal planning and control over land-use policies is the best way out of our current mess. This is, in many ways, the thrust of the current movement for "ecological management."[35]

This approach, however, will not work economically or politically. The United States has a long history of attempts to achieve "comprehensive planning." It has been tried in local land use, on the public lands, in planning for federal housing programs, as a requirement for spending federal transportation moneys, etc. It has never worked in any of these areas. Other countries around the world have gone much farther in their efforts to implement comprehensive land-use and other planning. Most of these nations are now in the process of dismantling the mistakes of the past.

Perhaps the United States should be acting in a similar fashion to dismantle the systems of federal land-use planning and regulation that have developed since the early 1970s. Yet it will not be an easy task. Federal control over land use is built into the basic structure of laws such as the Clean Air Act and the Water Pollution Control Act. Removing the land-use elements would mean rethinking the basic strategy of these laws and the fundamental relationship between the federal government and the states on which they are premised.

While the federal government has overreached in many areas, some federal roles and responsibilities may be worth preserving. The question we now face is whether to try to incrementally improve the federal air, water, endangered species, and other environmental and land-use laws or to repeal them altogether. The former approach would mean surgically keeping some federal roles, curtailing others, rolling back some land-use responsibilities to the states, and leaving others to the common law or to the private sector altogether.

A set of key questions thus will have to be answered in each of the major areas of environmental policy:

(1)   Should this area be regulated by government at any level?

(2)   To the degree that government regulation is appropriate, what level of government—federal, state, and/or local—should be ultimately responsible?

(3)   If a federal role is desirable, where should this responsibility be placed and how should it be administered?

The protection of endangered species, for example, may be a legitimate national responsibility in that it reflects a shared moral commitment of the whole nation. In that case, while the current law cries out for practical improvements and even basic changes in strategy, it may be that a new law would still require federal administration. Wetlands would seem to have less claim to protection as a moral obligation of the whole nation, and thus might represent an intermediate case.

The need for the federal government to undertake the main tasks of regulating air and water quality is still more doubtful. It is impossible to separate air and water policy from questions of what kind of society and what kind of land use we will have. Unless there is to be a single national policy in these matters, there will have to be the leeway to allow the political process in different states and localities to choose different answers. That will mean a significant decentralization of responsibility for land use—and thus also for air and water regulation. To be sure, the case for a major federal role may be strong where the relevant airsheds and watersheds cross state boundaries.

Whatever the level of government at which responsibility may come to rest, certain types of major improvements will have to be made in existing environmental legislation.

1. Benefits and costs must be considered. The absolutist framework of much existing federal environmental and land-use legislation, limiting administrators to one environmental object of concern to the exclusion of other social considerations, will have to be abandonned. It has always been in practice a fiction. It has served environmental and other litigants who could selectively sue, and thus drive government actions according to their priorities. It has served agency administrators who could invoke the law at their convenience. But absolutist fictions, such as the statutory mandate that acceptable levels of air quality cannot allow any impairment of human health, have warped and confused the policy debate. To be sure, paying attention to benefits and costs does not mean that any one group such as professional economists will have the exclusive role and capacity—based on assertions of unique technical skills—to decide their magnitudes.

2. Government should pay for the use of private property for social purposes. The debate over the definition of a "taking" has been going on for many years and failed to yield any precise resolution. The exact boundary will probably always be subject to judgment calls. However, many of the government actions currently being taken under laws such as the Endangered Species Act and for the purpose of wetlands protection are well outside the area of legitimate debate. Although the means is regulatory, they represent the putting to use by society of the property of a private owner. As a matter of basic equity, government should pay in that case. Requiring government to pay will also have the salutory consequence of forcing society to consider the real value of the new use sought for private property.

3. The federal government should not impose uniform "one size fits all" requirements across the United States. To the degree that ultimate responsibility remains at the federal level, there must be greater flexibility to craft local solutions tailored to local geographic, economic, political, and other circumstances.

Current requirements that every part of the nation achieve the same air quality, water quality, and other environmental and land-use standards do not reflect the wide range of costs. They do not, for example, reflect the greater difficulty of improving the air in Los Angeles versus other metropolitican areas. They also do not reflect legitimate differences in environmental and land use objectives of people living in diverse regions of the United States.

4. The federal government should devote greater efforts to improved scientific understanding and information dissemination. Over the past quarter century the federal government has been quick to impose far-reaching environmental regulations that had weak scientific justifications.[36] Proponents argued that, even though existing knowledge was poor, it was "better safe than sorry." However, this strategy comes at a high cost including greater risks in nonenvironmental areas; it requires a set of value judgments that each state and locality may want to make differently. A role for which the federal government is well suited is the conduct of scientific and other research to enable states and localities to make informed risk and regulatory judgments. The federal government has the ability to pool the resources of all the states in order to generate information of value throughout the United States.

In Search of a New Governing Paradigm

The federalization of land-use regulation should be seen in the context of the federal assumption of ever greater responsibilities in many other areas of government as well. The progressives argued early in this century that most social problems required the application of the expert skills of trained professionals. The very best of these professionals should be assembled where the most resources would be available and where their skills could be put to the widest use—at the federal level. Moreover, state boundaries were a crazy quilt that simply did not correspond to the realities of modern life. To the extent that the government pursued redistributionist objectives, it would also be necessary to locate much of the responsibility at the federal level.

Another key factor was that transportation and communications revolutions were linking diverse parts of the United States ever more closely together. They favored the development of the strongest citizen loyalties to the national community—to be an "American," not a "Virginian." If a resident of Philadelphia thinks that he or she may well be living in Chicago or Los Angeles five years from now, that person may prefer that the federal government assume the responsibility for setting national policies for housing, transportation, and other areas of concern.

However, the fundamental assumptions underlying the progressive scheme for government have been undercut in a number of respects in recent years.[37] The level of public trust in the skills and motives of professional groups has declined. Some of the redistributive roles of the welfare state have lost legitimacy. Confidence in the overall capacity of the federal government to conceive sound policies and to administer them rationally and effectively has eroded. With the end of the Cold War, the sense of national purpose associated with a common military purpose has diminished.

The current period is in many respects similar to the late nineteenth century, when there was also particularly strong discontent with existing instititions. The progressives saw a Congress that was the captive of the special interests, serving private greed more than the nation as a whole. The response in the progressive era represented probably the greatest shift in thinking about government and society—in the governing "paradigm"—over the 200-year history of the United States.

Today, however, it is the intellectual and institutional legacy of progressivism that is under challenge. The progressive design for the scientific management of society has become the old orthodoxy holding back change. To be sure, just what will replace the progressive scheme, what will be the new governing paradigm, is not yet clear. One can predict with some confidence, however, that it will involve significant elements of privatization of existing government functions. It will involve substantial decentralization—indeed, outright devolution to states and localities in many cases—of federal power.

Yet, most of the specifics remain to be resolved. One thing that is certain is that the future of federal land-use policy, and especially the system of federal federal land-use regulation that has emerged from the environmental legislation of the past quarter century, will be a leading arena for rethinking the progressive paradigm and the appropriate role for the federal government in American life.

Notes

1. See Robert H. Nelson, *Zoning and Property Rights: An Analysis of the American System of Land Use Regulation* (Cambridge: MIT Press, 1977).

2. P.L. 91-604, Sec. 110(a)(2)(B).

3. W. Wendell Fletcher, *The Land Use Implications of the Clean Air Act of 1970* and the Federal Water Pollution Control Act Amendments of 1972, *Congressional Research Service Report No. 74-176EP* (Washington, D.C.: October 4, 1974), p. 20.

4. P.L. 92-500, Sec. 208 (b)(2)(c).

5. Quoted in Frank J. Popper, *The Politics of Land Use Reform* (Madison: University of Wisconsin Press, 1981), p. 61.

6. Noreen Lyday, *The Law of the Land: Debating National Land Use.*

7. Fletcher, *The Land Use Implications of the Clean Air Act of 1970 and the Federal Water Pollution Control Act Amendments of 1972,* p. 1.

8. Paul R. Portney, ed., *Public Policies for Environmental Protection* (Washington, D.C.: Resources for the Future, 1990).

9. *Budget of the United States, Fiscal Year 1995* (Washington, D.C.: Government Printing Office, 1994), p. 137.

10. Ibid.

11. Normal Williams Jr., *American Planning Law: Land Use and the Police Power* (Chicago: Callaghan, 1975).

12. David Schoenbrun, "Goals Statutes or Rules Statutes: The Case of the Clean Air Act," *UCLA Law Review* Vol. 30 (1983); William Pederson, "Turning the Tide on Water Quality," *Ecology Law Quarterly* Vol. 15 (1988).

13. John McPhee, *Encounters with the Archdruid* (New York: Farrar Straus Giroux, 1971), p. 83.

14. Donald Worster, *The Wealth of Nature: Environmental History and the Ecological Imagination* (New York: Oxford University Press, 1993), p. 185. See also Robert H. Nelson, "Environmental Calvinism: The Judeo-Christian Roots of Ecotheology," in Roger E. Meiner and Bruce Yandle, eds., *Taking the Environment Seriously* (Lanham, Md.:Rowman and Littlefield, 1993).

15. Robert H. Abzug, *Cosmos Crumbling: American Reform and the Religious Imagination* (New York: Oxford University Press, 1994).

16. David Schoenbrod, "Goals Statutes or Rules Statutes: The Case of the Clean Air Act,"; Tom Tietenberg, *Environmental and Natural Resource Economics* (New York: HarperCollins, 1992); Joseph L. Bast, Peter J. Hill, and Richard C. Rue, *Eco-Sanity: A Common-Sense Guide to Environmentalism* (Lanham, MD: Madison Books, 1994).

17. Robert W. Crandall, *Controlling Industrial Pollution: The Economics and Politics of Clean Air* (Washington, D.C.: Brookings Institution, 1983).

18. Bruce A. Ackerman and William T. Hassler, *Clean Coal/Dirty Air: or How the Clean Air Act Becaome a Multibillion-Dollar Bailout for High Sulfur Coal Producers and What Should Be Done About It* (New Haven: Yale University Press, 1981).

19. Letter from Ann W. Richards, Governor of Texas, to Bruce Babbitt, Secretary of the Interior, September 12, 1994.

20. Jim Lyons, Washington director of the Mineral Policy Center, quoted in *High Country News*, October 17, 1994, p. 1.

21. Jessica Mathews, "Scorched Earth," *Washington Post,* October 18, 1994, p. A17.

22. Memorandum from Environmental Group lobbyists through Erik Olson (Natural Resources Defense Council), to John Adams, Peter Barie, Jay Hair, Fred Krup, Jane Perkins, and Carl Pope, on "Proposal for Legislative Strategy for the Rest of This Congress," March 4, 1994.

23. Mathews, *Scorced Earth.*

24. Nelson, *Zoning and Property Rights,* Ch. 1. See also William A. Fischel, *The Economics of Zoning Laws: A Property Rights Approach to American Land Use Controls* (Baltimore: John Hopkins University Press, 1985).

25. See Dwight Waldo, *The Administrative State: A Study of the Political Theory of American Public Administration* (New York: Holmes and Meier, 1984, first ed. 1948).

26. *A Standard State Zoning Enabling Act* (Washington, D.C.: U.S. Department of Commerce, 1924), sec. 3, p. 6.

27. Advisory Committee on Zoning, *A City Planning Primer* (Washington, D.C.: U.S. Department of Commerce, 1928), p. 14.

28. Seymour Toll, *Zoned American* (New York: Grossman, 1969).

29. Dennis J. Coyle, *Property Rights and the Constitution: Shaping Society Through Land Use Regulation* (Albany: SUNY Press, 1993).

30. Richard Babcock, *The Zoning Game: Municipal Practices and Policies* (Madison: University of Wisconsin Press, 1966).

31. Fred Bosselman and David Callies, *The Quiet Revolution in Land Use Control,* Prepared for the Council on Environmental Quality (Washington, D.C.: Government Printing Office, 1971).

32. Robert H. Nelson, *Public Land and Private Rights: The Failure of Scientific Management* (Lanham, Md.: Rowman and Littlefield, forthcoming).

33. United States Senate, *Report of the Committee on Interior and Insular Affairs to Accompany S. 268—Land Use Policy and Planning Assistance Act,* Report No. 93-197 (Washington, D.C.: Government Printing Office, 1973), p. 39.

34. Ibid., pp. 37, 38.

35. Robert B. Keiter, "NEPA and the Emerging Concept of Ecosystem Management on the Public Lands," *Land and Water Law Review,* 25 (1990).

36. See Roger E. Meiners and Bruce Yandle, eds., *Taking the Environment Seriously* (Lanham, Md.: Rowman and Littlefield, 1993).

37. Robert H. Nelson, "Government as Theatre: Toward a New Paradigm for the Public Lands," *University of Colorado Law Review* 65, No. 2 (1994).

Index

About the Political Economy Forum and the Authors

The Political Economy Research Center (PERC) is a nonprofit think tank in Bozeman, Montana. For over a decade, PERC has pioneered recognizing the value of the market, individual initiative, the importance of property rights, and voluntary activity. This approach is known as the New Resource Economics or free market environmentalism. PERC associates have applied this approach to a variety of issues, including resource development, water marketing, chemical risk, private provision of environmental amenities, global warming, ozone depletion, and endangered species protection.

In 1989, PERC first organized a forum aimed at applying the principles of political economy to important policy issues. The purpose of this forum is to bring together scholars in economics, law, political science, anthropology, history, and other disciplines to discuss and refine academic papers that explore new applications of political economy. It is increasingly evident that the interface between government and individuals in society is vital in determining the rate and direction of economic progress. Political economy analyzes this interface.

Donald J. Boudreaux is associate professor of law and economics at Clemson University. He received his M.A. in economics from New York University, his Ph.D. in economics from Auburn University, and his J.D. from the University of Virginia. He has published articles in *Regulation, Journal of Institutional and Theoretical Economics,* and numerous law reviews. His research interests in law and economics include antitrust and regulation.

Karol J. Ceplo is an adjunct professor of legal studies at Clemson University. She holds undergraduate and graduate degrees in English and modern languages from Rutgers University and received her J.D. degree from the University of Virginia in 1992. Her fields of interest include international law, business law, and environmental regulation.

Jody Lipford is an assistant professor of economics at Presbyterian College. He holds the M.A. and Ph.D. degrees in economics from Clemson University. With research interests in property rights economics and public choice, Jody has published articles in *Public Choice* and the *Journal of Institutional and Theoretical Economics*.

Hertha L. Lund is a third-year law student at the University of Montana Law School where she is law review editor. Once an active rancher, Lund, an award-winning journalist, was assistant editor of the *Farm Bureau News* in Washington where she covered agricultural policy and western issues. In 1994 she was a research fellow at PERC. She will be a clerk at the U.S. Claims Court in the fall of 1995.

Nancie G. Marzulla is president and founder of Defenders of Property Rights, a nonprofit public interest legal foundation dedicated to the preservation of constitutionally guaranteed property rights. She holds the M.P.A degree from the University of Colorado and the J.D. from the University of Colorado at Boulder School of Law. Nancie served as a special assistant and trial attorney in the U.S. Department of Justice Civil Rights Division, 1984-88.

Roger E. Meiners is a professor of law and economics at the University of Texas at Arlington. He has been a visiting scholar at PERC since 1992. He received his Ph.D. in economics from Virginia Polytechnic and State University and his J.D. from the University of Miami Law School. Roger previously taught at Clemson University, Emory University, the University of Miami, and Texas A&M University and was regional director of the Federal Trade Commission. He is the author of numerous articles on environmental policy and coauthor of *Taking the Environment Seriously, The Economic Consequences of Liability Rules,* and *Regulatory Reform in the Reagan Era.*

Robert H. Nelson, holder of the Ph.D in economics from Princeton University, is a professor at the School of Public Affairs at the University of Maryland and Senior Fellow of the Competitive Enterprise Institute. From 1975 to 1993, he was a member of the economics staff of the Office of Policy Analysis of the U.S. Department of the Interior. During these years, he was a visiting scholar at the Brookings Institution, a visiting senior fellow at the Woods Hole Oceanographic Institution, and a visiting scholar at PERC. His writing has appeared frequently in the popular press and professional journals. He is author of *Zoning and Property Rights, The Making of Federal Coal Policy,* and *Reaching for Heaven on Earth: The Theological Meaning of Economics.*

Erin O'Hara is an assistant professor at George Mason University School of Law where she is currently teaching Federal Courts and International Protection of Intellectual Property. Her research interests extend to takings and taxation and strategic judicial decision making. A graduate of Georgetown University Law Center, O'Hara was a law clerk for Chief Judge Dolores Sloviter of the U.S. Court of Appeals, Third Circuit. She has taught at the University of Chicago Law School and Clemson University.

Jeffrey J. Pompe is an assistant professor of economics at Francis Marion University. He received his Ph.D. degree in economics from Florida State University. His current research interests include coastal resource issues, common pool resources, and cultural economics. He has published scholarly articles in *Coastal Management, Ocean and Coastal Management, Society and Natural Resources,* and *Journal of Leisure Research.*

James R. Rinehart is Phillip N. Truluck Professor of Public Policy Economics at Francis Marion University where he directs the Center for Economic Education. He is coauthor of *American Education and the Dynamics of Choice* and has published articles dealing with beach nourishment and property values in *Society and Natural Resources,* and *Ocean and Coastal Management.* He received his Ph.D. in economics from the University of Virginia.

Lee Ann Welch is a first-year law student at the University of South Carolina School of Law. A graduate of the S.C. Governor's School for Science and Mathematics, Welch received her B.S. degree in biological sciences from Clemson University. She was a research assistant for Clemson's Legal Studies Group, has worked as a summer intern for Westvaco's Timberland Division, and was a research fellow at PERC.

Bruce Yandle is Alumni Distinguished Professor of Economics and Legal Studies at Clemson University and coordinator of the Center for Policy and Legal Studies. A member of PERC's academic advisory board, Bruce served as executive director of the Federal Trade Commission and as senior economist on the staff of the President's Council on Wage and Price Stability. He is author of *The Political Limits of Environmental Regulation* and coauthor/coeditor of *Environmental Use and the Market, Benefit/Cost Analysis of Social Regulation, Taking the Environment Seriously,* and *The Economic Consequences of Liability Rules.* He received his A.B. degree from Mercer University and his M.B.A and Ph.D. degrees from Georgia State University.